LEADING LEARNING
and
TEACHING

Stephen Dinham

Published in 2025 by Amba Press, Melbourne, Australia
www.ambapress.com.au

First published in 2016 by ACER Press, an imprint of
Australian Council for Educational Research Ltd

© Stephen Dinham 2025

This book is copyright. All rights reserved. Except under the conditions described in the *Copyright Act 1968* of Australia and subsequent amendments, and any exceptions permitted under the current statutory licence scheme administered by Copyright Agency (www.copyright.com.au), no part of this publication may be reproduced, stored in a retrieval system, transmitted, broadcast or communicated in any form or by any means, optical, digital, electronic, mechanical, photocopying, recording or otherwise, without the written permission of the publisher.

Edited by Carolyn Glascodine
Indexed by Julie King
Cover design, text design and typesetting by ACER Creative Services
Cover image © Alex Valent, used under license from Shutterstock.com

ISBN: 9781923569300 (pbk)
ISBN: 9781923569317 (ebk)

A catalogue record for this book is available from the National Library of Australia.

Foreword

The learning opportunities offered to aspiring, newly appointed or experienced principals are typically about the art and science of leadership, not the art and science of teaching. After all, the argument goes, educational leaders learn enough about the core business of assessment, curriculum and pedagogy when they are teachers. This knowledge provides the foundation from which they can venture into the new land of leadership learning—including the theories and skills of leadership developed in business and management. I am delighted to be writing a foreword to this book, *Leading Learning and Teaching*, which rejects this argument and treats engagement with deep and up-to-date knowledge of student and teacher learning as central to the development of educational leaders. In this foreword I explain and illustrate why I see this focus to be so important.

The assumption that the educational knowledge of aspiring and appointed educational leaders is sufficient is seen in the structure and curriculum of most leadership preparation programs. In North America, and typically in Australasia as well, graduate programs in educational leadership and administration are structurally separate from graduate programs in teaching and curriculum, with little overlap between the two in either curricula or faculty. Graduate leadership programs are usually taught by faculty specialising in leadership, human resources, policy, finance, law and politics, leaving little space in a crowded timetable for deepening the knowledge of learning and teaching of aspiring or experienced leaders.

The separation of leadership learning from learning more about the core educational business is increasingly problematic, because the depth of educational knowledge required to meet the ambitious goals set by politicians and policymakers is substantially greater than provided in either pre-service or on-the-job learning opportunities. Today's leaders are, in nearly every OECD jurisdiction, expected to achieve highly ambitious goals such as 'every child succeeding on intellectually challenging tasks'. The reason why that goal has not yet been met in any jurisdiction is that it requires learning how to overcome, in every school and classroom, the substantial equity challenges that prevent success. While moral commitment to reducing inequity is highly desirable in any educational leader, it is far from sufficient. In addition, every leader needs access to the educational knowledge and skills that would enable them to identify how features of school organisation and educational practice contribute to the perpetuation of inequity, and to lead their teams in the

Foreword

redesign of those features. This change process requires a sophisticated integration of deep educational knowledge and skill in social problem solving.

To make this more concrete, I take the example of student grouping in primary schools. Having been taught how to organise reading and mathematics programs by ability groups in pre-service teacher education, most educators assume that such grouping is essential for meeting children's learning needs. Yet new research on ability grouping is showing how, far from meeting students' learning needs, it locks them into differentially effective peer and teacher learning opportunities.[1] Furthermore, within-class ability grouping may account for much of the well-known association between social class and achievement. While external factors, such as poverty, are partly responsible for this association, research has uncovered particular features of class and school organisation that reinforce rather than unlock the social class-achievement association.[2] Leaders who know about the unintended negative effects of ability grouping are able to problematise the practice. Those who do not have access to this new knowledge are likely to continue to assume that ability grouping serves students' learning needs.

But while such knowledge is a good starting point, it is far from sufficient. Knowledge that renders the status quo problematic differs from the knowledge needed to design improved practices. How do teachers teach mixed-ability groups in ways that create genuine communities of learners? What types of problem-solving tasks are rich enough to support multiple solution strategies and rich peer learning conversations? How much pedagogical knowledge do teacher leaders need to support their teachers in this change and how much knowledge do senior leaders need to be able to support and evaluate the work of their teacher leaders?

While there is very little research providing direct answers to these questions, examples like this one suggest that the depth of educational knowledge required to meet today's ambitious educational goals is substantially greater than is typically available to a school's leadership team. But, once again, there is more required than knowledge of what is wrong and how to put it right. This knowledge must be integrated into a social problem-solving process in which the leader can engage others in evaluation and improvement of current practice. A small research study conducted by one of my current graduate students suggests how challenging this change process can be. After a high quality two-day course in mixed-ability teaching in maths, her follow-up study showed that only one of six curriculum leaders was able to shift the grouping practices of the teachers for whom they were responsible, despite all six leaders espousing such grouping. The difficulties were threefold: first, a two-day course did not provide sufficient opportunities to practise and gain confidence in the new pedagogy; second, the capability of the teacher leaders in leading improvement fell short of what was required of the task; and third, five of the six teacher leaders were unable to garner the active support of their senior leaders for the change.

The lesson I draw from this is that meeting the equity challenge requires multiple levels of leadership that can integrate deep educational knowledge with high level capabilities in the pursuit of improvement. The structural and curricular separation of these two aspects of leadership perpetuates the inequities that leaders and policymakers say they wish to reduce.

The implications of my argument go to the heart of what leadership is. Is it a mostly generic skill—a set of processes if you like—that can be taught and applied to the leadership of organisations engaged in very different types of work? Under this conception of leadership, the curriculum priority is teaching generic, rather than education specific, leadership knowledge and skills. Theories of change, cultural responsiveness, goal setting, and performance management, for example, are taught without simultaneously teaching or investigating the educational content knowledge required to apply these generic leadership processes to specific tasks in specific contexts. Teacher appraisal processes are taught without simultaneous consideration of the empirical and theoretical adequacy of the theories of effective teaching that underpin existing or planned appraisal procedures. In this more generic conception of leadership, we run the risk of focusing 'too much on decontextualised processes of interpersonal influence and too little on substantive task-related expertise'.[3]

My preferred conception of educational leadership recognises the importance of generic leadership processes but requires their integration with relevant educational knowledge, and skill in social problem solving. Improved teacher appraisal processes, for example, require knowledge and skill in appraisal processes (generic leadership knowledge), a defensible theory of effective teaching (educational knowledge) and skill in social problem solving. In earlier work I have called this a task-embedded conception of leadership. Under this conception, leadership is exercised when ideas or acts are recognised by others as capable of progressing important tasks or problems. Those who are knowledgeable about how to understand and resolve the relevant problems are more likely to be recognised for making such contributions, and thus more likely to exercise leadership, regardless of whether or not they hold a formal leadership role.[4]

Whether called instructional, learner-centred or student-centred leadership, there is a growing consensus that developing the quality and density of such leadership is central to achieving the equity and excellence goals set by many educational systems. While there is widespread recognition of how school management responsibilities can detract from the work of leading the improvement of teaching and learning, there is far less recognition of how progress is stymied by insufficient access to relevant educational expertise and capability in social problem solving. It cannot be assumed that the job of leadership development involves grafting generic leadership knowledge onto already adequate knowledge of learning and teaching. As *Leading Learning and Teaching* demonstrates, the job of leadership learning involves updating and deepening educational knowledge in the process of analysing and resolving context-specific educational problems.

Foreword

Stephen Dinham, the author of this book, has provided a resource in which knowledge of learning and teaching is integrated into, rather than separated from, the work of school leadership. The importance given to that knowledge is seen in the fact that eight of the twenty chapters provide an updated overview of the evidence about quality teaching and its impact on student learning and achievement. A further two chapters review teacher professional learning and the role leaders can play in its promotion and effectiveness. The lessons provided are central to the work of leadership at all levels of education—from teacher leaders, to school and system leaders to state and federal policymakers. While the numerous Australian reports and policies are not directly relevant to readers in other jurisdictions, the major messages certainly are. This book makes a substantial contribution to our understanding of just what is involved in developing more skilled and more effective leaders of teaching and learning.

Viviane Robinson
Distinguished Professor, The University of Auckland
December 2015

Endnotes

1. Rubie-Davies, C. M. (2014). *Becoming a high expectation teacher: Raising the bar.* Abingdon, Oxon: Routledge.
2. Schmidt, W. H., Burroughs, N. A., Zoido, P., & Houang, R. T. (2015). The role of schooling in perpetuating educational inequality: An international perspective, *Educational Researcher, 44*(7), 371–386.
3. Robinson, V. M. J. (2001). Embedding leadership in task performance. In K. Wong & C. Evers (Eds.), *Leadership for quality schooling: International perspectives* (pp. 90–102). London, England: Falmer Press.
4. Mumford, M. D., Zaccaro, S. J., Harding, F. D., Jacobs, T. O., & Fleishman, E. A. (2000). Leadership skills for a changing world: Solving complex social problems, *The Leadership Quarterly, 11*(1), 11–35.

Contents

FOREWORD	Viviane Robinson, Distinguished Professor, The University of Auckland	iii
INTRODUCTION		ix
ABOUT THE AUTHOR		xiii
ACKNOWLEDGEMENTS		xiv

PART A Research evidence on teaching for learning

1. What difference do schools make to student achievement? — 2
2. What works best in teaching? Evidence, myths, ideologies, habits, fads and fashions — 19
3. International patterns of student achievement: How do we measure achievement and how and why do these measurements vary? — 46
4. International and national emphases on quality teaching: What value is placed on quality teachers and quality teaching? — 64
5. How does teacher expertise develop? What are the differences between routine and adaptive expertise? — 82
6. What do quality teachers do? What does quality teaching look like? — 93
7. Teacher preparation: What are the shortcomings of 'traditional' approaches? What are 'clinical' approaches to teaching? — 113
8. What are students' perspectives on schooling, teaching and learning? — 124

PART B The importance and impact of educational leadership

9. How and why have thinking and approaches to leadership and educational leadership changed? — 133
10. What impact does leadership have on student outcomes? — 143

| 11 | What are the features and benefits of distributed and teacher leadership? | 180 |

PART C Professional learning in education

| 12 | What forms of professional learning are most effective? | 199 |
| 13 | What role can leaders play in promoting professional learning and development? What role can professional standards for teachers play? | 216 |

PART D School improvement and educational change

14	What are the forces, contexts and features of educational change? What role can leaders play?	232
15	What does it mean to be an authoritative leader?	252
16	What role does leadership play in turnaround schools? What school improvement strategies are most effective?	268
17	What strategies for leading teachers and teams are most effective? What are effective processes for teacher assessment and evaluation?	280

PART E Leadership preparation and development

18	What are current, effective approaches to school leadership preparation?	297
19	What are the potential benefits of professional standards for school leaders?	305
20	How can educational leaders be prepared?: A case study of the Master of Instructional Leadership at the University of Melbourne	318

REFERENCES 339

INDEX 355

Introduction

I have been researching, consulting, writing, presenting and providing professional learning for teachers, school leaders, departments of education, professional bodies and governments for several decades. Originally my research focused mainly on educational leadership and administration. I had completed the venerable Master of Educational Administration degree from the University of New England in the late 1980s before moving into teacher education following 14 years as a secondary teacher in New South Wales public schools.

I commenced a doctorate, again through the University of New England, which had as its focus teacher satisfaction and dissatisfaction, resignation and persistence.[1] This led to a larger series of studies into teacher satisfaction, motivation and mental health conducted with Catherine Scott and colleagues in Australia, New Zealand, England, the United States of America, Canada, Malta, Cyprus and other locations, which resulted in a considerable body of research and publications.[2]

Teachers' work and lives became a central interest for a period[3] and I, along with colleagues, became increasingly involved in researching effective or successful teaching.[4] I came to realise that my work on educational leadership, teachers and teaching was lacking a crucial element, that of student learning, and thus I became interested in the links between and impacts of leadership and teaching on student achievement.

Over the years that followed there were many complementary research projects and productive diversions into areas such as professional teaching standards, teacher development and appraisal, leadership preparation and effectiveness, teacher education, effective schools and organisational change. At the same time my focus moved from initial teacher education to postgraduate in-service education, working with experienced teachers and school leaders and supervising higher research degree students. I also became more interested and involved with the area of educational policy and had the opportunity to work in a range of states and countries, observing similarities, differences and connections in the organisation of schooling, educational policy and practice.

During this period I was gaining further experience as a tertiary teacher, leader, curriculum developer, evaluator and policymaker through the positions I held at universities, on professional bodies and through representation on key committees and projects. I worked on a variety of educational leadership programs at different universities and contributed to a range of professional development programs for school leaders offered by departments of education and other bodies. I became convinced there were deficiencies with many such programs, including their continued focus on management to the neglect of teaching and learning, the lack of an evidence-base to some of what was being advocated, and a failure to connect with and demonstrate the impact of various strategies and approaches on student learning.

To address these concerns I wrote *How to Get Your School Moving and Improving: An Evidence-Based Approach*, published in 2008.[5] This brought together my and others' research into what we know about—and more importantly, the interrelationships between—student learning, effective teaching, how leaders can promote teaching and learning, teacher satisfaction, motivation and stress, the key role of professional learning and the dynamics of school change and improvement. This book enjoyed a high degree of acceptance and has been used in many formal educational leadership programs, and more widely by aspiring and practising school leaders. In the interim I continued to research and to be involved in developments such as the Australian Professional Standards for Teachers[6] and the Australian Professional Standard for Principals[7], as well as providing leadership development programs for bodies such as the Bastow Institute of Educational Leadership in Victoria and various sectors and departments of education in Australia and overseas. I became increasingly convinced of the need for greater use of evidence in initial teacher education[8], teaching[9] and professional development for teachers and school leaders.[10]

In 2011, I joined the Melbourne Graduate School of Education (MGSE) at the University of Melbourne following a period as Research Director of the Teaching, Learning and Leadership program at the Australian Council for Educational Research. Drawing upon my experience at that time and taking advantage of the presence at MGSE of people such as John Hattie, Patrick Griffin, Lea Waters, Helen Stokes, Lawrie Drysdale and David Gurr, I began, with colleagues, to develop a new degree, the Master of Instructional Leadership (MIL). There was some debate over the name, but ultimately we wanted to distinguish our program from existing educational leadership and management programs, many of which I would characterise as 'doughnuts', with the missing central portion being teaching and student learning. If some find the label of 'instruction' or 'instructional' somewhat disconcerting, so be it; while the management responsibilities of school leaders are a fact of life, the core business of schools and educational leaders must be the facilitation of teaching and learning. Furthermore, it is not sufficient to hope that our strategies are successful. We need to be able to utilise and generate evidence so that impact on and growth in student learning can be measured to inform future action.

The Master of Instructional Leadership was launched in 2013 and met with immediate acceptance. It contains an embedded Professional Certificate in Instructional Leadership comprising two core MIL subjects taught by John Hattie and myself, and both the MIL and the Professional Certificate have proven popular with individual educators and with employers, with sponsored cohorts from departments of education, Catholic education systems, schools and professional bodies from across Australia and internationally.[a]

This book arises then from the above context and attempts to bring together essential research and understandings of how educators can lead teaching and learning. It critically examines the research evidence linking teaching with student outcomes. Of central interest is the role of leadership, and in particular instructional leadership, in promoting quality teaching and facilitating student learning. Key aspects include successful change management, the role and effectiveness of teacher professional learning and the importance of evidence, data and the measurement of impact. Further emphases include the current national and international contexts of educational theory, policy and practice[11] as these relate to leadership for teaching and learning. In my experience there has never been such a turbulent period in education, with competing pressures, agendas and ideologies all being brought to bear on the 'problems' of schooling, teaching and learning.

It is my hope that the book assists you in better understanding this current context, facilitates self-reflection, and provides a means for enhancing the capabilities of individual educators, teaching teams, schools and systems. This content and approach has met with acceptance and has proven valuable to both candidates involved in formal studies and to educators interested in improving their leadership effectiveness as evidenced by evaluations and more informal feedback. My wish and expectation is that you, too, will find this thinking and material informative and valuable in your professional practice.

Some of what you encounter in this book will be affirming, some may be new and some may well challenge your beliefs and practices. It is important for all of us to be prepared to consider, reconsider and revise our thinking and professional practice on an ongoing basis. In responding to a criticism that he had changed his opinion on monetary policy during the Great Depression, John Maynard Keynes has been quoted as saying 'When the facts change, I change my mind. What do you do, sir?'

In this introduction I have provided instances where my thinking has changed in the face of new evidence and greater experience. My views continue to change and that is as it should be. One of the themes running through this book is that we can never be complacent in education. We can never say we have worked it all out and that we can put our feet up, because the world continues to change, and each year we have a new group of learners and in some cases, teachers, to work with.

The big challenge lies in educating ourselves, our colleagues and those we are entrusted to teach, to the highest levels possible.

---

a   See Chapter 20.

Endnotes

1. Dinham, S. (1992). Human perspectives on the resignation of teachers from the New South Wales Department of School Education: Towards a model of teacher persistence. (Doctor of Philosophy thesis). University of New England, Armidale, New South Wales.
2. See, for example, Dinham, S., & Scott, C. (1998). A three domain model of teacher and school executive satisfaction. *Journal of Educational Administration, 36*(4), 362–378; Scott, C., Cox, S., & Dinham, S. (1999). The occupational motivation, satisfaction and health of English School Teachers. *Educational Psychology, 19*(3), 287–308; Dinham, S., & Scott, C. (2000). Moving into the third, outer domain of teacher satisfaction. *Journal of Educational Administration, 38*(4), 379–396.
3. Dinham, S. (1993). Teachers under stress. *Australian Educational Researcher, 20*(3), December, 1–16; Dinham, S. (1997). Teaching and teachers' families. *Australian Educational Researcher, AARE, August, 24*(2), 59–88; Dinham, S. (1997). Societal expectations, pressures and teaching. *Teaching and Teachers' Work, 5*(3), August, 1–8.
4. See Ayres, P., Dinham, S., & Sawyer, W. (2004). Effective teaching in the context of a Grade 12 high stakes external examination in New South Wales, Australia. *British Educational Research Journal, 30*(1), 141–165.
5. Dinham, S. (2008). *How to get your school moving and improving: An evidence-based approach*. Melbourne, Victoria: ACER Press.
6. Dinham, S., Ingvarson, L., Kleinhenz, E., & Anderson, M. (2009). *The Draft National Professional Standards Framework for Teachers and School Leaders*. Melbourne, Victoria: ACER.
7. See Dinham, S. (2011). *Pilot study to test the exposure draft of the National Professional Standard for Principals—Final report*. Melbourne, Victoria: AITSL. Dinham, S., Collarbone, P., Evans, M., & Mackay, A. (2013). The development and proposed use of a national standard for principals in Australia. *Educational Management, Administration and Leadership, 41*(4), 466–482.
8. Dinham, S. (2015). *Issues and perspectives relevant to the development of an approach to the accreditation of initial teacher education in Australia based on evidence of impact*. Melbourne, Victoria: AITSL.
9. McLean Davies, L., Anderson, M., Deans, J., Dinham, S., Griffin, P., Kameniar, B., Page, J., Reid, C., Rickards, F., Tayler, C., & Tyler, D. (2013). Masterly preparation: Clinical practice in a graduate pre-service teacher education program. *Journal of Education for Teaching, 39*(1), 93–106.
10. Dinham, S. (2013). Connecting instructional leadership with clinical teaching practice. *Australian Journal of Education, 57*(3), 220–231.
11. See Dinham, S. (2013). The quality teaching movement in Australia encounters difficult terrain: A personal perspective. *Australian Journal of Education, 57*(2), 91–106; Dinham, S. (2015). The worst of both worlds: How US and UK models are influencing education in Australia. *Educational Policy Analysis Archives, 23*(49), n.p. http://dx.doi.org/10.14507/epaa.v23.1865

About the author

Stephen Dinham OAM PhD has over 40 years of experience as a teacher, university academic, researcher, writer and consultant. He has conducted a wide range of research projects in the areas of educational leadership and change, effective pedagogy/quality teaching, student achievement, postgraduate supervision, professional teaching standards, teachers' professional development, middle-level leaders in schools, and teacher satisfaction, motivation and health. He has an extensive publication record (more than 340 publications): books, book chapters, refereed journal articles, and articles in professional journals.

Stephen is a frequent presenter at international, national and state conferences (over 520 presentations) and has worked as consultant with a wide range of educational bodies nationally and internationally.

Stephen's position at the time of writing was Professor of Teacher Education and Director of Learning and Teaching in the Melbourne Graduate School of Education, The University of Melbourne.

Acknowledgements

Many of the projects and publications I have cited in this book were undertaken with colleagues. I acknowledge all of these people, both for their input to this work, and for their contribution to the development of my knowledge and understanding.

I would like to thank Viviane Robinson for agreeing to write the foreword. I would also like to thank Patricia Collarbone, Alma Harris, John Hattie, David Hopkins and Ken Leithwood for reading the draft of this book and providing such positive support for what I have tried to achieve. I have cited the important work of each of these eminent educators, researchers and writers at various points in the text.

I would also like to thank my colleagues at the University of Melbourne Graduate School of Education, with whom I have worked in the development and implementation of the Master of Instructional Leadership degree and other related professional development programs for educational leaders. In particular, I would like to thank and acknowledge the contributions of Helen Stokes, Warren Marks, Sue Lazenby and Kerry Elliott to my MIL (Master of Instructional Leadership) subject, Leading Learning and Teaching.

My thanks also go to ACER Press for the professional way this book has been brought to fruition.

* * *

Dedication

This book is dedicated to my wife Dr Catherine Scott,
a true scholar and great teacher.

* * *

PART A

Research evidence on teaching for learning

CHAPTER 1

What difference do schools make to student achievement?

INTRODUCTION

This chapter provides a foundation and context for this book. We examine firstly the influence that schools can make to student achievement, including evidence for this, and how thinking in the field has changed.

We examine what research has revealed as the major influences on student achievement and the crucial influence of the classroom teacher is explored.

Drawing upon the findings of international meta-analyses, we consider the aspects of teaching that have greatest impact on student learning. Particular attention is paid to the labelling and categorisation of learners that is sometimes employed in an attempt to meet perceived needs of students, and the deleterious effects of such categorisation.

The role of leadership in promoting effective teaching and learning is then considered.

A broad overview from empirical research of how people learn also serves as a foundation for subsequent chapters.

Schools make almost no difference: the Coleman Report

Up until the mid-1960s the prevailing view was that schools made almost no difference to student attainment. What students could achieve was largely predetermined by heredity, where they lived, their socio-economic background and family circumstances. Measured 'IQ' was considered a powerful predictor of student achievement and seen as largely innate and fixed by the time young people got to school.[a] In other words, every student had his or her personal glass ceiling when it came to attainment. More than this, whole schools, suburbs, cultural and racial groups, and even regions were consigned to a particular category and likely future in society, with expectations for achievement and probable employment (or not) set accordingly. Students who didn't fit this pattern, for example young people from lower socio-economic status (SES) areas with high measured IQ, were seen as exceptions who proved the rule for most of their peers. It was hard to escape this social stratification, and as we shall see, one of the most damaging things we can do to people is to put them into categories and treat them accordingly.

In the United States of America and beyond, an influential and subsequently contentious publication[b] of the time was the so-called 'Coleman Report'[1] of 1966, *Equality of Educational Opportunity*, which concluded that the quality of schooling was responsible for only about 10 per cent of the variance in student achievement.[c] Many people today, including practising teachers, still subscribe, consciously or subconsciously, to various forms of biological-social determinism and stereotyping.[2]

This view that schools made little or no difference was reflected in the nature of Australia's schools, with public 'junior' high schools (and some systemic religious schools) providing various forms of 'technical' education for children of the working classes, prior to them entering lower-skilled occupations and trades, a pattern and structure termed 'tracking' still common in nations such as Germany, Austria and Switzerland[3] and prevalent, although less overt in other nations such as the USA.

Girls in these 'technical' secondary schools studied various 'home science' (cooking, sewing) and clerical subjects (bookkeeping, typing), while boys undertook 'industrial arts' subjects, such as woodwork, metalwork and technical drawing, to

---

a   See discussion of the 'Flynn Effect' later in this chapter.
b   The data used in the compilation of the Coleman Report has been subject to regular re-analysis and re-interpretation ever since.
c   An important technique for analysing the effect of categorical factors on a response is to perform an Analysis of Variance. An ANOVA decomposes the variability in the response variable amongst the different factors. Depending upon the type of analysis, it may be important to determine: (a) which factors have a significant effect on the response, and/or (b) how much of the variability in the response variable is attributable to each factor. http://www.statgraphics.com/analysis_of_variance.htm

prepare them for trade apprenticeships and semi-skilled labour. Many such schools were single-sex, which both reflected and reinforced stereotypes about accepted and expected careers for boys and girls.

In contrast, more affluent areas were served by government and private secondary 'matriculation' schools that were geared to preparation for 'white collar' work, university entrance and the professions. Although not as overtly powerful as in the UK, the 'class system' of the time in Australia was important in determining people's life chances.

At this time students tended to be streamed off into one of these broad pathways at the end of primary school or even earlier. Some gifted students from poorer backgrounds who passed special examinations were offered the 'opportunity' to attend 'better' primary and secondary schools. In reality however, most students and their families had little say—the decision was made for them by circumstances and the expectations for them held by others. 'Zoning' for government school attendance was rigidly applied, with government school students attending their local 'public' school. For students to escape this broad social categorisation and streaming, determination and sacrifice from their parents and long-distance commuting was required. Those students who emerged from the junior 'technical' highs and who aspired to university study and the professions were faced with long years of 'night school' or correspondence study, and lowly paid on-the-job education in accounting firms, legal offices and the like, to bridge the gap.

Introduction of comprehensive education

A major change to the situation described above was the introduction from the late 1950s to the mid-1960s of (near) universal 'comprehensive' education in Australia through a single model of secondary schooling accompanied by greater prevalence of coeducation.[4] The playing field still wasn't level, but some of the hills had been lowered, and this change made it possible for more young people to choose to study from the same range of subjects as students from 'better' areas. Girls and boys could also choose subjects previously not open to them such as the 'industrial arts' and 'home sciences' respectively, although take up across this divide was slow to gather pace. Students could now complete their secondary education through their local secondary school and qualify for matriculation, although in reality, in the less affluent areas only a small minority managed to complete post-compulsory education under these new arrangements. In more isolated areas, completing secondary school was still difficult and usually required boarding or commuting to complete the final years of high school, something that is still a challenge for some isolated students in remote areas.

As an example, in New South Wales (NSW) the Higher School Certificate (HSC) was awarded for the first time in 1967 to the first 'sixth form' classes (now Year 12). It was based on six years of secondary study (four years for the School Certificate and another two years for the Higher School Certificate), rather than the previous model of five years (three years for the 'Intermediate' and another two years for the 'Leaving Certificate'). Final results were still determined by external public examinations heavily influenced by universities, as was the curriculum.

Students could still leave school at 15 after third form (Year 9), however, and many did, 15 being the traditional age to enter apprenticeships, although increasingly, those who left school prior to sixth form (Year 12) now did so after fourth form (Year 10) at 16 with the School Certificate. The HSC was now the means for determining university entry, although only 20 per cent of students who had begun high school in 1962 completed the first HSC examinations in 1967, and university fees and a lack of family role models no doubt still deterred many students from attending university. (A teacher's scholarship was important in some of these school leavers gaining a tertiary education, especially women.)[5] Overall, fewer than half of those who completed the inaugural NSW HSC of 1967 entered university in the following year, but this situation would change.[6]

These patterns and developments were mirrored in other Australian jurisdictions as the post-World War II 'baby boomers' moved through schooling, and post-compulsory retention and the numbers of those entering tertiary education increased. Many of those who entered colleges and universities from the late 1960s onwards were first generation secondary school graduates and tertiary students, including me. In Australia, the abolition of university fees in the early 1970s was a factor in increased tertiary participation, although this incentive was undermined by the introduction of higher education 'contribution' fees and loans in later decades.

School effectiveness research

Another broad change influencing our thinking about student achievement came from school effectiveness research, largely from North America. In the post-World War II period the USA had invested heavily in education, education being seen as vital to the economic development and prosperity of the nation.

However, when school results were compared there was concern about the varying performance of students, especially those in large urban secondary schools, where considerable funds had been expended in the hope of improving opportunity and achievement. When 'like' schools were compared, despite similar clientele, resources, curricula and administration, some schools were clearly more successful than others when it came to student performance on standardised measures, and on other indicators such as high school completion and college entry. Whatever was responsible for this disparity, it wasn't just the students, and it wasn't just resources or structural arrangements.

To investigate school performance further, 'input-output' economic studies were carried out from the mid-1960s to the early 1970s, and were accompanied later by 'effective school' studies (early to late 1970s), which led to 'school improvement' studies (late 1970s to mid-1980s) and more recently, 'context variables' studies (late 1980s to the present).[7]

Rather than school performance being largely determined by the 'raw materials'—the students, resources and structures—other more intangible and contextual factors were clearly at work. While attention was focused for a time at the school level—including the influence of leadership—as researchers began to 'drill down', it was becoming apparent that student achievement also varied considerably *within* seemingly successful schools, and in fact in all schools. It was found that the differences within schools were actually greater than the overall differences in student achievement between schools. (This phenomenon remains true in most schools today.)

From the 1970s, the attention of some researchers turned more to what was happening within individual classrooms. By the late 1980s, the belief that schools, and by implication teachers, made no difference to student achievement had been powerfully refuted.

Influences on student achievement

As research continued into effective schools and successful teaching and the corpus of studies grew, evidence was mounting that not only did schools make a difference, but that the teacher was the major *in-school influence on student achievement*.

An important innovation for these burgeoning studies was the application of the technique of meta-analysis. Meta-analysis was developed from earlier approaches by Gene Glass in the 1970s.

> Meta-analysis refers to the analysis of analyses. I use it to refer to the statistical analysis of a large collection of results from individual studies for the purpose of integrating the findings. It connotes a rigorous alternative to the casual, narrative discussions of research studies which typify our attempts to make sense of the rapidly expanding research literature.[8]

Today, meta-analysis is the foundation methodology for analysing studies of teacher effectiveness, with 'effect size' a key unit of measurement.

> A meta-analysis combines the results from a number of studies to determine the average effect of a given technique. When conducting a meta-analysis, a researcher translates the results of a given study into a unit of measurement referred to as an effect size. An effect size expresses the increase or decrease in achievement of the experimental group (the group of students who are exposed to a specific instructional technique) in standard deviation units.[9]

What then are the main influences on student achievement and how can we explain the variance in students' performance? In answering these questions, I am drawing on the work of Professor John Hattie, previously from the University of Auckland, New Zealand, and now a colleague at the University of Melbourne.[10]

As a result of a meta-analysis of many thousands of studies, Hattie and his colleagues found six major sources of variance. It should be pointed out that these factors explain or account for a proportion of the variation in student achievement, not the proportion of the actual marks or scores achieved by students (a common misconception).

- **Students** account for about 50% of the variance of achievement: 'It is what students bring to the table that predicts achievement more than any other variable'.
- **Home** accounts for about 5–10% of the variance: 'the major effects of the home are already accounted for by the attributes of the student. The home effects are more related to the levels of expectation and encouragement, and certainly not a function of the involvement of the parents or caregivers in the management of schools'.
- **Schools** account for about 5–10% of the variance: 'the finances, the school size, the class size, the buildings are important as they must be there in some form for a school to exist, but that is about it'.
- **Principals** 'are already accounted for in the variance attributed to schools; their effect is mainly indirect through their influence on school climate and culture'. (As will be seen later, I think that the influence of principals and leadership generally may have been underestimated, at least in successful schools.)
- **Peer effects** account for 5–10% of the variance: 'It does not matter too much who you go to school with, and when students are taken from one school and put in another the influence of peers is minimal (of course, there are exceptions, but they do not make the norm)'.
- **Teachers** account for about 30% of the variance: 'It is what teachers know, do, and care about which is very powerful in this learning equation'.[11]

There is now considerable evidence that the major in-school influence on student achievement is the quality of the classroom teacher.[12] As Wright, Horn and Sanders stated in 1997:

> ... the most important factor affecting student learning is the teacher ... The immediate and clear implication of this finding is that seemingly more can be done to improve education by improving the effectiveness of teachers than by any other single factor'.[13]

However, research evidence is also clear on some related matters. Firstly, it takes time, support, learning and effort to develop from a 'novice', to a 'competent', and then to an 'expert' teacher, and not all teachers become experts. Secondly, teacher expertise varies considerably.[14] These phenomena are recognised in the Australian Professional Standards for Teachers introduced in 2011, which identify four levels of development or expertise: *Graduate, Proficient, Highly Accomplished* and *Lead*.[15] (Further reading on the development of teacher expertise is provided in Chapter 5.)

What works (best) in teaching?

There is now a large international research literature on student achievement. The technique of meta-analysis enables researchers to combine and integrate the findings from many studies.

Robert Marzano, a leading researcher in the field, has summarised the major factors affecting student achievement[16]:

FACTOR	EXAMPLE
School	• Guaranteed and viable curriculum • Challenging goals and effective feedback • Parent and community involvement • Safe and orderly environment • Collegiality and professionalism
Teacher	• Instructional strategies • Classroom management • Classroom curriculum design
Student	• Home atmosphere • Learned intelligence and background knowledge • Motivation

To help us to 'unpack' this further, John Hattie has provided a list of 150 effects on student achievement based on more than 800 meta-analyses containing over 50 000 studies, 150 000 effect sizes and over 240 million students.[17] Space precludes a detailed examination, but calculated effect sizes for the broad categories of teacher, curricula, teaching, student, home, and school, revealed the following. (Generally, an effect size (ES) less than 0.2 is considered weak or insignificant, 0.2–0.4 is small, 0.4–0.6 is moderate, and an effect size of 0.6 or above is considered large, although ES can be calculated and reported in slightly different ways. (Some texts, for example, give a large effect size as being 0.8 or more.)

CATEGORY	EFFECT SIZE
Teacher	0.50
Curricula	0.45
Teaching	0.43
Student	0.39
Home	0.35
School	0.23
Average	**0.40**

To disaggregate these findings, Hattie's 'top 25' influences on student learning—all of which have 'large' effects—from his list of 150 are as follows[18]:

RANK	INFLUENCE	EFFECT SIZE
1	Self-report grades/Student expectations	1.44
2	Piagetian programs	1.28
3	Response to intervention	1.07
4	Teacher credibility	0.90
5	Providing formative evaluation	0.90
6	Micro-teaching	0.88
7	Classroom discussion	0.82
8	Comprehensive interventions for learning disabled students	0.77
9	Teacher clarity	0.75
10	Feedback	0.75
11	Reciprocal teaching	0.74
12	Teacher–student relationships	0.72
13	Spaced versus mass practice	0.71
14	Meta-cognitive strategies	0.69
15	Acceleration	0.68
16	Classroom behavioural	0.68
17	Vocabulary programs	0.67
18	Repeated reading programs	0.67
19	Creativity programs	0.65
20	Prior achievement	0.65
21	Self-verbalisation and self-questioning	0.64
22	Study skills	0.63
23	Teaching strategies	0.62
24	Problem-solving teaching	0.61
25	Not labelling students	0.61

The list highlights yet again the importance of the classroom teacher and quality teaching. In considering Hattie's overall list of 150 influences and effect sizes for these, a number of conclusions can be drawn:
- The teacher and the quality of his or her teaching are major influences on student achievement, along with the individual student and his or her prior achievement (all have large effect sizes).
- School-based influences (beyond the classroom) have weaker effects on student achievement.
- Structural and organisational arrangements (open vs traditional classrooms; multi-age vs age-graded classes; ability grouping; gender; class size; mainstreaming) have negligible or small effects on student learning. It is the quality of teaching that occurs within these structural arrangements that is important.
- Examples of 'active teaching' (reciprocal teaching, feedback, teaching self-verbalisation, meta-cognition strategies, direct instruction, mastery learning, testing) have large to moderate effects on student achievement.
- Effect sizes are negligible or small for 'facilitatory' teaching (simulations and games, enquiry-based teaching, individualised instruction, problem-based learning, differentiated teaching for boys and girls, web-based learning, whole language reading, inductive teaching).
- Strategies to promote and remediate literacy figure prominently in Hattie's full list. Literacy is the foundation of student achievement.[19]
- While socio-economic status and home environment do have a moderate to large effect on student achievement (each with an ES of 0.52), this influence is outweighed by the quality of teaching students receive in the classroom (see various effect sizes for aspects of teaching).
- Overall, the quality of the teacher and the quality of teaching (large effect sizes) are much more important than structural or working conditions (negligible or small effect sizes), demonstrating the futility and waste of 'fiddling around the edges' of schooling without sufficiently addressing the quality of teachers and the quality of teaching within schools and classrooms.

It is because of findings like these that there has been so much attention paid to improving teacher education, the quality of teachers[20] and the quality of teaching in recent times.[21]

However, to return to an earlier point, it must be recognised that there is still not a level playing field in either education or life, and I can't see that changing much. Schooling still reflects and reinforces many social and economic divisions, and students, after all, spend less than 15 per cent of their time in school. Socio-economic status and family background still exert a powerful influence, not on innate student ability or capacity, but on expectations, support, opportunities and life choices.

In the highest performing nations, however, socio-economic factors have less influence on student achievement than in Australia, once again pointing to the importance of quality teaching rather than innate ability. In a paper for the Business Council of Australia, Lawrence Ingvarson, Elizabeth Kleinhenz and I noted[22]:

> Although Australia performs well on international measures of student achievement such as PISA (the OECD's Programme for International Student Assessment involving 400 000 15-year-olds in 57 countries), there are concerns over equity. Many students in Australia continue to struggle, including Indigenous students, where the performance gap with non-Indigenous students remains wide. Students' social backgrounds have a greater influence on educational results in Australia than in higher performing countries such as Finland and Canada.[23]

(Later chapters will explore the issue of Australia's performance on international measures of student achievement in more detail.)

Dangers and harm of categorisation

We will consider the issue of labelling and categorisation of students in more detail later, but it is worth considering here because the practice is so pervasive and deleterious. Hattie found that *not* labelling students had a large effect size in respect of their learning of 0.61.[24] One of the most harmful things we can do to a child is to categorise him or her as a particular type of person or learner.[d] I have seen classrooms where students as young as eight have been 'tested' to determine their 'learning style' and are labelled, and label themselves, according to this type—'I'm a ___ learner', 'I can do ___', 'I'm no good at ___', etc.

Any time we categorise students there are certain consequences:
1. There is a necessity to define the group and explain how membership will be determined—who is in and who is out. This can be quite arbitrary and differences between groups and individuals tend to be exaggerated to make the 'case'.[e]
2. There is a need to justify the existence of the group and to defend its existence, that is, why and how the group is 'different'.
3. Members of the group then inevitably receive 'special' treatment while others miss out.

---

d   Later we will examine the work of Carol Dweck and what she has described as 'entity thinking', or believing that one's capabilities are fixed, and how this can influence self-concept, effort and learning.

e   Many inventories used to categorise students lack psychometric rigour, validity and reliability. There are, for example, more than 70 extant models of supposed learning styles.

4. Members are usually told of their membership or 'label', which encourages entity thinking: 'gifted'[25], 'disadvantaged', 'learning difficulties', 'male', 'left-brain', 'kinaesthetic', for example, 'I'm a ___ learner', 'I'm a ___ type of personality', and so forth, setting up a 'self-fulfilling prophecy', rather than adopting an incremental approach to learning and development.
5. Catering to a particular perceived 'learning style' reinforces that style (ironically, learning styles, if they exist at all, are *learned*, not innate, and more likely, are simply preferences, and what we prefer is not always what's best for us) at the expense of other approaches.
6. Those so labelled (and frequently their families) see the role of teachers and others as recognising their particular abilities, rather than developing their capacities further, which they see as fixed.
7. Labelling and 'treatment' based on stereotypes (e.g., boys, girls) then reinforces those very stereotypes.

We should, by all means, attempt to meet the needs of young people (and not just their preferences), challenge them and enrich their learning through exposure to a variety of learning opportunities; we shouldn't just categorise them and limit their horizons through making them believe they are a particular fixed type of learner or person. Categorisation of students is another form of streaming or tracking.

The research evidence is clear that categorising learners and catering for supposed differences has a very weak to negative effect on learning.[26] Rather than limiting young people's horizons in this way, I believe that *with good teaching, it is possible to teach almost anybody almost anything.*

These issues aside, schooling and education remain our best chance for changing people's lives and society for the better. The data on all sorts of social and economic indicators and outcomes correlate strongly with educational achievement. For example, on average, the higher a person's level of educational attainment, the higher their income, the better their health, the longer their life expectancy, and the less chance they will end up in prison.

The best thing we can do for any young person is to provide them with a quality education. Intellectual capacity is not fixed and can be increased through education. Measured IQ has steadily risen over the past century—the so-called 'Flynn Effect'[27]—to the extent that IQ tests have to be periodically normalised so that the average score remains at 100. Overall, average IQ has risen by an astounding 30 points over the past century.[28] Young people are becoming 'smarter' over generations, and the major factor behind the almost universal rise in measured IQ is schooling, with health and nutrition also playing their part. Parental literacy, an outcome of schooling, also plays an important role[29] in compounding the effects of schooling.

Leadership also matters

We have confirmed the crucial importance of the teacher to student learning. The challenge for any educational leader, and the focus of this book, is to make things happen within individual classrooms. *A quality teacher in every classroom is the ultimate aim, but how to achieve this is the big question and challenge.* Lawrence Ingvarson, Elizabeth Kleinhenz and I noted in our report for the Business Council of Australia:

> Thus, the major challenge in improving teaching lies not so much in identifying and describing quality teaching, but in developing structures and approaches that ensure widespread use of successful teaching practices: *to make best practice, common practice.*[30] [Emphasis added]

This matter is taken up in greater detail in later chapters but overall, 'school leaders can play major roles in creating the conditions in which teachers can teach effectively and students can learn, although the influence of leadership on student achievement has perhaps been underestimated'.[31]

Today, leadership is seen as central and essential to delivering the changes, improvement and performance that society increasingly expects of all organisations, including schools. Because of this perceived importance, leadership has been the subject of widespread in-depth study and popular writing. The shelves of airport bookshops are filled with the latter.

What has become clear, though, is that leadership, including educational leadership, is a more contentious, complex, situated and dynamic phenomenon than previously thought.

The study of leadership has been through many phases and fashions, with various idealistic, empirical, theoretical and ideological stances: trait versus process leadership; assigned versus emergent leadership; bureaucratic versus charismatic leadership; administration/management versus leadership; transactional versus transformational versus instructional leadership; universal versus contextual/contingent leadership; 'born' versus 'learned' leadership; command versus relationships; line management versus distributed leadership, and so forth.[32]

Part of the confusion has been caused by the conflation of leaders (their attributes, knowledge and skills, i.e., entities) with *leadership* (the influence exercised by and the functions performed by leaders, i.e., behaviours and processes).

As noted, the prevailing view until the mid-1960s was that leaders and schools had very little influence on student achievement. Today, however, the pressure is on school leaders to be leaders of learning and not just managers or administrators, and for teaching and learning to be the prime focus of the school. (I know this sounds a strange thing to have to say, but the reality is that during the fixation with school management that occurred during the late 1980s to the 1990s, teachers, teaching and students barely rated a mention in in-service courses for school leaders. It felt wrong at the time and still does.)

While the administrative and management functions of school leaders are important and are not going to go away—and many would argue are increasing due to increased responsibilities and accountabilities—leaders need to find the time and means to focus on improving the quality of teaching and learning within their schools, i.e., to be *instructional leaders*. (When I use the term 'school leader', unless stated otherwise, I am referring to principals, deputies, others holding formal leadership positions in schools, and teacher leadership within and beyond the classroom, and not only principals.)

How People Learn

Two publications under the umbrella *How People Learn* were published in the late 1990s, as a result of the work of the Committee on Developments in the Science of Learning under the auspices of the National Research Council of the USA.[33] I recommend these to any educator interested in understanding learning and teaching, and who wishes to distinguish research evidence about learning and teaching from the fashions, fantasies, superstitions and ideological positioning that frequently confronts and confuses us.

Key findings from *How People Learn*
1. Students come to the classroom with preconceptions about how the world works. If their initial understanding is not engaged, they may fail to grasp the new concepts and information that are taught, or they may learn them for the purposes of a test but revert to their preconceptions outside the classroom.
2. To develop competence in an area of enquiry, students must:
   a. have a deep foundation of factual knowledge
   b. understand facts and ideas in the context of a conceptual framework
   c. organise knowledge in ways that facilitate retrieval and application.
3. A 'metacognitive' approach to instruction can help students learn to take control of their own learning by defining learning goals and monitoring their progress in achieving them.

Implications for teaching
1. Teachers must draw out and work with the pre-existing understandings that their students bring with them.
2. Teachers must teach some subject matter in depth, providing many examples in which the same concept is at work and providing a firm foundation of factual knowledge.
3. The teaching of metacognitive skills should be integrated into the curriculum in a variety of subject areas.

Designing classroom environments
1. Schools and classrooms must be learner-centred.
2. To provide a knowledge-centred classroom environment, attention must be given to what is taught (information, subject matter), why it is taught (understanding), and what competence or mastery looks like.
3. Formative assessments—ongoing assessments designed to make students' thinking visible to both teachers and students—are central. They permit the teacher to grasp the students' preconceptions, understand where the students are in the 'developmental corridor' from informal to formal thinking and design instruction accordingly. In the assessment-centred classroom environment, formative assessments help both teachers and students monitor progress.
4. Learning is influenced in fundamental ways by the context in which it takes place. A community-centred approach requires the development of norms for the classroom and school, as well as connections to the outside world, that support core learning values.

Applying the design framework to adult learning
Many approaches to teaching adults consistently violate principles for optimising learning. Professional development programs for teachers, for example, frequently:
- Are not learner-centred.
- Are not knowledge-centred.
- Are not assessment-centred.
- Are not community-centred.[34]

A recent publication entitled *The Science of Learning* by Deans for Impact in the US adds to the above, and also provides a valuable framework and foundation for what is to come in this book.[35] In brief, the report considers a number of key questions and provides 'cognitive principles' (shown below), as well as 'practical implications for the classroom' for each question, along with key supporting research references. Only ten pages, it is a terrific resource for discussions about learning and teaching:

1. **How do students understand new ideas?**
   - Students learn new ideas through reference to ideas they already know.
   - To learn, students must transfer information from their working memory (where it is consciously processed) to their long-term memory (where it can be stored and later retrieved). Students have limited working memory capacities …
   - Cognitive development does not progress through a fixed sequence of age-related stages …

2. **How do students learn and retain new information?**
   - Information is often withdrawn from the memory just as it went in. We usually want students to remember what information means and why it is important, so they should think about meaning when they encounter to-be-remembered material.
   - Practice is essential to learning new facts, but not all practice is equivalent.
3. **How do students solve problems?**
   - Each subject area has some set of facts that, if committed to long-term memory, aids problem-solving by freeing working memory resources and illuminating contexts in which existing knowledge and skills can be applied ...
   - Effective feedback is often essential to acquiring new knowledge and skills.
4. **How does learning transfer to new situations in or outside of the classroom?**
   - The transfer of knowledge or skills to a novel problem requires both knowledge of the problem's context and a deep understanding of the problem's underlying structure.
   - We understand new ideas via examples, but it's often hard to see the unifying underlying concepts in different examples.
5. **What motivates students to learn?**
   - Beliefs about intelligence are important predictors of student behaviour in school.
   - Self-determined motivation (a consequence of values or pure interest) leads to better long-term outcomes than controlled motivation (a consequence of reward/punishment or perceptions of self-worth).
   - The ability to monitor their own thinking can help students identify what they do and do not know, but people are often unable to accurately judge their own learning and understanding.
   - Students will be more motivated and successful in academic environments when they believe that they belong and are accepted in those environments.
6. **What are common misconceptions about how students think and learn?**
   - Students do not have different 'learning styles.'
   - Humans do not use only 10% of their brains.
   - People are not preferentially 'right-brained' or 'left-brained' in the use of their brains.
   - Novices and experts cannot think in all the same ways.
   - Cognitive development does not progress via a fixed progression of age-related stages.

We will examine the nature and importance of evidence-based professional learning for teachers and school leaders at various points in subsequent chapters of this book.

Endnotes

1. Coleman, J. (1966). *Equality of educational opportunity*. Ann Arbor, MI: Inter-University Consortium for Political and Social Research. http://www.icpsr.umich.edu/icpsrweb/ICPSR/studies/06389
2. Bransford, J., Brown, A., & Cocking, R. (2000). (Eds.). *How people learn: Brain, mind, experience, and school*. Washington, DC: National Academy Press. (p. 145)
3. Dinham, S. (2015). *Regulation or deregulation? Observations on education in Germany and Australia*. Keynote address at the Australian College of Educators National Conference, Brisbane, 24 September; Dinham, S. (2015). Regulation or deregulation? Observations on education in Germany and Australia. In *Educators on the edge: Big ideas for change and innovation*. Refereed Conference Proceedings ACE 2015 National Conference (pp. 3–15). Carlton South, Victoria: Australian College of Educators.
4. Campbell, C., & Sherington, G. (2013). *The comprehensive public high school: Historical perspectives*. New York, NY: Palgrave Macmillan.
5. Dinham, S. (1992). Human perspectives on the resignation of teachers from the New South Wales Department of School Education: Towards a model of teacher persistence. (Doctor of Philosophy thesis). University of New England, Armidale, New South Wales.
6. Campbell, C., & Sherington, G. (2013).
7. Reynolds. D., Teddlie, C., Creemers, B., Scheerens, J., & Townsend, T. (2000). An introduction to school effectiveness research. In C. Teddlie & D. Reynolds (Eds.), *The international handbook of school effectiveness research* (pp. 3–25). London, England: Falmer Press.
8. Glass, G. V. (1976). Primary, secondary, and meta-analysis of research. *Educational Researcher, 5*, 3–8. (p. 3)
9. Marzano, R., Pickering, D., & Pollock, J. (2005). *Classroom Instruction that works—Research-based strategies for increasing student achievement*. Upper Saddle River, NJ: Pearson. (p. 4)
10. Hattie, J. (2003). *Teachers make a difference: What is the research evidence?* Paper presented at ACER Annual Conference, October.
11. Hattie, J. (2003). (pp. 1–2); see also Hattie, J. (2009). *Visible learning*. London, England: Routledge; Hattie, J. (2012). *Visible learning for teachers*. London, England: Routledge.
12. OECD. (2005). *Teachers matter: Attracting, developing and retaining effective teachers*. Paris, France: OECD Publishing.
13. Wright, S., Horn, S., & Sanders, W. (1997). Teacher and classroom context effects on student achievement: Implications for Teacher Evaluation. *Journal of Personnel Evaluation in Education, 11*, 57–67.
14. See Berliner, D. (1988). *The development of expertise in pedagogy*. Washington, DC: AACTE Publications; Berliner, D. (2004). Describing the behaviour and documenting the accomplishments of expert teachers. *Bulletin of Science, Technology & Society, 24*(3), 200–212.
15. AITSL [Australian Institute for Teaching and School Leadership]. (2011). *Australian Professional Standards for Teachers*. Melbourne, Victoria: Author.
16. Marzano, R. (2003). *What works in schools—Translating research into action*. Alexandria, VA: ASCD. (p. 10)

17 Hattie, J. (2012). (p. 1)
18 Hattie, J. (2012). (p. 251)
19 Dinham, S. (2007). The lesson of Jonah. *Education Review, 17*(8), 5.
20 Dinham, S., Ingvarson, L., & Kleinhenz, E. (2008). Investing in teacher quality: Doing what matters most. In *Teaching talent: The best teachers for Australia's classrooms*. Melbourne, Victoria: Business Council of Australia.
21 Dinham, S. (2006). Teaching and teacher education: Some observations, reflections and possible solutions, *ED Ventures, 2*, 3–20.
22 Dinham, S., Ingvarson, L., & Kleinhenz, E. (2008). (pp. 5–53; 10)
23 McGaw, B. (2007). Crisis? The real challenges for Australian education. *Independent Education, 37*(2), 21–23.
24 Hattie, J. (2012). (p. 251)
25 See Scott, C. (2008). No gift for the talented: A lousy label for any child. *Professional Educator, 7*(1), 4–5.
26 Hattie, J. (2007). *Developing potentials for learning: Evidence, assessment, and progress*. EARLI Biennial Conference, Budapest, Hungary; Hattie, J. (2009); Hattie, J. (2012).
27 Flynn, J. R. (1984). The mean IQ of Americans: Massive gains 1932 to 1978, *Psychological Bulletin, 95*, 29–51.
28 Scott, C. (2015). *Learn to teach, teach to learn*. Port Melbourne, Victoria: Cambridge University Press. (p. 75)
29 Neisser, U. (1997). Rising scores on intelligence test. *American Scientist, 85*, 440–447.
30 Dinham, S., Ingvarson, L., & Kleinhenz, E. (2008). (p. 14)
31 Dinham, S. (2007). How schools get moving and keep improving: Leadership for teacher learning, student success and school renewal. *Australian Journal of Education, 51*(3), 263–275.
32 Dinham, S. (2007). The waves of leadership. *The Australian Educational Leader, 29*(3), 20–21, 27.
33 Bransford, J., Brown, A., & Cocking, R. (2000); Donovan, M., Bransford, J., & Pellegrino, J. (1999). (Eds.). *How people learn: Bridging research and practice*. Washington, DC: National Academy Press.
34 Bransford et al. (2000). (pp. 14–27)
35 Deans for Impact. (2015). *The science of learning*. Austin, TX: Deans for Impact.

CHAPTER 2

What works best in teaching? Evidence, myths, ideologies, habits, fads and fashions

INTRODUCTION

In Chapter 1 we considered from a macro level the development of research and thinking around the impacts that schools, teaching and leadership can have on student accomplishment.

This chapter builds on this understanding by examining in more detail what research has revealed about those strategies and the approaches that are *most* effective in moving students' learning forward. This is important because, as John Hattie has reminded us, almost everything works to some degree.[1] We also examine from a position of research evidence some of the less effective and even harmful strategies and approaches that some educators have embraced, and consider why such beliefs and practices persist.

As you proceed through this chapter, and indeed the book as a whole, I would encourage you to keep these 'big' questions in mind:
1. What evidence *affirms* your current knowledge in respect of teaching and learning?
2. What evidence is *new*?
3. What evidence have you found *challenging*?
4. What are the *implications* for your professional practice of your answers to the previous questions?

Four fundamentals of student achievement

At the conclusion of my book *How to Get Your School Moving and Improving*[2] I presented a simple yet powerful model for what I had observed and researched in the classrooms of successful teachers, successful school subject departments, cross-school working groups, successful schools and education systems across Australia and overseas.[3] I am revisiting this model at the beginning of this book because my subsequent research and experience in schools has only strengthened my conviction that these elements are fundamentally important. Figure 2.1 presents a simple diagram of the four fundamentals underpinning student achievement and thus successful schools. It will serve as an organising construct and touchstone for the remainder of this book.

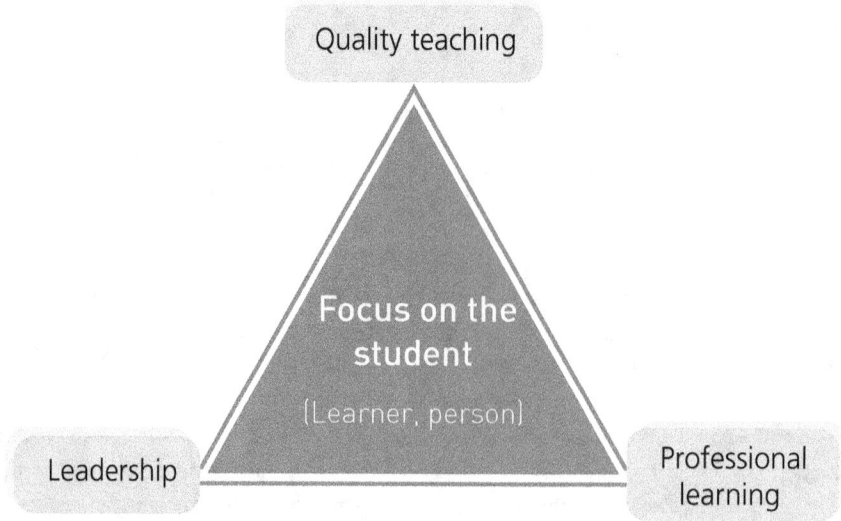

Figure 2.1: The four fundamentals of student achievement[4]

1 A central focus on students, both as learners and people

Successful teachers, faculties and teams, schools, and even education systems, have a central focus on knowing their students as both learners and people. In other words, they focus on the individual.

1. **The individual learner**—In terms of learning, each student's progress is assessed formatively, and summatively, and teachers are aware of where each student *has been* in terms of their learning, *where they are* at present in terms of what they can and can't do in respect of the standards and expectations held for them, and *what is needed* to move their learning forward. Constructive feedback and appropriate teaching strategies are part of the ongoing assessment of each student. Hattie has calculated an effect size of 0.54 for student-centred

teaching and 0.75 for teacher-to-student feedback, underlining the importance of knowing students as learners and acting on this knowledge.[5]

2. **The individual person**—The second aspect of this central focus is that every student is also known as a person. Hattie has calculated an effect size of 0.72 for teacher-student relationships.[6] It is important that every student feels that there is at least someone who knows about them, and cares about them. Some students can go weeks or longer without such personal contact or interest, particularly those students who don't stand out or draw attention to themselves because of their learning, conduct or other factors. Effective teachers find ways to communicate and connect with all their students. They know and use students' names and offer commendation or correction when appropriate. They keep records. They notice changes in a student's engagement, enthusiasm, work or even health, and intervene before small problems become bigger.

Some years ago I was engaged in a research project in a primary school. While I was in a Year 3 class, I heard a student ask the teacher whether she would 'still get my five minutes today?'. On asking the teacher what this was about, I was told that he had timetabled five minutes of 'face time' each week with every student. This occurred while the class was working on some activity or when another teacher was taking a lesson, and enabled the teacher and student to get to know each other better, for learning to be discussed, and to follow up any issues of concern. In other words, it enabled the teacher to know his students better as both learners and people, and for them to know him better. Obviously, appropriate professional distance is important here. Being too remote as a teacher is not helpful in establishing a healthy and productive teacher–student relationship, but nor is attempting to be too close and intrusive. The old adage holds true. As teachers, we should strive to be *friendly* but shouldn't try to be a *friend* to our students. Beginning teachers sometimes fall into the trap of the latter.

One could argue that five minutes a week is not very much but it is also accurate to say that this is probably five minutes more of teacher–student interaction than many students are currently receiving. The lesson I learned from this, and subsequently, is that such *one-to-one conferences can have a powerful effect on student learning and teaching.*

In some schools, however, there is a lack of relative balance between knowing students as learners and as people. In some schools the emphasis is more on the learning side. The school prides itself on the academic success of its students and those who don't measure up are ignored, put in a bottom class, or they can go elsewhere. School newsletters, websites and notice boards outside the school advertise academic success as defined by Australian Tertiary Admission Ranks (ATARs) and how many students enter university.

On the other hand, some schools, usually of lower SES, have lower expectations of their students. The language used here can be instructive. I have heard variations on all of these and more in my travels: 'Don't expect too much and you won't be disappointed'; 'This is a poor area and the best we can do is give our students the basics'; 'The local community doesn't value education'; 'The most important thing we can do is to boost students' self-esteem and make them feel better about themselves', and finally 'We are a welfare school'.

In my research it is clear that those schools that are most successful in terms of overall student achievement maintain that essential balance between 'academic' (learning) and 'welfare/wellbeing' (personal) aspects of schooling.[7]

Here are some questions I've used with various groups of educators that might be useful to consider now, and reconsider, as you proceed through this book:
1. Can we say that every student in our school is known as a *learner* and a *person*?
2. What are our *processes* to ensure this occurs and what is our *evidence*?
3. How do we *act* on this evidence?
4. Any there any *implications* of your answers to the previous questions?

2 Professional learning

A second broad factor responsible for successful teaching, learning, schools and systems is that of professional learning. It is no coincidence that the most effective teachers, subject faculties and schools are never satisfied with what they know. They never reach the point where they feel they can put their feet up and say they have it all worked out. There are always new challenges and every year, new students. These educators continually question what they do and how and why they do it, use evidence to inform this knowledge, and are always on the lookout for new strategies, resources and approaches to improve teaching and learning. Hattie has found professional development to have an effect size of 0.51 on student achievement. Teachers utilising micro-teaching to improve their practice has an effect size of 0.88. Providing teachers with formative evaluation and feedback on their performance has an even larger effect size of 0.90.[8] Robinson, Hohepa and Lloyd found from their meta-analyses that leaders 'promoting and participating in teacher learning and development' had a very large effect size of 0.84.[9]

Professional learning—one of the 'big levers' at our disposal—is essential to teacher development and school improvement. I can't see how we can change what teachers know and can do without it. Any change we introduce into a school or system must be accompanied and supported by relevant and effective professional learning, if it is to have any chance of success.

3 Leadership

Leadership is another 'big lever' in improving teaching and learning. Our earlier views of leadership have changed and we now recognise that leadership resides in all teachers and not just in those occupying formal leadership positions. Every time a teacher takes a class, runs an extra-curricular activity, works with a less experienced teacher or sits on a school committee or working party, to give but a few examples, they are exercising leadership.

Leadership, as with professional learning, is a powerful enabler in schools. It is possible to have good teachers and teaching without having a successful school, but in my experience it is impossible to have a successful school without good leadership. Hattie has identified an effect size of 0.39 for principals/school leaders[10], but as I have noted elsewhere, the effects of leaders and leadership are often widely variable, indirect, and therefore more difficult to measure than those for teaching.[11] Additionally, some forms of leadership, such as instructional leadership, have been found to have a greater effect on student learning than others, such as transformational leadership.[12] As we will see in later chapters, leadership is a group function which, over time, can lift a school's performance, but poor leadership can quickly undo this good work.

4 Quality teaching

Not surprisingly, quality teaching—our 'biggest lever'—has been found to be essential in facilitating successful student learning. There are two sides to the quality teaching coin: the qualities of the teacher and the quality or effectiveness of their teaching. There has been great interest in the quality of those entering teaching in recent times (and with the quality of initial teacher education programs[13]), as there has been for teaching performance or effectiveness. Hattie found an overall effect size of 0.48[14] for the quality of teaching, but research has also revealed the wide variation in teacher quality that can occur in any school. As noted in Chapter 1, while the teacher is the biggest *in-school* influence on student achievement, the big challenge is to get a quality teacher in every classroom, something I have described as being the biggest equity issue in education.

An evidence base for teaching and learning

We now consider the major focus of this chapter, the evidence base, or the lack of it, for teaching and learning. I have noted previously:

> It is given that teachers want their students to learn. Anything that promises to aid in the achievement of this is therefore attractive. Unfortunately education is subject to the same sorts of fads and fashions as the rest of society but in the case of teaching, real harm can come from adopting an untested strategy. There are well developed protocols prior to the introduction of any new drug or treatment in medicine yet educators readily experiment upon students—a situation where lives are also at stake—with unproven (or even disproved) methods. This is compounded by the fact that a scientific approach is rarely taken. Rather than changing one variable and measuring its impact, the tendency is to change a range of things simultaneously and hope for the best.[15]

We will now consider a number of areas where strongly held beliefs and common practices are challenged by current—and even long-standing—research.

Effects of socio-economic status are too powerful to be overcome

We considered the matter of socio-economic background and status in Chapter 1. It requires further examination because of the powerful influences thinking and mindsets about SES exert on schools, teachers and student achievement.

Hattie calculated an effect size of 0.52 for both socio-economic status (SES) and home environment on student achievement, meaning both have a moderate to large influence on student learning.[16] Each should be considered separately as there are high SES families that are dysfunctional and wonderful low SES families. In some cases, however, young people experience double jeopardy with low SES and a poor family background. To summarise, SES *is* about:
- foundations and advantage
- opportunity
- support
- role models and encouragement.

To be blunt, life isn't fair, or to put it another way, some people have certain advantages and others have disadvantages. Coming from a literacy-rich home background, having family members who have succeeded in school education and beyond who can act as role models and offer support and encouragement, having family and business networks and connections, can all advantage students in achieving schooling success. In short, possessing family social and financial capital can be advantageous in schooling and in life.

However, SES *is not* about:
- innate ability
- social-biological determinism
- potential.

As mentioned in Chapter 1, the notion of innate intelligence or ability has been questioned and refuted by phenomena such as the 'Flynn Effect', whereby measured intelligence has been found to increase over generations.[17] At various times people have attempted to prove or support the contention that one ethnic, cultural or racial group is inferior or superior to another. However, it has been found that within any such group there exists the same spread or distribution of ability, and any differences that are observed are not the result of innate or fixed differences, but of other factors. Catherine Scott has observed:

> Evidence ... confirms the role of the environment—particularly the cultural environment—in building minds. Everyone is getting more competent at using abstract thinking as a result of schooling, but disadvantaged minorities

are gaining at a faster rate as they come to experience the same learning environments as the majority.[18]

When we consider, for example, the relationship between SES and Australian students' scores for reading on PISA (Programme for International Student Assessment), there is a positive correlation between increased mean reading scores and increased SES. However, what this conceals is the wide variation in student achievement on this measure at any point on the SES continuum. SES certainly explains some of the variation in student test scores but it is reasonable to suggest, in line with the observation from Scott, that this variation is more associated with environmental factors than any form of innate dis/ability. In fact, poor performance on measures such as PISA is spread across the SES spectrum.[19]

Similarly one of the things revealed by NAPLAN testing (National Assessment Program—Literacy and Numeracy) in Australia is that many high SES schools—and by implication students at those schools—are not achieving at a level predicted by their SES, and thus while their performance overall is very good by national standards, it is actually sub-optimal in terms of adding value.[20] To put it another way, some of these well performing schools are 'coasting'.

Thus, generally speaking, and allowing for special types of schools at either end of the spectrum, in any school we have much the same spread of ability. The real problem arises when people make assumptions about students, schools and communities based upon SES and are not cognisant of this spread. Stereotyping, stigmatising and holding lesser expectations for students in low SES schools can be extremely damaging in terms of student achievement and their resultant life options and choices.

It can be instructive, not to mention disconcerting, to listen to how teachers, principals, education officials and community members speak about students, schools and their communities. A comment from a principal of a low SES school I overheard a few years ago horrified me:

> Principal to new teacher (2013): 'This is a working class school in a working class area. Don't expect too much and you won't be disappointed.'

I would urge you to challenge and not tolerate such comments, which are a reflection of values and beliefs that translate into attitudes and actions that condemn students to underachievement. As I have commented (many times) previously:

> Life isn't fair, but good teaching and good schools are the best means we have of overcoming disadvantage and opening the doors of opportunity for young people.

Content knowledge is seen by some as problematic

Until the mid-1960s to 1970s, curricula in Australia were centrally devised (at state or territory level) and content or knowledge centred, with frequent use of formal in-school and external testing. Teachers knew what they had to teach and when to teach it, regardless of the background of their students, the school or its location. There was little recognition of individual differences in either students or school contexts, and the notion of the development of values—let alone alternative values—was largely absent.

However, from the 1970s new curriculum documents de-emphasised knowledge and content and were based upon the principle of 'school based curriculum development' within broader frameworks, rather than centrally devised and assessed prescriptive content. In short, curriculum development moved from the 'centre' to schools, and to teachers, a paradigm shift many educators were in favour of but few appeared adequately prepared for.[21]

The 1960s had been a time of social questioning, activism and change and this was reflected in school curricula, which became more 'issues' based. The environment, multinational corporations, multiculturalism, 'rights' of various types, to name only some issues, became part of the curriculum. New curricula and associated teaching techniques recognised and privileged skills and values acquisition, diversity, experiential learning, cross-curricular thematic approaches, cooperative learning and 'group work', problem solving, critical thinking and more personalised learning. In literacy, the 'whole language' approach superseded 'phonics'—not for the first time—and the formal teaching of grammar receded.[22]

There had been of course a long history of 'progressivist', 'child-centred', 'constructivist', enquiry type approaches to teaching and schooling going back to the late 19th century but in schooling, things tend to go in and out of fashion, before being 'rediscovered'.[23]

Unfortunately in education there is a tendency to adopt positions and to formulate and advocate 'false dichotomies', and the result in this instance was that content or knowledge was seen by many as counter to the learning process. In primary education especially, this resulted in many cases in a largely 'content free' curriculum, particularly in the humanities, where teachers had wide choice and little guidance. Learning processes, issues and activities tended to be privileged over knowledge, and formal testing declined.

Catherine Scott and I observed an example of this paradigm in an upper primary class. Students had been asked to work in groups to research an aspect of Australian history and present this by means of an animation created using a digital camera. One group had chosen the First Fleet entering Sydney Harbour in January 1788. The small fleet of ships was being heroically led by Captain James Cook. Unfortunately, for both the students and Captain Cook, he had been killed in 1779. Was this error seen as significant? No, because 'the most important thing' was that the students had been 'engaged in the learning process'. In this way, means and ends have been confused, with activity and 'engagement' seen as more important than actual learning outcomes achieved. I have previously noted:

> Subject content knowledge has been portrayed by some as rote learning and recitation of facts, names, dates and places, and is seen as less worthy than critical thinking and the acknowledgement of multiple social realities. Learning to learn is seen as preferable to learning. Teacher-directed learning is seen as old-fashioned, even harmful, while student activity and choice is championed, regardless of what that activity or choice might entail.[24]

To support the above contention, Hattie found a minuscule effect size of only 0.04 for giving students control over their learning.[25]

In respect of 'factual knowledge', Willingham has noted:

> Data from the last thirty years lead to a conclusion that is not scientifically challengeable: thinking well requires knowing facts ... The very processes that teachers care about most—critical thinking processes such as reasoning and problem solving—are intimately intertwined with factual knowledge that is stored in long-term memory (not just found in the environment).[26]

This has taken a further twist with the widespread growth of and access to the Internet. It is argued by some that the teacher as expert—the 'sage on the stage'—is no longer needed, but rather teachers should be facilitators of learning—the 'guide by the side'—and in any case why should students need to learn anything, when virtually all of human knowledge is only a mouse click away. However, because of this context, the need for effective, knowledgeable teachers is greater than ever in order to assist students to navigate the mass of material 'out there'. Further, it is not a matter of a teacher being an expert in either content or pedagogy. As Shulman pointed out long ago[27], teachers need to be masters of both through what he termed pedagogic content knowledge. To put it another way, the best teachers 'know their stuff', and know how to teach it, as we will see later.[28]

Knowledge/content/outcomes, versus activity/process/engagement, is not the only false dichotomy bedevilling education. Student-centred rather than teacher-directed learning, as noted above, is another position many ascribe to, but as research shows, the two do not have to be mutually exclusive. The best teachers are both student-centred and teacher-directed. They are both 'sage' and 'guide'.[29]

Lack of an evidence base for teaching and learning: fads, myths, legends, ideology and wishful thinking

As noted earlier, it is admirable and expected that teachers will want their students to learn, but a problem arises when strategies and resources are adopted that in some cases have weak, unproven, or disproved effects, on student learning. Teachers and other educators need to be what I term 'critical consumers of research' in their selection of such approaches, but this is a challenge when time and knowledge are in short supply and 'quick fixes' to student learning, often advocated by various vested and/or commercial interests, are attractive. In other cases, some approaches are an ideological position on how learning and the world *should* be, in the views of some.

Discovery learning and constructivism

One such belief and approach is that of 'discovery learning' and its allied concept, 'constructivism'. It has become an ideology or article of faith for some that it is 'better' if students can discover and construct their own learning. Writing in the *American Psychologist*, Mayer reviewed the research evidence and commented:

> The debate about discovery has been replayed many times in education, but each time, the research evidence has favoured a guided approach to learning ... Today's proponents of discovery methods, who claim to draw their support from constructivist philosophy, are making inroads into educational practice. Yet a dispassionate review of the relevant research literatures shows that discovery-based practice is not as effective as guided discovery.[30]

However unguided discovery learning, problem-based learning, enquiry and constructivism are popular with many teachers and are common strategies in many classrooms, with students receiving little or no guidance as to the content, scope or standards required for satisfactory completion of a task. A variation is social constructivism where students work in small groups trying to discover what they need to know. Hattie found that problem-based learning has an effect size of only 0.15, whereas direct instruction, where the teacher is clear about their intentions and orchestrates the learning of the students accordingly, has an effect size of 0.59.[31] This is not to say that we don't want students to engage in problem solving or enquiry, just that such activities are most effective when students have been given a solid foundation of knowledge, skills and understanding that they can then *apply* to problems.[32]

Mayer concluded from his analysis that:

> As constructivism has become the dominant view of how students learn, it may seem obvious to equate active learning with active methods of instruction. Thus, educators who wish to use constructivist methods of instruction are often encouraged to focus on discovery learning—in which students are free

to work in a learning environment with little or no guidance. Under the banner of social constructivism, the call for discovery learning remains, but with a modest shift in form—students are expected to work in groups in a learning environment with little or no guidance ... The research ... shows that *the formula constructivism = hands-on activity is a formula for educational disaster.*[33] [Emphasis added]

Ken Rowe and I noted in a review of middle schooling for the New Zealand Ministry of Education:

> Whereas constructivism is an established, legitimate theory of learning and knowing ... it is not a theory of teaching. This has particular relevance for effective pedagogy during the middle years, especially given the strong advocacy in middle school teaching for 'hands-on', 'action-oriented', constructivist learning activities.[34]

In highlighting the inappropriateness of constructivism as an operational theory of teaching, Wilson commented:

> We largely ignore generations of professional experience and knowledge in favour of a slick postmodern theoretical approach, most often characterised by the misuse of the notion of constructivism.[35]

This is not the full extent of the fads and fashions, however. There is a raft of other approaches for which a research evidence base is either lacking or non-supportive. These include learning styles (see following), 'neuro-linguistic programming', multiple intelligences, 'thinking hats', brain exercise, emotional intelligence, the 'Mozart effect', so-called 21st century curriculum and associated skills, and 'digital natives'.[36]

Learning styles

The notion of the existence of learning styles has been around since the 1970s; there are now more than 70 extant models ranging from early childhood to higher education. An online search of 'learning styles' will yield more than 31 million hits. It has become a vast, lucrative industry, with inventories, manuals, video resources, in-service packages, websites, publications and workshops.[a]

---

a   An online search on 'learning styles workshops' will yield around 2.5 million hits, indicating the scope of the industry. On the other hand, 'learning styles criticism or critique' yields about 1.8 million results.

However, psychologists and neuroscientists agree there is little efficacy in these models, which rest on dubious evidential grounds. Of the very many publications supporting the existence and use of learning styles in teaching, most have not been subject to peer review. Hattie has noted that 'It is hard not to be sceptical about these learning preference claims'.[37]

Stahl has commented:

> I work with a lot of different schools and listen to a lot of teachers talk. Nowhere have I seen a greater conflict between 'craft knowledge' or what teachers know (or at least think they know) and 'academic knowledge' or what researchers know (or at least think they know) than in the area of learning styles ... The whole notion seems fairly intuitive. People are different. Certainly different people might learn differently from each other. It makes sense.[38]

However, there is a distinct lack of empirical support for the existence of learning styles:

> The reason researchers roll their eyes at learning styles is the utter failure to find that assessing children's learning styles and matching to instructional methods has any effect on their learning.[39]

The authors of an extensive review of the research evidence for learning styles concluded:

> Although the literature on learning styles is enormous, very few studies have even used an experimental methodology capable of testing the validity of learning styles applied to education. Moreover, of those that did use an appropriate method, several found results that flatly contradict the popular meshing hypothesis.
>
> We conclude therefore, that at present, *there is no adequate evidence base to justify incorporating learning styles assessments into general educational practice.*[40] [Emphasis added]

Yet as Scott has observed:

> Failure to find evidence for the utility of tailoring instruction to individuals' learning styles has not prevented this term from being a perennial inclusion in discussions about and recommendations on pedagogy. It also continues to influence what teachers do in their day-to-day work. Practitioners from preschool to university level attempt to apply the theory in classrooms, administering the unreliable tests, criticised by so many, to their students, using the results as a guide to classroom practice and encouraging or requiring

students to apply the results to understanding, controlling and explaining their own learning.[41]

References to learning styles still abound in many curriculum documents at system and school level, despite the lack of evidence for their existence. When I have pointed this out to educators, the usual response is that it 'doesn't matter'. However, it does matter, because of the problems and harm that can be caused by the categorisation, labelling and limiting of learning experiences of students through the continued belief in and application of so-called learning styles. Would we tolerate doctors continuing to use a disproved, harmful treatment?

Multiple intelligences

In 2013 Bennett exposed the lack of evidence for many of these educational fads and the harm they can do.[42] Unfortunately, these approaches are popular, particularly in primary schools, and are often thrown together in what Howard Gardner of 'multiple intelligences' (MI) fame terms 'dazzling promiscuity'. In fairness to Gardner, he is highly critical of how his work has been reified and misused in education:

> I learned that an entire state in Australia had adapted an education programme based in part on MI theory. The more I learned about this programme, the less comfortable I was … much of it was a mishmash of practices, with neither scientific foundation nor clinical warrant. Left-brain and right-brain contrasts, sensory learning styles, 'neuro-linguistic programming', and MI approaches commingled with dazzling promiscuity.[43]

Myers-Briggs, etc.

Another form of categorisation occurs through the use of various forms of personality tests sometimes administered to students. The danger lies with how the results of such tests are used and whether this use engenders 'entity thinking' or fixed mindsets in students[44] [b] and stereotyping and fixed, inappropriate expectations for students held by teachers. Paul has commented:

> Millions of people worldwide take personality tests each year to direct their education, to decide on a career, to determine if they'll be hired, to join the armed forces, and to settle legal disputes … the sheer number of tests administered obscures a simple fact: they don't work. Most personality tests are seriously flawed, and sometimes unequivocally wrong. They fail the field's own standards of validity and reliability.[45]

---

b   Dweck's work in this area is discussed later in this chapter.

Neuromyths

There is much information and misinformation about the brain and learning. Dekker and colleagues tested some of the 'neuromyths' held by teachers—which they define as beliefs 'loosely based on scientific facts'—and the possible effects of these on teachers and their teaching:

> A large observational survey design was used to assess general knowledge of the brain and neuromyths. The sample comprised 242 primary and secondary school teachers who were interested in the neuroscience of learning ... Participants completed an online survey containing 32 statements about the brain and its influence on learning, of which 15 were neuromyths ... Results showed that on average, teachers believed 49% of the neuromyths, *particularly myths related to commercialized educational programs.* ...
>
> These findings suggest that *teachers who are enthusiastic about the possible application of neuroscience findings in the classroom find it difficult to distinguish pseudoscience from scientific facts.*[46] [Emphases added]

One of the best sources of factual information in respect of the brain and learning is still *How People Learn: Brain, mind, experience and school* (2000) mentioned previously.[47] It is well worth following up. More recently *Learn to Teach, Teach to Learn* (2015) is also worthy of consultation.[48] Each goes into much more detail on the evidence for learning than is possible here.

Harm can be done

As Stahl[49], Bennett[50] and others have noted, these approaches are intrinsically appealing but the fact is, learning is not so simple. Aside from wasting teachers' and students' time and the schools' money, the real cost of dabbling with such unsupported strategies is that students are not being taught what they need to know, coupled with the harm caused by arbitrary, invalid labelling, categorisation and stereotyping. Through such practices students can come to see their abilities as fixed or limited, something Carol Dweck has termed 'entity thinking'[51] (see following page). This can powerfully constrain future learning. Those convinced that they have a natural, innate talent for something will be disappointed when they come to expect success without effort, while those who believe they don't have a talent for something may be put off from even trying.

I have noted previously that:

> ... one of the most damaging things we can do to people is to put them into categories and treat them accordingly.[52]

Hattie found that *not* labelling students has a large effect size of 0.61 for student learning[53], yet categorisation is something approaches such as learning styles, thinking hats, multiple intelligences, personality types[54] and so forth, are predicated on.

Entity versus malleable theory of intelligence

Carol Dweck identified and refuted a number of harmful, invalid beliefs about students and schooling:

- the belief that students with high ability are more likely to display mastery-oriented qualities
- the belief that success in school directly fosters mastery-oriented qualities
- the belief that praise, particularly praising a student's intelligence, encourages mastery-oriented qualities
- the belief that students' confidence in their intelligence is the key to mastery-oriented qualities.[55]

Dweck goes on to contrast 'two frameworks for understanding intelligence and achievement':

- **The theory of fixed intelligence**—Some people believe that their intelligence is a fixed trait. They have a certain amount of it and that's that. We call this an 'entity theory' of intelligence because intelligence is portrayed as an entity that dwells within us that we can't change.
- **The theory of malleable intelligence**—Other people have a very different definition of intelligence. For them intelligence is not a fixed trait that they simply possess, but something they can cultivate through learning. We call this an 'incremental theory' of intelligence because intelligence is portrayed as something that can be increased through one's efforts.[56]

The concepts of entity intelligence and its counterpart, malleable intelligence, have great significance to teaching and learning. One implication is that we need to avoid giving students the view that their ability is fixed. This applies equally whether they are currently able to perform at a high level, or a low level, in any area or subject.

Telling someone they are a 'natural' at something can be equally harmful as telling them they are 'hopeless'. I will wager that everyone reading this has at some time been told or been given a message that they are no good at something. Whether we are talking about sport, music, mathematics, languages or any other area, such a belief can powerfully constrain future success in that area of endeavour and create a barrier to further participation and improvement.

The implication for teaching is that we need to concentrate on communicating to students how their *current performance* on any task or in any subject compares to the standard expected. This must be accompanied by constructive feedback to help them understand what is required to improve their learning and performance. To use the example of so-called 'gifted and talented students', by all means challenge them, accelerate their learning, and find ways to further develop their capabilities. On the other hand, if you can avoid it, don't tell them that they are gifted and perhaps more importantly, don't tell their parents. This may seem confusing. If a person is an expert in any area, surely they are aware of this. However, ask any high achieving person and they will invariably tell you about the long hours of practice, the sacrifices, the coaching and the dedication required to be successful. To some degree it is an insult to label such people as naturals. On the other hand, I have heard a teacher say to a student 'You're no good at maths and I shouldn't be surprised because your brother wasn't either'. Such comments set up entity thinking, with all the attendant dangers and problems identified by Dweck.

Thus it is important to carefully consider how and what we communicate to students about their achievements. We need to concentrate on what they can do at a particular time and not give a message that their ability is fixed forever.

What about self-esteem?

Research shows that student self-esteem or self-concept can have moderate or greater effects on student learning (Hattie found an effect size of 0.47 for student self-concept[57]).

Some teachers have been convinced therefore, that if self-esteem can be boosted to higher levels, this will result in enhanced learning, a classic case of 'putting the cart before the horse' or confusing cause and effect. Conversely, it is thought that any form of criticism, correction or failure will harm students' self-esteem and thus learning, and should therefore be avoided. The downside of this is that students can gain an inflated view of their capacities, which can lead to the entity thinking mentioned previously.[58] I've observed schools where no one receives a 'bad' or failing mark, red pens are not used to correct work because 'red is an angry colour', and 'merit' certificates are thrown around like confetti for meeting normal expectations such as sitting quietly when eating one's lunch. In short, rampant, devalued, 'positive reinforcement' abounds.

However, the best way to legitimately boost self-esteem is for students to receive regular constructive, developmental feedback, something known to have one of the most powerful effects on learning.[59] If students can see and feel themselves achieving, even in small increments, this can then lead to an increase in self-concept/esteem that sets up a cycle for further improvement. However empty, inauthentic, unwarranted praise ultimately hampers both learning and self-esteem.[60]

Authentic achievement, no matter how small, is thus the best way to engender self-concept and self-esteem. This can then serve as a foundation for further achievement. When students have their self-esteem boosted artificially in inauthentic ways, they can be confused about their actual ability and the air can quickly come out of the self-esteem balloon when they hit the wide world and meet real-life challenges.[61] Unwarranted self-esteem boosting works against building perseverance and resilience in students, qualities necessary to meet challenges in schooling and later life.[62]

Comment: what do students think?

A key point to consider: have students been asked what they think of all this, especially the various uses of categorisation? Their answers will be instructive. In my experience, students will put up with such methods, even when they know them to be invalid. There are many students who have been very successful in various areas out of school (music, sport, drama, for example), yet were not considered to possess such ability within school because of judgements made by teachers. Some young people are also late developers, and this development can be hindered by their negative experiences in school.

We now turn to strategies and techniques that *have* been found to be powerful agents for student learning.

Self-report grades

The highest influence of all on student achievement, according to Hattie's meta-analyses, was self-report(ed) grades, with an effect size of 1.44, an effect beyond very large and in the 'radioactive' category.[63]

Hattie notes:

> Overall, students have reasonably accurate understandings of their levels of achievement ... [however]
>
> There are at least two groups that are not as good at predicting their performance and who do not always predict in the right direction: minority students and lower achieving students ... They tend to underestimate their achievement and, over time, they come to believe their lower estimates and lose the confidence to take on more challenging tasks ...
>
> Student reflection of their performance alone makes no difference. Emphasising accurate calibration is more effective than rewarding improved performance. The message is that teachers need to provide opportunities for students to be involved in predicting their performance; clearly, making the learning intentions and success criteria transparent, having high, but appropriate, expectations, and providing feedback at the appropriate levels ... is critical to building confidence in successfully taking on challenging tasks. Educating students to have high, challenging, appropriate expectations is among the most powerful influence in enhancing student achievement.[64]

I have developed and successfully used the following approach to using self-report grades with a range of teachers and school leaders across Australia; in turn, they have used it with their students. I don't advocate that it be used for every lesson or activity, but experience has shown it is a powerful training, analytic and cognitive exercise. It requires both teachers and students to think about what they are doing and what success looks like.

There are six steps in the process:

1. **Carefully explain to students an assignment or learning activity, including key terms and directions**—This is always a good way to start and requires the teacher to be clear in their learning intentions. Checking for student understanding of key terms and directions is essential in this step. If students are unclear about what they have to do, poor performance is almost guaranteed.
2. **Provide students with the assessment rubric, including criteria and the marking/assessment scale/method for each item/criterion**—This step is about students having a clear idea of the expectations for the activity, the elements of what is required, and what acceptable performance looks like. Where students are unsure of the standard required, this can lead to confusion. Providing examples of unacceptable, acceptable and superior performance on a task can be a powerful aid to successfully completing the task and to improvement.[c] The old technique of 'compare and contrast' can be valuable here: 'Here are three examples of responses to 'x'. Which is the best and why?'
   - *Optional:* Jointly discuss and determine criteria to be used with students. [A useful activity once students are familiar with the approach. This promotes deeper thinking about the task and can engage, empower and show respect to students.]
3. **Students complete the activity (individually or in groups) using the rubric as a guide**—This is the most powerful use of a rubric, to guide completion of a task rather than just assessing how a task or criterion of the task has been performed.
4. **Students assess their work using the rubric**—An interesting phenomenon sometimes occurs with this step—students can be quite self-critical (see Hattie's previous comments about minority and lower performing students); some students will be 'harder' on themselves than their teacher might be.
   - *Optional:* Students assess another student's work and discuss the work with that student.
5. **Teacher assesses each student's work, providing feedback using the rubric**—It is important here that the teacher's assessments are congruent with the earlier instructions, the rubric and standards expected. For example, it is counter-productive and 'unfair' (students have low tolerance for unfairness)

---

c This is not 'cheating', although I have heard it labelled as such. Regardless of what we are attempting to learn, it is always advantageous to be able to see what good performance looks like.

to introduce additional criteria at this stage, for example, 'I'm reducing your mark by 25% because your work is untidy', 'I'm taking off 5 marks because you were noisy', or 'I'm taking off 10 marks because I find you obnoxious', if these were not part of the original criteria/rubric.
6. **Student and teacher discuss/compare their assessments**—A most important step where discussion and moderation ('give and take') can occur. It is powerful if the teacher (and student) is prepared to listen to evidence and to be flexible, e.g., 'Yes, I think you are right, it is a B rather than a C'.
    - *One-to-one conferences are powerful:* As seen in Chapter 1, the one-to-one conference between teacher and student is important in the teacher knowing the student as a learner and person, and vice versa, and for individualised feedback to be given.

In my experience, if you start to use this process with students, expect them to ask 'Will we get to assess our own work?' in the future. The lasting benefits include students (and yourself) thinking more deeply about an activity and checking for understanding, being more aware of required standards, using rubrics or criteria to guide the work, engaging in self-assessment prior to submission and assessment by the teacher, and constructive feedback, discussion and adjustment to assessment where necessary.

Direct teaching/instruction

Direct teaching/instruction (ES = 0.59) is described by Hattie thus:

> In a nutshell: The teacher decides the learning intentions and success criteria, makes them transparent to the students, demonstrates by modelling, evaluates if they understand what they had been told by checking for understanding, and re-telling them what they had been told by tying it all together with closure.[65]

It is a mistake to confuse this approach with that of didactic teaching, yet some have chosen to conflate the two. The approach by Hattie above is congruent and compatible with the six-step process for self-report grades I have outlined. In both cases—self-report grades and direct instruction—it is really about the teacher orchestrating the learning, and not merely lecturing or having a rigid approach to the transmission of information. If done well, it promotes a 'growth mindset'.[66]

The importance of spaced practice

Another strategy with a large measured effect size (ES = 0.71[67]) in respect of student learning is that of 'spaced' practice. Once again, some people seem to be ideologically opposed to the notion of practice, equating it with drills and rote learning. Spaced practice means structuring the learning experience so that students have the opportunity to receive instruction, perform a task, receive feedback to improve their performance and then complete the task again, rather than simply performing it once, that is 'mass' practice.

Reeves has noted in respect of practice:

> Research shows the value of deliberate practice across fields such as music to athletics: ... children and adults need deliberate practice in order to achieve their objectives ... The components of deliberate practice include performance that is based on a particular element of the task, expert coaching, feedback, careful and accurate self-assessment, and—this is the key—the opportunity to apply feedback immediately for improved performance.[68]

Thus, if you are a soccer coach, you don't have your players practise soccer by playing a game of soccer. You isolate the essential, discrete skills and strategies (e.g., heading the ball, kicking the ball with either foot, where to position on corners, etc.), coach your players in these skills, let them perform the skill, give them constructive feedback—note the reference to self-assessment once again ('careful and accurate self-assessment')—and let them perform the task once more, that is engage in further 'spaced' practice. Then it might be time to play a game.

Feedback

Teacher-to-student feedback does not have the largest effect size of those strategies and approaches at our disposal (ES = 0.75, number 10 on Hattie's list of 150 influences on student learning[69]), but in some ways it *is* a 'silver bullet', simply because there are so many opportunities for feedback, and in many cases, feedback is done so poorly.

I have noted:

> Look at learning or mastery in fields as diverse as sports, the arts, languages, the sciences or recreational activities and it's easy to see how important feedback is to learning and accomplishment. An expert teacher, mentor or coach can readily explain, demonstrate and detect flaws in performance. He or she can also identify talent and potential, and build on these.
>
> In contrast, trial and error learning or poor teaching are less effective and take longer. If performance flaws are not detected and corrected, these can become ingrained and will be much harder to eradicate later. Learners who don't receive instruction, encouragement and correction can become disillusioned and quit due to lack of progress.[70]

The issue of feedback has rightly received a lot of attention and there are various approaches, all worthy of consideration. Based upon my research experience, I believe there are four key questions students require answers to, if their learning is to move forward:

The four questions of students[d]
- What can I do?
- What can't I do?
- How does my work compare with that of others?
- How can I do better?

Keeping in mind previous advice about avoiding entity thinking, students need to know what they can do at the present time ('ticks') and what they can't do ('crosses'), again, at the present time and not for all time. For many students, this is where feedback begins and ends, and has little impact, at least of a positive nature, on learning.

'How does my work compare with that of others?' is really about the standards expected for the student at his or her stage of schooling. It is more than just position in the class or year, and has the potential to be useful, especially if a technique like self-report grades is employed.

However, the most important question and answer, and one that in my experience students rarely receive, is 'How can I do better?' This is where constructive feedback that assists the student to improve their performance needs to be provided. I have had teachers say to me 'I can tell them when they are right, and I can tell them when they are wrong, but I find it hard to tell them how they can improve'. If that's the case, then the teacher is more a referee (assessor) than a coach (teacher).

Here is a powerful, instructive quote from a 14-year-old student:

> I really hate it when you wait for weeks to get back some piece of work and then it says 'Well done. B', and there are a few scribbles here and there. *You don't know what you're supposed to do to get any better.*[71] [Emphasis added]

Nuthall offered some salutary comments on this issue, pointing out that based on his research in New Zealand primary classrooms, students received the majority of their feedback not from their teacher but from other students, with much of this feedback being incorrect.[72]

It should be pointed out that feedback can take many forms, and not just marks or grades. It can be verbal, graphical, and can even be communicated through body language. There is some suggestion that if you want students to read your written feedback, don't put a mark or grade on their work, because otherwise that is what they will fixate on, and entity thinking may well kick in, that is, '20 out of 20. The teacher

---

d It is arguable that we all need answers to these questions, whatever our role.

has recognised that I am a genius', or alternatively, 'Eight out of 20. The teacher is hopeless'. I should point out that such thinking is not restricted to school students. I have had the situation where a postgraduate education student commented upon a mark that I awarded them: 'This can't be right, I'm a high distinction student', usually followed by a request for a re-assessment.

A structured approach to considering feedback

In working with teachers, schools and university faculties, I have successfully used the following process to begin a productive, professional conversation about feedback:

1. **What are our present approaches—formal and informal—to student feedback? Conduct an audit.** This could well involve classroom observation of teaching. For example, who receives the majority of feedback? The 'bright' girls or boys? Those who are misbehaving? Those at the front of the room? And what of the feedback itself—is it predominantly negative or is it constructive? Examine some examples of written feedback provided to students. Does it answer the four questions mentioned previously? How frequently and in what forms is feedback provided? Do students have the opportunity to provide feedback on this feedback, that is, what Argyris has termed 'double-loop' feedback?[73]

2. **Are our assessment methods and criteria clear, valid and reliable? Identify the links between assessment and feedback.** One area where I believe the professional development of educators is generally lacking is in the area of assessment. Constructing valid and reliable assessment tasks is not easy, and not all teachers have this knowledge. The second point is also important. Feedback should be congruent with instructions for the assessment task, as noted previously.

3. **Do our students understand what is meant by feedback?** This is vital if student learning is to be moved forward. Just as with the wording of the assessment task itself, we need to check for understanding of the feedback provided. Scales, marks, terminology, and further instructions and suggestions provided to students all need to be checked for understanding.

4. **Is the feedback our students receive infrequent, unfocused, unhelpful, inconsistent or negative?** We have already discussed the importance of practice. Irregular or infrequent feedback is less effective in improving student performance. Examples of unfocused feedback include statements such as: 'concentrate'; 'revise your work'; 'try harder'. These statements are unhelpful. Inconsistent feedback also confuses students. For example, I observed some written work a primary student had submitted to her teacher. It came back

with a mark of 6.5 out of 10 and the single comment 'Not enough detail'. (There was not much detail in the teacher's comment, but we'll ignore that.) The next time the student submitted similar work, it again came back with 6.5 out of 10 and the comment 'Too much detail'. Negative feedback speaks for itself. It is unhelpful in showing students what they need to do to improve their work. Unrelenting negative feedback can also demoralise and dishearten.

5. **Is the feedback we provide focused, comprehensive, consistent and improvement oriented, addressing the four key questions raised above? (especially, 'How can I do better?')** This is the key to effective, constructive, developmental feedback, and moves beyond assessment *of* learning towards the goal of assessment *for* learning, that is, from judgement to development.

6. **How does the feedback our students receive relate to parental feedback through reports, interviews and parent–teacher nights? Is feedback to students and parents consistent?** In my experience most parents/caregivers would like to assist their children to improve their work if they are shown how, and if they understand what the work is about. One thing that gets parents 'offside' is hearing very little about how their child is progressing, and then receiving a message that their child's work or behaviour is unacceptable, and has been for some time. The other thing we need to pay attention to is how we report on students' progress to parents. Some means of reporting are almost incomprehensible and worse, inconsistent when the child, for example, has been receiving high grades ('distinctions') and then some form of moderation or normalisation occurs and they end up with a middle grade ('C') on their report. I have experienced this with my own children. A final aspect is where parents do not have an English speaking background. Some of the most successful low SES schools I've studied have been very effective at translating and interpreting key information for parents on a regular basis, and not just through annual rituals such as parent–teacher nights and school reports, but on a more regular and 'need to know' basis.[74]

7. **How can we provide our students with improved feedback?** This then becomes the plan for improvement. Once we have completed our audit, we can examine what is known about effective feedback and put a plan into place. Some educators that I have worked with have engaged in a benchmarking exercise, whereby a pre-test is given at the beginning of a unit of work, a program of feedback is then implemented during the unit, and another assessment is given at the end of the work, enabling student growth and an effect size to be calculated, if desired.

8. **How will we know if it works? What evidence will we need?** Here we need to think about what success will look like and how it will be measured. Any time we plan an activity or longer unit of work we need to think about the outcomes that are intended for the work and how these will be achieved, demonstrated and assessed. Finally, it is important to evaluate and learn from this process and to modify our strategies for future work.

The answers to the above questions will provide an important foundation for improving the quality of teaching and student achievement in our schools. However, we need to consider a cautionary note. *Feedback is only one part of the equation. It is not a substitute or remedy for poor teaching.*

Concluding remarks

This chapter considered the key question of what works *best* in teaching. A strong thread running through the discussion has been the need for teachers to be critical consumers of research and to be evidence-based in their practice, both in respect of evidence informing what they do, and in respect of generating evidence of their students', and therefore, their success.

We need to concentrate on the strategies and approaches that have been found to have *most* impact on student achievement, and to question and disregard practices that not only have been found to be ineffective, but in some cases are known to be harmful.

Endnotes

1. Hattie, J. (2009). *Visible learning: A synthesis of over 800 meta-analyses relating to achievement.* London, England: Routledge.
2. Dinham, S. (2008a). *How to get your school moving and improving: An evidence-based approach.* Melbourne, Victoria: ACER Press.
3. Dinham, S. (2008a). (pp. 138–141)
4. Dinham, S. (2008a). (p. 140)
5. Hattie, J. (2012). *Visible learning for teachers.* London, England: Routledge. (pp. 251–252)
6. Hattie, J. (2012). (p. 251)
7. See Dinham, S. (2008); Dinham, S. (2007). How schools get moving and keep improving: Leadership for teacher learning, student success and school renewal. *Australian Journal of Education, 51*(3), 263–275; Ayres, P., Dinham, S., & Sawyer, W. (2000). Successful senior secondary teaching. *Quality Teaching Series*, No. 1, Australian College of Education, September, 1–20.
8. Hattie, J. (2012). (p. 251)
9. Robinson, V., Hohepa, M., & Lloyd, C. (2009). *School leadership and student outcomes: Identifying what works and why.* Wellington, New Zealand: New Zealand Ministry of Education. (p. 39)
10. Hattie, J. (2012). (p. 252)

11 Dinham, S. (2007). How schools get moving and keep improving: Leadership for teacher learning, student success and school renewal. *Australian Journal of Education, 51*(3), 263–275.

12 Robinson, V., Lloyd, C., & Rowe, K. (2008). The impact of leadership on student outcomes: An analysis of the differential effects of leadership types. *Educational Administration Quarterly, 44*(5), 635–674.

13 Teacher Education Ministerial Advisory Group. (2014). *Action now: Classroom ready teachers.* Canberra, Australia: Department of Education; Dinham, S. (2015). *Issues and perspectives relevant to the development of an approach to the accreditation of initial teacher education in Australia based on evidence of impact.* Melbourne, Victoria: AITSL.

14 Hattie, J. (2012). (p. 252)

15 Dinham, S. (2014). Primary schooling in Australia: Pseudo-science plus extras times growing inequality equals decline. In Australian College of Educators. (2014). *What counts as quality in education?* (pp. 3–15). Carlton South, Victoria: Australian College of Educators. (p. 10). Reprinted with permission.

16 Hattie, J. (2012). (p. 252)

17 Flynn, J. R. (1984). The mean IQ of Americans: Massive gains 1932 to 1978. *Psychological Bulletin, 95,* 29–51.

18 Scott, C. (2015). *Learn to teach, teach to learn.* Port Melbourne, Victoria: Cambridge University Press. (p. 77)

19 Thomson, S., De Bortoli, L., & Buckley, S. (2013). *PISA in brief: Highlights from the full Australian Report: PISA 2012: How Australia measures up.* Melbourne, Australia: ACER.

20 Australian Curriculum, Assessment and Reporting Authority (2014). *NAPLAN Achievement in Reading, Persuasive Writing, Language Conventions and Numeracy: National report for 2014.* Sydney, New South Wales: ACARA.

21 Brady, L. (1987). *Curriculum development.* (2nd ed.). New York, NY: Prentice Hall. (pp. 3–20)

22 Scott, C. (2009). How the ghosts of the nineteenth century still haunt education. *Policy Futures in Education, 7*(1), 75–87; McGuinness, D. (1997). *Why our children can't read and what we can do about it.* New York, NY: Simon & Schuster.

23 Scott, C. (2009); Christodoulou, D. (2014). *Seven myths about education.* London, England: Routledge. (pp. 11–14)

24 Dinham, S. (2008a). (pp. 95–96)

25 Hattie, J. (2012). (p. 254)

26 Willingham, D. (2009). *Why students don't like school.* San Francisco, CA: Jossey-Bass. (p. 47)

27 Shulman, L. (1986). Those who understand: Knowledge growth in teaching. *Educational Researcher, 15*(2), 4–14.

28 Ayres, P., Dinham, S., & Sawyer, W. (2004). Effective teaching in the context of a Grade 12 high stakes external examination in New South Wales, Australia. *British Educational Research Journal, 30*(1), 141–165.

29 Christodoulou, D. (2014). (pp. 27–42); Ayres, P., Dinham, S., & Sawyer, W. (2004); Dinham, S. (2008). (p. 95)

30 Mayer, R. (2004). Should there be a three-strikes rule against pure discovery learning? *American Psychologist, 59*(1), 14–19. (p. 18)

31 Hattie, J. (2012). (pp. 251, 253)

32 Ayres, P., Dinham, S., & Sawyer, W. (2004); McCulla, N., Dinham, S., & Scott, C. (2007). Stepping out from the crowd: Some findings from the NSW Quality Teaching

Awards on Seeking Recognition for Professional Accomplishment. *Unicorn Online Refereed Article*, ORA 51, 3–32.

33 Mayer, R. (2004). (p. 17); see also Kirschner, P., Sweller, J., & Clark, R. (2006). Why minimal guidance during instruction does not work: An analysis of the failure of constructivist, discovery, problem-based, experiential, and inquiry-based teaching. *Educational Psychologist, 41*(2), 75–86. Copyright © 2004 American Psychological Association. Reproduced with permission.

34 Dinham, S., & Rowe, K. (2007). *Teaching and learning in middle schooling: A review of the literature—A Report to the New Zealand Ministry of Education*. Melbourne, Victoria: ACER. (p. 58)

35 Wilson, B. (2005). *Unlocking potential*. Paper presented at the 2005 Australian and New Zealand School of Government (ANZSOG) conference, University of Sydney, 29 September (pp. 2–3).

36 See, for example, Bennett, T. (2013). *Teacher proof—Why research in education doesn't always mean what it claims, and what you can do about it*. Milton Park, Oxon: Routledge; Scott, C. (2015).

37 Hattie, J. (2009). (p. 197)

38 Stahl, S. (1999). Different strokes for different folks? A critique of learning styles. *American Educator, Fall*, 1–5, 1.

39 Stahl, S. (1999). (p. 1)

40 Pashler, H., McDaniel, M., Rohrer, D., & Bjork, R. (2008). Learning styles—Concepts and evidence. *Psychological Science in the Public Interest, 9*(3), 105–119. (p. 105)

41 Scott, C. (2010). The enduring appeal of 'learning styles'. *Australian Journal of Education, 54*(1), 5–17. (p. 8)

42 Bennett, T. (2013).

43 Gardner, H., cited in Demos (2004). *About learning: Report of the Learning Working Group*. London, England: Demos. (p. 15)

44 Dweck, C. (2000). *Self-theories—Their role in motivation, personality and development*. Philadelphia, PA: Psychology Press.

45 Paul, A. (2004). *The cult of personality: How personality tests are leading us to miseducate our children, mismanage our companies, and misunderstand ourselves*. New York, NY: Free Press.

46 Dekker, S., Lee, N., Howard-Jones, P., & Jolles, J. (2012). Neuromyths in education: Prevalence and predictors of misconceptions among teachers. *Frontiers in Psychology, 3*(429), 1–8. (p. 1)

47 Bransford, J., Brown, A., & Cocking, R. (Eds.). (2000). *How people learn*. Washington, DC: National Academy Press.

48 Scott, C. (2015).

49 Stahl, S. (1999).

50 Bennett, T. (2013).

51 Dweck, C. (2000).

52 Dinham, S. (2008a). (p. 1)

53 Hattie, J. (2012). (p. 251)

54 See Paul, A. (2004).

55 Dweck, C. (2000). (pp. 1–2)

56 Dweck, C. (2000). (pp. 2–3)

57 Hattie, J. (2012). (p. 252)

58 Dweck, C. (2000).

59 Dinham, S. (2008b). Feedback on feedback. *Teacher*, May, 20–23; Hattie, J. (2012). (pp. 115–137)
60 Scott, C., & Dinham, S. (2005). Parenting, teaching and self-esteem. *Australian Educational Leader*, 27(1), 28–30; Dinham, S., & Scott, C. (2007). Parenting, teaching and leadership styles. *The Australian Educational Leader*, 29(1), 30–32, 45.
61 Dinham, S. (2010). The perils of self-esteem boosting, *Leadership in Focus*, Summer, 20, 23–25.
62 Stewart, D., Sun, J., Patterson, C., Lemerle, K., & Hardie, M. (2004). Promoting and building resilience in primary school communities: Evidence from a comprehensive 'health promoting school' approach. *International Journal of Mental Health Promotion*, 6(3), 26–33.
63 Hattie, J. (2009). (pp. 43–44); Hattie, J. (2012). (pp. 53–54)
64 Hattie, J. (2012). (pp. 53–54)
65 Hattie, J. (2009). (pp. 205–206)
66 Dweck, C. (2000).
67 Hattie, J. (2012). (p. 251)
68 Reeves, D. (2010). *Transforming professional development into student results*. Alexandria, VA: ASCD. (p. 66)
69 Hattie, J. (2012). (p. 251)
70 Dinham, S. (2008b).
71 Glasson, T. (2009). *Improving student achievement*. Carlton South, Victoria: Curriculum Corporation. (p. 53)
72 Nuthall, G. (2007). *The hidden lives of learners*. Wellington, New Zealand: NZCER.
73 Argyris, C. (1982). *Reasoning, learning, and action*. San Francisco, CA: Jossey-Bass.
74 See Dinham, S. (2007). *Leadership for exceptional educational outcomes*. Teneriffe, Qld: Post Pressed.

CHAPTER 3

International patterns of student achievement: How do we measure achievement and how and why do these measurements vary?

INTRODUCTION

In this chapter we consider the notion of student achievement, and how it can be defined and measured. We will examine the commonly utilised international measures of achievement and what these reveal, both internationally and for Australia, and how and why these measurements vary, both at any point in time and over time. Influences or factors in such achievement will be explored.

This macro level of analysis or 'big picture' will provide a foundation for the chapters that follow.

A broad(er) conception of student achievement

Student achievement is often equated with performance on standardised tests, both international and national. However, this is a narrow conceptualisation. In making judgements about schooling effectiveness, we need to consider the full range of intended outcomes for schooling and the degree to which these are being achieved or not before drawing conclusions about the performance of a school, system, state or nation.

In the case of Australia, a particularly useful document is the *Melbourne Declaration on Educational Goals for Young Australians* (2008).[1] This declaration has been formulated and agreed to by all Australian education ministers and is binding, in the sense that every school, system, state and territory, along with the Commonwealth, has 'signed off' on both the goals themselves and their pursuit. (This declaration followed similar declarations in 1999 (*The Adelaide Declaration*) and the *Hobart Declaration* of 1989.)[a]

The Melbourne Declaration states that:

> As a nation Australia values the central role of education in building a democratic, equitable and just society—a society that is prosperous, cohesive and culturally diverse, and that values Australia's Indigenous cultures as a key part of the nation's history, present and future.[2]

The Melbourne Declaration speaks of the economic, social and personal outcomes of schooling, and not just those outcomes revealed through testing. As such, I believe it to be an excellent frame for the sorts of emphases and evidence we might utilise at a class, school, system level, or above, to both guide the pursuit of the stated outcomes and to judge our success at achieving these. I find it disappointing that given we have agreed to pursue these outcomes in every school and for every student in Australia, there appears to be a very low level of recognition, and therefore use of the Declaration, in day-to-day schooling.

In terms of the breadth and depth of these goals, the Melbourne Declaration states:

> In the 21st century Australia's capacity to provide a high quality of life for all will depend on the ability to compete in the global economy on knowledge and innovation. Education equips young people with the knowledge, understanding, skills and values to take advantage of opportunity and to face the challenges of this era with confidence.
>
> Schools play a vital role in promoting the intellectual, physical, social, emotional, moral, spiritual and aesthetic development and wellbeing of young Australians, and in ensuring the nation's ongoing economic prosperity and

---

a   Because education is essentially a state and territory responsibility under the Australian Constitution, it is necessary to gain agreement for such national statements and goals.

social cohesion. Schools share this responsibility with students, parents, carers, families, the community, business and other education and training providers.[3]

The goals themselves are simple, yet powerful:

Improving educational outcomes for all young Australians is central to the nation's social and economic prosperity and will position young people to live fulfilling, productive and responsible lives.

Young Australians are therefore placed at the centre of the Melbourne Declaration on Educational Goals.

These goals are:

Goal 1:
Australian schooling promotes equity and excellence.

Goal 2:
All young Australians become:
- successful *learners*
- confident and creative *individuals*
- active and informed *citizens*.[4] [Emphasis added]

Goal 1 comprises the twin aims of raising overall student performance ('excellence') and addressing aspects of disadvantage that result in poor student performance ('equity'). Excellence is sometimes referred to as 'raising the bar', and equity as 'closing the gap'. This is something of a balancing act, in that increasing 'excellence' might result in widening of the 'equity' gap if those at 'the bottom' are left behind, while a major focus on equity could result in 'closing the gap', yet 'lowering the bar'.

In respect of goal 2, becoming 'successful learners' doesn't mean that every student obtains a high Australian Tertiary Admission Rank (ATAR) or university entrance, but it does mean that all students:

- develop their capacity to learn and play an active role in their own learning
- have the essential skills in literacy and numeracy and are creative and productive users of technology, especially ICT, as a foundation for success in all learning areas
- are able to think deeply and logically, and obtain and evaluate evidence in a disciplined way as the result of studying fundamental disciplines
- are creative, innovative and resourceful, and are able to solve problems in ways that draw upon a range of learning areas and disciplines
- are able to plan activities independently, collaborate, work in teams and communicate ideas

- are able to make sense of their world and think about how things have become the way they are
- are on a pathway towards continued success in further education, training or employment, and acquire the skills to make informed learning and employment decisions throughout their lives
- are motivated to reach their full potential.[5]

These goals are unmistakably aspirational, as they should be. We cannot have different expectations for different groups of students. We cannot guarantee all students will achieve the above ends to achieve a uniform, high standard, but we need to provide all students with the opportunity to do so.

In addition to what might be termed the 'academic domain' of successful learning, the Melbourne Declaration expands on what it means to be a 'confident and creative individual' (what could be called the 'personal' domain of achievement), and what it means to be an 'active and informed citizen' (the 'social' domain). In other words, student achievement is defined and described in terms more broadly and holistically than just performance on external tests.

Thus, the two goals together act as both more of a global conception of student achievement, and as a useful frame for identifying and employing strategies, and engendering and measuring success at varying levels, from the individual student, to the classroom, school, system, state or territory, and to the nation.

Below are some questions based upon the goals that school staff I have worked with have found useful.

Some key questions to consider in your school

1. What are we doing about promoting *excellence* in our school? How are we going?
2. What are we doing about addressing *equity* in our school? How are we going?
3. What are we doing to ensure every student experiences *success as a learner*? How are we going?
4. What are we doing to ensure that every student becomes a *confident and creative individual*? How are we going?
5. What are we doing to ensure that every student becomes an *active and informed citizen*? How are we going?
6. Overall, to what extent are we *addressing and achieving* the Melbourne Goals?
7. What are the *implications* of our answers to the above questions? What is the *evidence* telling us?

We now consider the major international measures of student achievement, and how Australia has performed on these, over time and more recently.

International measures of student achievement

PISA

Arguably the highest profile and influential measure of student achievement and national performance is PISA, the Programme for International Student Assessment and an initiative of the Organisation for Economic Co-operation and Development (OECD). It has been implemented since 2000 on a three-year cycle, with 15-year-old students from randomly selected schools. In the most recent iteration in 2012, more than 510 000 students from 65 economies participated, a sample representing about 28 million 15-year-olds worldwide.[6]

> **Features of PISA**[b]
> PISA is unique because it develops tests which are not directly linked to the school curriculum. The tests are designed to assess to what extent students at the end of compulsory education, can apply their knowledge to real-life situations and be equipped for full participation in society. The information collected through background questionnaires also provides context which can help analysts interpret the results …
>
> Since the year 2000, every three years, fifteen-year-old students from randomly selected schools worldwide take tests in the key subjects: reading, mathematics and science, with a focus on one subject in each year of assessment. In 2012, some economies also participated in the optional assessments of Problem Solving and Financial Literacy.
>
> Students take a test that lasts 2 hours. The tests are a mixture of open-ended and multiple-choice questions that are organised in groups based on a passage setting out a real-life situation. A total of about 390 minutes of test items are covered. Students take different combinations of different tests.
>
> The students and their school principals also answer questionnaires to provide information about the students' backgrounds, schools and learning experiences and about the broader school system and learning environment.[7]

In Australia, 14 481 students comprised the sample for PISA in 2012.[8] In summary, Australia's performance was as follows:

Mathematical Literacy
- Australia achieved an average score of 504 points in the PISA 2012 mathematical literacy assessment, which was significantly higher than the OECD average of 494 score points.

---

b   See http://www.oecd.org/pisa/aboutpisa/ for a short video explaining PISA.

International patterns of student achievement

- Sixteen countries scored significantly higher in mathematical literacy than Australia. Shanghai-China achieved the highest score, with an average score of 613 points. The difference between Shanghai-China's and Australia's mean scores represents just over three years of schooling ...
- The range of mathematical literacy scores between the lowest and highest performing students (students who scored between the 5th and 95th percentiles) was wider for Australian students (315 score points) than the OECD average (301 score points).[9]

Scientific Literacy
- Australia achieved an average score of 521 points in the PISA 2012 scientific literacy assessment, which was significantly higher than the OECD average of 501 score points.
- Seven countries performed significantly higher than Australia. Shanghai-China achieved the highest score, with an average score of 580 points. In terms of schooling, Shanghai-China performed almost two years higher than Australia ...
- Australia showed a comparatively wide distribution of students' performance in scientific literacy, with 329 score points between students in the 5th and 95th percentiles, compared to 304 score points across OECD countries.[10]

Reading Literacy
- Australia achieved an average score of 512 points in the PISA 2012 reading literacy assessment, which was significantly higher than the OECD average of 496 score points.
- Nine countries scored significantly higher in reading literacy than Australia. Shanghai-China achieved the highest score. The difference between Shanghai-China's and Australia's mean scores represents more than one-and-a-half years of schooling ...
- Australia's spread of 318 score points between the lowest and highest performing students was wider than the OECD average of 310 score points.[11]

There was considerable variation in performance across the various Australian jurisdictions of PISA, as is the case with other international and national measures of student achievement:

Variation in Mathematical Literacy
- The Australian Capital Territory, Western Australia, New South Wales and Queensland significantly outperformed the OECD average. Victoria and South Australia achieved at a level not significantly different to the

OECD average, while Tasmania and the Northern Territory performed at a level significantly lower than the OECD average ...
- The difference in mean mathematical literacy between the highest and lowest performing jurisdictions is 66 score points, the equivalent of almost two years of schooling.[12]

Variation in Scientific Literacy
- The performances of Tasmania and the Northern Territory were not significantly different to the OECD average, while all other jurisdictions performed at a significantly higher level ...
- The difference in mean scientific literacy between the highest and lowest performing jurisdictions is 52 score points, the equivalent of one-and-a-half years of schooling.[13]

Variation in Reading Literacy
- The Australian Capital Territory, Western Australia, Victoria, New South Wales and Queensland performed significantly higher than the OECD average in reading literacy, while South Australia's score was not significantly different. Tasmania and the Northern Territory achieved at a significantly lower level than the OECD average...
- The difference in mean reading literacy between the highest and lowest performing jurisdictions is 59 score points, the equivalent of more than one-and-a-half years of schooling.[14]

Thomson, De Bortoli and Buckley have provided a further breakdown of Australia's PISA 2012 results that are outside the scope of this chapter, but in brief they compared results for:
- males and females
- Indigenous students
- school sectors
- geographic location of schools
- socio-economic background
- immigrant background
- language background.[15]

Of the above, the performance of Indigenous students is of great concern. In mathematical literacy the mean for Indigenous students in PISA 2102 was 417, compared with non-Indigenous students' mean of 507 and the OECD average of 494 points. In scientific literacy, Indigenous students had a mean of 440, compared with non-Indigenous students' mean of 524, the difference equivalent to 2.5 years of schooling. In reading literacy, Indigenous students recorded a mean of 428, with non-Indigenous students having a mean of 515, the difference once again being equivalent to 2.5 years of schooling.[16]

The influence of socioeconomic status on Australia's PISA results is also of concern, being greater than for other participants in PISA overall. Australia has been described as being a high performing yet low equity nation on PISA. In PISA mathematical literacy, the mean score for the highest SES quartile in 2012 was 550, 29 points higher than the second SES quartile, 58 higher than the third SES quartile and 87 points higher than the mean for the fourth SES quartile, a difference equivalent to 2.5 years of schooling. In PISA scientific literacy, the mean scores were similar, with 567 for students in the first SES quartile, 88 points higher than students in the lowest quartile, a difference equivalent to 2.5 years of schooling. In PISA reading literacy, students in the highest SES quartile averaged 557 points, 86 points higher than students in the lowest SES quartile, once again a difference equivalent to 2.5 years of schooling.[17]

Obviously, for some students, disadvantage is compounded. For example, a lower SES Indigenous student living in a remote area with English as a second or third language, a common scenario, is facing some severe hurdles not associated with 'innate' ability.

The other aspect of Australia's performance on PISA is that of changes over time, and the results are not good, with significant decline in mean performance on mathematical literacy since PISA 2003, with the greatest falls associated with Indigenous students. In scientific literacy, mean scores have not changed significantly between PISA 2006 and PISA 2012, while Australia's mean scores on reading literacy have declined significantly between PISA 2000 and PISA 2012. This decline was hardest felt between the 70th and 90th percentiles of student performance. Clearly, the statistically significant decline in mathematical and reading literacy and the lack of growth in scientific literacy should be of concern, as should the decline in the mean performance of Indigenous students and the growing influence of SES status and equity.[18]

Other aspects of Australian schooling revealed by PISA 2012 are also worthy of consideration, and highly relevant to this book. One such aspect is the environment in Australia's schools and related conditions for learning:

- Australian schools, on average, reported a higher frequency of students not listening, noise and disorder, and teachers needing to wait a long time for students to quieten down compared to the OECD average ...
- Australia's jurisdictions, in general, had access to a high quality of resources compared to the OECD average. However, 38% of Northern Territory principals reported that a lack of access to science laboratory equipment affected learning 'to some extent' or 'a lot', while 52% of principals in the Australian Capital Territory and 30% of Tasmanian principals reported learning being affected 'to some extent' or 'a lot' by inadequate internet

connections. Thirty-two per cent of principals in the Australian Capital Territory and 29% of principals in the Northern Territory reported problems with a shortage or inadequacy of instructional materials.
- ... While teacher morale is perceived by principals to be highest in Australian Capital Territory schools, it is below the OECD average in Northern Territory schools.
- On average, over 20% of Australian students felt that they did not belong, were not happy or were not satisfied at school.[19]

Finland and the Asian 'PISA powerhouses'

When the first PISA results for 2000 were released, there was a sudden interest in Finland, which had performed a lot better than either the Finnish or anyone else had expected. International attention (and travel) was focused on Finland and its education system in the hope of discovering the 'secret' to its success.[c]

In later iterations of PISA, however, attention has focused more on the emerging 'PISA powerhouses' of Shanghai, Singapore, Hong Kong, South Korea, and so forth. In 2012 Catherine Scott and I wrote of this new fixation: 'Our Asian schooling infatuation: The problem of PISA envy'.[20]

TIMSS and PIRLS

Two other significant international testing regimes are the Trends in International Mathematics and Science Study (TIMSS) and the Progress in International Reading Literacy Study (PIRLS).[d] Thomson and colleagues (2012) have provided an overview of the two programs:

> TIMSS has been conducted at Year 4 and Year 8 on a four-year cycle since 1995 and PIRLS at Year 4 on a five-year cycle since 2001. In 2011, the cycles for TIMSS and PIRLS coincided for the first time and participating countries were offered an unprecedented opportunity to conduct both TIMSS and PIRLS with their Year 4 students. Australia was one of a group of countries that chose to have the same sample of Year 4 students participate in TIMSS and PIRLS, thus obtaining results for students in reading, mathematics and science. As in previous cycles, Australia also participated in TIMSS at Year 8.
>
> Australia has participated in TIMSS since its inception, providing rich data about trends in mathematics and science achievement over 16 years.

---

c   See an engaging discussion of the Finland PISA experience from the well known Finnish educational expert Pasi Sahlberg: http://www.youtube.com/watch?v=TdgS--9Zg_0

d   See http://www.iea.nl/; https://www.acer.edu.au/files/TIMSS-PIRLS_Australian-Highlights.pdf

This is the first time that Australia has participated in PIRLS, or indeed any international study of reading achievement at this level.[21]

Unlike PISA, TIMSS and PIRLS are curriculum focused, with three levels of curriculum: the 'intended curriculum' (at national or system level); the 'implemented curriculum' (as interpreted and delivered by classroom teachers), and the 'attained curriculum' (as learned by students).[22]

In 2011, the most recent round of TIMSS and PIRLS, 48 countries (plus 9 benchmarking jurisdictions) participated in PIRLS, and 52 countries (plus 7 benchmarking) participating in Year 4 TIMSS, with 45 countries (plus 14 benchmarking) participating in Year 8 TIMSS. In Australia, a stratified random sample of primary (N = 280) and secondary schools (N = 290) took part in TIMSS and PIRLS in 2011.[23] An overview of Australia's performance follows.

PIRLS: Year 4 Reading 2011
- Hong Kong, Finland, the Russian Federation and Singapore were the top-performing countries of PIRLS 2011, scoring well in excess of the High international benchmark of 550. The scores for these countries were not significantly different to each other but were significantly higher than all other countries.
- Australia's average score of 527 score points was similar to the score for Bulgaria, New Zealand, Slovenia, Austria, Lithuania and Poland. It was, however, significantly lower than the average score for 21 other countries, including Ireland and Northern Ireland, the United States, England and Canada, as well as the participating Asian countries Hong Kong, Singapore and Chinese Taipei.
- Internationally, female students performed at a significantly higher level in PIRLS than male students, other than in Colombia, Italy, France, Spain and Israel. The gender gap was, on average, 17 score points, and it was 17 score points in Australia.
- The range of average scores across the states was 49 score points between the Australian Capital Territory and the Northern Territory.
- The performance of students in the Australian Capital Territory was significantly higher than that of students in all other states.
- The performance of students in New South Wales and Victoria were not significantly different to each other, and both scored significantly higher than students in the remaining states, with the exception of Tasmania.[24]

TIMSS: Year 4 Mathematics 2011
- Singapore, Korea and Hong Kong were the top-performing countries of TIMSS 2011, scoring well in excess of the High international benchmark

of 550. The scores for these countries were not significantly different from each other but were significantly higher than all other countries.
- Australia's achievement score of 516 was significantly higher than that of 27 countries, including Sweden and New Zealand, but below that of 17 countries, including most of the Asian countries, England and the United States.
- Australia's average Year 4 mathematics score in TIMSS 2011 was not significantly different to the achieved score in TIMSS 2007, but Australia's 2011 score was a significant 21 points higher than in TIMSS 1995.
- The range of scores was 56 score points, just over half a standard deviation, between the Australian Capital Territory and the Northern Territory.
- The performance of students in the Australian Capital Territory was significantly higher than that of students in all states except Victoria.
- The performance of students in Victoria and New South Wales were not significantly different to each other, but were significantly higher than performance of students in all remaining states with the exception of Tasmania.[25]

TIMSS: Year 4 Science 2011
- Korea and Singapore were the top-performing countries of TIMSS 2011, scoring well in excess of the High international benchmark of 550. The scores for these countries were not significantly different to each other but were significantly higher than all other countries. The next highest performing country was Finland, which had higher achievement than all remaining countries.
- Australia's achievement score of 516 was significantly higher than that of 23 countries, including Belgium and New Zealand, but below that of 18 countries, including most of the Asian countries, England and the United States.
- Australia's average Year 4 science score in TIMSS 2011 was significantly lower than the achieved score in TIMSS 2007, but Australia's 2011 score was not significantly different to the score in TIMSS 1995.
- The range of scores was 56 score points, just over half a standard deviation, between the Australian Capital Territory and the Northern Territory.
- The performance of students in the Australian Capital Territory was significantly higher than that of students in all other states. The performance of students in Victoria and New South Wales was not significantly different to each other, but were significantly higher than performance of students in all remaining states, with the exception of Tasmania.[26]

TIMSS: Year 8 Mathematics 2011

- Korea, Singapore and Chinese Taipei were the top-performing countries of TIMSS 2011, with an average score higher than the High international benchmark of 550. The scores for these countries were not significantly different to each other but were significantly higher than all other countries.
- Australia's achievement score of 505 was significantly higher than that of 27 countries, including New Zealand and Sweden, and below that of 6 countries, including the high-performing Asian countries listed above as well as the Russian Federation.
- Australia's average Year 8 mathematics score in TIMSS 2011 was not significantly different to the achieved score in TIMSS 1995, although there have been some small fluctuations over the 16 years.
- The range of scores was 70 score points, almost three-quarters of a standard deviation, between the Australian Capital Territory and the Northern Territory.
- The performance of students in the Australian Capital Territory was significantly higher than that of students in all states other than New South Wales.
- Students in New South Wales significantly outperformed students in South Australia, Tasmania and the Northern Territory, and students in Victoria and Queensland also significantly outperformed students in Tasmania and the Northern Territory.[27]

TIMSS: Year 8 Science 2011

- Singapore had the highest average achievement across participating countries, with a score about halfway between the High and Advanced benchmarks. The next highest performing countries—Chinese Taipei, Korea and Japan—had higher levels of achievement than all countries other than Singapore, with average scores just higher than the High benchmark.
- Australia's achievement score of 519 was significantly higher than that of 26 countries, including Italy and Ukraine, and below that of 9 countries, including the high-performing Asian countries listed above as well as Finland, Slovenia, the Russian Federation, Hong Kong and England. The score for New Zealand and the United States was not significantly different to that of Australia.
- Australia's average Year 8 science score in TIMSS 2011 was not significantly different to the achieved score in TIMSS 1995, although there have been some fluctuations over the 16 years.
- Science is the only cognitive area in which there has been a significant gender difference in Australia in each assessment since 1995, in favour of males.

- The range of scores was 70 score points, almost three-quarters of a standard deviation, between the Australian Capital Territory and the Northern Territory.
- The score for students in the Australian Capital Territory was not significantly different to that of students in New South Wales, but was significantly higher than that of students in all other states.
- Students in New South Wales significantly outperformed students in South Australia, Tasmania and the Northern Territory, and students in Queensland also significantly outperformed students in Tasmania and the Northern Territory.[28]

Australia's performance overall on PISA, TIMSS and PIRLS: Is primary education problematic?

There was concern when Australia's 2011 results for the international testing programs TIMSS and PIRLS were released. In Year 4 TIMMS Australia came 18th out of 50 countries in mathematics and 25th out of 50 in science. However, in Year 8 TIMMS, Australia did better in relative terms and was placed 12th out of 42 participating nations in both maths and science.

In Year 4 PIRLS a similar pattern was evident with Australia placed 27th out of 45 nations for reading. However, for the most recently available PISA data (2012, for 15-year-olds), Australia was placed equal 13th out of 53 for reading literacy.[29]

Caution needs to be exercised when inferring from such rankings—differences between nations are sometimes small and the metrics are different—but the overall trends should be of concern.

- Why does Australia do relatively more poorly on these international measures of achievement in the primary years? For example, Australia outperforms both the United States of America and the United Kingdom on every measure of PISA, yet is clearly outperformed by these nations on Year 4 TIMMS and Year 4 PIRLS.
- Why does Australia appear to make up ground against other countries between the middle primary and middle secondary years (although as noted previously, there is also a general decline for Australia's scores on PISA both absolutely and relatively against other nations[30])?
- Is this discrepancy the result of 'poorer' teaching in the primary years and/or 'better' teaching in the secondary years, or are there other factors that might account for these differences?

> ### Summary of Australia's Performance on TIMSS (2011), PIRLS (2011) and PISA (2012):
>
> » TIMSS (*Trends in International Mathematics and Science Study*)
>   - Year 4 Maths: 18th out of 50 countries
>   - Year 4 Science: 25th out of 50 countries
>   - Year 8 Maths & Science: 12th out of 42 countries
> » PIRLS (*Progress in International Reading Literacy Study*)
>   - Year 4 Reading: 27th out of 45 countries
> » PISA (*Programme for International Student Assessment*) (15-year-olds)
>   - Reading Literacy: = 13th out of 52 countries.
>   - Mathematical Literacy: 19th out of 53
>   - Scientific Literacy: = 16th out of 55
>   - Computer-based Mathematical Literacy and Digital Reading literacy: 13th out of 32.

In a paper presented at a national conference of the Australian College of Educators in 2014, I examined in detail the possible reasons for Australia's seemingly poorer performance on primary achievement in comparison with secondary achievement. Space precludes a full coverage, but I identified a numbers of potential reasons for this disparity, some of which have been discussed earlier in this book. Each of the following tends to be more prevalent in primary than in secondary schools, overall:

1. Content knowledge is seen by some as problematic.
2. There is a lack of an evidence base for teaching and learning.
3. Expectations on primary teachers are unrealistic and untenable.
4. A degree of specialisation is needed in primary teaching.
5. Self-esteem needs to be boosted and there is a lack of constructive, developmental feedback.[31]

To paraphrase my concluding remarks to the paper, I noted that it should not be construed as an intended criticism of either primary teachers or teachers in general. There has been too much of blaming teachers for things outside their control, coupled with simplistic measures purported to improve the quality of teachers and the quality of teaching through rewarding, testing, judging, 'fixing' or removing 'underperforming' teachers.[32]

Concluding remarks

Australia's performance on international measures of student achievement, while good overall, is cause for concern. The variations in performance associated with SES, indigeneity, geolocation, sector, and in some cases, gender, are greater than for similar nations, and equity gaps appear to be widening as overall performance declines in both absolute and relative terms. The primary–secondary performance disparity is, as noted, concerning, and in need of further investigation and action.

This raises questions about how primary teaching in particular is conceptualised and enacted in schools, given the increasing expectations held for both schools and teachers. There is a need for strong, evidence-based teacher pre-service education and ongoing professional development (see later chapters). There is a need to question from a basis of firm evidence the foundations for what teachers do in schools and to test empirically what are presently regarded as 'facts'.[33] There is a need to question from a basis of evidence and to drive out the folklore, dogma, ritual and untested assumptions underpinning primary teaching and schooling more generally. There is a need to reject the pseudo-science and the shiny products people want to sell educators, and for educators to be 'critical consumers' of research, as noted previously.

There is a need to equip teachers with knowledge and tools for effective teaching and learning and for teachers to adopt a clinical, diagnostic approach to individual student assessment and learning.[34] There is a need for teachers with high intellectual capacity and strong content and pedagogic content knowledge. It is not sufficient to just like young people and to want to be a teacher. There is also a need for school leaders with strong instructional leadership capability who can lead teaching and learning.[35]

There is a need to rethink and reinstate the philosophical bases and moral purposes of schooling and to focus on agreed outcomes, not only academic but also personal and social, as noted in the Melbourne Declaration[36], and not just on activities in the hope these will 'engage' students. While it is important to consider international and national measures of student achievement, too great a focus on external test results alone can be counter-productive.[37]

There is a need to use intelligently the vast amount of extant educational research rather than grasping at 'quick fixes' promoted by economists, policy advisers and the corporate sector to deliver enhanced learning. Complex problems require complex solutions. There is a need to break the cycle of teachers teaching the way they were taught. 'Forget everything you've learned at uni' and 'don't expect too much and you won't be disappointed' are not the ways to move teaching and learning forward, yet for beginning teachers this is frequently their introduction to teaching.

It is important that we recognise the inequalities that exist in Australian society. Many young people enter primary education with disadvantages associated with health, poverty, family background, geographic location and the lack of any form of pre-school education. Primary school teachers are in the front line of dealing with the effects of such disadvantage as they attempt to meet the needs of their students and the expectations society has for them. Many primary schools serving such students are also disadvantaged and financially impoverished.

The primary years of schooling, in particular, are vital in setting up young people for successful lives. There are wonderful practitioners in primary and secondary education and many pockets of excellence, but as a whole we can do better. It is debatable whether primary education today is more effective overall than it was 50 years ago, in part because of the issues raised above. Competing dichotomous ideologies—the 'literacy wars' fought over 'whole language' versus 'phonics' for example—and the widespread, unquestioned acceptance of educational fads, coupled with the overcrowding of the primary curriculum through the unreasonable shifting of expanding social responsibilities to schools, has created an untenable situation. Teachers and young people deserve better.

Wilkinson and Pickett have demonstrated that inequality in society is worse for everyone—or in other words, as they put it in their book title, 'more equal societies almost always do better'—and their data indicate that Australia is becoming a less rather than more equitable society.[38] This puts further pressure on schools and thus there is a need to ensure that schools are resourced as well and as equitably as possible, according to need, and that spending is targeted to those things that are known to add most value to teaching and learning.

Ken Boston, a member of the Gonski Review committee that examined funding for schooling in Australia[39], was blunt in his assessment:

> [T]he decline in the performance of our schools in reading, mathematics and science across the past decade or more ... [is a situation that] is entirely self-inflicted ...
>
> Independent international studies of Australian school performance show that we are in trouble and have been so for at least two generations of schooling. Our business model for school funding—based on the funding of sectors rather than the funding of schools according to the job to be done—has comprehensively failed in the long term.
>
> It has failed for two reasons. First, it has led to Australia having one of the most socially segregated education systems in the OECD. Across the world, there is a positive correlation between socioeconomic advantage and educational performance: in Australia, socioeconomic disadvantage has a greater adverse effect on educational achievement than in any other comparable OECD country ...
>
> Second, there is no real competition between sectors. The sector-based business model has failed to create an even playing field on which government, Catholic and independent schools can compete to drive up school performance.[40]

Finally, let me add that this is not an argument or call for some form of 'back to basics' movement but more, as the late Garth Boomer noted, it highlights the need to 'go forward to fundamentals'.[41]

Endnotes

1. Ministerial Council on Education, Employment, Training and Youth Affairs [MCEETYA]. (2008). *Melbourne Declaration on Educational Goals for Young Australians*. Canberra, Australia: Australian Government. Melbourne Declaration on Educational Goals for Young Australians is reproduced with permission of Education Services Australia as the legal entity for Education Council.
2. MCEETYA. (2008). (p. 4)
3. MCEETYA. (2008). (p. 4)
4. MCEETYA. (2008). (p. 7)
5. MCEETYA. (2008). (p. 9)
6. OECD. (n.d.). About PISA. http://www.oecd.org/pisa/aboutpisa/
7. OECD. (n.d.). 'What makes PISA different' and 'What Assessment involves'. https://www.oecd.org/pisa/aboutpisa/
8. Thomson, S., De Bortoli, L., & Buckley, S. (2013). *PISA in brief: Highlights from the full Australian Report: PISA 2012: How Australia measures up*. Melbourne, Victoria: ACER.
9. Thomson, S. et al. (2013). (p. 7)
10. Thomson, S. et al. (2013). (p. 8)
11. Thomson, S. et al. (2013). (p. 9)
12. Thomson, S. et al. (2013). (p. 10)
13. Thomson, S. et al. (2013). (p. 11)
14. Thomson, S. et al. (2013). (p. 12)
15. Thomson, S. et al. (2013). (pp. 16–22)
16. Thomson, S. et al. (2013). (p. 18)
17. Thomson, S. et al. (2013). (p. 21)
18. Thomson, S. et al. (2013). (pp. 22–23)
19. Thomson, S. et al. (2013). (p. 25)
20. Dinham, S., & Scott, C. (2012). Our Asian schooling infatuation: The problem of PISA envy, *The Conversation*, September (n.p.). https://theconversation.edu.au/our-asian-schooling-infatuation-the-problem-of-pisa-envy-9435
21. Thomson, S., Hillman, K., Wernert, N., Schmid, M., Buckley, S., & Munene, A. (2012). *Highlights from TIMSS & PIRLS 2011 from Australia's perspective*. Melbourne, Victoria: ACER. (p. 1)
22. Thomson, S. et al. (2012). (p. 2)
23. Thomson, S. et al. (2012). (pp. 2–3)
24. Thomson, S. et al. (2012). (pp. 7–8)
25. Thomson, S. et al. (2012). (pp. 9–10)
26. Thomson, S. et al. (2012). (pp. 11–12)
27. Thomson, S. et al. (2012). (pp. 13–14)
28. Thomson, S. et al. (2012). (pp. 15–16)
29. Thomson, S. et al. (2012); Thomson, S. et al. (2013).
30. OECD. (2011). *Education at a glance: OECD indicators*. Paris, France: OECD Publishing.

31 See Dinham, S. (2014). Primary schooling in Australia: Pseudo-science plus extras times growing inequality equals decline. In *What counts as quality in education?* (pp. 8–15). Carlton South, Victoria: Australian College of Educators; Dinham, S. (2015). Pseudo-science, inequality and decline. *Journal of Professional Learning*, Semester 1, n.p.
32 Dinham, S. (2013). The quality teaching movement in Australia encounters difficult terrain: A personal perspective. *Australian Journal of Education, 57*(2), 91–106.
33 See Sahlberg, P. (2014). *Facts, true facts and research in improving education system.* Paper presented to the British Education Research Association, London, 21 May.
34 McLean Davies, L., Anderson, M., Deans, J., Dinham, S., Griffin, P., Kameniar, B., Page, J., Reid, C., Rickards, F., Tayler, C. & Tyler, D. (2013). 'Masterly Preparation: Clinical practice in a graduate pre-service teacher education program. *Journal of Education for Teaching, 39*(1), 93–106; National Council for Accreditation of Teacher Education (2010). *Transforming teacher education through clinical practice: A national strategy to prepare effective teachers.* Washington, DC: Author.
35 Dinham, S. (2013). Connecting instructional leadership with clinical teaching practice. *Australian Journal of Education, 57*(3), 220–231.
36 MCEETYA. (2008).
37 See Berliner, D., Glass, G., & Associates. (2014). *50 myths & lies that threaten America's public schools.* New York, NY: Teachers College Press. (pp. 12–17)
38 Wilkinson, R., & Pickett, K. (2009). *The spirit level: Why more equal societies almost always do better.* London, England: Allen Lane.
39 Australian Government (2011). *Review of funding for schooling—Final report.* Canberra, Australia: Department of Education, Employment and Workplace Relations.
40 Boston, K. (2013). School results tell the story too well: The funding model has failed. *The Australian,* 16 February, p. 16.
41 Cited in Brock, P. (2005, September 21). *The Garth Boomer Memorial Lecture.* Australian Curriculum Studies Conference, University of the Sunshine Coast.

CHAPTER 4

International and national emphases on quality teaching: What value is placed on quality teachers and quality teaching?

INTRODUCTION

As we have established, there is now widespread acceptance that the quality of the teacher is the biggest in-school influence on student achievement. While decades of research have given a clear picture of what good teaching looks like, research has also shown that teacher quality varies widely, and more so within than between schools.[1]

Ensuring a quality teacher in every classroom, although aspirational, is essential in terms of equity and improving the life chances of every young person. It also has wider social, political and economic ramifications. While factors such as socio-economic status (SES) and family background can each have moderate to large effects on student achievement, these are not life sentences.[2]

With the recognition of the importance of the teacher, coupled with research evidence that schools can make a significant difference to student attainment and acknowledgement that good teaching is our best means of overcoming disadvantage associated with the socio-economic and cultural backgrounds of students the 'quality teaching movement' gained traction. This major international emphasis on improving teacher effectiveness during the 1980s was stimulated in part by some influential OECD reports (see below).

Once international measures of student achievement such as TIMSS, PIRLS, and especially PISA gained prominence and 'league tables' of top-performing countries became available, there was increasing concern for the need to improve teaching in order to improve both student achievement and national performance. Nations such as the United States of America and Germany experienced a blow to their national pride when they were ranked relatively poorly on these measures, and reacted in different ways, with the US calling into question the validity and reliability of the measures (denial, then blame), while Germany immediately sought to redress the situation (shock, then action).[3] As noted, other nations such as Finland, and later the Asian 'PISA powerhouses', became overnight success stories.

Educational attainment was increasingly seen as a major factor in the economic growth and status of nations. In Australia, bodies such as the Business Council of Australia[4] and the Productivity Commission[5] have taken a keen interest in teacher quality, teaching quality and student achievement, accompanied by numerous inquiries and reports.

Some of the related concerns that emerged both internationally and in Australia, and continue to attract attention, include:
- attracting high-quality candidates to teaching
- retaining quality teachers and reducing attrition, especially in the first years of teaching
- reforming teacher education
- addressing areas of shortage, especially STEM (science, technology, engineering, mathematics)
- effective teacher workforce planning
- identifying the attributes and actions of effective teachers
- improving in-service professional development for teachers
- building a profession through sufficient remuneration and recognition for the 'best' teachers
- the introduction of professional teaching standards with associated teacher appraisal mechanisms
- better professional development for school principals, particularly in instructional leadership
- curriculum reform
- wider use of standardised testing, with results used as a proxy for teacher, schooling, system and national effectiveness
- measuring the impact of teaching and different teaching approaches and strategies on student learning
- research into the 'science' of learning and its implications for teaching
- greater public investment in education and scrutiny on the return from this investment
- 'upscaling' quality teaching—a quality teacher in every classroom
- educating teachers for the challenge of diversity
- teacher engagement with school change and education reform
- teaching '21st century' students
- the role of technology in teaching and learning
- teaching and learning environments.

These issues will be addressed, both in the international and Australian contexts, in this and subsequent chapters.

Key international reports and findings on quality teaching

In improving the quality of teachers, teaching and learning, the nature and effectiveness of initial teacher education (ITE) is of great importance, although this alone is insufficient. If the effectiveness of teachers and teaching is to be improved, it is necessary to address issues of quality and performance at every key point of leverage. These issues include the quality of those entering ITE programs, the quality of such programs, the quality of university–school partnerships and professional experience, the quality of induction and support for beginning teachers, the quality of ongoing supervision and professional learning for teachers, the quality of school leadership—in an integrated approach[6], rather than relying on 'quick fix' solutions found wanting, or simplistic, unreliable 'one shot' measures such as setting minimum entry scores for teacher candidates.[7]

One of the most influential bodies in respect of quality teaching and education more generally has been the Organisation for Economic Co-operation and Development (OECD). There has been a succession of important OECD reports into matters pertaining to teacher quality and the teaching profession going back to the 1980s. The sheer number of publications is indicative of the interest in, and concern for improving teaching.[a]

In 2011 the OECD reported on the *International Summit on the Teaching Profession*, which brought together:

> ... education ministers, union leaders and other teacher leaders from high-performing and rapidly improving education systems to review how best to improve teacher quality and the quality of teaching and learning.[8]

The report on the summit provides a useful high-level summary of some of the major issues concerning the quality of teaching internationally:

- **How teachers are recruited into the profession and trained initially.** In face of widespread shortages that, in many countries, will soon grow as large cohorts retire, intelligent incentive structures are needed to attract qualified graduates into the teaching force. Pay levels can be part of this equation. However, countries that have succeeded in making teaching an attractive profession have often done so not just through pay, but by raising the status of teaching, offering real career prospects, and giving teachers responsibility as professionals and leaders of reform. This requires teacher education that helps teachers to become innovators and researchers in education, not just deliverers of the curriculum.

---

a   See the OECD library for a wealth of relevant publications: http://www.oecd-ilibrary.org/

- **How teachers are developed in service and supported.** Surveys show large variations across and within countries in the extent of professional development. Not only the quantity but also the nature of this activity is critical. Often, the professional development of teachers is disjointed in one-off courses, while teachers in TALIS[b] reported that the most effective development is through longer programs that upgrade their qualifications or involve collaborative research into improving teaching effectiveness ...
- **How teachers are evaluated and compensated.** Results from TALIS show that, at its best, appraisal and feedback is supportive in a way that is welcomed by teachers. It can also help lead to self-improvement and be part of efforts to involve teachers in improving schools. At present, most teachers do not feel that school leaders use appraisal to recognise good performance, which suggests that a key component of appraisal is appropriate training for those conducting the appraisals. A connected issue, which also requires sensitive handling, is the criteria used to link rewards with performance. Whatever system is used must be fair, based on multiple measures, and transparently applied in ways that involve the teaching profession.
- **How teachers are engaged in reform.** Fundamental changes to the status quo can cause uncertainties that trigger resistance from stakeholders; and without the active and willing engagement of teachers, most educational reforms fail. The chances for success in reform can improve through effective consultation, a willingness to compromise and, above all, through the involvement of teachers in the planning and implementation of reform. In moving beyond consultation to involvement, the reform process becomes oriented towards transforming schools into learning organisations, with teaching professionals in the lead.[9]

The quality teaching movement in Australia: a personal view

Concerns about teacher quality in Australia have abounded for decades. In Australia there has been, on average, one major state or national enquiry into teacher education every year for the past 30 years, the most recent, and potentially most far-reaching—if it is fully implemented—being the Teacher Education Ministerial Advisory Group (TEMAG) enquiry and its subsequent report *Action Now: Classroom Ready Teachers* (2014). No other program of professional preparation has been thought to warrant such scrutiny.[10]

---

b   The OECD Teaching and Learning International Study (TALIS).

Recently there has been a growing chorus of criticism, and even signs of panic, over teacher education, teachers and school performance. Data from international surveys and reports have been used selectively, both to paint a grim picture of the problem and to prescribe remedies. Many journeys have been made to and from Finland, and more latterly Asia, to learn the secret of teaching and student success.

'Experts' from business, government and the field of economics in particular, have weighed into the debate. There has been a concerted push by state and federal governments and educational systems to enact policies and processes to quickly drive improvement in teacher quality. As part of this agenda, it has been determined that all Australian teachers will undergo annual performance reviews.[11]

Australia's increasing fixation with international measures of student achievement and our seeking to emulate the current star performers are having dysfunctional consequences, not least of which is an erosion of our self-belief and confidence as educators.

The lowering of standards for entry to teacher education, in some cases, and the oversupply of teachers in some areas, are combining to work against teacher status and quality. The persistent and increasing 'battering' of the teaching profession[12] is cause for concern and there is a need for educators to find their voice in the current debate and policy context.[13]

As noted, there is now a significant international emphasis on improving teacher quality through bodies such as the Organisation for Economic Co-operation and Development (OECD) and the United Nations Educational, Scientific and Cultural Organization (UNESCO), as well as through various reports on the 'best' performing schools and school systems.[14]

In Australia, developments from 2007 such as the National Assessment Program—Literacy and Numeracy (NAPLAN), the Australian Curriculum and Reporting Authority (ACARA), National Partnerships, the Australian Government Quality Teaching Program (AGQTP) and the Australian Institute for Teaching and School Leadership (AITSL) have all played a part, both in reflecting and strengthening this focus on the teacher and teaching.

However, there are growing and worrying signs in Australia that the quality teaching movement, recently so promising, is in danger of being diverted and disrupted. There are signs that the gains made since the agreement and introduction of key national initiatives dating from 2007 are at risk, both because of the pursuit of other agendas, and a failure to heed the lessons from decades of empirical work.

The recognition of teachers as the biggest in-school influence on student achievement led to a reasonable expectation that there would be an increased focus on and investment in teachers' professional learning and development. However, it is apparent that rather than being seen as education's most important asset, teachers are now being blamed when students fail to learn or to reach the standards set for them individually and collectively.

When teachers are subject to criticism there is an understandable tendency to defend, rationalise and deflect. Rather than mutual understanding and collaboration, this can lead to finger pointing and blame. The effects of socio-economic status (SES) in Australia are cited by some as being too powerful to overcome and, as has been noted, there is panic over international league tables of student achievement. Confused thinking thus abounds.

What are the supposed problems with education?

I have previously identified some of the thinking and beliefs that are that are driving current developments in education internationally. The following appeared in an article in *Education Policy Analysis Archives*:

> The myths, 'facts' or beliefs underpinning the 'crisis' in education in the US, the UK, Australia and elsewhere are many but are typified in the following[15]:
> 1. Public education is failing.
> 2. International testing is a true barometer of the decline in public schooling.
> 3. Private schools are better than public schools.
> 4. Government funded independent and for-profit schools are better than private schools.
> 5. Greater autonomy for public schools will lift performance [yet].
> 6. Greater accountability will lift public school performance.
> 7. Money is not the answer—increased spending on public education has not resulted in improvement in student achievement.
> 8. The teacher is the biggest influence on and is therefore responsible for student achievement.
> 9. Merit pay/payment by results is the solution to improving teacher quality.
> 10. Removing tenure and dismissing poor teachers will lead to greater student achievement.
> 11. Schools should be resourced on the basis of results.
> 12. The curriculum is a captive of the 'left'.
> 13. Schools are not producing the skills and capabilities required by industry.
> 14. 21st century skills are not being taught in 21st century schools.
> 15. Technology changes everything.
> 16. Teacher education is ineffective and the value of a teaching credential is questionable.
> 17. The effects of poverty are too difficult to overcome.
> 18. Educational research offers no solutions.
> 19. Non-educators should lead (public) schools.
> 20. Choice, competition, privatisation and the free market are the answers to almost any question about education.[16]

Simplistic solutions that haven't worked elsewhere

There has been a growing raft of ill-informed solutions to the above 'problems' of teacher quality and education more generally. These measures have included:
- sacking the 'bottom' 5% of teachers[17], whoever they are, and somehow replacing them with better teachers
- paying teachers by 'results', however these are determined and measured
- punishing and rewarding schools on the basis of 'performance', whatever this means
- giving principals more autonomy and power to hire and fire
- bonus pay for the 'top' 10% of teachers, if they can be identified
- raising entry standards for teacher candidates
- exit tests for teacher graduates
- allowing non-educators to become principals.

At the same time, there have been substantial cuts to some federal and state education budgets. In essence, the message is 'do better with less, or else'.

All this is happening in spite of the fact that Australia still performs well on international measures of student achievement such as PISA, although we certainly cannot rest on our laurels. As noted, there are signs of decline, and the equity achievement gap appears to be widening, as is the apparent disparity between primary and secondary achievement noted earlier.[18] We are, however, ahead of the USA on PISA, to use that one measure. This said, we still heed the recipes and exhortations of US economists, educators, politicians and education big business to be more like the USA.

Nowhere in any of these proposed solutions is there recognition of the need to provide ongoing effective professional learning for teachers to enable them to continue to develop and upgrade their skills, and to be recognised and rewarded for this growth. Everyone assumes someone else will fund and provide this. Nowhere is there the means to provide educational leaders en masse with the knowledge and skills they need to be true leaders of learning. What is apparent is a blanket stigmatisation of teachers, principals, teacher educators and education system leaders. There is an assumption in these criticisms, for example, that all teachers, teacher candidates and teacher education courses are equally ineffective. Reality is quite different, as the most recent review of teacher education pointed out.[19]

The work of John Hattie, in particular, has been misinterpreted and used to criticise teachers, teacher education and teaching. His recognition of teachers' importance has been misused to imply that it is the teacher's fault when students fail to learn. The words 'in school' have been mislaid, by accident or design, and we now frequently hear of the teacher being 'the biggest influence on student achievement', which is untrue.

Instead of a collegial opening up of classrooms and professional practice, what follows is a view that because of their importance, we need greater control over and surveillance of teachers, to the extent that some principals are said to engage in a growing practice of snap inspections of classrooms, sometimes accompanied by video-taking, to 'catch' teachers performing badly. As we tend to mimic what others do overseas, we can expect to see this practice in Australian schools.

> One of the more dubious practices in U.S. schools is administrators dropping into classrooms with clipboards, laptops, or iPads, filling out checklists or rubrics, and sending them to teachers without any human contact. This kind of one-way feedback is superficial, bureaucratic, annoying, and highly unlikely to make a difference. Another ineffective practice is giving teachers a score on each short observation ... This increases the teacher's anxiety and is the opposite of good coaching.[20]

Rather than careful, collaborative planning and constructive, improvement-oriented feedback, we see arbitrary, unfocused, impressionistic teacher 'assessment', with an overall demand to lift performance, while simultaneously cutting education budgets and removing specialist assistance provided by people such as literacy and numeracy coaches and regional network staff.

Hattie's position on direct instruction has been misconstrued as advocating didactic, 'traditional' teacher-centred 'chalk and talk' approaches, rather than its intended meaning of teachers having clear intentions of what they are trying to achieve with every student, and planning, orchestrating and assessing learning in their classrooms accordingly.[21]

Similarly, the role of professional standards for teachers[22] has been twisted by some to be more about standardising, judging and dismissing teachers, than developing and recognising them, that is, a *judgemental* rather than *developmental* purpose and application. Instead of being done *with* and *for* teachers, many measures advocated and hastily and poorly implemented in the quest to improve teaching and learning are essentially being done *to* teachers and *without* their involvement, almost guaranteeing resistance, minimal compliance and inefficiency.

As I have noted, I believe that the biggest equity issue in Australian education is a quality teacher in every classroom.[23] However, to achieve this we need to address teacher quality at every key point of potential influence or 'leverage'.[24] Simplistic, quick-fix, populist solutions promulgated by economists, business representatives, educational advisers and politicians who are out of touch with teaching and the extant body of research on teaching and learning capture the headlines, feed the panic and reinforce misconceptions, while providing little guidance or positive substance for the profession.

A battered profession

Everyone has been to school and seems to have a view on education and, as noted, teaching has increasingly become the 'battered profession'. I have been involved with researching teacher satisfaction, dissatisfaction, and mental health and associated areas such as teacher status internationally and in Australia since the early 1990s, and things have not improved since that time.[25] On a daily basis we hear damning statements—denigration, abuse, misinformed criticism—about the dire state of education. In the main these statements are made not by educators but by politicians, education bureaucrats, the media, members of the corporate sector and other self-appointed experts. The standard of those entering and practising teaching is generalised and criticised as poor, and university faculties of education are said to be staffed by out-of-touch ideologues who produce graduates unfit for teaching. Teacher unions are seen as nothing more than self-serving rabbles, and (largely public) schools as war zones. Our school students are fit for neither society nor work. Such views, if expressed often enough, enter popular consciousness and become accepted as truth. The 'manufactured crisis' in education identified by Berliner and Biddle in 1995[26] can become a self-fulfilling prophecy, as, for example, when people are convinced to take their children out of public schools, and high-quality candidates are deterred from entering teaching.

Much of this criticism is directed at public education but other sectors are also targets and victims. And the worst part is that, by and large, the profession accepts it, although sometimes, unhelpfully, it turns upon itself, particularly across the public–private and SES divides as well as upon matters of ideology.

For over 40 years *Phi Delta Kappan* (PDK) and Gallup have polled the US public on their attitudes towards public education.[27] One of their perennial findings is that while there is widespread concern about public education *generally*, those surveyed invariably report a high level of support, satisfaction and appreciation for their *local* public school. These findings are instructive in understanding how we as a society regard education, teachers and schooling.

There are, however, real concerns, and educators encounter these on a daily basis. Despite our overall good performance as a nation on international and national measures of student performance, we can, and need to, improve. In particular, we need to address the impact of disadvantage and inequity on student development and achievement, which is larger than we would like it to be and, as noted, is greater than in other OECD nations.[28]

There is an ongoing need to focus—through evidence—on the nature and impact of our pedagogical practices and the roles that teachers' preparation and professional learning, professional standards, leadership, and appraisal and development processes can play in improving teaching and learning. However, addressing these real concerns is made more difficult by the prevailing climate of criticism and the fact that every time a social problem emerges it is passed to schools for resolution, with the result that schools are constantly battling pressures to simultaneously address the 'basics' as well as the 'extras' society seems unwilling or unable to deal with. In essence, 'we trust you less' yet 'we entrust you with more'.

Critics of education make simplistic pronouncements that disregard decades of research and the many great achievements of our teachers and schools. Our accumulated expertise and wisdom in education is totally disregarded, yet when I speak with international colleagues they frequently express admiration for what we have achieved in Australian education. These people look to Australia for leadership, research and guidance, while the self-styled experts urge us to copy Shanghai and the like, or worse still, the USA, on the basis of their 'research', which usually consists of selectively using statistics from reports completed by others, and making flying, stage-managed visits to schools to discover the 'secret' to their success.

Our home-grown critics persistently argue that education is 'broken' and must be 'fixed', and as noted previously, the quality teaching movement, once so promising, appears to have been hijacked.[29] It is hardly surprising that educators have lost self-confidence after years of such treatment.

Entry to the profession

Unfortunately, the quality teaching movement is also being put at risk through the related issues of the widening range of entry standards to teaching, the varying quality of teacher education programs and the uncapping of Commonwealth-funded places for teacher education candidates.

Despite all the talk about improving the quality of teachers and teaching in Australia—and partly because of the poor publicity around teachers and teaching—the general downward slide of entry standards to undergraduate teacher training courses continues. While the best-performing nations such as Finland and South Korea draw their teachers from the top quartile of school leavers or higher[30], some Australian universities have dropped their ATAR (Australian Tertiary Admission Rank[c]) entry levels to the 45th percentile and even lower, with various 'bonus' schemes reducing these levels still further.[31]

Teacher education is typically the largest undergraduate professional program in most universities and is thus a significant source of university revenue. Unfortunately, in some universities, in order to fill the desired number of places and reach financial targets, minimum entry levels are set far too low. Additionally, when universities experience an overall shortfall in student applications, often this 'load' is shifted to teacher education, usually against the wishes of education faculties, further driving down entry standards and in some cases, leading to teacher oversupply, especially in primary initial teacher education (ITE).

This has been exacerbated in recent years with the 'uncapping' of undergraduate Commonwealth Supported Places (CSP[d]) from 2012. Some universities have reacted

---

c   ATAR—a percentile ranking of high school graduates' final assessed performance.

d   These places are substantially subsidised by the Australian Government so that students pay only the 'student contribution' portion for their units of study and their degree overall.

to this 'free for all' by greatly expanding their offers and places for teacher candidates, at a time when there is an oversupply of primary teachers and long waiting lists for teacher employment more generally. At present, more than 75 per cent of teachers on waiting lists around the country—there are more than 40 000 in New South Wales alone—are seeking primary positions, yet around 50 per cent of the 16 000 teachers graduating every year in Australia are primary-trained. However, there are teacher shortages in areas such as secondary mathematics, science, technology, languages and English, and for special needs and early childhood teachers.[32] Put simply, we are training too many primary teachers and these resources would be better spent targeting areas of shortage. We are also misleading people about their chances of gaining employment, something which has both financial and personal cost and is, to say the least, ethically questionable if not unconscionable.

Overall, this situation has a number of serious consequences. Students with higher ATARs who might otherwise be attracted to teaching could feel they are 'wasting' their marks if they accept a place in an education course that could have been 'bought' with a much lower ATAR. There is a powerful view that one must 'spend' all one's ATAR. More broadly, lower entry scores reinforce the perceived low status of teachers and teaching.

Meanwhile, those accepted with low ATARs[e] are likely to find completing their course challenging and teaching itself difficult. If they do manage to complete their course, they will find themselves teaching students who are potential '90+' ATAR performers—something that will present challenges for both teacher and student.

It needs to be recognised that, contrary to popular thinking, entry scores to undergraduate teacher training courses vary widely. While some universities do set minimum entry standards as low as the 40s, others require ATARs of over 90. This discrepancy is widening, particularly with the entry of some TAFE and private colleges to teacher education, and cannot be allowed to continue if we are serious about improving the quality of teaching and learning in Australian schools.

Where candidates cannot meet minimum standards for admission, bridging programs may need to be provided to enable candidates to demonstrate capability at the standard required, but universities and other providers must not be permitted to enrol candidates below 70–75 ATAR or equivalent into undergraduate teacher education programs. Making excuses and exceptions is the beginning of a 'slippery slope' that can lead to the acceptance of candidates with very low ATARs, thereby reinforcing unproductive cycles we need to break.

---

e   Increasingly, teaching in Australia is becoming a graduate entry profession, which should ease the fixation with ATARs. South Australia has recently determined that all commencing teachers will have completed a Masters of Teaching and some universities have been graduate entry only for quite some time.

Accreditation of teacher education courses

It needs to be recognised that the quality of teacher education courses is variable, with this variation widening, based on published entry standards. Processes for 'nationally consistent' accreditation of teacher education courses, which are currently being introduced[33] and revised in the light of the TEMAG recommendations[34], need to address the issue of course quality and in particular, the effectiveness of graduating teachers and their impact on student learning.[35] There needs to be a rigorous, evidence-based process for course accreditation rather than the minimalist, competency-based approach that currently predominates. TEMAG called for:

> An overhauled national accreditation process for initial teacher education programs ... [with] Full program accreditation contingent upon robust evidence of successful graduate outcomes against the [Australian] Professional Standards [for Teachers] ... [and] Strengthened accreditation requiring providers to demonstrate that program design and delivery is underpinned by solid research and includes measures of program effectiveness.[36]

If we are to continue to offer teaching as an undergraduate qualification—and I don't think we should for reasons I will outline below—we must set firm minimum acceptable standards for entry as part of an approach to improve teacher and teaching quality.

Many will cite equity issues in that high school students from particular backgrounds and geographic locations experience disadvantage, which is reflected in their final ATAR. It is important to recognise this and to seek to attract a broadly representative teaching service, but accepting candidates with very low levels of secondary school achievement into teaching is not the way to achieve it. It risks setting such people up for failure, and in many cases, those who do manage to pass their ITE course will go back to the same sorts of disadvantaged schools that they have come from.

Some teacher educators maintain that entry standards to teacher education are irrelevant and that it is what teachers exit with that is most important[37], but this is simplistic thinking; *both* are important. However, there is a need for other measures of suitability for teaching to augment ATAR scores above minimum levels, to ensure that those selected into teaching have the attributes needed to succeed in their courses and in their careers.[f][38]

---

f   The University of Melbourne has developed and implemented an instrument, *Teacher Selector*, for the purpose of providing a broader assessment of teacher education candidates' attributes, motivations, and suitability for teaching. See https://teacherselector.com.au/; Bowles, T., Hattie, J., Dinham, S., Scull, J., & Clinton, J. (2014). Proposing a comprehensive model for identifying teacher candidates, *Australian Educational Researcher, 41*(4), 365–380.

However, I do believe that the practice of taking people straight from school, training them as teachers and then sending them back to school, often to the same geographical area that they have come from, is no longer appropriate. Graduate entry teaching degrees, particularly Master of Teaching courses—as opposed to the old one-year diplomas in education—are attracting candidates with high-level undergraduate academic performance who are older, more experienced and who have made a mature decision to become a teacher.[39]

Serious attention to the standards required for entry to teaching is long overdue. If entry requirements to undergraduate programs are allowed to continue to decline as they have over the past few years, there will be a heavy price. All the effort around improving the quality of teachers, the quality of teaching and student achievement in this country will be undermined. As noted, the quality of teachers and of teaching needs to be addressed at each key point of leverage, but the quality of those entering the profession is of crucial importance for everything that follows.

It is time for the profession to speak and for the nation to act

Those involved with all aspects of education need to find their voice to reject the misinformed, persistent, harmful rhetoric and indeed bullying that at present is going largely unchallenged in the public arena and, worse still, informing education policy. In doing so, it is imperative that evidence-based reasoning is employed, rather than defensive, apologetic excuse making.

In engaging with the wider community and stakeholders to promote the cause of education, professionalism is essential. Educators need to work with the media and key bodies to ensure that the evidence and 'good news stories' get out there to counter the fixation with the tiny proportion of students, teachers and schools that are so easy and tempting to sensationalise. Taking our lead from the PDK findings on the US public's views on education, we need to think globally yet act locally to raise awareness of the many great things schools achieve on a daily basis, often against significant odds.

We cannot ignore the effects on learning and development of socio-economic status, family background, geographic location, indigeneity, and the uneven level of funding and other resources available to schools, but this is not a reason to give up; quite the opposite. It should strengthen our resolve.

We also need to be realistic. Every teacher is not going to be able to bring every student to an average or above average level of performance—a statistical and practical impossibility—but the vast majority of teachers and principals will try very hard to do this. Life is not fair, but education can make it fairer. As I have noted, good teaching and good schools are the best means we have of overcoming disadvantage and opening the doors of opportunity for young people. We must hold to this belief.

Much attention has been given to the Gonski Review[40] recommendations on school funding in Australia. The fact is that we have a highly inequitable, opaque and inefficient means of allocating funding to schools that has been cobbled together over time.⁴¹ An ideal scheme would be lean, powerful, efficient and fair in achieving its aims. It will be difficult to achieve this from the position where we currently find ourselves, which is the outcome of ad hoc, politically influenced decision making over many decades.

There is a lack of will to make the necessary hard decisions on school funding because of fear of alienating elements of the electorate. Whenever there is debate about a more equitable funding system, politicians are forced to offer a guarantee that whatever the new process or formula, no school will be worse off. In other words, equity comes a distant second to votes. This guarantees that little will change and that inequalities will be perpetuated if not exacerbated.

We also need to address the present salary and career structures for teachers, which are inefficient, inconsistent, 19th century industrial artefacts that see teachers' salaries peak too soon and at too low a level. I have written extensively on the need to integrate the Australian Professional Standards for Teachers introduced in 2011 with authentic, efficient assessment and accreditation processes and with industrial awards, to provide incentive, guidance, reward and recognition to teachers who continue their professional learning and improve their performance.⁴²

We are at a crucial point in our development as a country, and the national initiatives around enhancing the quality of teaching introduced by the first Rudd Labor government in 2007 have been substantial and significant. We are, however, at a crossroads. We have the opportunity through these initiatives and agreements to take the necessary next steps down the road of ensuring effective professional learning for all teachers and principals and quality teaching for all Australian students, but we badly need strong, informed, bipartisan support rather than the fragmentation, push back and politicking that is increasingly occurring in education.⁴³ It is time education ceased to be used as a political football. It is too important for that.

This is unfortunately complicated and exacerbated by the situation whereby education is constitutionally largely a state and territory responsibility, yet funded substantially through the Commonwealth tax system. The 'rail gauge mentality' of the 19th century[g] is apparently alive and well.⁴⁴ Australia has a population of about 24 million, yet is bedevilled by wasteful duplication, mistrust, competition, and in some instances, petty jealousies.

We need to be cognisant of decades of empirical work in educational research rather than dismissive. We need to stop adopting quick-fix solutions that have been found wanting elsewhere. Education as a whole is performing much better than many of the corporations and governments that seek to criticise it.

---

g Australia is 'famous' for developing different rail gauges within the various colonies during the 19th century prior to Federation in 1901, such that with the development of national trade, trains were unable to travel from one state to another. This has become a metaphor for the distrust, rivalry, lack of agreement and non-cooperation between the states and territories that persists.

Above all, as a nation we need to recognise education as our most important investment in facilitating personal, social and economic prosperity, and not as a cost or a commodity to be purchased by those with the most social and financial capital.

Many are convinced that there is a crisis in Australian schooling, and this has eroded our self-belief and confidence. As a result, we are tempted to seize upon quick, cheap, simple solutions when what we need is comprehensive evidence-based improvement and action to create a system and career structure for promoting effective teaching and for recognising and rewarding effective teachers.

Linda Darling-Hammond has identified what such a coherent systematic approach requires:

1. *Common statewide* [or national] *standards* for teaching that are related to meaningful student learning and are shared across the profession;
2. *Performance-based assessments, based on the standards,* guiding state functions such as teacher operation, licensure, and advanced certification;
3. *Local evaluation systems aligned to the same standards,* for evaluating on-the-job teaching based on multiple measures of teaching practice and student learning;
4. *Support structures* to ensure trained evaluators, mentoring for teachers who need additional assistance, and fair decisions about personnel actions; and
5. *Aligned professional learning opportunities* that support the improvement of teachers and teaching quality.[45]

Fortunately, most of the key national elements are largely in place, with developmental work proceeding through AITSL and other bodies, but we are not there yet and the temptation will be to do these things quickly and cheaply, which will severely compromise their impact.

We need to remind ourselves we have much to be proud of in Australian education and we need to be prepared to recognise, understand and build upon that foundation and not let others undermine and pull it down.

It is time for the profession as a whole to speak up, to state what it believes in, and to question from a basis of evidence the externally proposed remedies to the perceived problems of teachers, teaching and schools in Australia. If we fail to do this, the outcomes will be neither pleasant nor productive and we can expect to continue to slide down the international student achievement league tables, with the resultant negativity feeding upon itself. If this occurs, we will all be the poorer for it.

Endnotes

1   See Cochran-Smith, M., & Zeichner, K. (Eds.). (2005). *Studying teacher education.* New Jersey: Lawrence Erlbaum; Dinham, S. (2008). *How to get your school moving and improving: An evidence-based approach.* Melbourne, Victoria: ACER Press; Hattie, J.

(2009). *Visible learning: A synthesis of over 800 meta-analyses relating to achievement.* London, England: Routledge; Rowe, K. (2003). *The importance of teacher quality as a key determinant of students' experiences and outcomes of schooling.* Discussion paper prepared for the Interim Committee of the NSW Institute of Teachers. Sydney, New South Wales: NSWIT.
2. Hattie, J. (2009). (pp. 61–63)
3. Dinham, S. (2015). *Regulation or deregulation? Observations on Education in Germany and Australia.* Keynote address, Australian College of Educators National Conference, Brisbane, 24 September.
4. Dinham, S., Ingvarson, L., & Kleinhenz, E. (2008). Investing in teacher quality: Doing what matters most. In *Teaching talent: The best teachers for Australia's classrooms.* Melbourne, Victoria: Business Council of Australia.
5. Productivity Commission. (2012). *Schools workforce, research report.* Canberra, Australia: Australian Government.
6. Dinham, S. (2008). *Driving improvement in the quality of Australian education: Points of leverage,* Australian College of Educators, Victorian Branch Oration, University of Melbourne, 15 August; Teacher Education Ministerial Advisory Group. (2014). *Action now: Classroom ready teachers.* Canberra, Australia: Department of Education.
7. Dinham, S. (2013). The quality teaching movement in Australia encounters difficult terrain: A personal perspective. *Australian Journal of Education, 57*(2), 91–106.
8. OECD. (2011). *Building a high quality teaching profession: Lessons from around the world. International Summit on the Teaching Profession.* Paris, France: OECD Publishing. (p. 5) ... DOI: http://dx.doi.org/10.1787/9789264113046-en
9. OECD. (2011). (pp. 5–6)
10. Dinham, S. (2006). Teaching and teacher education: Some observations, reflections and possible solutions, *ED Ventures, 2,* 3–20; Dinham, S. (2013); Dinham, S. (2008).
11. AITSL [Australian Institute for Teaching and School Leadership]. (2012). *Australian Teacher Performance and Development Framework.* Melbourne, Victoria: Author.
12. Scott, C., & Dinham, S. (2013). A 'battered' profession. *Sheilas,* 14 February, n.p. http://sheilas.org.au/2013/02/a-battered-profession/
13. Dinham, S. (2013).
14. Barber, M., and Mourshed, M. (2007). *How the world's best-performing school systems come out on top.* New York, NY: McKinsey & Company.
15. After: AACTE [American Association of Colleges for Teacher Education] (2012). *Educator preparation: Myths and facts.* Washington, DC: Author. https://www.aau.edu/WorkArea/DownloadAsset.aspx?id=13450; Benn, M. (2012). *School wars—The battle for Britain's education.* London, England: Verso; Berliner, D., Glass, G., & Associates. (2014). *50 myths & lies that threaten America's public schools.* New York, NY: Teachers College Press; Brill, S. (2011). *Class warfare—Inside the fight to fix America's schools.* New York, NY: Simon & Schuster; Christodoulou, D. (2014). *Seven myths about education.* London, England: Routledge; Dinham, S. (2013). The quality teaching movement in Australia encounters difficult terrain: A personal perspective. *Australian Journal of Education, 57*(2), 91–106; Hopkins, D. (2013). *Exploding the myths of school reform.* Melbourne, Victoria: ACER Press; Ravitch, D. (2010). *The death and life of the great American school system.* New York, NY: Basic Books; Ravitch, D. (2014). *Reign of Error—The hoax of the privatization movement and the danger to America's public schools.* New York, NY: Knopf; Lubienski, C., & Lubienski, S. (2013). *The public school advantage: Why public schools outperform private schools.* Chicago, IL: University of Chicago Press.
16. Dinham, S. (2015). The worst of both worlds: How US and UK models are influencing education in Australia. *Educational Policy Analysis Archives, 23*(49), 1–20. http://dx.doi.org/10.14507/epaa.v23.1865 (p. 3)

17 Victoria Department of Education and Early Childhood Development. (2012). *New directions for school leadership and teaching profession.* Melbourne, Victoria: DEECD.

18 Dinham, S. (2014). Primary schooling in Australia: Pseudo-science plus extras times growing inequality equals decline. In Australian College of Educators. (2014). *What counts as quality in education?* Carlton South, Victoria: Australian College of Educators. (pp. 8–15)

19 Teacher Education Ministerial Advisory Group [TEMAG]. (2014). *Action now: Classroom ready teachers.* Canberra, Australia: Australia Department of Education.

20 Marshall, K. (2012). Let's cancel the dog-and-pony show, *Phi Delta Kappan, 94*(3), 19–23. (p. 21)

21 Hattie, J. (2009). (pp. 204–207)

22 AITSL [Australian Institute for Teaching and School Leadership]. (2011). *National [Australian] Professional Standards for Teachers.* Melbourne, Victoria: Author.

23 Dinham, S. (2011). Improving the quality of teaching in Australia. *Education Canada, 51*(1), 34–38.

24 Dinham, S. (2008).

25 See, as a sample: Dinham, S. (1992). Human perspectives on the resignation of teachers from the New South Wales Department of School Education: Towards a model of teacher persistence. (Doctor of Philosophy thesis). University of New England, Armidale, New South Wales; Dinham, S. (1993). Teachers under stress. *Australian Educational Researcher, 20*(3), December, 1–16; Dinham, S. (1995). Time to focus on teacher satisfaction, *Unicorn, 21*(3), September, 64–75; Dinham, S. (1997). Societal expectations, pressures and teaching. *Teaching and Teachers' Work, 5*(3), August, 1–8; Dinham, S. (1997). Teaching and teachers' families. *Australian Educational Researcher,* AARE, August, 24(2), 59–88; Scott, C., Cox, S., & Dinham, S. (1999). The occupational motivation, satisfaction and health of English school teachers. *Educational Psychology, 19*(3), 287–308; Dinham, S., & Scott, C. (1998). A three domain model of teacher and school executive satisfaction. *Journal of Educational Administration, 36*(4), 362–378; Dinham, S., & Scott, C. (2000). Moving into the third, outer domain of teacher satisfaction. *Journal of Educational Administration, 38*(4), 379–396; Scott, C., Stone, B., & Dinham, S. (2001). 'I love teaching but ...' International patterns of teacher discontent. *Education Policy Analysis Archives, 9*(28), 1–7; Dinham, S., & Scott, C. (2002). Pressure points: School executive and educational change. *Journal of Educational Enquiry, 3*(2), 35–52; Scott, C., & Dinham, S. (2002). The beatings will continue until quality improves: Carrots and sticks in the search for educational improvement. *Teacher Development, 6*(1), 15–31; Scott, C., & Dinham, S. (2003). The development of scales to measure teacher and school executive occupational satisfaction. *Journal of Educational Administration, 41*(1), 74–86.

26 Berliner, D., & Biddle, B. (1995). *The manufactured crisis: Myths, fraud, and the attack on America's public schools.* Cambridge, MA: Perseus.

27 See *PDK* (2012). A nation divided: Results of the 44th annual PDK/Gallup Poll of the Public's Attitudes Towards the Public Schools. *Phi Delta Kappan, 94*(1), [special edition].

28 Thomson, S., Hillman, K., Wernert, N., Schmid, M., Buckley, S., & Munene, A. (2012). *Highlights from TIMSS & PIRLS 2011 from Australia's Perspective.* Melbourne, Victoria: ACER.

29 Dinham, S. (2012). A political education: Hijacking the quality teaching movement, *The Conversation,* August, (n.p.). http://theconversation.edu.au/a-political-education-hijacking-the-quality-teaching-movement-9017; Dinham, S. (2012). The hijacking of the quality teaching movement. *Professional Educator, 11*(7), 8–11.

30 Dinham, S., Ingvarson, L., & Kleinhenz, E. (2008). Investing in teacher quality: Doing what matters most. In *Teaching talent: The best teachers for Australia's classrooms*. Melbourne, Victoria: Business Council of Australia.
31 Preiss, B., & Butt, C. (2013, January 18). Teacher entry ranking tumbles. *The Age*.
32 Productivity Commission. (2012). *Schools workforce, research report*. Canberra, Australia: Australian Government.
33 AITSL [Australian Institute for Teaching and School Leadership]. (2011). *Accreditation of initial teacher education programs in Australia*. Melbourne, Victoria: Author.
34 TEMAG. (2014).
35 See Dinham, S. (2015). *Issues and perspectives relevant to the development of an approach to the accreditation of initial teacher education in Australia based on evidence of impact*. Melbourne, Victoria: AITSL.
36 TEMAG. (2014). (p. vii)
37 See Tovey, J. (2013, February 19). High marks 'not the key' to better teachers. *The Age*.
38 Bowles, T., Hattie, J., Dinham, S., Scull, J., & Clinton, J. (2014). Proposing a comprehensive model for identifying teacher candidates. *Australian Educational Researcher, 41*(4), 365–380.
39 See McLean Davies, L., Anderson, M., Deans, J., Dinham, S., Griffin, P., Kameniar, B., Page, J., Reid, C., Rickards, F., Tayler, C. & Tyler, D. (2013). Masterly preparation: Clinical practice in a graduate pre-service teacher education program. *Journal of Education for Teaching, 39*(1), 93–106; Scott, C., Kleinhenz, E., Weldon, P., Reid, K., & Dinham, S. (2010). *Master of teaching MGSE: Evaluation report*. Melbourne, Victoria: ACER.
40 Australian Government. (2011). *Review of funding for schooling*. Canberra: Australian Government.
41 Dowling, A. (2008). Unhelpfully complex and exceedingly opaque: Australia's school funding system. *Australian Journal of Education, 52*(2), 129–150.
42 See Dinham, S. (2011). *Let's get serious about teacher quality: The need for a new career architecture for Australia's teachers*. Dean's Lecture Series, University of Melbourne, MGSE, 27 September. http://web.education.unimelb.edu.au/news/lectures/pdf/S Dinham PowerPoint 27.9.11.pdf; Dinham, S., Ingvarson, L., & Kleinhenz, E. (2008).
43 Tomazin, F. (2013, February 24). Victoria throws education reforms into disarray. *The Age*.
44 Clancy, L. (2004). *Culture and customs of Australia*. Westport, CT: Greenwood Press. (p. 15)
45 Darling-Hammond, L. (2012). *Creating a comprehensive system for evaluating and supporting effective teaching*. Stanford, CA: Stanford Center for Opportunity Policy in Education.

CHAPTER 5

How does teacher expertise develop? What are the differences between routine and adaptive expertise?

INTRODUCTION

In this chapter we look at the research literature on expertise generally and how it can develop, before considering the development of teacher expertise. The broad characteristics of expert teachers are highlighted. These are examined in greater detail in Chapter 6. We also examine the important distinction between routine and adaptive expertise and its implications for teaching.

How teacher expertise develops

General findings on expertise

Work on the development of teacher expertise is a sub-set of work on expertise generally. It has been found that it takes around eight to ten years to become expert at anything, child prodigies aside.[1] Malcolm Gladwell estimated a minimum commitment of 10 000 hours of practice to reach an expert level of performance in any field.[2] Self-motivation, encouragement and support from others, expert coaching or instruction coupled with constructive feedback, extensive practice and sacrifice are usually required to reach the highest levels of expertise.

In the 1980s Hubert and Stuart Dreyfus developed a five-stage model of the activities involved in skills acquisition, which proved popular and has since gone through various iterations.[3] Dreyfus and Dreyfus drew on cases from foreign language acquisition, learning to play chess, and flight instruction to develop their initial five-stage model.[a]

Later, as a result of further development, these stages were modified as[4]:

> **Stage 1: Novice**—Normally, the instruction process begins with the instructor decomposing the task environment into context-free features that the beginner can recognize without the desired skill. The beginner is then given rules for determining actions on the basis of these features ...
>
> **Stage 2: Advanced Beginner**—As the novice gains experience actually coping with real situations and begins to develop an understanding of the relevant context, he or she begins to note, or an instructor points out, perspicuous examples of meaningful additional aspects of the situation or domain. After seeing a sufficient number of examples, the student learns to recognize these new aspects. Instructional maxims can then refer to these new situational aspects ...
>
> **Stage 3: Competence**—With more experience, the number of potentially relevant elements and procedures that the learner is able to recognize and follow becomes overwhelming. At this point, because a sense of what is important in any particular situation is missing, performance becomes nerve-wracking and exhausting, and the student might well wonder how anybody ever masters the skill ...
>
> As students learn to restrict themselves to only a few of the vast number of possibly relevant features and aspects, understanding and decision making becomes easier ...

---

a   The five stages or levels of skills acquisition in their initial model were identified as: *(1) Novice, (2) Competence, (3) Proficiency, (4) Expertise, and (5) Mastery.*

Stage 4: Proficiency—As the competent performer becomes more and more emotionally involved in a task, it becomes increasingly difficult for him or her to draw back and adopt the detached, rule-following stance of the beginner. If the detached stance of the novice and advanced beginner is replaced by involvement, and the learner accepts the anxiety of choice, he or she is set for further skill advancement ...

Stage 5: Expertise—The proficient performer, immersed in the world of his or her skilful activity, sees what needs to be done but decides how to do it. The expert not only sees what needs to be achieved; thanks to his or her vast repertoire of situational discriminations, he or she also sees immediately how to achieve this goal. Thus, the ability to make more subtle and refined discriminations is what distinguishes the expert from the proficient performer.

It is important to note that the above developmental framework is predicated on the learner receiving expert instruction and feedback from an 'instructor', especially in the earlier stages. This is in contrast to trial-and-error learning or attempting to teach oneself.

Dreyfus and Dreyfus were concerned with four key mental functions performed by practitioners:

- **Recollection**—which ranges from Non-situational (Novice) to Situational (Master)
- **Recognition**—Decomposed (Novice) to Holistic (Master)
- **Decision**—Analytical (Novice) to Intuitive (Master)
- **Awareness**—Monitoring (Novice) to Absorbed (Master)[5]

Overall, the behaviour of novices tends to be rule or 'maxim' governed, while the behaviour of experts or masters tends to be governed mainly by personal and professional knowledge. Novice chess players for example, think about rules and simple moves, while experts who know the rules think more deeply about complex strategies involving many potential moves and the possible consequences of these.

Experts tend to be skilled at reading context and noticing detail or 'cues', while novices barely notice detail and context and how all parts of the context fit together.

Novices need structure, while experts or masters need autonomy, and may find rules and structure inhibiting. The implication is that it is a mistake to treat a novice like an expert or master, and vice versa.

Because experts seem to come up with the right option so quickly, and seemingly without thinking or analysing a situation, there is a tendency to see them as 'naturals', 'born' with a high degree of skill, but as we will see, this is more a matter of training, coaching, feedback and improvement over time. They just make a task look easy through their mastery. An implication of this that we pick up later, is that experts, including expert teachers, often find it difficult to articulate what they do, simply because their responses to situations, including challenging, changing situations, seem to be automatic. An elite tennis player doesn't try to recall what the coaching manual says when the ball is coming towards them. Experts thus seem to have more time to make decisions than do novices.

The National Research Council of the USA provided the following distinguishing, generic characteristics for experts that are congruent with the findings from Dreyfus and Dreyfus above:

1. Experts notice features and meaningful patterns of information that are not noticed by novices.
2. Experts have acquired a great deal of content knowledge that is organised in ways that reflect a deep understanding of their subject matter.
3. Experts' knowledge cannot be reduced to sets of isolated facts or propositions but instead, reflects contexts of applicability; that is, the knowledge is 'conditionalised' on a set of circumstances.
4. Experts are able to flexibly retrieve important aspects of their knowledge with little attentional effort.
5. Though experts know their disciplines thoroughly, this does not guarantee that they are able to teach others.[b]
6. Experts have varying levels of flexibility in their approach to new situations.[6]

Expert teachers

Similar results have been found for 'expert teachers' that are congruent with the work of Dreyfus and Dreyfus and the National Research Council of the USA outlined above. John Hattie and Dick Jaeger identified five major dimensions of excellent teachers, underpinned by 16 prototypic attributes[7]:

A. Can identify essential representations of their subject(s)
  A1. Expert teachers have deeper representations about teaching and learning.
  A2. Expert teachers adopt a problem-solving stance to their work.
  A3. Expert teachers can anticipate, plan, and improvise as required by the situation.
  A4. Expert teachers are better decision-makers and can identify what decisions are important and which are less important decisions.

B. Guiding learning through classroom interactions
  B5. Expert teachers are proficient at creating an optimal classroom climate for learning.

---

b   A finding with important implications for teacher preparation and teaching.

B6. Expert teachers have a multidimensionally complex perception of classroom situations.

B7. Expert teachers are more context-dependent and have high situation cognition.

C. Monitoring learning and provide feedback

C8. Expert teachers are more adept at monitoring student problems and assessing their level of understanding and progress, and they provide much more relevant, useful feedback.

C9. Expert teachers are more adept at developing and testing hypotheses about learning difficulties or instructional strategies.

C10. Expert teachers are more automatic.

D. Attending to affective attributes

D11. Expert teachers have high respect for students.

D12. Expert teachers are passionate about teaching and learning.

E. Influencing student outcomes

E13. Expert teachers engage students in learning and develop in their students' self-regulation, involvement in mastery learning, enhanced self-efficacy, and self-esteem as learners.

E14. Expert teachers provide adequate challenging tasks and goals for students.

E15. Expert teachers have positive influences on students' achievement.

E16. Expert teachers enhance surface and deep learning.

It needs to be emphasised that progression from novice to expert is neither automatic nor merely the result of accumulated experience. Further, as noted above, being an expert teacher is not a matter of being a 'born teacher'—there is no such thing[8]—nor is it of personality, intelligence, memory or some form of general ability. Marzano has noted that:

> Relatively speaking, it was not that long ago that expertise was considered something that could not be developed. To illustrate, as a result of his historical analysis of perceptions of expertise, Murray concluded that it was generally believed that talent was considered 'a gift from the gods' …
>
> Over time, the fallacies in this perspective emerged. Ericsson and Charness explain that 'it is curious how little empirical evidence supports the talent view of expert and exceptional performance'. They note that over the centuries, the talent hypothesis was inevitably challenged once it became evident that individuals could 'dramatically increase their performance through education and training if they have the necessary drive and motivation'.
>
> … If expertise is not a function of talent or intelligence, then what are its determiners? The research points to two critical factors: *a well-articulated knowledge base and deliberate practice.*[9] [Emphasis added]

Marzano goes on to note that while there has been almost an 'exponential' increase in the knowledge base for education, especially pedagogy, a weakness in this work has been insufficient understanding of how teachers, including expert teachers, combine these strategies in dynamic and diverse classroom contexts.[10] It is not just a matter of knowing a suitable strategy, but selecting and implementing the best, most appropriate strategy, or more realistically, the best combination of strategies, to move learning forward for both individuals and groups within a class in the same way that a master chess player considers a range of possible 'moves' before settling on the one he or she believes to be most effective, given the context of the game, and even the state of a series of games.

Marzano also implies that a lesson is not an entity, but a process that involves a range of 'segments', which also require planning in sequence. He notes nine of these types:

1. Communicating learning goals, tracking student progress and celebrating success
2. Establishing or maintaining rules and procedures
3. Introducing new content (critical input lessons)
4. Knowledge [from] practising and deepening lessons
5. Hypothesis generating and testing lessons (knowledge application lessons)
6. Increasing student engagement
7. Recognising and acknowledging adherents and lack of adherence to classroom rules and procedures
8. Establishing and maintaining effective relationships with students
9. Communicating high expectations for every student.

These nine segments are organised into three categories: segments involving routine events, segments involving academic content, and segments involving issues that must be addressed as they occur.[11]

A key aspect of successful teaching is recognising that lessons will not always go to plan for a variety of reasons, and that the teacher needs to monitor the progress of the lesson and the various strategies being employed, and be prepared to modify, augment, or even abandon strategies if it is clear they are not working. We will consider the issue of 'adaptive expertise' later in this chapter.

Marzano's second factor—in addition to a well-articulated knowledge base—in developing teacher expertise is providing opportunities for teachers to engage in 'deliberate practice'[c]:

---

c   We considered the importance of practice in Chapter 2, including the relative impacts on learning of 'spaced' versus 'mass' practice.

> Where a comprehensive knowledge of pedagogy is important to developing expertise, deliberate practice is the vehicle that transforms knowledge into behaviour ... Deliberate practice has at least three defining characteristics: (1) clear and focused tasks, (2) clear criteria for success, and (3) the motivation to engage in deliberate practice ... Necessary resources include an identified cadre of expert teachers, time for expert teachers and aspiring teachers to interact about effective teaching, and time for expert teachers and aspiring teachers to observe each other teaching.[12]

The above goes beyond the 'normal', still common, approach of teachers rarely seeing each other teach and thus rarely gaining constructive, focused feedback on their performance. There may, however, be an annual ritual of 'performance appraisal', which inevitably, most teachers 'pass'. For many teachers, where some form of observation occurs, it is tokenistic and reliant on 'gut feelings' of whether someone is a 'good' teacher, or not. However, as we shall see, the best teachers are comfortable about, and even relish, working collaboratively, opening up their classrooms to others, and giving each other feedback.

While attaining expert teacher status can take a substantial amount of time, this is more a matter of 'rich' experience, working and talking with colleagues and supervisors, targeted professional learning, trial and error and experimentation, role modelling, feedback and reflection.

There is a saying that while some teachers have 25 years of experience, other teachers have the same year of experience 25 times over. In other words, not all teachers will reach expert status and none will do so automatically. Some teachers will actually regress in their effectiveness over time. However, all teachers are capable of learning how to be more effective, including highly experienced and even 'stale' teachers, as we will see from research cited in later chapters.

David Berliner is an authority in the field of the development of teaching expertise. In reviewing the research literature, including his own work, he concluded:

> Experts in teaching share characteristics of experts in more prestigious fields such as chess, medical diagnosis, and physics problem solving. Thus, there is no basis to believe that there are differences in the sophistication of the cognitive processes used by teachers and experts in other fields. This is an important conclusion for educators who are generally held in low esteem by the public.
>
> ... we now have evidence that those who are identified as experts through National Board Certification do, in fact, behave in classrooms as experts are expected to. They also have learned the skills required to increase their students' test scores beyond that of non-experts. The related fields of research on teaching, teacher education, and public policy concerned with teachers have all benefited enormously from the study of expertise in teaching. And

the psychological study of expertise across different fields is richer for having this literature on expertise in pedagogy available.[13]

How long does it take to become an expert teacher?
In considering how long it takes to develop expertise in teaching, Berliner concluded that moving from novice status to achieving competence as a teacher takes around two to three years. The development of a high level of skill, however, takes five to seven years and a great deal of work.[14] Such findings are congruent with the Australian Professional Standards for Teachers (APST) introduced in 2011, which recognise four levels of expertise: *Graduate*, *Proficient*, *Highly Accomplished*, and *Lead*.[15] 'Novices' are required to pass initial teacher education courses designed to meet the Graduate standards. Beginning teachers are then required to meet the Proficient standards in their first year or so of teaching, depending on whether they are in full-time or partial employment. Reaching the voluntary level of Highly Accomplished expertise and performance could conceivably take around five years of teaching, while the voluntary Lead level might take around seven years or more to obtain and could be considered equivalent to an 'expert' level of accomplishment and performance, although some might meet these standards more quickly.

In a paper for the Business Council of Australia (BCA), *Investing in Teacher Quality: Doing What Matters Most*, Lawrence Ingvarson, Elizabeth Kleinhenz and I considered a new salary and career structure for Australia's teachers[16] based on four such levels of performance. (We later wrote the early drafts of the APST.[17]) We suggested that once such a system of four levels of standards, coupled with suitable salary and career structures, had worked its way through and reached equilibrium, approximately 60 per cent of teachers might be in the Proficient band, either qualifying for or having received certification for full registration. Another 30 per cent might occupy the Highly Accomplished band, while the 10 per cent of remaining teachers might be in the Lead class. This would be consistent with what we know about the development and distribution of teacher expertise, but should be criterion referenced, in that anyone who demonstrated they had met the standard could be certified at that level, rather than limiting those who can be recognised as a result of a quota system and/or a minimum time requirement to present for certification, given that the ultimate aim of such a salary and career structure would be to drive, recognise and reward quality teaching.

The importance of routine
Berliner and colleagues conducted a number of research studies involving novice teachers, 'advanced beginners', and expert teachers, who were required to plan and implement a lesson in a laboratory situation. The lesson was videoed and the participants were then asked to articulate their thinking and justify their actions taken during the teaching of the lessons. The findings were somewhat surprising:

Despite the fact that the experts performing this task were judged to be better teachers on a number of dimensions, the task triggered a good deal of anger among them. One of them quit the study, another broke down and cried in the middle of the study, and all were unhappy they participated.[d]

They all reported their fears about performing well when we moved them from their own classrooms to the laboratory situation we had created for them to teach in.

Furthermore, we had allocated 30 minutes for planning, enough for the advanced beginners and the novices to feel comfortable. But the experts claimed they needed more time. One suggested 3 hours, and another claimed to need 3 weeks to prepare that material. Our interviews revealed that experts rarely entered their classrooms without having taken the time they need to (a) thoroughly understand the content they will teach and (b) plan one or more activities to teach that content.

The experts also noted that they did not know the students in this situation[e] and that their pedagogical expertise depended, in part, on knowing their students well.[18]

It was evident in the above experiments that one factor in the success of expert teachers, in addition to knowing their students well, are the routines they establish in their classrooms. In the laboratory situation, the familiar contexts and associated routines that the expert teachers and their students were accustomed to were absent, leading to anxiety and less effective than usual performance. Ayres, Dinham and Sawyer[19] found the establishment and maintenance of classroom routines, which are not to be confused with regimentation, was an important factor in the effectiveness of expert teachers. (We will consider the findings from that study of successful senior secondary teachers in the following chapter.)

Routine and adaptive expertise

An interesting aspect on the research evidence on expertise, and by implication that on teacher expertise, is provided by the concept of 'adaptive expertise', and its counterpart, 'routine' or 'classic' expertise. The term adaptive expertise was first developed by Hatano and Inagaki[20], who famously illustrated the concept by considering two types of Japanese sushi experts. One is adept at replicating the same recipes time and again, that is, he or she possesses routine expertise. The second,

---

d   Recall Carol Dweck's findings reported in Chapter 2 about those labelled experts fearing exposure.

e   You will also recall the emphasis in Chapter 2 on successful teachers knowing their students as 'learners' and 'people'. These findings support that contention.

equally skilled in the technical aspects of the art, is able to create new recipes, or in other words, possesses adaptive expertise.

In *How People Learn*, Bransford, Brown and Cocking noted that:

> Adaptive experts are able to approach new situations flexibly and to learn throughout their lifetimes. They not only use what they have learned, they are metacognitive and continually question their current levels of expertise and attempt to move beyond them. They don't simply attempt to do the same things more efficiently; they attempt to do things better. The major challenge for theories of learning is to understand how particular kinds of learning experiences develop adaptive expertise or 'virtuosos'.[21]

An implication of the above is that adaptive experts are more likely, by definition, to be more innovative and open to change. They also need to be able to identify and articulate problems that require solutions. To achieve change in their professional practice, they need to be able to identify areas where their current expertise is deficient and to be open to new professional learning. Routine experts, on the other hand, are capable of high levels of performance—'artisans'—but find it difficult to change and innovate—to be 'virtuosos'—either because they don't see the need for such change or because they don't know how to go about adapting their professional knowledge and practice. A further implication is that adaptive experts not only need to be able to identify the need for change in their own practice, but to plan and implement change collaboratively through working with others, who may or may not be adaptive in their outlook.

As we will see in later chapters, many of the effective teachers and other leaders researched and profiled, fall into the category of adaptive experts. They are never satisfied with what they know or can do and are always attuned and open to new ideas and opportunities, while being willing to undergo the necessary professional learning to solve problems, address issues and improve their professional practice.

Endnotes

1   Simon, H., & Chase, W. (1973). Skill in chess. *American Scientist, 61*(4), 394–403.
2   Gladwell, M. (2008). *Outliers: The story of success.* New York, NY: Little, Brown and Company.
3   Dreyfus, S., & Dreyfus, H. (1980). *A five-stage model of the mental activities involved in directed skills acquisition.* Berkeley, CA: Operations Research Center, University of California. (pp. 1–18)
4   See Dreyfus, S. (2004). The five-stage model of adult skill acquisition. *Bulletin of Science, Technology & Society, 24*(3), 177–181.
5   Dreyfus, S., & Dreyfus, H. (1980). (p. 15)

6   Bransford, J., Brown, A., & Cocking, R. (2000). (Eds.). *How people learn*. Washington, DC: National Academy Press. (p. 31). Reprinted with permission by the National Academy of Sciences, Courtesy of the National Academies Press, Washington, D.C.
7   Hattie, J. (2003). *Teachers make a difference: What is the research evidence?* Paper presented at ACER Annual Conference, October. (pp. 5–9).
8   Scott, C., & Dinham, S. (2008). Born not made: The nativist myth and teachers' thinking. *Teacher Development, 12*(2), 127–136.
9   Marzano, R. (2010). Developing Expert Teachers. In Marzano, R. (Ed.), *On excellence in teaching* (pp. 213–245). Bloomington, IN: Solution Tree Press. (p. 216)
10 Marzano, R. (2010). (p. 217)
11 Marzano, R. (2010). (pp. 218–219)
12 Marzano, R. (2010). (p. 232)
13 Berliner, D. (2004). Describing the behaviour and documenting the accomplishments of expert teachers. *Bulletin of Science, Technology & Society, 24*(3), 200–212. (p. 210). Copyright © 2004 by D. Berliner. All text extracts from this article are reprinted by Permission of Sage Publications, Inc.
14 Berliner, D. (2004). (p. 201)
15 AITSL [Australian Institute for Teaching and School Leadership]. (2011). *Australian professional standards for teachers*. Melbourne, Victoria: Author.
16 Dinham, S., Ingvarson, L., & Kleinhenz, E. (2008). Investing in teacher quality: Doing what matters most. In *Teaching talent: The best teachers for Australia's classrooms* (pp. 5–53). Melbourne, Victoria: Business Council of Australia. (p. 10)
17 Dinham, S., Ingvarson, L., Kleinhenz, E., & Anderson, M. (2009). *The Draft National Professional Standards Framework for Teachers and School Leaders*. Melbourne, Victoria: ACER.
18 Berliner, D. (2004). (p. 202)
19 See Ayres, P., Dinham, S., & Sawyer, W. (1998). *The identification of successful teaching methodologies in the NSW Higher School Certificate: A research report for the NSW Department of Education and Training*. Penrith: University of Western Sydney, Nepean; Ayres, P., Dinham, S., & Sawyer, W. (2000). Successful senior secondary teaching, *Quality Teaching Series*, No. 1, Australian College of Education, September, 1–20.
20 Hatano, G., & Inagaki, K. (1986). Two courses of expertise. *Child Development and Education in Japan*, 262–272.
21 Bransford, J., Brown, A., & Cocking, R. (2000). (p. 48)

CHAPTER 6

What do quality teachers do? What does quality teaching look like?

INTRODUCTION

The importance of the teacher, teaching strategies that have greatest (and lesser) impact on student learning, the development of teacher expertise, and general attributes of 'expert' teachers have been examined in previous chapters.

Although teachers' work is highly complex and is carried out across a variety of contexts, there is a strong consensus on what quality teachers know and do.[1] As noted, the big challenge lies in upscaling, with the ultimate aim of having a quality or highly effective teacher in every classroom.[2]

This chapter takes a closer look at the qualities and actions of successful teachers before presenting the findings from a research project investigating successful senior secondary teachers, along with findings from a broader project, designed both to recognise and research quality teaching, involving teachers from various sectors and levels of education.

What is quality teaching?

A team from Durham University conducted a review of the research literature in an attempt to answer the question 'What makes great teaching?'.[3] However, rather than listing attributes and actions of quality teachers, the authors were concerned with measuring the impacts of teaching on student outcomes, something ignored or simplistically addressed in earlier work on teacher and teaching effectiveness. This situation of ignoring the effects of teaching on learning can lead to the situation where one could say 'I taught them, but they didn't learn'. As noted, it is important to consider more holistic outcomes and evidence when we consider the effects of teaching on learning, including evidence from the 'academic', 'personal', and 'social domains'[4] of learning and development.

In defining 'great teaching', the authors commented:

> Great teaching is defined as that which leads to improved student progress ... We define effective teaching as that which leads to improved student achievement using outcomes that matter to their future success. Defining effective teaching is not easy. The research keeps coming back to this critical point: student progress is the yardstick by which teacher quality should be assessed. Ultimately, for a judgement about whether teaching is effective, to be seen as trustworthy, it must be checked against the progress being made by students.[5]

The authors identified six components of 'great' teaching, as indicated by student outcomes, which can be utilised when assessing teaching quality:

> Good quality teaching will likely involve a combination of these attributes manifested at different times; the very best teachers are those that demonstrate all of these features.

1. **(Pedagogical) content knowledge** (Strong evidence of impact on student outcomes)

    The most effective teachers have deep knowledge of the subjects they teach, and when teachers' knowledge falls below a certain level it is a significant impediment to students' learning. As well as a strong understanding of the material being taught, teachers must also understand the ways students think about the content, be able to evaluate the thinking behind students' own methods, and identify students' common misconceptions.

2. **Quality of instruction** (Strong evidence of impact on student outcomes)

    Includes elements such as effective questioning and use of assessment by teachers. Specific practices, like reviewing previous learning, providing model responses for students, giving adequate time for

practice to embed skills securely and progressively introducing new learning (scaffolding) are also elements of high quality instruction.
3. **Classroom climate** (Moderate evidence of impact on student outcomes)
Covers quality of interactions between teachers and students, and teacher expectations: the need to create a classroom that is constantly demanding more, but still recognising students' self-worth. It also involves attributing student success to effort rather than ability and valuing resilience to failure (grit).
4. **Classroom management** (Moderate evidence of impact on student outcomes)
A teacher's abilities to make efficient use of lesson time, to coordinate classroom resources and space, and to manage students' behaviour with clear rules that are consistently enforced, are all relevant to maximising the learning that can take place. These environmental factors are necessary for good learning rather than its direct components.
5. **Teacher beliefs** (Some evidence of impact on student outcomes)
Why teachers adopt particular practices, the purposes they aim to achieve, their theories about what learning is and how it happens and their conceptual models of the nature and role of teaching in the learning process all seem to be important.
6. **Professional behaviours** (Some evidence of impact on student outcomes)
Behaviours exhibited by teachers such as reflecting on and developing professional practice, participation in professional development, supporting colleagues, and liaising and communicating with parents.[6]

The authors of the report advocated the assessment of teacher quality through the use of multiple measures, rather than the simplistic and unreliable method of relying on student performance on high stakes testing, or some form of 'gut instinct' assessment arising from limited and unfocused observation of teaching.

According to the report, approaches to assessing teachers that demonstrate 'moderate' reliability include:
1. classroom observations by peers, principals or external evaluators
2. 'value added' models (assessing gains in student achievement)
3. student ratings.

On the other hand, approaches or measures with 'limited evidence' in respect of validity include:
4. principal (or head-teacher) judgement
5. teacher self-reports
6. analysis of classroom artefacts and teacher portfolios.[7]

The above is instructive, because some of those measures listed above with 'limited evidence' are those that still appear to be prevalent in schools, including principal's assessments that don't rely on systematic observation.

Case study of successful teaching

In order to now get a richer view of quality teaching from the 'chalkface', the findings from a study of successful senior (Years 11 and 12) secondary teaching in government (public) schools in New South Wales (NSW), Australia, are explored. These findings remain fresh and relevant, based on subsequent work, and will be related to other material in this book and what we know about 'expert' teachers more generally.

Context

The NSW Higher School Certificate (HSC) is a high stakes credential first awarded in 1967. Although it has changed over the years in terms of how student performance in Years 11 and 12 is measured and reported, since that time it has remained the prime mechanism for measuring overall senior secondary achievement and allocating students to places in courses at NSW and other universities. Rather than being an overall 'mark' as it once was, the HSC today is a ranking exercise based on a combination of performance on in-school assessments and external examinations, which after moderation, results in an Australian Tertiary Admission Rank (ATAR).

In the minds of students, parents, the media and the community, great importance is placed upon the ATAR 'score' (actually a percentile ranking) that HSC students (and students in other Australian territories and states) achieve. Schools are judged, and some choose to promote themselves, on the basis of the performance of their students at the HSC. University entry scores also contribute to the status of courses, faculties and universities as a whole, with medicine, for example, typically requiring an ATAR of more than 99.5.

The study

The study was commissioned by the NSW Department of Education and conducted by Paul Ayres, Wayne Sawyer and me, who were all on the academic staff of the then University of Western Sydney at the time. All three of us had previously been experienced HSC teachers in different subject areas.

The aims of the study were to:

- identify the relationship between teaching methods and HSC outcomes for students,
- identify the characteristics of successful HSC teaching methodology, and
- consider the implications of the study findings for improving teacher efficiency.[8]

In designing the study, we were guided by the finding from the literature that experts often find it difficult to articulate what they do, something that tended to rule out some form of survey to ask teachers about their practices (see earlier comment about the low validity of teacher self-report measures). We decided, therefore, that we needed to do several things: identify some highly successful senior secondary teachers, observe them teach, and talk to them and others about their teaching. This would be costly and would limit the number of teachers we could include in the study, given our time and financial budgets.

We were given access to confidential HSC performance data for government schools for the period under study, and teachers were selected by first identifying a number of faculties (subject departments) that had demonstrated significant success at the HSC in certain subjects over a period of time (at least five years). Success was defined as having students in the top 1 per cent of HSC courses (subjects often have several courses or levels of difficulty, and we looked at all courses, including lower level/ability courses).

We then used a variety of statistical 'filters' to eliminate variables other than the teacher as the cause for this success. We did this by: comparing results achieved by other teachers with the same students at the same school; external comparisons within a course, especially for courses like languages with small numbers sitting the HSC; additional controls for academic selectivity (some secondary schools in NSW are academically selective with potential students undertaking a competitive examination at the end of year 6—these schools would be expected to achieve higher results) and socio-economic status (SES) through comparing 'like with like' schools; observing the clustering of results over the time period, and considering who was teaching these classes in different years.

Thus, it was performance within a school over time by a teacher, as well as absolute performance in terms of statewide HSC results, which determined possible inclusion in the study.

Because of budgetary limitations and the desire to cover as best we could both the range of subjects and the types of secondary schools across the state, we finally settled on teachers in subject departments in 32 schools—18 metropolitan (Sydney) and 14 non-metropolitan (regional urban and rural). Of the 32 subject departments, 7 were in academically selective high schools and 25 in comprehensive high schools. Because of the method used to select teachers and the need to cover the major subject areas[a] and broad socio-economic diversity of the state in a representative fashion, we did not claim that the teachers chosen were the 'best' HSC teachers in NSW; merely that they appeared to be highly successful according to the criteria and data

---

[a] Twelve subjects were represented in the study: Ancient History, Biology, Business Studies, English, Legal Studies, Mathematics, Modern History, Music, Personal Development Health and Physical Education (PDHPE), Physics, Society and Culture, Visual Arts.

at our disposal, which comprised both internal assessment and external examination. As will be seen, we felt we could have chosen another equally successful group of teachers had we the resources to do so.

Due to various constraints, we were able to visit only 17 of the 32 schools. Twenty-five teachers took part in the study, where the typical methodology was to observe each teacher for two lessons or more, usually teaching Year 11 classes, and then interview the teacher both about the lesson observed and more generally about their teaching and professional development. We also sat in staff rooms and spoke to other teachers, head teachers (heads of department; eight study teachers were themselves HoDs) and in some cases, students. Sixty-eight per cent of the teachers were women, broadly reflecting the distribution of women and men in secondary teaching in NSW, and most were very experienced, with an average of 17 years in their present school.[b]

We had a number of concerns about the method we employed. The first was that the teachers we identified might not have been 'expert' teachers at all, but promoters of 'rote learning', 'textbook teachers', and 'exam crammers' who 'taught to the test'. This was not the case with any of the teachers we observed, however. The second concern was that these teachers might have been talented isolates, 'high fliers' or 'lone rangers', not well integrated into their faculties or schools. Once again, our findings proved otherwise. The third concern was that because of the limited time available, we would not be able to get an accurate view of their teaching—they would 'put on a show' for our benefit. This too was unfounded.

In the early stages, all three of us observed lessons until we were satisfied that the method and protocols (lesson observation schedules, interview questions, other structured and unstructured observations) were working successfully. After this pilot phase, usually only one of us was in the room. Even when all three were observing classes, it was obvious that once we were introduced to or observed by the class—the real reason for our presence was not provided to the students—the class and teacher quickly got down to work and we were ignored. A number of teachers actually told us they had no intention of doing anything out of the ordinary for us, but would give their 'regular' lesson. We told them we were happy with that.

Some teachers appeared nervous, but this soon vanished once the lesson started. In fact, we found that it was a feature of many of these teachers' teaching that others were frequently in the room for various purposes—students were used to teachers dropping in and out—and thus we didn't feel we were a distraction to either teachers or students.

A final point to add that is frequently overlooked in research reports is that we genuinely enjoyed the research process. In this and other studies where I have had the opportunity to watch expert teachers at work (see later in this chapter, for example),

---

b   As noted, due to the methodology employed, teachers had to be at their present school for at least five years in order to be selected.

it is always illuminating and often inspiring. As an experienced teacher, I always see something that makes me reflect on my own teaching, as well as learning more about teaching generally, and there is something special about watching someone who is a master of their profession in action.

Factors contributing to senior secondary teaching success

We analysed our data using accepted content analysis techniques, and utilised spreadsheets to record the frequency of various observation and interview phenomena.[9] As a result of this process, seven broad factors were identified as contributing to HSC teaching success. The essential features of each will be described:
- School background
- Subject faculty (department)
- Personal qualities
- Relationships with students
- Professional development
- Teaching—resources, planning
- Teaching strategies.

1   School background

When we spoke to the selected teachers and their colleagues, there was a marked tendency to talk of the students at their school positively, regardless of how the school might have been regarded in the wider community. Terms used to describe students included 'motivated', 'friendly', 'disciplined', 'focused on learning', and just 'good kids'. A general finding drawn from this and other studies (see later chapters) is that positive attitudes are both indicative of a healthy school culture and 'contagious', in that they set up something of a self-fulfilling prophecy or upward cycle. Unfortunately, experience has shown that the reverse is also true. Students and schools can be talked down easier than they can be talked up. Attitudes, expectations and mindsets are powerful influences in schools, for good or bad.

Consistent with the positive way that students were regarded and described, the teachers in the faculties (once again, not just those selected for study but also others we spoke with) described their fellow teachers as 'supportive', 'hard working' and 'caring'. They also commented how school leaders provided support for their subject or faculty. Some spoke of the support of the community for their subject area.

Faculty members also commented about whole or cross-school approaches to curriculum and pedagogy that they saw as contributing to student success at the HSC.

In the light of research findings about factors leading to student achievement identified by writers such as Hattie and Marzano earlier, school-based factors were reported by those involved with the HSC study to be influential, but of lesser importance overall in the success of individual teachers and students. In other words, helpful, but not essential conditions for student success.

2 Subject faculty

As noted, we had wondered whether the teachers we selected for the study might have been misfits or loners, with their head stuck in a textbook in a corner of the staffroom. However, the message we got very quickly was how important subject departments or faculties—in other words, their colleagues—were to the success of these individual teachers. In fact, a number of study teachers and other faculty members told us that while we had identified one teacher as being successful, there were others who were equally effective in the faculty, and in the school generally. This was not said with any sense of criticism, professional jealousy or complaint but rather as free recognition of others' professional capacity. 'We do a lot of things together here', was a frequent comment.

Ways in which the faculty as a group influenced the success of individual teachers and their students included:

- **The faculty acting as a team** through sharing programs, resources and teaching ideas.
- **Faculty members setting the climate for all individuals within the faculty**; this could be summed up as: 'We are professional, we have high expectations, we will help you as much as possible, but we expect you to play your part, meet our standards and support us in what we are trying to achieve'.
- **Whole-faculty approaches to programming**, with staff sharing responsibility for curriculum development.
- **The faculty having achieved a certain profile and identity within the school**, leading to comments from others like: 'The teachers in the Science faculty are up to date, innovative, hard-working and successful', and so forth.
- **Faculty success breeding success**. This was one of those 'ah ha' moments that sometimes occurs with research. When we asked faculty members and those teachers selected for the study why they thought their students were successful at the HSC, a majority stated—independently—that they laid the groundwork for HSC success by attracting talented junior students into the subject in Years 11–12 through their teaching in Years 7–10; 'setting up' students for HSC success through thorough teaching of fundamental knowledge and skills in Years 7–10, and through the subject having gained the status of a 'dominant culture' within the school, so that undertaking the subject was a sign of aspiration and ambition on the part of students, who expected to 'work hard and do well'.
- **Whole-faculty rapport with students**. As part of a strong and distinct faculty ethos and culture, there was general positive rapport with students that was observed in classrooms, staff rooms and in the school generally. There was obvious mutual respect and even affection between staff and students. A key, instructive observation was how staff members were prepared to assist the students of their fellow faculty members. One situation I observed illustrated this. I was sitting in a staff room used by visual arts teachers when a senior student knocked at the door. The student spoke briefly to her class teacher, asking for

some assistance. The teacher listened carefully before saying something along the lines of 'You really need to speak to Mrs ___' she's the expert on that', at which point Mrs ___ stopped what she was doing and went to the student's assistance. This phenomenon was repeated elsewhere in the study and indicates a number of things: these teachers were willing to speak with students during their breaks, something that is not always the case; teachers were prepared to admit they didn't know everything, once again, not universal among teachers; these teachers were comfortable about deferring to the superior knowledge of a colleague, and finally, that a teacher was willing to help someone who wasn't their student. After observing this phenomenon a number of times, we came to the conclusion that this practice was analogous to a medical professional referring a patient to a specialist colleague.

There were other faculty features identified by teachers as being influential in their students' HSC success:

- Faculties were well organised with easy access to resources.
- The faculty had a general sense of enthusiasm and vitality.
- Faculty members 'loved' their subject and saw it as important to students.
- Faculties were very experienced.
- Faculty members were well prepared and up to date.
- The faculty aimed to give their subject(s) a high profile within the school.
- Faculties sometimes focused on specific purposes appropriate to the particular needs of students, e.g., Indigenous students.

Overall, the faculty emerged as being more influential in the success of individual teachers than we had expected. Once again, in line with other research literature, faculty-based factors were confirmed to influence teacher effectiveness and student achievement, more so than general school factors, although the influence was less than that of the individual teacher, which is to where this discussion now turns.

3 Teachers' personal qualities

Teachers' personal qualities emerged as an important factor in this research project. Key aspects are detailed below, although there was understandable overlap with the factor of 'Relationships with Students', which follows.

- **Orientation to subject**—the individual teacher's mastery of content knowledge and their belief that this was a key factor in their success was one of the key findings of the study. Strong subject content knowledge was evident in the lessons observed across the curriculum: 'You've got to know your stuff' was the most common response from teachers to questions about HSC success. This was also a strong factor influencing student confidence in the teacher, and student success at the HSC. Teachers' love and passion for their subject was important in motivating students. In another one of those 'ah ha' moments, teacher after teacher told us that their particular subject (English, Maths, Legal Studies, or whatever) was 'the most important subject' students undertook, the reason being that it was essential and would prepare them for life. This belief gave weight and even passion to their teaching and teachers were constantly communicating to their students and reinforcing their belief in the importance and relevance of their subject.

- **Orientation to students**—approachability in and out of class was the important trait most readily identified here by these teachers. They demonstrated a willingness to relax and to be themselves with students and were regarded by students as 'real people', and not remote, unapproachable authority figures.
- **Orientation to work**—teachers described themselves and were described by others as hard-working and committed. Good organisation on the part of the teacher was seen as a key factor contributing to student confidence and success.

4 Relationships with students

Strong positive relationships with students formed an important background against which effective teaching occurred. Positive teacher–student relationships and effective teaching are mutually reinforcing and in this case it was hard to discern cause and effect, with each being in evidence.

Aspects of positive relationships with students exhibited by the teachers included:
- **Being themselves**—teachers showed willingness and capacity to relax in the classroom and not be remote, yet were still unmistakably in control.
- **Relating to students as people**—it was apparent that the teachers had established appropriate personal and professional 'distance' with their students. Teachers took a personal interest in things such as sport, music and other student accomplishments through conversations in the playground and classroom, without prying too deeply or giving away too much personal information about themselves. They were friendly to their students without trying to be a friend.
- **Mutual respect and discipline**—classes were calm and orderly and had a sense of purpose, with students interacting informally within unspoken, yet agreed limits. We saw no instance where a teacher needed to discipline a student. There was a jointly held expectation concerning what was acceptable behaviour. Students appeared to feel that they were respected for being 'seniors' and responded accordingly.
- **Teacher availability and approachability**—teachers were prepared and happy to take questions, help students and see them out of class time. Students saw teachers as being there to help if needed. They were not afraid to ask for assistance and didn't fear being ridiculed for asking a 'dumb question'.

5 Teachers' professional development

These teachers had achieved a certain profile, credibility and reputation within, and in some cases beyond their school. Their expertise was recognised and sometimes sought out by others. Some had taken the lead in providing professional development within their school and through their involvement with professional associations outside the school.

A number of teachers mentioned how teachers from other schools would sometimes contact them to request copies of their teaching programs because of their success, usually after the HSC results were released, but that these approaches were usually rebuffed. Aside from a reluctance to hand over their work to others, there was a view expressed that 'It's not just the program … but what you do with it', to use the words of one teacher in the study.

- **Networking**—most of these teachers were active professional networkers, which assisted both their professional learning and the learning of others. This occurred through membership of various groups, associations and committees. An interesting finding of the study was the high degree to which teachers were involved in professional practice in their 'host discipline'. For example, visual arts teachers were artists, music teachers were musicians, legal studies teachers were involved with the legal profession, science teachers were amateur astronomers, and so forth. Thus, rather than being a maths teacher, someone might consider themselves a mathematician who teaches. These connections with their discipline were beneficial in keeping these teachers in touch with developments in their field and added richness and current relevance to their teaching.
- **In-school professional development**—around half the teachers saw their professional development as being based largely within their faculty. When teachers had been involved in in-service learning off-site, there was usually some form of demonstration or reporting back to fellow staff. Sometimes a head teacher or another mentor on staff was nominated by teachers as having been an important source of professional learning. Where teachers were in small faculties or were the only teacher of a subject in the school, as was the case with teachers of music and biology in the study, professional development, mentors and networks were often external to the school. Larger faculties tended to be more self-contained.
- **Development through experience**—almost all of the teachers spoke of their accumulated experience as being important in their success, although they also recognised that experience or time alone was not sufficient to guarantee effectiveness. 'Rich' experience, professional learning and help from others were seen as necessary for development as an effective teacher, over and above time in the job.
- **Out-of-school professional development**—for those teachers who nominated out-of-school activities as the major source of their professional learning (around half of those studied), formal courses that provided 'subject content' were seen as most valuable by two-thirds of these teachers, while the remaining third nominated

courses about 'pedagogic content' or teaching strategies as being most valuable. While most of the teachers in the study took advantage of regular in-service, some teachers sought out particular courses to enrich their teaching, e.g., one Ancient History teacher undertook a university course on hieroglyphics in her own time; other teachers planned their holidays to visit sites they would be teaching about.

6 Resources and planning
- **Planning**—over half the teachers identified planning as a key aspect of their success, both in terms of content and strategies, although content planning—what to teach—was more common.
- **Resources**—teachers were highly critical and selective users of resources—what I have termed 'critical consumers'—and many had developed their own materials for teaching in collaboration with colleagues. Textbooks alone were seen as inadequate, both because these did not contain topical material and because they were not considered sufficiently challenging or innovative.

7 Teaching strategies
The identification of teaching strategies leading to HSC success was the central aim of the study. While it was possible to identify particular strategies and approaches that were more prominent in certain subject areas such as English[10], overall, these successful teachers had far more in common than not.

Men and women teachers also had much in common in terms of both personal qualities and teaching strategies. There were no discernible 'male' or 'female' teaching styles or approaches.

What does come through from the study findings was that these people were not, and did not consider themselves, born teachers. They did, however, have a passion for learning about their subject—and teaching itself—and an enthusiasm to pass on to students what they know and 'love' about it. Overall, they possessed both deep content knowledge and what Shulman termed 'pedagogic content knowledge'[11]—they knew what to teach and how to teach it. They also had an expert's understanding of the HSC processes, including the curriculum, what HSC examiners looked for, and the standards required.

What follows is a description of teaching strategies employed by the teachers. As suggested by the literature, these teachers were not able to recall or describe fully the strategies they employed in the lessons that were observed.[12] Like experts in other fields and teachers in other studies, their actions and interventions frequently appeared to be 'arational' and characterised by automaticity. However, like other experts, they saw more detail in their classrooms than would novice teachers, and were thus able to provide an appropriate intervention or variation in technique almost unthinkingly and instantaneously.[13]

In the discussion of teaching strategies that follows, there is inevitably some overlap with the previous sections.

a) Classroom climate
Aspects of classroom climate observed in these teachers' classes included:
- unspoken expectation for students to demonstrate 'on task' behaviour, yet acceptable 'off-task' behaviour tolerated
- often rapid rate of progress in lessons, yet students able to cope
- in class, 'face-to-face' time, seen as precious, rather than out of class, home time
- community or group learning was more common than expected
- teacher enthusiasm and energy
- teacher reinforcement of students; feedback; recognition of student work and achievements
- regular routine and some repetition seen as important in providing structure and order
- teacher interest in students' lives, as well as individual progress; some informal time in class
- development of an ethos of student-student cooperation and sharing in the classroom, despite supposed competitive aspects of the HSC.

b) HSC focus
- Lessons were classed as 'HSC dominated' in half the lessons observed, in that the HSC was referred to or its requirements were addressed specifically.
- Half the teachers felt regular practice on specific HSC exam components was important; providing 'tips' and strategies to tackle the course and exam.
- On the whole, the HSC was seen as a common goal, with rituals and rules that had to be met and faced; teacher and students were on the 'same side', working together.
- Teachers went 'beyond' the HSC in many instances, 'teaching for understanding' rather than to pass an exam.
- Half the teachers felt their HSC marking experience was vital to their success (i.e., knowing marking standards, what markers looked for—most non-metropolitan teachers lacked this experience, an equity issue for these teachers and their students, marking the HSC being commonly described by those who had the opportunity as 'great PD (personal development)').
- Teachers were not 'exam crammers'.

c) Building understanding
- The inter-relatedness of the subject: teachers continually linked different areas and topics of the subject, previous lessons, to develop a 'big picture'; emphasis on finding multiple solutions rather than advocating or practising one 'best way'; use of previous knowledge to find these solutions.
- Using students' responses: use of student responses as building blocks; teacher drawing out responses without providing the answer.

- Facilitating thinking through applying knowledge and solving problems: emphasis on applying knowledge in class time using reasoning, independent thinking and group work.
- Interpretation: emphasis on interpretation, rather than reproduction of knowledge.
- DARTS: (Direct Activities Related to Texts)[14] e.g., cloze, prediction, categorising, labelling, sequencing exercises.
- Games, simulations and stories: e.g., scenarios, role plays, songs, setting up a business.

d) Note-making

- Building notes: through teacher facilitation; recording student discussion, directed note-making and student summaries; from student research, from student presentations; filling in gaps in knowledge.
- Independent note-making: little class time devoted to note 'taking', notes rarely distributed; independent 'note-making' and thinking encouraged, e.g., by having students complete notes from research/discussion, directed note-making (see above), student note-sharing from seminars or group work, allowing students latitude to decide what to record depending on individual need, reviewing class work in the student's 'own words', making own notes which the teacher checked—all leading to student 'ownership' of notes and obviating the need for further note-making and summaries out of class time.

e) Writing essays and organising information

- 'Big' essays or projects often seen as worthless: emphasis instead was on writing within the time scale or parameters of the HSC exam (e.g., write 250 words in 10 minutes); work on essay technique; provision of positive essay examples (e.g., 'this paper is worth 18/20 because …').
- Answering problems: importance of 'stretching', 'challenging' students, and not 'talking down to', or 'leading by the hand'; teachers refused to provide 'ready-made' solutions to problems; students were encouraged to find solutions using foundation provided by teacher.

f) Questioning

Some of us may have been told that closed questions are 'bad' (only one answer; 'guess what's in the teacher's head'; stifles discussion) and open questions are 'good' (a number of possible answers, interpretations; promotes discussion and thinking).

However, when the lesson observations were coded, there were many examples of closed questions, along with many open questions, which seemed to contradict the view about the importance of 'good' teachers emphasising reasoning, understanding, thinking and interpretation through the use of open questions.

After analysis and reflection, the key to this apparent contradiction was discovered. These teachers used different forms of questioning depending on the stage of the lesson, and whether the teacher was teaching the whole class or if students were working alone or in small groups.

Teachers tended to use closed questions when talking to the whole group and at the beginning and end of lessons to link, revise and test understanding. This also occurred at certain break points in lessons when students were passing from one activity to the next.

Open questions tended to be used when teachers wanted students to explore, interpret, predict or explain individually or in small groups. No teacher was able to tell us that they were using this approach, but virtually all did, and it makes perfect sense in hindsight.

- Whole-class questioning: closed questions dominated whole class discussion (assessment, review, linking, building).
- Open questions: used for individuals and groups to promote deeper thinking.

g) Whole-class discussion, group work and independent student activity
- Discussion: climate of open debate, presentation of different views, respect for all opinions, 'filtered' through the teacher.
- Group work: small groups (2–3 students) used in a third of observed lessons; two-thirds of teachers said they used this technique, but virtually all did, according to their students; groups used for making deductions from source material, learning from each other, finding out for themselves, solving problems; teachers used this time for one-to-one assistance for students, prompting, challenging, providing individual feedback.
- Independent student activity: included presentations of seminars by students, peer teaching, individual out-of-class research.

h) Assessment
Two things that characterised the teaching of these successful teachers were frequent, varied assessment, and frequent, constructive feedback designed to help students to understand what they can and can't do, and what they need to do in order to do better.[15] Assessment and feedback each took a variety of forms, both informal and formal.
- Techniques: short tests, quizzes, instant feedback for teacher and students; student work marked while students worked; sometimes whole lesson used for evaluation; providing a lot of feedback seen as important; monitoring of every student's progress.

i) Other strategies
A variety of other strategies were observed or reported by teachers.
- Question/answer/explain; pattern of demonstration/application, portion of lesson as lecture; concrete aids to recall (mind-maps, time-lines, colours, graphs, songs); having students use imagination (visualisation, drawing parallels with today,

imagining, role playing); students using board to demonstrate; taking students to out of school lectures, extra-curricular activities (e.g., mock trials), using real-world examples.

Findings from a program to recognise and research quality teaching

To underline the commonality of findings regarding successful or expert teaching, I will briefly examine the findings of another project.

Between 2000 and 2007 I chaired the development and implementation of the NSW Minister for Education and Training and the Australian College of Educators (NSW) Quality Teaching Awards (QTA).[16]

The twin aims of the QTA were to *recognise* and *research* 'quality teachers', drawn from early childhood education, through primary, secondary, TAFE and universities and from government and non-government sectors, in NSW.

In brief, teachers self-nominated (although we found that many had been encouraged to do so) and were required to complete an application form, provide details of professional referees who could be contacted, and complete a portfolio that was based upon the *Standards for Professional Practice for Accomplished Teaching in Australia* that were developed collaboratively by the Australian College of Educators (ACE), the Australian Association for Research in Education (AARE) and the Australian Curriculum Studies Association (ACSA).[17] [c]

Once this material—applications, referees' reports, portfolios—had been assessed, possibly the most important step occurred, whereby shortlisted teachers were required to be observed teaching, and their colleagues, supervisors, students, and in some cases community members, were interviewed. We left it to the teachers themselves to plan the day during which the visit would take place. We provided some guidelines in terms of the number of lessons to be observed, and some of the key people to be interviewed, but left the rest of the organisation to the discretion of the teacher.

This visitation step was seen as essential in terms of validation of the award winners and to complete the necessary research. There are many awards for teaching in existence, but very few actually involve observation of teaching. Teams of two educators visited each finalist and conducted the observations and interviews[d] using

---

c These standards were a forerunner of the present Australian Professional Standards for Teachers (AITSL, 2011).

d After the first year, QTA winners were invited to be part of the two-person visitation teams. This provided both further recognition and their expert input to the assessment process. Those who are part of the assessment teams described it as both inspiring and instructive. One implication of this is that there is great value in educators having the opportunity to move out of their context and to observe and interact with other educators. The focus of the QTA provided the framework for both reflection and discussion on quality teaching.

protocols prepared for that purpose. The recording of observations, interviews and other data in a handbook designed for the purpose was an important source of evidence, both for decision-making and for research.

The majority of candidates were successful at this stage but some were not, and, in the case of the latter, it was apparent that what had been provided in the form of written evidence was contradicted by what we saw in the field. Having said that, we observed some wonderful educators from across the spectrum, from early childhood, through to university teachers, and in many diverse settings across the state.[e]

Budgetary and logistical constraints meant that in any one year, up to 60 Quality Teaching Awards could be presented. The presentation of the awards by the Minister for Education took place at Government House in Sydney, a most spectacular and auspicious setting for the awards.

It was apparent that for many QTA recipients, this was a professional and personal highlight, receiving such an award in such a setting and with their families present.

Space precludes a more detailed examination of the operation of the awards but there are a number of observations that are relevant to a wider discussion about quality teaching. The first is that many of the recipients could be described as 'hidden treasures', in that they were little known outside their immediate context and tended to be modest and self-effacing. Some reported, with no false modesty, that they didn't think that what they were doing was out of the ordinary, due to their lack of a frame of reference with other teachers' performance. The implication here is that the passion, talent and experience of such teachers needs to be shared with others in pre-service and in-service courses and more generally. They need to network with others and to serve as role models and exemplars throughout the wider profession.

A second implication is that in the main these people were very focused on classroom teaching. Despite greater awareness of the importance of the classroom teacher, the last few decades of educational change has tended to distract teachers from teaching itself in favour of the administrative and social responsibilities being placed on schools. Although many recipients had such responsibilities, they were still teaching-focused, seeing it as their 'core business'.

A further implication was that the practice of preparing the nomination and engaging in the awards process was actually highly rewarding and affirming for the vast majority of those who took part, despite the work involved. We have written elsewhere about the benefits of the portfolio, and in particular a portfolio based upon professional teaching standards[18], but in brief, the reflection engendered by having to marshal one's thoughts about teaching and to provide evidence and

---

e   Some of the outstanding tertiary teachers, for example, had no formal teaching qualifications, and had engaged in self-directed learning in areas such as curriculum development, assessment and the use of technologies.

justification of professional teaching practice against a standards framework, proved to be important in promoting reflection and further development. Some teachers mentioned the fact that they had underestimated what they actually achieved, until they had time to reflect and document this achievement. Others reported that they were influenced to revisit their philosophy of teaching as a result of completing the QTA requirements.

The Quality Teaching Awards process and findings also underlined the importance of context in making judgements about teachers' professional accomplishments. By visiting these teachers in their workplaces and talking with their colleagues, students and others, as well as observing their teaching, and interviewing them afterwards, it became apparent that each was operating in a distinct professional context with its own challenges. They had modified their teaching, or in other words, demonstrated 'adaptive expertise', to meet these challenges. Obviously teachers can find themselves in a variety of socio-economic, geographic and cultural settings, and it is difficult to prepare people to be 'classroom ready' for all of these, but one of the implications of this is that pre-service education, in particular, needs as much as possible to expose people to a range of such contexts, or at least make them aware of the possible contexts, in which they may be operating in the future.

What follows is a brief summary from the research aspect of the awards, which highlights the attributes of the QTA recipients. It should be noted that these aspects of expert teaching were found to be largely generic from early childhood through to university level, but there are also specific attributes depending on the level of education the teacher is operating within and other contextual factors. It is how the teacher adapts to these that possibly makes the difference between being a good and an expert teacher.

In summary, the research found that these teachers demonstrated:

1. A high level of knowledge, imagination, passion, and belief in, and for, their field.
2. An overriding commitment to, and high aspirations for, their students' learning.
3. A rich repertoire of skills, methods and approaches on which they are able to draw to provide the right 'mix' for the specific needs of individual students.
4. A detailed understanding of the context in which they are working; of the specific expectations of the community; and of the needs of the cohort of students for whom they are responsible.
5. A capacity to respond appropriately to students, individually and collectively, and to the context, through their teaching practice.
6. A refusal to let anything get in the way of their own or their students' learning, and what they perceive as needing to be addressed.

7. A capacity to engender a high level of respect and even affection from their students and colleagues, a byproduct of their hard work and professionalism.
8. A great capacity for engagement in professional learning through self-initiated involvement in various combinations of professional development activities, some provided by the employing authority; others sought out by the individual.
9. A great capacity to contribute to the professional learning of others, and a willingness to do so.
10. Moral leadership and professionalism, in that they exemplify high values and qualities and seek to encourage these in others.[19]

Note: The Quality Teaching Awards concluded in 2011 after 10 years of operation. By the end of 2011, 473 teachers, comprising nine early childhood educators, 130 primary teachers, 157 secondary teachers, 112 TAFE teachers and 65 university teachers had received a QTA. The Australian Professional Standards for Teachers had been released in 2011 and there were other forms of recognition becoming available to educators. For these and other reasons, it was determined to wind up the awards, but there is a legacy of research, recognition, and positive focus on teaching that continues.[20]

Concluding remarks

This chapter sought to provide a detailed examination of what quality teaching looks like and what quality teachers do, through examination of both more general research literature and through case studies of two projects that involved identification and research of highly successful teachers.

Consistent findings that emerged lend confidence to the contention raised earlier that while we do have a good idea of what quality teaching is, the big challenge and question is how can we promote quality teaching more widely. This question of up-scaling[21] is taken up in subsequent chapters concerned with the preparation and professional development of both teachers and other educational leaders.

Endnotes

1 OECD. (2005). *Teachers matter—Attracting, developing and retaining effective teachers.* Paris, France: OECD Publishing.
2 See Dinham, S. (2011). *Let's get serious about teacher quality.* Melbourne, Victoria: Melbourne Graduate School of Education. https://www.youtube.com/watch?v=hT49plkJ7Ek
3 Coe, R., Aloisi, C., Higgins, S., & Major, L. (2014). *What makes great teaching? Review of the underpinning research.* Durham University: Centre for Evaluation and Monitoring & The Sutton Trust. http://www.suttontrust.com/wp-content/uploads/2014/10/What-Makes-Great-Teaching-REPORT.pdf

4   Ministerial Council on Education, Employment, Training and Youth Affairs [MCEETYA]. (2008). *Melbourne Declaration on Educational Goals for Young Australians*. Canberra, Australia: Australian Government.
5   Coe, R. et al. (2014). (p. 2)
6   Coe, R. et al. (2014). (pp. 2–30)
7   Coe, R. et al. (2014). (pp. 3–4)
8   Ayres, P., Dinham, S., & Sawyer, W. (1999). *Successful teaching in the NSW Higher School Certificate*. Sydney: NSW Department of Education and Training. See also Ayres, P., Dinham, S., & Sawyer, W. (2004). Effective teaching in the context of a Grade 12 high stakes external examination in New South Wales, Australia. *British Educational Research Journal, 30*(1), 141–165.
9   Ayres, P., Dinham, S., & Sawyer, W. (1997). *The identification of successful teaching methodologies in the NSW Higher School Certificate: Identifying the successful teachers*. Penrith: University of Western Sydney, Nepean.
10 Sawyer, W., Ayres, P., & Dinham, S. (2001). What does an effective Year 12 English teacher look like? *English in Australia, 129*(30), 51–63.
11 Shulman, L. (1986). Those who understand: Knowledge growth in teaching. *Educational Researcher, 15*(2), 4–14.
12 Berliner, D. (2004). Describing the behaviour and documenting the accomplishments of expert teachers. *Bulletin of Science, Technology & Society, 24*(3), 200–212.
13 Bransford, J., Brown, A., & Cocking, R. (Eds.). (2000). *How people learn*. Washington, DC: National Academy Press. (pp. 31–50)
14 Lunzer, E., & Gardner, K. (1984). *Learning from the written word*. London, England: Oliver & Boyd.
15 Dinham, S. (2008). Feedback on feedback. *Teacher*, May, 20–23.
16 Dinham, S. (2002). NSW Quality Teaching Awards—Research, rigour and transparency. *Unicorn, 28*(1), 5–9.
17 Brock, P. (2000). *Standards for Professional Practice for Accomplished Teaching in Australia*. Canberra: Australian College of Education. [now Educators]
18 Dinham, S., & Scott, C. (2003). Benefits to teachers of the professional learning portfolio: A case study. *Teacher Development, 7*(2), 187–202; Bergin, M., Dinham, S., Scott, C., & Brock, P. (2002). *The heart of teaching: Report on the 2001 Quality Teaching Awards Project*. Sydney: Australian College of Educators, NSW Chapter.
19 Dinham, S. (2002). (pp. 1–2); McCulla, N., Dinham, S., & Scott, C. (2007). Stepping out from the crowd: Some findings from the NSW Quality Teaching Awards on seeking recognition for professional accomplishment. *Unicorn Online Refereed Article*, ORA 51, 3–32. Reprinted with permission.
20 McCulla, N., Dinham, S., Brock, P., & Scott, C. (2015). Identifying, validating and recognising the work of accomplished teachers: Reflections on a decade of research and experience within the NSW Minister for Education and Training & Australian College of Educators' Quality Teaching Award, *ACE NSW Refereed Research Monograph*, 1–52.
21 Elmore, R. (1996). Getting to scale with good educational practice. *Harvard Educational Review, 66*(1), 1–26.

CHAPTER 7

Teacher preparation: What are the shortcomings of 'traditional' approaches? What are 'clinical' approaches to teaching?

INTRODUCTION

In Chapter 4 we considered pre-service teacher education as part of an overall approach to improving teaching quality and thus student outcomes. The role that initial teacher education (ITE) plays in developing and retaining effective teachers is obviously important. We discussed some of the common debates over standards of entry to the teaching profession. There have also been concerns over the quality and impact of initial teacher education courses and their methods of accreditation to ensure that these attract high-quality candidates suited to teaching, and that the courses produce graduates who are 'classroom ready'[1] and have met the standards expected of a graduate teacher.[2]

However, the point was also made that we need to address teacher quality at every key point of leverage[3] and should avoid adopting, 'quick fix', simplistic 'solutions' to the 'problem' of teacher quality. While ITE is important, teachers' professional learning needs to be ongoing, something that characterises the most successful and effective teachers.

In this chapter we examine some of the deficiencies of so-called traditional approaches to ITE, as well as emerging approaches to teaching and teacher education that can be termed 'clinical'. An important consideration in these new approaches is how ITE providers, schools and other educational bodies can work more collaboratively and

> effectively to develop and support beginning teachers. We all have an obligation to bring on the next generation of educators, as well as improving the teaching of existing teachers.
>
> A case study of an ITE program at the University of Melbourne illustrates some of these newer approaches, including clinical teaching and the structures and processes adopted to ensure closer alignment and common purpose between schools and ITE providers.

Ongoing concerns with initial teacher education[5]

The ultimate worth of any initial teacher education program should be judged on the basis of the collective impact of its graduates on student learning:

> Teaching teachers is certainly among the most demanding kinds of professional preparation: teacher educators must constantly model practices; construct powerful learning experiences; thoughtfully support progress, understanding, and practice; carefully assess students' progress and understandings; and help link theory and practice.[5]

However, there have been consistent concerns over teacher pre-service education for decades, both within Australia[6] and internationally.[7] The basic model of university or college coursework plus practice teaching rounds in its various manifestations has been found wanting.[8] Despite attempts to rectify this situation, only a minority of beginning teachers in Australia rate themselves as being 'well' or 'very well' prepared when they begin full-time teaching.[9] An international study by Catherine Scott and I found similar findings in New South Wales, England, Canada, the United States of America and New Zealand.[10]

In Australia, as noted previously, there has been, on average, one major state or national enquiry into teacher education every year for the past 30 years. Inevitably and unfortunately, 'Each inquiry reaches much the same conclusions and makes much the same recommendations, yet little changes'.[11] *Action Now: Classroom Ready Teachers*[12], is the latest in a long line of such inquiries and reports but in this case, there appears greater will for substantive change. Time will tell.

Darling-Hammond and Baratz-Snowden provide a succinct summary of the concerns over ITE:

> In the recent past, traditional teacher preparation often has been criticised for being overly theoretical, having little connection to practice, offering fragmented and incoherent courses, and lacking in a clear, shared conception of teaching among the faculty. Programs that are largely a collection of unrelated courses and that lack a common conception of teaching and learning have been found to be feeble agents for [affecting] practice among new teachers.[13]

However, in response:

> Beginning in the late 1980s, teacher education reforms began to produce program designs representing more integrated, coherent programs that emphasise a consistent vision of good teaching ... The programs teach teachers to do more than simply implement particular techniques; they help teachers to think pedagogically, reason through dilemmas, investigate problems, and analyse student learning to develop appropriate curriculum for a diverse group of learners.[14]

There has been growing recognition that teachers need to be able to assess or 'diagnose' individual student learning and provide appropriate 'prescriptions' or interventions for improvement, that is, to be clinical, evidence-based, interventionist practitioners in the nature of health professionals.[15] Teachers have been told for decades that they need to cater for individual student differences and to 'personalise' learning, but generally they have not been shown or taught how to do this in effective ways.[16] Assessment of individual students is the key to personalising learning.

Darling-Hammond and Baratz-Snowden have noted that successful clinical teacher education programs exhibit the following characteristics:

- clarity of goals, including the use of standards guiding the performances and practices to be developed;
- modelling of good practices by more expert teachers in which teachers make their thinking visible;
- frequent opportunities for practice with continuous formative feedback and coaching;
- multiple opportunities to relate classroom work to university coursework;
- graduated responsibility for all aspects of classroom teaching, and
- structured opportunities to reflect on practice with an eye towards improving it.[17]

Such an approach seeks to address the criticisms outlined previously and goes far beyond the traditional notion of sending the least experienced teachers to the most 'difficult' schools in some form of 'baptism by fire', 'apprenticeship', or 'survival of the fittest', equipped only with a limited 'toolkit' of teaching and classroom management strategies.[a]

Alter and Coggshall have provided a useful overview of what they see as the five key characteristics of a clinical practice profession more generally:

---

a   The language sometimes used to describe beginning teaching is instructive, and often has military overtones: 'raw recruits', 'survival', 'baptism of fire', the 'chalkface'.

1. **Centrality of clients:** Clinical practice involves the direct observation and treatment of patients or clients.
2. **Knowledge domains:** The work of clinical practice professionals is highly complex, requiring general and specialised knowledge and skills as well as theoretical, practical and technical understanding not possessed by lay people.
3. **Use of evidence and judgement in practice:** In clinical practice professions, determining the best course of treatment requires knowing an individual client (through observation, questioning and other diagnostic or evidence collection techniques) as well as knowing what research has shown to work with other clients in similar situations.
4. **Community and standards of practice:** Clinical practice professions form a professional community that monitors quality, distributes knowledge and creates standards of practice. Professionals and professional organisations, including training institutions, are held accountable to these standards of practice.
5. **Education for clinical practice:** Prior to being granted full access to practice, clinical practice professionals must successfully complete rigorous academic and practical training. Candidates must learn to work effectively with clients, obtain a high degree of knowledge, and understand how to use evidence and judgement in practice, and comprehend and value the standards of their respective professional communities.[18]

It should be noted that there is some resistance among educators to the use of the term 'clinical', as there is to 'pedagogy', and 'evidence'. In the context described here clinical practice should not be taken to mean diagnosing deficiency in students. It means being able to expertly assess the learning development of every student, their strengths and weaknesses, at a point in time and over time, and to provide constructive feedback and personalised strategies to move their learning forward.[19]

Despite the conclusions drawn by Darling-Hammond and Baratz-Snowden concerning the overarching characteristics of successful or effective ITE programs outlined above[20], the area remains contested, especially at the level of operational detail, with debates often concerned more with program structure—undergraduate or graduate entry, length of program, traditional versus alternative pathways, funding, time in schools—than with program quality, or impact on matters such as teacher recruitment and retention, graduate teacher effectiveness and student learning.

Cochran-Smith and Zeichner concluded from a major study into teacher education conducted for the American Educational Research Association:

> Studies comparing the effectiveness of various kinds of traditional and alternative teacher education programs and 4-year versus 5-year programs in relation to a variety of outcomes generally provide conflicting findings about

the efficacy of different forms of teacher preparation and do not enable us to identify the specific program features that are related to the achievement of particular outcomes. Across the studies, there is a lack of information about the programs, about the teachers who enter the programs, and about the places teachers teach after program completion. These omissions, together with the vague criteria often used to assess teaching, limit the value of these studies in helping us understand the relative impact of different kinds of alternative and traditional programs on aspects of teacher quality and student learning.[21]

A further difficulty in evaluating program impact lies in the early teaching experiences of ITE program graduates. Periods of casual or emergency teaching, short-term contracts or gaps in employment, may well result in the 'deskilling' of beginning teachers. This often fragmented and disjointed beginning to teachers' careers can also be compounded when they encounter unsupportive and in some cases demoralised experienced teachers and negative school cultures, characterised by expressions such as 'forget everything you've learned at uni', 'don't expect too much and you won't be disappointed', and 'we tried that in 1975 and it didn't work'.[22] As Zeichner and Tabachnick found[23], the effects of university teacher education can be 'washed out' by school experience, regardless of whether it is predominantly negative or positive, making it difficult to measure the longer-term impact of ITE programs.

Not surprisingly, Hattie concluded from his meta-analyses from research on the measured effects of teacher education programs on student outcomes: 'So much more is needed on this topic'.[24]

Addressing clinical practice in a graduate entry pre-service teacher education program: the Master of Teaching at the University of Melbourne[b]

In 2008, the Melbourne Graduate School of Education (MGSE) at the University of Melbourne began phasing out its undergraduate pre-service teacher education degrees and introduced a new graduate entry program, the Master of Teaching (M Teach), with streams for early childhood, primary and secondary educators.

The design of the M Teach, a two-year full-time equivalent program, was heavily influenced by the concerns over traditional approaches to teacher education outlined above, and by developments at leading teacher education institutions worldwide. MGSE staff visited and interacted with faculty at Stanford University (USA), University of Virginia (USA), Ontario Institute for Studies of Education (Canada) and Queensland University of Technology (Australia), as well as benchmarking the new program with other leading international educational institutions that employed elements of clinical approaches to teacher education and teaching.

---

b   This section is based upon McLean Davies, L. et al. (2013) and Dinham, S. (2013).

Space precludes a detailed explanation of the development and features of the M Teach, but one of the key principles underpinning the program is the focus upon evidence or data about learners to improve teaching practice and, thereby, to lead to enhanced student learning and development. A second important principle is that in order to break the cycle of teachers teaching as they were taught and new teachers being drawn into this prevailing culture, there needs to be much more alignment, mutual understanding and collaboration between the university and schools and early childhood settings.

Some additional key features of the M Teach include:
- Teacher candidates spend two days per week in a school or early childhood centre from early in their studies and attend university for the remaining three days.
- Teacher candidates also undertake placements in block rounds of up to four weeks in each semester.
- Placement sites (base schools, placement schools and early childhood centres) are arranged in neighbourhood groups (or networks in early childhood) that have been carefully chosen and where staff members have a sound understanding of the program and the respective stream.
- The university provides funding for one staff member at each of 40 base schools/centres, called a teaching fellow[c], to be released from 50 per cent of their regular duties and to work across their partnership group/network with M Teach candidates, and mentor (supervising) teachers for the placement days each week to ensure the coherent and consistent operation of the placement.
- The teaching fellow is joined by a dedicated university-based clinical specialist[d], who supports teacher candidates one day per week at university as they seek to meet the needs of individual learners. In most instances, clinical specialists are also involved in the teaching of academic university-based subjects and are thus well placed to make links between theory and practice.
- In order to further embed the links between theory and practice within the program, clinical specialists, with the support of teaching fellows, organise and deliver a seminar series that runs throughout each semester at a placement/network site.
- These partnerships play a key role in supporting the clinical premise of the M Teach, which posits that teachers who use a specific form of evidence-based, diagnostic, interventionist teaching have a positive effect on student learning outcomes. The program facilitates the role of the teacher to work in teams and

---

c   Teaching fellows: expert teachers from the base school (the central school in a partnership school group) spend two and a half days per week mentoring candidates and supporting mentor / supervising teachers.

d   Clinical specialists: university experts work closely with a Teaching Fellow and are on-site in schools one day per week to help link university theory and classroom practice.

use data to enhance decision-making about teaching and learning strategies for individual students, groups and classes.
- Assessment of student work as evidence of learning with resultant improvement oriented feedback lies at the core of M Teach subjects, a key underlining principle being that with a data-driven, evidence-based approach to teaching and learning, teachers can manipulate the learning environment and scaffold learning for every student, whatever the student's current development or intellectual capacity.[e]

To bring together and strengthen learning in the program, an initiative called the Clinical Praxis Examination was introduced in 2010. It was refined in 2011 and has undergone further development. It now forms a key component of the M Teach program. This assessment task requires candidates, and those supporting them, to consider theory and research in the context of practice. Teacher candidates are asked to identify a student on whom they wish to focus and, in considering what knowledge or skill they are planning to enhance, construct a developmental continuum that lays out the sequence of ideas, concepts and/or skills necessary to assist the student to undertake the task or develop the intended outcomes. They are also asked to consider what might come next so the student can continue to learn beyond the teaching target if necessary. The teacher candidate then identifies the student's strengths, as well as what they are ready to learn.

The assessment of the student's current capabilities and identification of appropriate teaching and learning strategies is undertaken with the input of mentor teachers, clinical specialists and teaching fellows. This happens within the context of teaching the class; in this way the candidate is asked to simultaneously attend to whole-class teaching and respond to the student's learning. This approach reflects the understanding that expert/master teachers are able to differentiate and attend the learning needs of individual students within a whole-class context.

There are five key questions that underpin and guide the MGSE approach to clinical judgement:
1. What is the learner ready to learn and what evidence supports this?
2. What are the possible evidence/research-based interventions?
3. What teaching strategies are preferred and how will they be implemented?
4. What is the expected impact on learning and how will this be evaluated?
5. What happened and how can this be interpreted?

As Figure 7.1 illustrates, this is a circular process that builds upon itself. After addressing the fifth question, the teacher is once again at the point of asking: 'What is the learner ready to learn, and what evidence supports this?', and the cycle continues.

---

e   For more detail see http://education.unimelb.edu.au/study_with_us/become_a_teacher

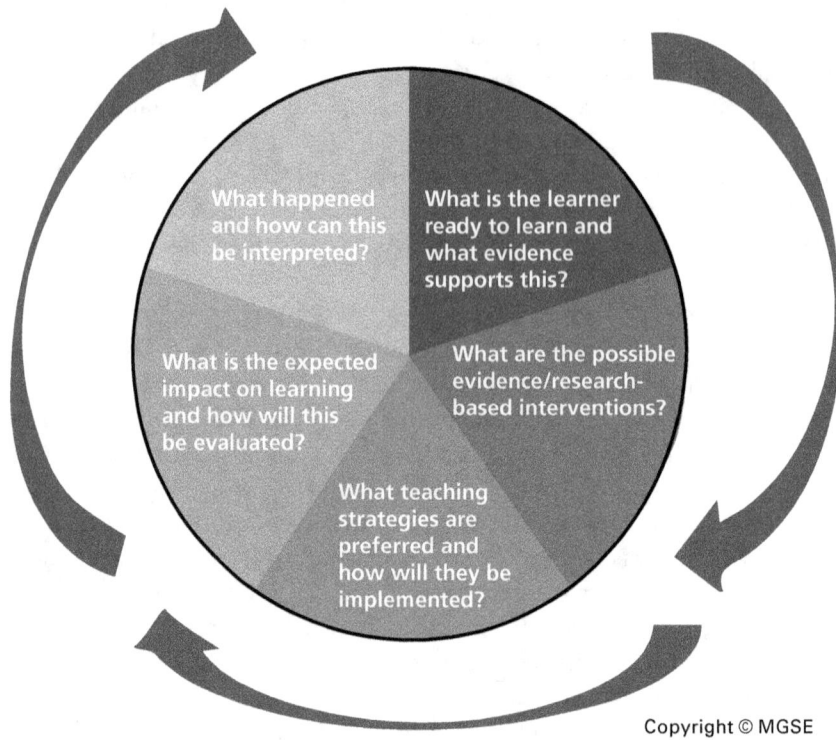

Figure 7.1: Questions underpinning clinical teaching practice[25]

The five questions are in some ways deceptively simple, yet some experienced teachers will find them difficult to answer. To do so requires three types of knowledge:
- knowledge of particular subject content
- knowledge of pedagogy
- knowledge of the individual student.

When combined, this produces what Shulman termed 'pedagogic content knowledge'.[26]

A key question concerning the M Teach is the extent to which it is making a difference. A study by the Australian Education Union asked 1545 new primary and secondary teachers from across Australia about their satisfaction with their initial training as preparation for the 'real life' of a classroom. On average, on a five-point scale, 40–45 per cent claimed that they were 'well' [4] or 'very well' [5] prepared when they began teaching.[27] This figure is similar to the findings from earlier, much larger samples of teachers in NSW, England, USA and New Zealand, which found only around 42 per cent of teachers rated themselves as 'well' or 'very well' prepared by their pre-service program at the time they commenced teaching.[28]

When the first graduates of the MGSE M Teach (primary and secondary) were asked the same question in a survey as part of an external evaluation conducted by the Australian Council for Educational Research (ACER) late in 2010, 90 per cent claimed that they were 'well' or 'very well' prepared when they began teaching. Principals and other school leaders also reported finding M Teach candidates and graduates to be more mature, confident and capable than those from other universities. The ACER evaluation found:

> All respondents [primary and secondary graduates, Clinical Specialists, Teaching Fellows, Mentor Teachers, Principals, other stakeholders] agreed that the [M Teach] program had impressive strengths. There was general agreement about the value of the program, as evident in the:
> - Integration of theory and practice.
> - Emphasis on evidence-based practice.
> - Increased awareness and engagement with aspects of the profession by Teacher Candidates.
> - Development of Candidates, who come into the profession with knowledge of 'best practice'.
> - Emphasis on deep reflection and on reflective practice in the course giving Candidates an opportunity to change as they go along; this links to improvements of teaching standards.
> - Recognition that Candidates have an important role to play in increasing standards in the profession. High levels of support for Candidates from Clinical Specialists, Teaching Fellows and school-based staff.[29]

This represents a significant advance, both on what MGSE was achieving in its ITE programs before the M Teach, and in comparison with courses from other universities and nations. One of the major implications, however, of the adoption of a clinical model, is the need for more research of the impact of teacher education on the subsequent learning of the students of the teacher candidates and graduates. This research has commenced and will provide vital data for the further development of all streams of the M Teach and more widely. The need for more research on the impact of teacher education programs on the capacity of graduates to impact student learning is implicit in the TEMAG review of teacher education[30], although measuring such impacts requires further work.[31]

Concluding remarks

There is strong evidence to consider teachers' professional development as a continuum rather than something that ceases on graduation from an ITE course. In particular, there needs to be ongoing cooperation between ITE providers, beginning teachers and school systems to ensure a coherent transition to teaching.

There is also a need to ensure and assure the quality and impact of teacher education courses. It is essential that rigorous and evidence-based approaches to the accreditation of teacher education courses be utilised and that there is mutual understanding and collaboration between ITE providers and school staff in matters such as school placements and the assessment of ITE candidates. One of the pleasing and possibly unforeseen outcomes of the development of the Master of Teaching program at MGSE, has been the extent to which this closer collaboration has resulted in staff such as mentor teachers reporting their own professional growth through involvement with the program.

Clinical approaches to teaching show potential. As noted, this should not be construed as a deficit model, in that such approaches are conceived as being only about diagnosing learning difficulties. Any competent medical professional, for example, will spend time with a patient or client undertaking a full assessment, both strengths and weaknesses and changes in condition, depending on the issue concerned, before any treatment is prescribed. Likewise, clinical approaches to teaching are predicated on a full and evidence-based assessment of students' learning before an appropriate research-based intervention, response, or strategy is selected and implemented.

However, experience with the Master of Teaching at the University of Melbourne has also shown that a factor in the success of and transfer of new approaches to teaching is the need for understanding and support by educational leaders in schools, if prevailing mindsets and practices are to change.

Endnotes

1. Teacher Education Ministerial Advisory Group [TEMAG]. (2014). *Action now: Classroom ready teachers*. Canberra, Australia: Department of Education.
2. AITSL [Australian Institute for Teaching and School Leadership]. (2011). *National [Australian] Professional Standards for Teachers*. Melbourne, Victoria: Author.
3. Dinham, S. (2008). Driving improvement in the quality of Australian education: Points of leverage. Australian College of Educators, Victorian Branch Oration, University of Melbourne, 15 August.
4. This section draws upon: Dinham, S. (2013). Connecting instructional leadership with clinical teaching practice. *Australian Journal of Education, 57*(3), 220–231; and a recent stimulus paper developed for AITSL: Dinham, S. (2015). *Issues and perspectives relevant to the development of an approach to the accreditation of initial teacher education in Australia based on evidence of impact*. Melbourne, Victoria: AITSL.
5. Darling-Hammond, L., Hammerness, K., with Grossman, P., Rust, F., & Shulman, L. (2005). The design of teacher education programs (pp. 390–441). In L. Darling-Hammond, & J. Bransford (Eds.), *Preparing teachers for a changing world: What teachers should learn and be able to do*. San Francisco, CA: Jossey-Bass. (p. 441)
6. See Dinham, S. (2006). Teaching and teacher education: Some observations, reflections and possible solutions. *ED Ventures, 2*, 3–20.
7. Labaree, D. F. (2004). *The trouble with ED Schools*. New Haven, CT: Yale University Press.
8. Hattie, J. (2009). *Visible learning: A synthesis of over 800 meta-analyses relating to achievement*. London, England: Routledge. (pp. 109–112)

9   Australian Education Union. (2009). *New Educators Survey 2008*. Melbourne, Victoria: Author.
10 See Dinham, S., & Scott, C. (2000). Moving into the third, outer domain of teacher satisfaction. *Journal of Educational Administration*, 38, 379–396; Scott, C., Stone, B., & Dinham, S. (2001). 'I love teaching but ...' International patterns of teacher discontent. *Education Policy Analysis Archives*, 9, 1–7. See also US Department of Education. (2011). *Our future, teachers: The Obama administration's plan for teacher education reform and improvement*. Washington, DC: US Department of Education.
11 Dinham, S. (2006). (p. 1)
12 TEMAG. (2014).
13 Darling-Hammond, L., & Baratz-Snowden, J. (2005). (Eds.). *A good teacher in every classroom*. San Francisco, CA: Jossey-Bass. (p. 37). All extracts from this publication have been reproduced with permission.
14 Darling-Hammond, L., & Baratz-Snowden, J. (2005). (p. 37)
15 McLean Davies, L., Anderson, M., Deans, J., Dinham, S., Griffin, P., Kameniar, B., Page, J., Reid, C., Rickards, F., Tayler, C. & Tyler, D. (2013). Masterly preparation: Clinical practice in a graduate pre-service teacher education program. *Journal of Education for Teaching*, 39(1), 93–106; National Council for Accreditation of Teacher Education. (2010). *Transforming teacher education through clinical practice: A national strategy to prepare effective teachers*. Washington, DC: National Council for Accreditation of Teacher Education.
16 Hattie, J. (2009). (p. 198)
17 Darling-Hammond, L., & Baratz-Snowden, J. (2005). (p. 43)
18 Alter, J., & Coggshall, J. G. (2009). *Teaching as a clinical practice profession: Implications for teacher preparation and state policy*. New York, NJ: National Comprehensive Center for Teacher Quality. (p. 3)
19 Dinham, S. (2008). Feedback on feedback. *Teacher*, May, 20–23.
20 Darling-Hammond, L., & Baratz-Snowden, J. (2005).
21 Cochran-Smith, M., & Zeichner, K. (2005). (Eds.). *Studying teacher education*. Mahwah, NJ: Lawrence Erlbaum. (p. 29)
22 Dinham, S. (2014). Primary schooling in Australia: Pseudo-science plus extras times growing inequality equals decline. In Australian College of Educators. *What counts as quality in education?* (pp. 8–15). Carlton South, Victoria: Australian College of Educators. (p. 13)
23 Zeichner, K., & Tabachnick, B. (1981). Are the effects of university teacher education 'washed out' by school experience? *Journal of Teacher Education*, 32(3), 7–11.
24 Hattie, J. (2009). (p. 112)
25 McLean Davies, L., Dickson, B., Rickards, F., Dinham, S., Conroy, J., & Davis, R. (2015). Teaching as a clinical profession: translational practices in initial teacher education – an international perspective, *Journal of Education for Teaching*, 41(5), 514–528. (p. 525). Copyright is held by Melbourne Graduate School of Education (The University of Melbourne) from the Master of Teaching program.
26 Shulman, L. (1986). Those who understand: Knowledge growth in teaching. *Educational Researcher*, 15(2), 4–14.
27 Australian Education Union. (2009).
28 Dinham, S., & Scott, C. (2000).
29 Scott, C., Kleinhenz, E., Weldon, P., Reid, K., & Dinham, S. (2010). *Master of teaching MGSE: Evaluation report*. Melbourne, Victoria: ACER. (p. 4)
30 TEMAG. (2014).
31 Dinham, S. (2015).

CHAPTER 8

What are students' perspectives on schooling, teaching and learning?

INTRODUCTION

Too often we have concentrated on teaching rather than learning, but even in our discussions about learning, the student perspective is often lacking or undervalued. It sounds strange to note that so many teachers have learnt about teaching and how to teach, without talking with students about their learning. Perhaps this reflects earlier thinking about children being 'seen and not heard', but as we will see, not listening to students represents both a loss of another source of evidence and a missed opportunity.

There is a history of not engaging students in discussion about their own learning, but rather, adopting the position that educators know best, and that there is little to learn from students. However as will be noted later, where students *are* given the opportunity to provide feedback on their teaching and learning, and schooling more generally, *and* they see this feedback acted upon, their feedback tends to be increasingly constructive and positive.[1] On the other hand, when students are not readily offered the opportunity to provide such feedback, and they see it not being acted upon in any case, invariably such feedback is negative and unhelpful.

This is not to say that in calling for greater attention to student perspectives, I am advocating giving students 'control' over their learning[2], something Hattie found had an effect size of only 0.04[3]. Rather I am advocating allowing and encouraging students to feed back to teachers important information that can be used to assess and 'know' students, and to modify teaching and improve learning effectiveness, as well as to improve the educational climate in a school or other educational institution more generally.

What are the benefits of listening to students?
Reflecting the above discussion, Rudduck has concisely encapsulated many of the benefits of and conditions for effective student 'voice':

> Student voice is most successful when it enables students to feel that they are members of a learning community, that they matter, and that they have something valuable to offer.[4]

It needs to be recognised that while there are those who are strong advocates for increased attention to student voice in its various forms, in line with the general approach emphasised in this book, we need to be sure of the research evidence before adopting this or any other strategy. It should also be noted that what can be termed student voice is often conflated with other notions such as democratic schools and student participation. Cook-Sather has considered the research evidence and has commented:

> The research literature ... tells us that when adults listen to and learn from students, teachers can teach better and students can learn better: a focus on student participation in processes of analysing and revising teaching and learning approaches 'can enhance [student] progress and learning'.[5] In particular, consulting with, listening to, and working with students help teachers build relationships with students, access the student experience of school, learn what facilitates student learning, and begin to address deeply entrenched social inequities.[6]

We know from research that relationships between teachers and students have a very large effect size (0.72) in respect of student achievement. It would stand to reason that anything that would facilitate this relationship should be worth pursuing. Classroom discussion also has a very large effect size (0.82), and this is one way that good teachers monitor their students and discover how they feel about the teaching they are receiving and their learning.[7] Cook-Sather has noted:

> when teachers make the effort to get to know students and let students know them, and when a relationship of mutual respect emerges as a result of that process, students are more willing to learn and open to learning, and they are also more willing to enter into a collaborative relationship with teachers. Such forms of caring and engaged relationships are particularly important for students who feel alienated from mainstream school culture, such as those at risk of cutting class or dropping out of school, but they are important for all students. When students are taken seriously and attended to as knowledgeable participants in conversations about teaching and learning, when they have collegial relationships with adults, they feel empowered and motivated to participate constructively in their education.[8]

Bahou, in another review of the research literature, has identified a number of 'key issues in [student] voice':

Authenticity—refers to the credibility students perceive in teachers' and school leaders' commitment to the processes of student participation ... Although students have been predominantly the 'missing voice' in research and discussions on school improvement ... privileging student voice must not come at the expense of teachers' voices ...

Inclusion—within schools has come to mean lifting barriers to learning and shifting students' self-perceptions, teachers' attitudes and practices, and school structures to benefit the entire diversity of students ... At the heart of any debate about voice is power and how it is negotiated through the intersection of positions of class, age, gender and ethnicity ...

Power—... the highest form of participation occurs when young people and adults work together towards the former's desired goals. Hart's (1992) widely cited 'ladder of youth participation' describes young people's involvement that ranges from the non-participation on the lower rungs of tokenism and manipulation to the middle participatory rungs of consulted and informed to the highest forms of involvement of young-person-initiated activities and decision-making shared with adults ...

Engaging Students in Research—The idea of students researching their own education, school or community and developing their own questions as a precursor to action is recent and still rare. Questions such as, 'Who conducts research on whom?', 'For whose benefit?', and 'For what kind of knowledge?', are at the heart of examining whose voice matters. The emergence of SAR[a] reflects two things: a shift towards school-based research in collaboration with external researchers ... and the fact that previous student voice initiatives had not gone far enough in cultivating agency in students ... As the 'missing voice' in educational reform ..., a review of the disparate SAR literature ... revealed common aims to:
1. Address issues that matter to students;
2. Create new knowledge about education for critical evaluation and action;
3. Set an agenda for students to make a difference;
4. Enable students to develop a kind of professionalism whereby student voices can be taken seriously by adults;
5. Enhance the conditions and processes of learning and teaching.[9]

Bahou does, however, point out some problems with SAR activities. Firstly, the volunteer research students might not be representative and might also receive certain

---

a   SAR: students as researchers

privileges and kudos for their involvement that sets them apart from their peers, something that is always an issue for student participation in school governance generally. Who participates is an ongoing concern. Many years ago I was involved in a study of comprehensive secondary schools that appeared to be characterised by effective communication. One school selected as a case study was 'famous' for its ongoing involvement with, and success in, a popular statewide 'Rock Eisteddfod' of the time. This was a large school and when we spoke to the staff and students it was apparent that only a small fraction of the school population was actually involved in this major annual event. The same school was also well known for its student representative council but, once again, few students and staff were involved with this, and the students who were, were hardly representative. Most students expressed alienation from both ventures.[10]

Bahou has also expressed concern that 'more explicit attention to the relationship between students' learning processes and what they are learning' is needed. Bahou was also critical of the fact that lower SES students and alienated students are often excluded from 'most student voice research'[11]. Given that the effects of disadvantage on education in Australia are more severe than in comparable countries and that Indigenous students are particularly affected, it would seem important that the views and experiences of low SES and disaffected students, including Indigenous students and their communities, are included in any such research.

Donovan has elaborated on the above situation:

> For decades, there has been a consistent stream of research and statistical evaluation highlighting the underachievement of Aboriginal and Torres Strait Islander students in Australian schools ...
>
> Over the last 40 years, much research has been conducted in an attempt to understand why so many more Aboriginal students experience difficulties in school. Several features of the educational system have been identified as potential contributors to this problem. These include the poor attendance rates of Aboriginal students, ... low expectations of Aboriginal students' academic achievement by teachers, ... limited knowledge of teachers about Aboriginal society and cultures, ... poor quality relationships between schools and Aboriginal communities, ... lack of engagement of Aboriginal students in schools ... and the quality of pedagogy in the classroom ...
>
> Many of these identified features intersect and impact on teachers' educational practices when working with Aboriginal students. For many Aboriginal students, their culture is rarely represented in the classroom, which can lead to poor relationships with the teachers due to limited connection between the teacher and the Aboriginal students' identity. This disconnection can lead to Aboriginal students disengaging from their teacher.[12]

Listening to students (and their communities)

As part of knowing every student as a learner and a person, we need to be regularly 'taking the pulse' of what is happening in our classes and schools. We also need to be communicating respectfully and openly with the various groups that make up our school community.

We need to utilise means to monitor the views of our staff, both teaching and professional, along with our students and community members, as part of a broader evidence-based approach to school improvement.

Heeding the cautionary notes above, we need to ensure that those consulted are representative, and not just the most able, articulate, assertive, attractive or privileged. We also need to ensure that diverse views are respected and that people see that their views have been considered and have contributed to school planning and operation. Whenever we seek the views of others in this way there is always the challenge of varying responses and how these are handled. For example, in higher education it is common in student surveys to have a group of students who 'love' one approach, while another group 'hates' it—that is, bi-modal responses or views—with the average being in the middle, despite few supporting that position.

Fortunately, there are many quality instruments that can measure various aspects of what could be termed the quality of school life.[b] Many of these are surveys that have been psychometrically validated and normed, enabling comparisons at a point in time with other schools and for the same (and other schools) over time.

Using student surveys

Student surveys of teaching performance are now common in tertiary education settings where students are asked to rate their course, the subjects they undertake, aspects of the teaching they receive, their own learning and the resources and infrastructure available to them, through using a university-wide common instrument.[13]

Student surveys of teacher performance in schools are less common, sometimes less valid, and often more contentious overall. Studies suggest that student ratings of teachers are not sufficiently reliable to be used for decision-making below Year 3, but have greater potential utility in upper primary and secondary grades. Students in those year levels are better placed to make comments about teachers' expectations, their treatment of and relationships with students of different backgrounds and abilities, and more general aspects of schooling, teaching and learning, such as school climate and student engagement, although students may not have a sufficient frame of reference or knowledge to make judgements about teachers' content or pedagogic knowledge.[14]

---

b   The Australian Council for Educational Research, the publisher of this book and a former employer, has literally dozens of instruments at its disposal that can be used to measure and thus benchmark many aspects of school climate and culture, student, staff and community satisfaction, quality of teaching, and so forth. See https://www.acer.edu.au/

An allied concern is the level of preparedness and willingness of teachers in schools to seek and utilise feedback or ratings from their students. As noted previously, there is evidence that when students have the opportunity to provide their teachers with regular feedback *and* see that this is acted upon, the quality and the utility of such feedback increases. (See the *Tripod Student Surveys* developed at Harvard University in 2001 by Donald Ferguson and validated by the *Measures of Effective Teaching Project* (MET) in 2013[c].)

When students have had the chance to provide feedback and their perspectives on their school, the research on how they perceive the environment and climate of their school can be instructive:

> To date, school climate has been described almost exclusively in terms of the behaviour of administrators and teachers. For example, collegiality and principal leadership are measures used to characterise the school as a workplace. However, schools are also workplaces for students. And, not surprisingly, we find that students are very much aware of and sensitive to the overall ambience of their schools. They have identified their own 'student measures' of school climate:
> - visibility and accessibility of the Principal;
> - the collective message and level of support students receive from teachers and staff members generally;
> - the perceived degree of safety or violence;
> - types of interactions between student groups;
> - student behaviour generally;
> - the availability of extracurricular activities;
> - mechanisms for student input into decisions;
> - the general condition of school facilities, and
> - the latitude for students whose second language is English to speak their own native language in informal settings (and their access to at least one adult with whom they can communicate).[15]

A crucial matter is how school leaders utilise and act (and are seen to act) on the results of such surveys, and other sources of evidence. As schools develop a 'culture of evidence'[16] and use this evidence to inform current practices, professional learning and future developments, it is important to be open about findings from student voice—and that of staff and the community—and not to rationalise or attempt to explain away unwanted or unfavourable findings. One can't improve by making excuses.

---

c   See http://tripoded.com/about-us-2/

Concluding remarks

Research demonstrates the positive contribution that consideration of student perspectives can make to student–teacher relationships, student achievement, and overall school effectiveness. It is important, however, that school staff do not feel threatened by student input and feedback. An adversarial or defensive climate will be unhelpful and could prove to be counterproductive and even damaging.

While students, particularly younger students, may not have the experience and perspective of experienced teachers, students do have a keen sensitivity to teacher fairness and effectiveness. They know the teachers who care about them, those who are well prepared, and those who are dedicated. They also know those teachers who, for whatever reasons, are poorly performing. Students talk with each other extensively and differentiate between their teachers. In secondary education, they sometimes choose elective subjects on the basis of what they know about the teachers concerned.[17]

When students have been involved in research, the attribute of teachers they overwhelmingly see as most important in facilitating their personal growth and academic development is that of caring.

> It's mostly the way that the teachers treat you as a student—or as a person, actually. Because sometimes they're just like, 'Here's the work. Do this.' And it is not really good because people are just like, there.[18]

There are, however, differences in the perceptions of caring between high- and low-achieving students, according to Phelan, Locke Davidson and Cao:

> High achievers often associate caring with assistance in academic matters. Such help demonstrates that teachers are aware of and concerned about helping students meet long-term educational goals ...
>
> Low-achieving students equate caring with certain personality traits (e.g., patience, humour, tolerance, ability to listen) and a readiness to give person-to-person academic assistance. Low-achieving students frequently express a preference for direct, personal interaction ...
>
> For these [low-achieving] students, caring means the expression of interest and concern that goes beyond assistance with schoolwork. Explicit statements affirming their value and worth as individuals and demonstrating teachers like them personally are important.
>
> The perception of teachers as caring or not appears to have direct consequences—particularly for low-achieving students. If the teacher is viewed as *not* caring, students report a lack of incentive to do schoolwork or to participate in class.[19]

Further, high-achieving students are more likely to turn to friends and family members for assistance with their work if this is not forthcoming from teachers, while low-achieving students may, without access to such people and experience, withdraw and disengage, falling further behind and widening achievement gaps.[20]

Endnotes

1. Rudduck, J. (2007). Student voice, student engagement, and school reform. In D. Thiessen & A. Cook-Sather (Eds.), *International handbook of student experience in elementary and secondary school* (pp. 587–610). Dordrecht, Netherlands: Springer. All extracts from this publication have been reproduced with permission by Springer.
2. Cook-Sather, A. (2009). Introduction learning from the student's perspective: Why it's important, what to expect, and important guidelines. In A. Cook-Sather (Ed.), *Learning from the student's perspective: A sourcebook for effective teaching* (pp. 1–20). Boulder, CO: Paradigm Publishers.
3. Hattie, J. (2012). *Visible learning for teachers*. London, England: Routledge. (p. 254)
4. Rudduck, J. (2007). (p. 587)
5. Rudduck, J., & Flutter, J. (2004). *How to improve your school: Giving pupils a voice*. London, England: Continuum. (p. 11)
6. Cook-Sather, A. (2009). (pp. 238–239)
7. Hattie, J. (2012). (p. 251)
8. Cook-Sather, A. (2009). (p. 239)
9. Bahou, L. (2011). Rethinking the challenges and possibilities of student voice and agency. *Educate*, Special Issue, January, 2–14. http://www.educatejournal.org/index.php/educate/article/view/286
10. Dinham, S., Cairney, T., Craigie, D., & Wilson, S. (1995). School climate and leadership: Research into three secondary schools. *Journal of Educational Administration*, 33(4), 36–58.
11. Bahou, L. (2011). (p. 8)
12. Donovan, M. (2015). Aboriginal student stories, the missing voice, to guide us towards change. *The Australian Educational Researcher*, July, 1–13. (p. 2)
13. Richardson, J. (2005). Instruments for obtaining student feedback: A review of the literature. *Assessment & Evaluation in Higher Education*, 30(4), 387–415.
14. See Goe, L., Bell, C., & Little, O. (2008). *Approaches to evaluating teacher effectiveness: A research synthesis*. Washington, DC: National Comprehensive Center for Teacher Quality.
15. Phelan, P., Locke Davidson, A., & Cao, H. (1992). Speaking up: Students' perspectives on school. *Phi Delta Kappan*, May, 695–704. (p. 701). Reprinted with permission of Phi Delta Kappan International, www.pdkintl.org. All rights reserved.
16. Council for the Accreditation of Educator Preparation. (2015). *CAEP Evidence Guide*. Washington, DC: Author. (p. 2)
17. Ayres, P., Dinham, S., & Sawyer, W. (2004). Effective Teaching in the context of a Grade 12 high stakes external examination in New South Wales, Australia. *British Educational Research Journal*, 30(1), 141–165.
18. Phelan, P. et al. (1992). (p. 698)
19. Phelan, P. et al. (1992). (p. 698)
20. Phelan, P. et al. (1992). (p. 700)

PART B

The importance and impact of educational leadership

CHAPTER 9

How and why have thinking and approaches to leadership and educational leadership changed?

INTRODUCTION

Leaders and leadership have been a topic of fascination for as long as people have inhabited the earth. As well as more objective study, leaders have been the subject of emotional responses ranging from adoration, even idolatry, to fear and hatred.

Even before these records could be written down, great leaders were the subject of oral history, legend and depiction in various ways. Many of these leaders were absolute rulers who exercised the power of life and death over both their followers and their enemies. Most were male but there were occasional females such as Cleopatra, Boudicca, Joan of Arc or Catherine the Great.

While some led through the power they exercised over others, others led through the power of ideas and knowledge, including religion, and some through discovery, both geographic and scientific.

Thus, the study, if it can be called that, of leaders and leadership goes back thousands of years, but more formal studies of administration and formal organisations go back only a little over a century, although organisations such as the Catholic Church, reputed to be the oldest formal organisation in the world, are far older than these formal studies.

This chapter traces the development of our understanding of leaders and leadership as well as considering the specialised field of educational leadership, providing a foundation for what follows in Part B.

Defining leadership

Airport bookshelves are full of books on leadership, no doubt in an attempt to catch the eye of the travelling businessperson or government official.[a] Many of these appeal by purporting to reveal the six or seven or eight attributes or actions of successful leaders, promising a 'quick fix' in only one to two hundred pages. Over the past 60 years or so there have been something in excess of 80 conceptions, definitions or models of leadership[1], evidence of what the leading educational leadership researcher Ken Leithwood has described as 'adjectival leadership'[2]; that is, put an adjective in front of the word leadership and you have 'discovered' a new field, and possibly a new source of fame and/or income.

What then, given this plethora of models and definitions, are the agreed dimensions of leadership? Various definitions over time have emphasised:
- Leadership as a *focus of group processes*
- Leadership from a *personality perspective*
- Leadership as *acts or behaviours*
- Leadership as a *transformational process*
- Leadership from a *skills perspective*.[3]

In considering these approaches, Northouse has provided the following useful definition and components of leadership:

> *Leadership is a process whereby an individual influences a group of individuals to achieve a common goal.*
>
> Defining leadership as a *process* means that it is not a trait or characteristic that resides in the leader but a transactional event that occurs between the leader and his or her followers. *Process* implies that a leader affects and is affected by followers. It emphasises that leadership is not a linear, one-way event but rather an interactive event. When leadership is defined in this manner, it becomes available to everyone. It is not restricted to only the formally designated leader in a group.
>
> Leadership involves *influence*; it is concerned with how the leader affects followers. Influence is the *sine qua non* of leadership. Without influence, leadership does not exist.
>
> Leadership occurs in *groups*. Groups are the context in which leadership takes place. Leadership involves influencing a group of individuals who have a common purpose. This can be a small task group, a community group, or a large group encompassing the entire organisation ...
>
> Leadership includes attention to *goals*. This means that leadership has to do with directing a group of individuals towards accomplishing some task

---

a   A Google search on 'leadership' will yield over three-quarters of a billion results.

or end. Leaders direct their energies towards individuals who are trying to achieve something together. Therefore, leadership occurs and has its effects in context where individuals are moving towards a goal.[4] [Emphasis added]

Trait approaches to leadership

As noted, our earliest conceptions of leadership came from stories and records of 'great' historical figures, and no doubt some embellishment of these people and their deeds occurred down through the ages. Some, such as King Arthur and his 'knights of the round table', may not have even existed, although the Arthurian legend influences our conceptions of appropriate 'knightly' values, virtue and behaviour to this day.

These figures from history and legend appeared to be 'larger than life', in terms of their personal and physical attributes, their wisdom, bravery and accomplishments, and thus there was an understandable tendency to regard these people as 'born leaders', incapable of being emulated by common people. Many of these leaders *had* been granted their power and position through succession and inheritance and were, in fact, leaders by dint of their birthright, so the 'born' part in some cases was correct, at least in lineage, if not in capability. It was believed by some, including the leaders themselves, that they had been chosen by a higher power to lead their people and to dominate others, and that they both gained and exercised their power through a 'god-given' right that included absolute control over the lives of others, land and property.

Thus, this 'trait' view of leaders was probably the first theory or approach to leadership. Personal characteristics that assisted these people to lead their followers and maintain their power over others included their height and physical strength, their wisdom or intelligence, their powers of oratory and persuasion, their skill with weapons, their resilience in the face of adversity, and in some cases their ability to foresee the future and exercise power over others through the 'dark arts' of sorcery or through acting on behalf of a higher power.

Obviously, this 'trait' form of leadership does not equate to the conception of leadership as a process and group function towards achieving a common goal, as outlined above by Northouse. Additionally, the focus of this approach is more on the leader, than on leadership. By implication, the trait approach also means that leadership is neither open to all nor that leadership can be learnt.

Assigned versus emergent leadership and personal versus positional power

When we see a police officer on the street, a referee at sporting event or a judge in court, it is natural for most of us to respond to the position held, rather than the person, whom we may not know personally or professionally. We recognise their authority as being legitimate.

Thus, someone who occupies an assigned position in an organisational hierarchy will be able to expect a certain amount of respect and compliance from those they are meant to lead, simply because of the position they occupy. This is a key principle behind 'line management'.

Assigned leadership leads to what has been termed 'position power'. However, in many settings, including schools, assigned leadership and positional power will only take you so far. When people ask the reasons behind a decision, a leader responding by saying: 'Because I'm the Principal'; 'It's my call', 'What I say goes', or even 'It's my way or the highway', will not only be less than optimal in ensuring the successful completion of a task but might prove to be counterproductive in the long run. Such leadership, as we will see later, can infantilise followers, cause unhealthy dependence on the leader, stifle innovation, and engender minimum 'get-by' performance; that is, doing just enough to satisfy the 'boss' or what is referred to in the organisational behaviour literature as 'satisficing' behaviour.[5]

Usually there is a 'honeymoon' period when a person is appointed to a formal position of responsibility and authority, but if someone is going to be an effective leader, he or she is going to have to earn their followers' trust and cooperation beyond this. This is termed 'emergent leadership', in that 'personal power' develops over time as a result of the ongoing communication and interaction between the leader and his or her followers and as group tasks are successfully completed.[6]

Another distinction between assigned and emergent leadership is that with the latter, as people are trusted and entrusted with greater responsibility by the leader, new leadership capability and personal power can emerge from within the group of followers through what has been termed distributed leadership. We will consider the phenomenon of distributive or distributed leadership later.

French and Raven provided a typology of five 'bases of power' that augments the previous discussion on personal and positional power:

- **Referent power**—based on followers' identification and liking for the leader ...
- **Expert power**—based on followers' perceptions of the leader's competence ...
- **Legitimate power**—associated with having status or formal job authority ...
- **Reward power**—derived from having the capacity to provide rewards to others ...
- **Coercive power**—derived from having the capacity to penalise or punish others.[7]

Of the types of power bases noted above, referent power and expert power could be seen as aspects of personal power, while the remaining types can be seen to flow from positional power or assigned leadership. This is not to say of course, that certain leaders might not draw their power to lead from several sources.

Leadership versus management

A perennial discussion centres on the differences between management and leadership. English has commented upon the 'management/leadership binary' in the context of education:

> The confusion between management and leadership continues to plague issues of preparation and performance in educational administration. Educational leaders do not perform in a social or organisational vacuum. Administrative positions exist within educational organisations, schools, colleges, and other related agencies. These positions are connected to other positions and to large organisational boundaries and functions. The dichotomy between leaders and management has become a point of contestation.[8]

Management does share commonalities with leadership. Managers also have leadership responsibilities in many cases, and leaders have management responsibilities. Each involves working with and influencing people in order to achieve certain objectives.

Despite these commonalities, Northouse has noted:

> But leadership is also different from management. Whereas the study of leadership can be traced back to Aristotle, management emerged around the turn of the 20th century with the advent of our industrialised society. Management was created as a way to reduce chaos in organisations and to make them run more effectively and efficiently. The primary functions of management, as first identified by Fayol (1916)[9], were planning, organising, staffing, and controlling. These functions are still representative of the field of management today.[10]

Kotterman has also considered the differences between leadership and management. He begins by considering the conventional, simplistic, dichotomist wisdom:

> Whereas leaders are seen as charismatic and often are admired and held in high esteem, managers frequently are thought of as the organisation's taskmasters with a whip in one hand and a bullhorn for screaming out orders in the other hand.[11]

But reality is not so simple:

> It is unusual for one person to have the skills to serve as both an inspiring leader and a professional manager. In large, complex organisations, these two distinct roles are even more difficult to assimilate in one person, and the tendency is to set leadership skills aside in favour of managing the workplace. Too often, senior managers believe they are leading when in fact they are managing ...
>
> This does not mean that managers cannot demonstrate leadership qualities. Managers may lead by example or lead a project or team, but they still end up performing the functions of management. Successful management is a really tough, challenging, and very important job. It should be given its due respect.
>
> Real leadership is tough, too, but it should not be confused with management.[12]

In a distinction that I believe would ring fairly true for educators, Kotter compared management and leadership, and noted that management is primarily about producing 'order and consistency'. This is achieved through the key functions of planning and budgeting, organising and staffing, and controlling and problem solving. Leadership, on the other hand, is primarily about producing 'change and movement'. This is achieved through establishing direction, aligning people, and motivating and inspiring.[13] Educational leaders have responsibility for all the above management functions, but as we will see, the most effective try and emphasise their leadership responsibilities.

We now move to consideration of leadership in education, where the lines between management and leadership are perhaps even more blurred than suggested above.

Leadership in education[14]

There have been several distinctive waves of conceptualising leadership—including educational leadership—over the past century.

As noted, earlier views and prescriptions of leadership were heavily influenced by portraits of 'great leaders', larger-than-life heroic figures few of us could hope to emulate but people we could all look to for inspiration.

With the growth of formal—as opposed to traditional—organisations, attention began to be focused on matters of administration and governance, the finer details and functions of running an organisation. Weber's notion of 'rational bureaucracy'[15] was later influential, with the leader almost sanitised and homogenised through the objective application of standard tasks and organising procedures that governed the behaviour and work of everyone in the organisation from top to bottom.[b]

As our knowledge of organisations grew, models, theories and typologies of leadership were developed and the notion of contingency, or fitting a particular type of leadership to a particular context or problem, was developed. In other words, the 'one size fits all' model of leadership was questioned.

In education, educational administration was a wave that began in the 1950s and built sharply from the 1960s. In Australia and internationally, the late Professor Bill Walker was a major influence, with thousands of educational leaders—including myself—completing courses in education administration, often by distance education, through the pioneering work in this field carried out at the University of New England in northern New South Wales, while many other Australian educators made the trek to North American universities to study similar courses.

The next development or wave from the 1980s was the result of heavy influence from the corporate world of modern business. Business and management degrees exploded in popularity, and degrees in educational management—as opposed to the earlier degrees in educational administration—began to appear. We saw much greater emphasis on educational strategic planning, quality assurance, mission and vision statements, value-added measures, measurable outcomes, management by objectives, competition, entrepreneurial activity and marketing schools. The language, techniques and mindsets of the corporate sector became pre-eminent in education at this time. This was the way of the future. Aspiring educational leaders polished their resumes and practised their interview technique, being mindful of the need to present as solid corporate citizens, and the 'self-managing' school[16] was the 'Holy Grail'.

At this time, it was not unusual to sit through hours, even days of staff development, where teaching, learning and students barely rated a mention, although there was talk of budgets, marketing, clients and stakeholders. In this respect, the 1980s–1990s represented something of a wasted decades in education.

Meanwhile, there was a new wave building and it came out of the effective schools literature of the 1970s. This new form went by the names of 'successful teaching', 'quality teaching' and 'pedagogy'. While educational management paradigms had been dominant, work had been going on in the background looking at what really added value in schools, and the answer wasn't management. Study after study and

---

b   Today the word 'bureaucracy' (and bureaucrat) is usually considered a pejorative but in Weber's conception it was meant to emphasise objectivity and the fact that there were rules and processes to govern the behaviour of all within the organisation the equivalent of the 'Rule of Law'. Critics of bureaucracy will point to the inflexibility and administrative clutter of complex organisations but proponents of bureaucracy will respond that Weber's concept or model of bureaucracy has never been implemented in its purest form. It is people and their behaviour that cause problems, according to the latter.

major meta-analyses confirmed that individual teachers made a major difference to student achievement, often working collaboratively in teams and supported by educational leaders. Suddenly, there was a realisation that the prime focus of schools was and should be teaching and learning—an absurd thing to have to say. Educational leaders had to refocus from managing their school to being leaders of teaching and learning—that is, instructional leaders—and new models and frameworks for quality teaching, 'productive pedagogy' and the like, came to prominence along with the use of professional teaching standards and later, teacher certification against these.

Institutes or colleges of teaching—teacher regulatory authorities—were established in the various states and territories, with the umbrella organisation the Australasian Teacher Regulatory Authorities (ATRA) established in 2005. Various awards for quality teaching became available at national and state level, including the New South Wales Minister for Education and Training Quality Teaching Awards introduced in 2000, which I had the pleasure of chairing.

Funding and support for quality teaching later become available through such measures as the Australian National Schools Network (ANSN) (early 1990s), the Australian Government Quality Teaching Program (AGQTP) (2000–13), the National Institute for Quality Teaching and School Leadership (NIQTSL) (2004), later renamed Teaching Australia (2005), and more recently becoming the Australian Institute for Teaching and School Leadership (AITSL, 2010). After a decade or more of disempowerment, criticism and reactivity, teachers and school leaders responded favourably to the new professional (action) learning opportunities opening to them which were largely focused on improvements in teaching and thereby student learning, although the initial emphasis was more on improving teaching than understanding learning.

This is not to imply that educational management is no longer important, but that we are seeing a new form of leadership. Despite the fact that their management responsibilities won't go away, the most effective school leaders are making the leadership of teaching and learning their prime focus and are empowering others through their leadership to revitalise and lift teaching and learning in schools.

Effective student welfare programs and procedures are recognised as foundational to academic achievement, with the two aspects not being dichotomous, and with high expectations for all. Educational leadership, both formal and distributive, is now fundamental in creating the conditions where teachers can teach and students can learn. Leaders also play a key role in facilitating teachers' professional learning.

Concluding remarks

Summary of the stages and changing views on leadership, including educational leadership

- 'Great Man'/trait theory [Aristotle?]
- Administration/Management [Henri Fayol, 1916][17]
- Scientific management [Frederick Taylor, 1911][18]
- Bureaucracy [Max Weber, 1905c][19]
- Behavioural theory [Elton Mayo, 1933][20]
- Leadership styles/typologies [Fred Fiedler, 1960s][21]
- Contingency theories [Lawrence and Lorsch [mid-1960s][22]
- Instructional leadership (phase 1) [1970s–]
- Transformational leadership [late 1970s–]
- Educational management [1980s–]
- Distributive/distributed leadership [1990s–]
- Leading learning communities [1990s–]
- Instructional leadership (phase 2) [2000–]

Above is a generalised summary I have made of some of the major phases or stages in the development of our understanding of leadership, including educational leadership. As I have pointed out in earlier work[23], at times these emphases have overlapped, influenced each other and even run in parallel, but it is clear that in the field of education, the present focus for educational leaders is on instructional leadership, or the leading of teaching for learning. However, instructional leadership builds and draws upon everything that has preceded it, including past and contemporary broader leadership theory and practice.

Endnotes

1. See Northouse, P. (2007). *Leadership* (4th ed.). Thousand Oaks, CA: Sage. (p. 2). All extracts from this publication have been reproduced with permission by SAGE Publications (US).
2. See, for example, Leithwood, K., & Duke, D. (1999). A century's quest to understand school leadership. In J. Murphy, & K. Louis (Eds.), *Handbook of research on educational administration*. San Francisco, CA: Jossey-Bass.
3. Northouse, P. (2007). (p. 2)
4. Northouse, P. (2007). (p. 3)

---

c Because of delays in the translation of Weber's work into English, and other languages, his impact was felt more from the 1930s.

5   Gibson, J., Ivancevich, J., & Donnelly, J. (1994). *Organizations: Behavior, structure, processes* (8th ed.). Burr Ridge, IL: Irwin. (p. 613)
6   Bligh, M., & Meindl, J. (2005). The cultural ecology of leadership: An analysis of popular leadership books. In D. Messick & R. Kramer. *The psychology of leadership*. Mahwah, NJ: Lawrence Erlbaum. (p. 12)
7   Cited in Northouse, P. (2007). (p. 8)
8   English, F. (2005). Introduction: A metadiscursive perspective on the landscape of educational leadership in the 21st century. In English, F., (Ed.), *The Sage handbook of educational leadership*. Thousand Oaks, CA: Sage Publications. (pp. xi–xii)
9   Fayol, H. (1916). *Administration industrielle et générale; prévoyance, organisation, commandement, coordination, contrôle* (in French). Paris: H. Dunod et E. Pinat.
10 Northouse, P. (2007). (pp. 9–10)
11 Kotterman, J. (2006). Leadership versus management: What's the difference? *The Journal for Quality and Participation, 29*(2), 13–17. (p. 13)
12 Kotterman, J. (2006). (p. 16)
13 Kotter, J. (1990). *A force for change: How leadership differs from management*. New York, NJ: Free Press. (pp. 3–8)
14 This section is based on Dinham, S. (2007). The waves of leadership. *The Australian Educational Leader, 29*(3), 20–21, 27.
15 Weber, M. (1905). *The Protestant ethic and the spirit of capitalism (*in German *Die protestantische Ethik und der Geist des Kapitalismus)*; Weber, M. (1930). *The Protestant ethic and the spirit of capitalism*. (first translated to English by Talcott Parsons). London, England: Allen & Unwin.
16 Caldwell, B., & Spinks, J. (1988). *The self-managing school*. London, England: Falmer Press.
17 Fayol, H. (1916).
18 Taylor, F. (1911). *The principles of scientific management*. New York, NY: Harper & Brothers.
19 Weber, M. (1905), (1930).
20 Mayo, E. (1933). *The human problems of an industrial civilisation*. New York, NY: Macmillan.
21 Fiedler, F. (1965). Engineer the job to fit the manager. *Harvard Business Review, 43*, 115–122.
22 Lawrence, P., & Lorsch, J. (1967). Differentiation and integration in complex organisation. *Administrative Science Quarterly, 12*(1), 1–47.
23 Dinham, S. (2007).

CHAPTER 10

What impact does leadership have on student outcomes?

INTRODUCTION

Leadership is increasingly recognised internationally as a vital factor in improving school effectiveness, teacher quality and student achievement.[1] As a result, over the past 15 years or so in particular, there has been greater attention paid to formulating professional standards[2], models, profiles and frameworks for school leadership, both to articulate the breadth and depth of leaders' roles and to inform professional learning, selection, appraisal and accountability processes.[3]

There has also been greater recognition that teachers exercise leadership.[4] As teachers become more experienced and adept, it is likely and indeed expected that their leadership involvement and influence will increase and move beyond the classroom, across the school and more widely into the profession. This widening and deepening leadership role for teachers is recognised in professional standards for teachers.

For those teachers who seek appointment to formal positions of responsibility in schools, such as coordinators, heads of faculties and assistant principals, leadership expectations held for them are greater, and articulated in both duty statements and higher levels of professional standards, such as the *Highly Accomplished* and *Lead* levels in Australia.[5]

In considering professional frameworks and standards for principals and the accompanying research, as noted, while principals will continue to be required to perform a variety of managerial functions, they have been found to be most effective where they place major emphasis on 'instructional leadership'. Hattie concluded from his meta-analytic work that:

> School leaders who focus on students' achievement and instructional strategies are the most effective ... It is leaders who place more attention on teaching and focused achievement domains ... who have the higher effects.[6]

We will now consider those effects in greater detail.

How educational leaders influence teaching and learning

The crucial importance of the teacher to student learning has long been recognised.[7] The challenge for any educational leader is to make things happen within individual classrooms, and across their school or area of responsibility. Wahlstrom and Seashore Louis have commented:

> In the current era of accountability, a principal's responsibility for the quality of teachers' work is simply a fact of life. How to achieve influence over work settings (classrooms) in which they rarely participate is a key dilemma.[8]

Despite the smaller (i.e., than for teachers and teaching), yet still significant measured effects on student learning for school-based factors beyond the classroom—Hattie has calculated an effect size of 0.39 for principals/school leaders[9]—research evidence has confirmed that 'school leaders can play major roles in creating the conditions in which teachers can teach effectively and students can learn'.[10]

As a result of extensive meta-analytic work, Marzano, Waters and McNulty concluded:

> A highly effective school leader can have a dramatic influence on the overall academic achievement of students ... Leadership has long been perceived to be important to the effective functioning of organisations in general and, more recently, of schools in particular. However some researchers and theorists assert that at best research on school leadership is equivocal and at worst demonstrates that leadership has no effect on student achievement. In contrast, a meta-analysis of 35 years of research indicates that school leadership has a substantial effect on student achievement and provides guidance for experienced and aspiring principals alike.[11]

The emergence, decline and re-emergence of instructional leadership

A key to understanding this apparent conundrum—that is, whether educational leadership is important for learning or not—is to distinguish between different approaches to, or types of leadership. Effective management of day-to-day school functions involving budgeting, facilities, teacher hiring and evaluation, planning and accountability, can result in a well-run school, but if this is the extent or main focus of leadership, there may be little effect on improving student achievement, at least at a whole school level. This situation has led to calls for what has been termed 'instructional leadership', or leadership for teaching and learning. Robinson, Lloyd and Rowe noted that:

> Instructional leadership theory has its empirical origins in studies undertaken during the late 1970's and 80's of schools in poor urban communities where students succeeded despite the odds ... these schools typically had strong instructional leadership, including a learning climate free of disruption, a system of clear teaching objectives, and high teacher expectations for students.[12]

Hallinger (2005) proposed three dimensions for instructional leadership from his review of the field:

- defining the school's mission,
- managing the instructional program, and
- promoting a positive school learning climate.[13]

Hallinger (2005) also observed that despite interest in instructional leadership arising from research into effective schools going back as far as the late 1970s:

> During the mid-1990s, however, attention shifted somewhat away from effective schools and instructional leadership. Interest in these topics was displaced by concepts such as school restructuring and transformational leadership.[14]

For a time, 'transformational leadership'—which goes back to James McGregor Burns' work on how some leaders 'engage with staff in ways that inspired them to new levels of energy, commitment and moral purpose'[15]—became prominent and instructional leadership was relegated, and to some degree discounted as outdated, as noted in the previous chapter. (Unfortunately, the term instruction—more commonly used in the United States of America—does have technical, transmissive connotations that some find off-putting.)

To compound matters, during the 1990s, there was great enthusiasm for system and school restructuring and for corporate models and approaches, as discussed in the previous chapter.[16] Yet how schools are structured (or restructured) has been found to be a weak driver of improvement in student outcomes, despite great enthusiasm for structural arrangements such as middle schools, mixed ability groupings and 'open classrooms'. It is the quality of teaching that occurs within such structures, and the leadership that guides and supports it, that is most important in improving student achievement.[17] Too often, schools make structural or organisational changes in the hope that these will lead to improved teacher and student performance, without addressing the bigger issue of teacher quality and its impact on learning. A highly effective teacher can work within almost any structural arrangement, while a poor teacher will not suddenly become a good one due to some change in how their class or school is organised.

However, despite the enthusiasm for both school restructuring and transformational leadership, the findings from international meta-analytic work comparing the impact of various approaches to educational leadership, along with wider developments and concerns over quality teaching and student performance noted in earlier chapters, caused a re-examination of the worth of instructional leadership. Robinson, Lloyd and Rowe concluded from their meta-analysis of empirical work on the impact of various leadership approaches:

> The comparison between instructional and transformational leadership showed that the impact [on student outcomes] of the former is three to four times that of the latter. The reason is that transformational leadership is more focused on the relationship between leaders and followers than on the educational work of school leadership, and the quality of these relationships is not predictive of the quality of student outcomes. Educational leadership involves not only building collegial teams, a loyal and cohesive staff, and sharing an inspirational vision. It also involves focusing such relationships on some very specific pedagogical work, and the leadership practices involved are better captured by measures of instructional leadership than of transformational leadership.[18]

Thus, while the need for instructional leadership had been formally recognised for three decades or more[19], the approach has only regained prominence within the last 15 years or so. With a growing focus on the importance of the quality of teaching to student achievement—as revealed through international student testing regimes such as the OECD Programme for International Student Assessment (PISA, introduced in 2000), Progress in International Reading Literacy Study (PIRLS), and Trends in International Mathematics and Science Study (TIMSS)—instructional leadership is once more assuming centre stage. Rankings and performance on such measures have, increasingly, become matters of concern and importance in many countries, as noted in Chapters 3 and 4.[20]

In Australia, one could argue that the imperative for instructional leadership only (re)gained momentum in the context of the National Assessment Program—Literacy and Numeracy (NAPLAN) tests introduced in 2008, and with the establishment of the My School website[a] in 2010 (which lists NAPLAN results for every school in Australia along with other information). National student testing and publication of school performance and student growth data certainly gained people's attention, although outcomes other than those from standardised testing (i.e., academic, personal, social) are considered by many to be equally or even more important.[21]

---

a   http://www.myschool.edu.au/

However, there is now little doubt that educational leaders are receiving a clear message as to both their importance and their obligation to improving teaching and learning.

An international review by Barber and Mourshed found:

> High-performing ['top' 15%] principals focus more on instructional leadership and developing teachers. They see their biggest challenges as improving teaching and curriculum, and they believe that their ability to coach others and support their development is the most important skill of a good school leader.[22]

The review found that a thorough knowledge of teaching and learning on behalf of leaders is essential if teachers are to be developed and supported to be able to move forward the learning of every student in their care:

> Leadership focused on teaching, learning, and people is critical to the current and future success of schools.[23]

Clearly, there is a growing hunger on the part of many aspiring and practising school leaders—as well as pressure from external sources such as educational systems—to be better equipped to lead teaching and learning, the prime rationale for this book. Implicit in many new leadership preparation programs[b] is the notion of action learning[c], whereby participants are supported and guided to undertake change projects in their schools to improve teaching and learning and to measure the impact of these interventions[24], and not just to read or hear about theory and research.[d] However, Robinson, Lloyd and Rowe's conclusions support the continued existence of a common disconnect between approaches to leadership and approaches to improving student outcomes, although:

> Fortunately, the gulf between the two fields is beginning to be bridged by a resurgence of interest in instructional leadership and calls for more focus on the knowledge and skills that leaders need to support teacher learning about how to raise achievement while reducing disparity ... it seems clear that if we are to learn more about how leadership supports teachers in improving student outcomes, we need to measure how leaders attempt to influence the teaching

---

b   See two programs I have been involved with: http://education.unimelb.edu.au/study_with_us/professional_development/course_list/instructional_leadership; http://www.bastow.vic.edu.au/courses/leading-instructional-practice

c   We will consider action learning in Part C.

d   There is a saying in Ukraine that translates as 'Theory without practice is sterile. Practice without theory is blind'.

practices that matter. The source of our leadership indicators should be our knowledge of how teachers make a difference to students rather than various theories of leader–follower relations.[25]

Leithwood, Seashore Louis and Wahlstrom, in reviewing the research literature on leadership and school achievement, found:

> [T]he total (direct and indirect) effects of leadership on student learning account for about a quarter of total school effects ...
>
> Leadership is second only to classroom instruction among all school-related factors that contribute to what students learn at school.
>
> Leadership effects are usually largest where and when they are needed most [that is, in the most challenging schools and circumstances, or coming off a 'low base'].[26]

Today, leadership is seen as central and essential to delivering the changes, improvement and performance society increasingly expects of all organisations, including schools. What has become clear, though, is that leadership generally, and educational leadership in particular, is a more contentious, complex, situated and dynamic phenomenon than previously thought.

We now turn to three case studies to illustrate and build upon the above understandings and views on leadership. The first is the result of a major meta-analysis and study carried out in New Zealand as part of a 'Best Evidence Synthesis' series of reviews of international literature. The second is a large study of school leadership in England and is included to provide 'high level' findings on the importance of leadership. The third is a more in-depth study 'on the ground' in schools, carried out in one state in Australia.

Together, the three studies provide a substantial foundation to assist in considering the question of the impact of school leadership on student outcomes.

School leadership and student outcomes: the Best Evidence Synthesis

A major review of the impact of leadership for student outcomes utilising meta-analytic and other techniques was carried for the New Zealand Ministry of Education by Robinson, Hohepa and Lloyd as part of the Best Evidence Synthesis Iterations.[27]

The report on the review was extensive, but one of the most illuminating findings, apart from the distinction between transformational and pedagogical or instructional leadership noted previously[28], was the evidence presented in respect of the impact on student learning of five key leadership dimensions (see Figure 10.1).

(The authors also identified three dimensions from indirect evidence that were not assigned an effect size, which will be mentioned briefly later.)

Drawing on their findings, Robinson et al. noted:

> Our primary conclusion is that pedagogically focused leadership has a substantial impact on student outcomes. The more leaders focus their influence, their learning, and their relationships with teachers on the core business of teaching and learning, the greater their influence on student outcomes.[29]

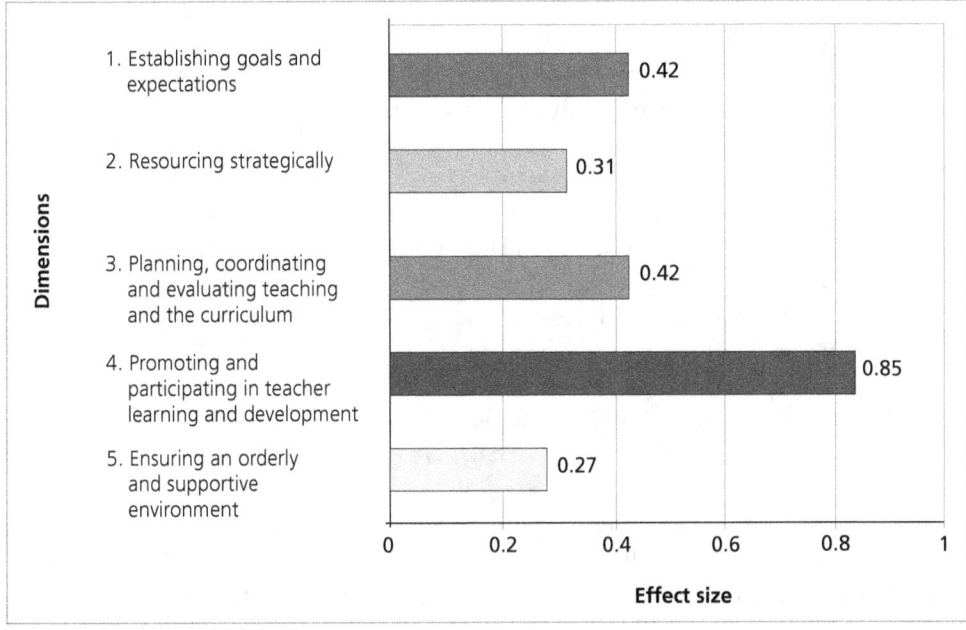

Figure 10.1: Relative impact of five leadership dimensions on student outcomes[30]

The five leadership dimensions

1 Establishing goals and expectations

This dimension is about the exercise of leadership through the setting and communicating of goals for teacher and student learning. The mean effect size for this dimension (0.42) was second equal highest. An effect of this magnitude can be interpreted as moderate and educationally significant.

Effective goal setting requires that leaders:
- establish the importance of the goals;
- ensure that the goals are clear;
- develop staff commitment to the goals.

> Leaders establish the importance of goals by communicating how they are linked to pedagogical, philosophical, and moral purposes. They gain agreement that the goals are realistic and win collective commitment to achieving them.[31]

Both the goals themselves, and the process of determining them, are important. Imposed goals are less likely to be inculcated at a personal or school level, than goals that are collaboratively determined. To put it another way, input to, 'buy-in' and 'ownership' of goals are important. (The input of students and community members to the formulation of school goals can also be important but is often overlooked.)

2 Resourcing strategically

Leadership is also exercised through obtaining and allocating material, intellectual, and human resources. As the word 'strategically' signals, this dimension is not about securing resources per se but about securing and allocating resources *that are aligned to pedagogical purposes*. At all levels of the education system, leaders play a vital role in working with teachers to identify and develop appropriate teaching and learning resources and in ensuring that these are readily available. The mean effect size for this dimension [ES = 0.31] indicates that it has a small indirect impact on student outcomes …

When identifying and obtaining resources, leaders in high-performing schools:
- use clear criteria that are aligned to pedagogical and philosophical purposes;
- ensure sustained funding for pedagogical priorities.[32]

An implication of this leadership dimension is that just because a school has good resources, doesn't mean it will be effective. The reverse also applies. The key notion is that of *targeting* the use of resources, both financial and other, to where these will have most pedagogical impact, something that was recognised in the Gonski Review of school funding in Australia, which called for such targeted—and not just additional—spending.[33]

Once again, there are advantages in involving school staff and others in these deliberations.

3 Planning, coordinating, and evaluating teaching and the curriculum

This dimension is about leaders' emphasis on improving the quality of teaching and the curriculum. The mean effect size obtained was the same as for Dimension 1 [ES = 0.42], which should be interpreted as meaning that this set of leadership practices has a moderate and educationally significant impact on student outcomes. Leaders in high-performing schools are distinguished from their counterparts in otherwise similar, low-performing schools by their personal involvement in planning, coordinating, and evaluating teaching and teachers.

When planning, coordinating, and evaluating teaching and the curriculum, leaders in high-performing schools:
- promote collegial discussions of teaching and how it impacts on student achievement;
- provide active oversight and coordination of the teaching programme;
- observe in classrooms and provide feedback that teachers describe as useful;
- ensure systematic monitoring of student progress and use of assessment results for programme improvement.[34]

This dimension is at the heart of being an instructional leader, rather than a school manager or administrator. The leaders outlined in the AESOP study later in this chapter, for example, took an active interest in this important dimension, and used professional learning as an important means of facilitating and supporting planning, coordinating and evaluating teaching and the curriculum.

4 Promoting and participating in teacher learning and development

Of all the dimensions derived from the meta-analysis, this dimension produced the largest estimated effect size [ES = 0.84]. This means that this set of leadership practices has a large, very educationally significant effect on student outcomes. The practices involved in this dimension include participation in, as well as promotion of, formal and informal opportunities for teacher learning and development. Leaders can participate in teacher professional learning as leaders, as learners, or as both …

Leadership promotes teacher learning via communities that are focused on improving student success. To establish such communities, leaders may need to challenge or change cultures that are not focused on collegial discussion of the relationship between what is taught and what is learned.

When promoting and participating in teacher learning and development, leaders in high-performing schools:
- ensure an intensive focus on the teaching–learning relationship;
- promote collective responsibility and accountability for student achievement and well-being;
- provide useful advice about how to solve teaching problems.[35]

Once again, this is a very important finding and one that is consistent with studies cited in this book. As noted in Chapter 2, I consider professional learning to be one of the 'big levers' in promoting student achievement. I can't see how it is possible to change schools, lift their performance and improve student outcomes without engaging staff in professional learning. To achieve change and improvement, we need to change what people know, can do, and even believe and value.

5   Ensuring an orderly and supportive environment

Leadership can facilitate the achievement of important academic and social goals by creating an environment that is conducive to success. An orderly environment makes it possible for teachers to focus on teaching and students to focus on learning. This dimension, derived from forward mapping studies, has a small mean effect size [ES = 0.27]. The indicators for this dimension include a focus on cultural understanding and a respect for difference; provision of a safe, orderly environment and a clear discipline code; and minimal interruption to teaching time. Other indicators include protection of staff from unreasonable parental and official pressures and early and effective conflict resolution.

The findings suggest that leaders of effective schools succeed in establishing a safe and supportive environment by means of clear and consistently enforced social expectations and discipline codes …

When ensuring an orderly and supportive environment, leaders in high-performing schools:
- protect teaching time;
- ensure consistent discipline routines;
- identify and resolve conflicts quickly and effectively.[36]

Something I've observed in schools that are attempting to improve and 'turn around', is an initial focus on achieving discipline and order, including aspects such as wearing of uniforms, behaviour and attendance. This is understandable, but in some ways it is 'putting the cart before the horse'. I have often been asked by beginning teachers the question 'What is the most effective classroom management strategy?' My answer, which no doubt often disappoints, is always the same. The best classroom management strategy is a well-prepared lesson, and if this is not successful, you need to evaluate the lesson and make modifications to your teaching on the basis of this. Thus, the view of the beginning teacher that: 'I'll get them under control, and then I'll teach them', is missing the point.

To some degree, an orderly school environment is a product of some of the leadership dimensions noted above. However, as will be noted in the AESOP study below, a central focus on students and their wellbeing, coupled with appropriate and well-understood rules, responsibilities and processes, is essential in developing a high performing school, and as we have seen with the successful senior secondary teaching project, those successful teachers made good use of routine and order, although ultimately it was their superior teaching that obviated the need for overt student 'discipline'.[37]

As noted, Robinson, Hohepa and Lloyd also identified a number of other leadership dimensions, which, while significant, were not assigned effect sizes. These were:

1. Creating educationally powerful connections.
2. Engaging in constructive problem talk.
3. Selecting, developing and using smart tools.[38]

Of the three, 'creating educationally powerful connections' was seen to be particularly prominent in the leadership of those leaders in the AESOP study outlined later in this chapter. Engaging in professional 'problem talk' was also a feature of a number of projects I've been involved with. Finally, the use of data gathering and analysis tools of various types was also common in the AESOP schools.[39]

The Effective Leadership and Pupil Outcomes Project[40]

The findings of *The Effective Leadership and Pupil Outcomes Project* are very consistent with both the synthesis carried out by Robinson et al., and with the AESOP study findings that follow. In the words of the authors:

> The Effective Leadership and Pupil Outcomes Project is the largest and most extensive study of contemporary leadership to be conducted in England to date. Its sampling methods and innovative mixed methods design have enabled it to examine the work of head teachers [principals] and other school leaders in a range of primary and secondary schools nationally ...
>
> The study focussed on schools that were identified to have significantly raised pupil attainment levels over a relatively short three year period (2003–2005) ... Through a combination of statistical analysis of national data sets on pupils' attainment three groups of schools were identified, all of which had made sustained improvements in academic outcomes but from different starting points. Low start, Moderate start and High start.[41]

The report authors made a number of 'claims' based upon the results of the project:

Claim 1: Almost all successful leaders draw on the same repertoire of 'basic' leadership practices:
- Building vision and setting direction
- Understanding and developing people
- Designing the organisation
- Managing and supporting the teaching and learning program

Claim 2: The same 'basic' leadership values and practices are enacted in contextually sensitive ways:
- Leaders' experience [less-experienced head teachers instigated more change and accomplished more]
- School socioeconomic status
- School improvement group [emphasis, type, composition of group important].

Claim 3: School leaders improve teaching and learning indirectly and most powerfully through their influence on staff ability, motivation and the conditions of teachers' work.

Claim 4: School leadership has a greater influence on schools and students when it is widely distributed.

Claim 5: Some patterns of distribution are more effective than others ['fatter', not 'flatter' distribution; the former achieved through consultation being most effective, the second and less effective achieved through delegation]

Claim 6: A small handful of personal traits explain a high proportion of the variation in leadership effectiveness.
- Diagnosis and differentiation [diagnosis of needs, differentiating of responses, coordinating activities]
- Values and Virtue [importance of leadership values of care, equity, achievement for all; high ideals, moral commitment][42]

We will now examine the degree to which a project carried out in Australia is congruent with the above framework, with the findings of the best evidence synthesis carried out by Robinson et al.[43] and with the prevailing research on the importance of leadership in schools.

An Exceptional Schooling Outcomes Project

Background to the study[44]

AESOP (An Exceptional Schooling Outcomes Project) aimed to investigate junior secondary education (Years 7 to 10), rather than senior secondary education (Years 11 and 12), the latter being the subject of an earlier study.[45]

It was decided to investigate the junior secondary years because this stage of schooling had been relatively neglected and was seen as something of a 'black hole'.

The junior secondary years represent a transition from the traditional model of primary school to secondary schooling, with its multiple teachers and discrete subjects. The junior secondary years also mark the period during which the physical, emotional and social development of young people intensifies. Alienation and disengagement from schooling can occur at this time, to the extent that some students leave (or are encouraged to leave) school once they pass the age for compulsory attendance. Achievement gaps, already evident at the beginning, and by the end of primary school, can widen during the junior secondary years[e]. One response to these perceived problems of upper primary/lower secondary schooling has been the so-called middle school movement.[46]

---

e Something confirmed by NAPLAN test results.

AESOP was a far larger project than the study of successful senior secondary teachers that preceded it, and was funded by the Australian Research Council. The major research partners were the then New South Wales Department of Education and Training (NSW DET), the University of Western Sydney[f], and the University of New England.

As noted, the project was designed to investigate processes leading to exceptional educational outcomes in Years 7–10 in NSW government (public) schools. Exceptional educational achievement was defined using the rubric of the three interrelated domains or principles outlined in *The Adelaide Declaration on National Goals for* [Australian] *Schooling in the Twenty-first Century*[g] [47] that is, schools should:
1. 'develop fully the talents of all students'
2. attain 'high standards of knowledge, skills and understanding through a comprehensive and balanced curriculum'
3. be 'socially just'.

Thus, we were concerned with conceptualising student achievement in a more holistic sense, rather than focusing on academic results alone.

Originally, our major focus was to be on subject departments (faculties)[h], but as a result of our discussions and our desire to utilise the framework of the Adelaide Goals, we decided to include teams responsible for cross- or whole-school programs.

Research sites were thus to be of two types: departments responsible for teaching certain subjects in Years 7 to 10 (which we decided would be around 80% of sites), and teams responsible for cross-school programs in Years 7 to 10 (the remaining 20% of sites).

How the case study sites were selected

Our budget and methodology meant we could study around 50 sites across the state. Selection of sites where exceptional outcomes were thought to be occurring was time consuming and complex. The project methodology employed a case study approach whereby quantitative data (e.g., public examination performance, various 'value-adding' measures of student achievement growth) and qualitative data (e.g., nomination from parent groups, principals, DET officers) were used to select a sample of sites where schools *appeared* to have been achieving exceptional educational outcomes over and above what might be expected based upon factors

---

f   Now Western Sydney University.

g   The Adelaide Goals preceded the Melbourne Goals (2008) mentioned previously but had substantially the same emphases on academic, personal and social outcomes.

h   The previous study of successful senior secondary teachers had revealed the importance of faculties and teams behind the success of individual teachers and their students, and we wanted to explore this more.

such as socio-economic status, either within faculty-based subject areas or with cross-school programs, over at least a four-year period.

Triangulation and analysis of quantitative and qualitative selection data occurred, with sites selected to provide a sample of socio-economic types, rural–urban distribution, size of school, and spread of subject areas and programs. As with the previous senior teaching study, there was no claim that these sites were the 'best', but based upon our selection criteria, they could be considered to be among the best in the state on a range of measures, confirmation or otherwise of which would come later.

Eventually, 50 sites were selected for study at 38 secondary schools, with some schools being selected for (potentially) exceptional educational achievement in two or more areas. In all, the project took six years from conception to publication of findings.

How AESOP data were obtained and analysed

The overall aim of the project was:

> To identify and analyse processes in NSW public schooling, Years 7 to 10, producing exceptional educational outcomes to assist national renewal in junior secondary education.

The following study questions were developed in respect of the above aim:

1. What are the variables and processes leading to outstanding educational outcomes—in the possible areas of personal identity, academic success and social attainment in the study site(s)?
2. Is it possible to identify the relationship(s), if any, between 'academic success', 'personal identity' and 'social attainment' as achieved through subject departments and/or other formal groups and special programs and initiatives?
3. What organisational and institutional factors—NSW DET, District, School, Leadership, Community, Faculty, other groups and individuals—contribute to and constrain this success?
4. To what degree and through what means, if any, are the outstanding educational outcomes of the sites shared or shareable with others within and beyond the school?[48]

Participation on the part of schools, teams, and individuals, was voluntary. Site visit research teams consisted of a university academic who acted as site team leader, another academic with expertise in the area under investigation (e.g., a maths education specialist), a head teacher (faculty head) from another school in the district with expertise in the subject under investigation, and the Chief Education Officer (School Improvement) from the local DET district. Additional academics and head teachers were included in multi-site visits.

Having an academic leading the research teams was important, as we realised early on that some school staff had suspicions about the study, seeing it as a departmental school 'review' or inspection by stealth, rather than a research project.

It is also worth noting that the faculty head teachers who were part of the site case study teams universally described the experience as a career highlight, and one of the 'best' professional development activities they had ever undertaken. They enjoyed the whole experience of visiting another school, observing lessons, speaking with staff, students and community members, examining resources, making observations of various sorts and being part of a research team and the recognition this entailed. Site visits gave them the time and opportunity not only to learn, but also to reflect and question their own professional practice. A view commonly expressed was that after the site visit, the department heads were going, even rushing, back to their own schools to make changes in the light of what they had seen in these sites and schools. (I think there are important implications for teacher professional development in this unexpected finding.)

Site teams were expected to undertake the following in four days or more:
- interview the Principal about the outstanding faculty/program
- interview the head teacher/leader of the outstanding faculty/program
- with classroom teacher approval, visit classes to observe students at work, and discuss pedagogy and related matters with those teachers
- hold a faculty forum (faculty/program staff meeting)
- conduct student focus discussions with two year groups—Years 7 and 8, and Years 9 and 10
- conduct a parent forum
- team leader to organise additional discussions with the Principal and perhaps the head teacher as needed
- team to investigate any documents that are held and used by the faculty/program, e.g. policy documents, newsletters, management plans, programs etc.
- provide verbal feedback to the faculty/program staff and Principal on the last day of the visit.

Site teams observed, interviewed, investigated and discussed intensively over the week, using protocols to record data and observations. Most interviews and focus groups were audiotaped. In country areas, teams usually stayed at the same accommodation and discussions took place 'after hours' as members came to an understanding of what they were encountering.

Teams collaboratively completed a detailed report in electronic format, usually within a month of the site visit. These reports were not provided to schools for reasons of confidentiality and concerns over the use of report findings—a few schools had publicised the fact that they had been selected for the study as proof of their effectiveness and success—but principals and relevant staff were provided with a verbal briefing of the broad findings for their school on the final day of the visit, feedback they appeared to find useful and affirming in almost all cases.

Report data were analysed using the NUD*IST[49] software program and accepted grounded theory procedures[50], with seven major reports completed, one of which was concerned with leadership.[i]

As a result of the AESOP project, a range of conference presentations and symposia were presented over the course of the study, in Australia and overseas. The major outcome of the project, however, was the set of seven books, which were provided to every public secondary school in NSW and made available for general sale. There were also additional publications in the leadership area.[51]

How does leadership contribute to outstanding educational outcomes in junior secondary schooling?

Leadership, both positional (principals, deputy principals, other school executives, relevant head teachers) and distributed (key classroom teachers and others), was found in this study to be a major factor in the outstanding outcomes achieved by students, teachers and schools.

Once again, as with the study of successful senior secondary teaching, there were surprises in the findings. It was expected that head teachers (faculty heads) and whole-school program leaders would be important to the success of faculties and teams, and this was confirmed.[52] What was unexpected was the extent to which principals were found to have influenced the achievements of these faculties and teams—there were no specific questions asked about the Principal's role in facilitating student or faculty achievement in our protocols and data about leadership emerged inductively—leading to the hypothesis that the influence of leaders, and especially principals, on student achievement may have been underestimated, possibly because this influence is indirect and difficult to measure. Another way to look at this is that in many or most schools, the influence exerted by the Principal and other leaders on student achievement might be in line with the general literature, but that this influence has the potential to be far greater, for better or worse, with commensurate effects on teacher quality and student achievement.

In light of the points raised above, it should be noted that while the vast majority of the 50 sites, (arguably 46 or 47), were confirmed to be achieving exceptional educational outcomes as defined by the project, some were not. In most cases this was due to a lack of suitable data for selection, especially for subject areas where examination/value added data were not available.

---

i English Education; ESL/Literacy Education; Mathematics Education; Science Education; Equity Programs; Student Welfare Programs; Leadership. See http://simerr.une.edu.au/pages/projects/3aesop.pdf; Dinham, S. (2007). *Leadership for exceptional educational outcomes*. Teneriffe, Qld.: Post Pressed.

The discussion that follows concentrates on principal leadership, although there were parallels across the various levels and types of leadership. Leadership by deputy principals, head teachers, other executive and teacher leadership is considered in more detail elsewhere.[53]

Approximately equal numbers of male and female principals were represented in the 38 schools. No differences between the leadership styles or attributes of men or women principals (or other leaders) were discerned.

From analysis of data on principal leadership from the site reports, seven categories of principal leadership attributes and practices contributing to exceptional educational outcomes were derived. Each is discussed below, with the core category Focus on Students and Their Learning being discussed last. Inevitably, there is some overlap between each of the broad categories, with each attribute or approach being related to others through the actions of principals and their teams.

1 External awareness and engagement

Principals of schools where sites achieving exceptional outcomes were provisionally identified and validated exhibited a keen awareness and understanding of the wider environment and a positive attitude towards engaging with it.

At a time when so much is imposed on schools and many teachers and executives feel overwhelmed by change, defensive and disempowered[54], it was apparent that principals in these schools possessed and demonstrated a positive attitude towards change. Rather than perceiving change as a threat, principals were open to the opportunities offered by change. Even with mandated change, principals looked for how they could adapt and improve what they were already doing to meet new requirements, and considered ways in which their school might benefit from being in the forefront of change. As one site report[j] for a school identified for successful student welfare programs noted:

> 'Even with mandated requirements, the Principal doesn't resort to line management, but draws out the positive aspects for the school of whatever is being required and 'sells' the change. What others would see as a problem, he sees as an opportunity. This positive mindset is contagious. As the Principal noted: "We do what we have to do, but we do it with gusto if we see that it helps".'

Instead of attempting to keep change at bay, these principals exposed their school to the opportunities and challenges brought by change. Rather than being inward looking, they sought out, fostered, and utilised external networks and resources to assist with change. It was observed by a staff member that her school participated

---

j As noted, site reports were completed collaboratively by the university and DET members of the case study teams.

in 'every trial and pilot program' because of the benefits derived from being in the vanguard of change.

The external links principals sought to develop ranged from the local community through to the international level. These principals were found to be entrepreneurial in obtaining financial and in-kind support from the system, government, community, and the corporate sector. They skilfully utilised such support and resources to realise their vision for the school. One site report for a school identified for ICT across the curriculum noted:

> 'Personal networking [by the Principal] has been core to developing community perceptions of [...] as a school displaying excellence in ICT across the curriculum. This has been fundamental in [the school] achieving and maintaining *Apple Distinguished School* status as well as opening up opportunities to trial DET ICT initiatives such as broadband communications.'

These leaders placed a high priority on establishing and maintaining good communications and relationships with external stakeholders. In schools with high proportions of non-English speaking background parents and community members, emphasis was placed on communication, through the use of interpreters, translators and community liaison officers. School signage and communications utilised the predominant languages of the community. Representatives of various disadvantaged groups spoke positively of the respect shown to them by the Principal and the school. They felt informed, valued and listened to, with the school open to them and their concerns.

As part of their open, outward perspective, these principals were prepared to seek outside assistance when they couldn't solve problems. They were not afraid to 'put their hand up' for help and didn't see this as a sign of failure or inadequacy. A powerful example of this was detailed in the site report for one school. The Principal had earned considerable staff respect for his handling of a crisis created by a small group of, in his words, 'angry, aggressive ... students' [of a certain cultural background]. At that time he was handling up to 20 'serious incident' reports each year and concluded:

> 'When I reflected on it I thought that perhaps the way we were managing some of these situations was contributing to them. The other situation was that basically whenever there was a problem they looked for me or [the Deputy Principal] and sometimes that took five or ten minutes ... [The Principal took the issue to District Office] I put my hand up and said "I'm going under!". And I'll be honest with you, there are several elements to this. By the time I came here I had been a principal for three years, but the enormity of this task was [too much] ... Dealing day-to-day with crises and nothing else took its toll and I was really afraid we were going to have a death. If it wasn't me it'd be someone else. By that stage I'd been spat on, chased ... I nearly had a brick through my head ...

people were looking to me for leadership, and I honestly didn't have the answers. So, my response was to ... change our practices ... [but] It was bigger than I could handle. At that stage I thought I was on my own ... [but the District Office training program and assistance] has been able to facilitate my growth and the school's growth.'

Shortly after the training program there was a critical incident that utilised the new processes adopted by the school 'for real'. With some satisfaction the Principal said:

'People [now] know the language of how to deal with kids in certain situations ... body language ... we no longer go in singly, we go in twos, we know how to separate fights, we know how to do a whole range of things. The feedback from my executive is the best feedback that I've got, and that's something that has changed the culture of the school.'

Allied to openness to change and opportunity, these leaders possessed positive attitudes that tended to be 'contagious'. They realised negativity can be self-handicapping ('misery loves company') and attempted to drive it out. Their positive approach motivated others and acted as a form of organisational energy to keep the school moving and improving. This was not blind, unthinking 'Pollyanna' optimism or always looking 'on the bright side of life', but was based on a realistic appraisal of the situation. Their positive approach was seen as authentic rather than a mechanism for manipulation or control.

2   A bias towards innovation and action

Three broad approaches were discerned in the actions of the principals of schools where sites achieving exceptional outcomes were identified. These principals:
1. used their powers and the rules and boundaries of the 'system' creatively
2. exhibited a bias towards experimentation and risk taking
3. demonstrated strength, consistency, yet flexibility in decision-making and the application of policy and procedures.

The schools tended to have a strong executive structure with clear, well-understood responsibilities. Rather than being dictatorial or autocratic, principals were seen to use these structures and responsibilities responsibly and effectively. They utilised the discretion available to them and pushed against administrative and systemic constraints when necessary. They creatively used resources at their disposal to support innovative programs and encouraged and supported staff to leave their 'comfort zones'. At times, they tended to be ahead of the system and profession and acted as 'ground breakers'. They had earned a certain amount of credibility with system officials who tended to give special dispensation, support or approval to new approaches, even 'turning a blind eye' on occasion. Some even appeared to operate on the principle that 'it is easier to gain forgiveness than permission' from their superiors. (When I mention this point in presentations, principals smile and nod, while system officials look apprehensive.)

In line with their outward-looking, positive nature, these principals were found to be informed risk-takers. When an opportunity or problem arose, or even if things appeared to be going well, they were prepared to experiment and to offer support to those proposing initiatives. They were also prepared to risk time, money and failure, and empowered others to do the same. One Principal commented: 'People are allowed to make mistakes here'. Staff at other schools made similar comments. These principals didn't say 'yes' to every request, but they do use 'yes' to empower and recognise others. (Less effective principals I've observed use 'no' as a means of controlling staff.)

These principals didn't dismiss a good idea because they hadn't thought of it, and were not threatened by confident, talented staff. Their attitude could be summed up as 'Let's give it a go', although this decision was based on a rapid, yet full consideration of the issue under deliberation.

Site reports at three separate schools illustrated this approach:

'The Principal's leadership style is a critical precursor to the process being undertaken at [the school]. She is a risk-taker and is prepared to "work the system" to achieve her goals.'

'Leadership at the school is outstanding. The Principal cultivates the trust of his staff by showing support for them to take risks and they return that trust by a willingness to improve processes that will benefit students. The Principal takes a strong role in selection of staff.'

'The senior Executive of the school, and in particular the Principal, is held in high regard. The Principal is described [by staff] as a leader who provides subtle guidance and direction and allows people to try new ideas if they will improve students' learning.'

Principals were found to have a major influence on the development and application of school policies and programs. Some leaders and staff characterised these as 'zero tolerance', but in reality this was more a case of having clear guidelines, effective communication, and consistent application, with everyone knowing where he or she 'stands'. In this respect, the standard and routine things were done well. Students knew what to do and who to seek help from when problems arose and often this understanding began in primary 'feeder' schools, with visits from key secondary staff and orientation visits to the secondary school playing an important role in easing the Year 6 to 7 primary–secondary transition.

However, this is not to imply rigidity, with principals and other leaders prepared to consider every case on its merits and to exercise discretion and compassion when needed. We saw and heard of many examples of such flexibility and compassion (see below). These leaders are able to sustain flexibility and innovation despite system accountabilities and constraints.

3 Personal qualities and relationships

Principals at the outstanding sites were found to possess and utilise high-level interpersonal skills and were liked and respected, often, but not always, by all. Their motives and actions were trusted by others. They used people's names when out and about in the school and showed interest in what others were doing. They demonstrated empathy and compassion and were available at short notice when needed. They were seen to work for the school rather than for themselves and modelled 'do as I do', rather than 'do as I say'. They epitomised the notion of the 'servant leader', while being unmistakably in control.

Students, staff and community members spoke positively of principals who were 'open', 'honest', 'fair', 'friendly' and 'approachable'. They valued the fact that the principal would 'listen' to them and hear what they had to say, thus showing respect. A head teacher (faculty head) at one school noted:

> '[The Principal] has attracted creative people in the past five years. He is very supportive of staff, a great mentor. He creates a strong learning culture at the school. He knows the system and works well at district level ... He is highly visible in the school. Everyone feels they are special, and valued as people. He sets a very positive tone in the school.'

A school counsellor [psychologist] at the same school commented:

> '[The Principal] is one of the best I have worked with. Students know they can speak to him. He is highly approachable. He can speak in a nice tone to staff, parents and students. He is not authoritarian but he does set parameters. He is a good listener, supportive and encouraging. He will not contradict any proposal you present for his consideration but may suggest ideas to build on your proposal. He leads and guides rather than dictates.'

A Year 11 student at another school spoke of the personal qualities of her principal:

> 'The Principal is a nice guy. He talks to us. He even knows our name. You often see him out walking around in the playground.'

[The site report from this Principal noted:] 'Parents, too, spoke about 'his open door policy' commenting that they felt comfortable phoning the Principal to discuss issues relating to their own children or the school.'

A site report from another school noted:

'The school Principal has a genuine concern for the wellbeing of the students and an excellent rapport with both staff and students. He appears to make a considerable effort to get out of his office and has a high profile around the school.'

These leaders were seen to possess and exhibit the characteristics they expect of others, such as honesty, fairness, compassion, commitment, reliability, hard work, trustworthiness and professionalism. They provide a 'good example'. They also tended to have a social justice agenda, believing in education for social good and the importance of putting students first. A site report noted:

'The Principal creates a school culture in which recognition of differences is central. She sees herself as having a vocation of social justice that permeates much of the school. She believes in the dignity of humanity, has a sense of social justice and is able to translate this into effective action.'

Another site report noted:

'[The Principal] sets a very positive tone at the school. He is not a "micro-manager", and gives staff "space" and discretion to develop initiatives. He is seen as a person who can influence and role model rather than demand compliance. He is not defensive, not authoritarian and gives a measure of autonomy while overseeing effectively. He puts the focus on the enterprise, rather than on himself and ... models openness and self-evaluation. He cultivates a climate of trust. He places great trust in his staff and strongly supports them in any initiatives. The trust he places in his staff is returned, as indicated by a willingness to participate in process improvement and innovative problem solving.'

A research team at another school reported on what has been termed 'moral' or 'authentic' leadership[55]:

'An important part of the success of this school, as with any school, is attributable to the role of the Principal. The Principal ... models quality interpersonal relationships and has an established presence and role in the management of student welfare programs. The professional and interpersonal dynamics which he nurtures and encourages in the faculties of the school lead to constant concern and productive dialogue about welfare and curriculum areas. During his interview the Principal articulated his drive to develop "programs that are fair to kids".'

Intellectual capacity is a factor frequently overlooked in discussions on successful leadership and quality teaching. These principals were generally seen to possess a high degree of intelligence and imagination. They were good judges of individuals, astute, and were able to balance 'big picture' issues with finer detail. They had good recall of the multitude of issues, facts and problems that make up the work of the principal and could pick up the threads of previous, often truncated conversations. They could deal with many issues concurrently and knew when to consult and to build consensus and when to be decisive and to act alone. They understood school, departmental and community 'politics' and had the courage to make unpopular decisions when these were in the best long-term interests of the school.

They were good communicators and listeners and provided prompt feedback and appropriate recognition to staff. Their support for staff was frequently noted in site visit reports. They made themselves available and were prepared to 'drop everything' and 'roll their sleeves up' to assist when and where necessary. In this way, they 'led from the front'. We were told of various instances where crises had occurred (sudden death of staff or students, violent incidents, tragedies of various sorts) where the principal had stepped into a difficult situation to take control and had supported staff and students to work through the issue.

4 Vision, expectations and a culture of success

These principals did not attempt to 'build Rome in a day'. They recognised the imperative for change and improvement but also realised that over-burdened and at times dispirited staff cannot be given more than they can reasonably be expected to handle. However, this does not preclude them from being decisive when necessary and 'pushing' staff at times.

Recognition of context is important, but it's also important not to be so bound up in context that one fails to see the wider environment or to act. Context can be like quicksand. These leaders managed to have a broader perspective, yet recognised and addressed local context.

These leaders also possessed a long-term vision and agenda and were prepared to work towards this. Put simply, I like to define vision as 'knowing where you are going'. There is no point in trying to stand still or to keep change at bay, as the world will pass you by and the organisation will be disadvantaged if you do.

These principals set meaningful, achievable goals rather than short-term targets. The norm for principals was six to seven years in their current school, and when they had not been in their position for this length of time, had often served in the same school as a deputy principal or faculty head, helping them to 'know the territory'. An implication is that 'quick fixes' or 'flurries of change'[56] are unlikely to be successful. It takes time to break existing patterns of thought, behaviour and practice and to achieve effective and sustainable change. In a number of sites, the school had been in decline prior to the appointment of the Principal, suffering a fall in reputation and losing students, staff and resources. It had taken time and much effort, but things have 'turned around' such that some of these schools were now full to capacity with the Principal having to deal with the politics of not being able to accommodate all requests for enrolment.

These leaders identified and nurtured the 'seeds' for change and school improvement. They recognised and valued the history of the school and used what has been achieved or what exists as a platform for further school improvement, thereby releasing latent 'organisational energy'. The site report for one school identified for ICT, which had previously been in decline but was now 'bursting at the seams' with students, noted:

> 'The current educational outcomes have their antecedents in the appointment of the current Principal [five years previously]. Staff universally point to her leadership, as well as the influence of others, on the school achieving outstanding educational outcomes since her appointment ... Clearly, the process is being driven from the top. The Principal has championed the infusion of ICT since her arrival ... She is aware of the potential of ICT as a tool for learning and discovery.'

An aspect of the vision demonstrated by principals was the ability to see the 'big picture' and to communicate this to staff. A site team noted:

> 'The Principal's leadership provides key input on critical issues, supports the positive culture of the school and helps to establish "big picture issues" as priorities. Under the current Principal, [the school] has a commitment to student welfare, with an emphasis on continual improvement and ensuring quality communication with parents.'

One way this vision is communicated and becomes reality is through the expectations of the Principal. It was found that these leaders had high and clearly understood expectations of others (and importantly, themselves) and did not easily accept 'second best'. As noted by one member of staff:

> 'The Principal has expectations and standards which are passed on and these things happen'.

> [The Principal himself stated:] 'If you don't have someone 'shaking the tree' you can get the same lessons for the twentieth time'.

Another Principal commented: 'I talk about performance all the time, give credit to teachers, ensure they know I am pleased'. This was confirmed by the site report for the school, which noted: '[The Principal] is up-front and clear on expectations'. The report also noted:

> 'Strong and clear leadership was evident across the school. The Principal articulates the school's vision and models the characteristics of community which are ascribed to by all stakeholders.'

A deputy principal from another school reported:

'We are here to develop clear policies and a safe and secure environment. We want to remove inconsistency faster so that everything runs smoothly. We need ways of doing things that are agreed on. There is a clear expectation that you do your job the best you can—a structure is in place and an agreed-upon way of doing things ... Part of it is to supervise and help teachers set priorities so we all actively engage in a cycle of improvement and development ... What is most important is dogged persistence. Following the same procedures is important. Having documents and policies is common sense but many schools don't do it.'

The Principal from the above school concurred, the research team noting:

'To [the Principal], the key to running a successful school is "commitment and high expectations, particularly of the head teachers. Kids don't want to be patronised. They want a disciplined place with rules and consequences. Over the years a school loses energy ... All schools need good structures and systems in place. Teachers should have the belief that kids can learn".'

These leaders were aware of the importance and value of providing professional, pleasant facilities and of treating staff professionally, expecting a high standard of professionalism in return. Principals placed a high priority on school cleanliness and a pleasant environment. It was considered important that graffiti and mess were dealt with promptly, with gardens, seating and shade areas improved and maintained. Staffrooms, classrooms and other spaces were clean and pleasant, with resources diverted for improved furniture and fittings. These principals realised the importance of school pride, identification with the school, and its reputation in the community. Students and staff responded to this and spoke in positive terms of the school. Even in the large urban schools visited by the research team, it was rare to see rubbish or evidence of vandalism.

One school encapsulated much of the above. The school was well over a century old and had a mixture of buildings from different eras. The site was a cramped one in a highly urbanised area. Prior to the appointment of the Principal the school had been feeling the effects of competition from other schools and systems and had been in decline. However, this has been turned around and there was now pressure on facilities. The Principal (and the previous Principal) had instigated refurbishment of the staff common room. The staff now referred to this as the 'Qantas Club' and they could be seen meeting and working with other staff and students in the pleasant surroundings. A cappuccino machine was installed. The old, dusty, open canteen had been walled in with translucent sheeting, rubber industrial floor coverings placed over the bare concrete, and aluminium cafe tables and chairs installed. Pot plants had been provided and older, internet-linked computers arranged around one wall. The canteen was now in effect an 'Internet cafe' and senior common room. A roster system ensured that students without home Internet access had priority use of computers. Students responded positively to this situation and graffiti and damage were minimal. Despite its large student population, the site visit team was impressed with the cleanliness of the school. The effect of all of this had been to lift both pride and expectations for behaviour in the school.

A further way vision and expectations for the school were communicated was through recognition of staff and student achievement. Principals saw and maintained teaching and learning as the central purpose of the school (see 'Focus on students, learning and teaching' below) and were observed to take every opportunity to recognise student and staff achievement and to 'talk up the school'. They utilised a variety of means including assemblies, newsletters, announcements, awards, letters, personal approaches, visits to classrooms and the local press. They had helped to create a positive school climate of high expectations and striving for success. They sought ways for every student to feel and be successful and for every teacher to receive appropriate recognition. Such recognition was perceived by students and staff as authentic and received in good humour. It eventually makes an impact and an upward cycle is set in motion. One site report for a central school (K to Year 10) noted:

> 'When he arrived ... the Principal was struck by the extent to which [School] assemblies were occasions for berating students rather than celebrating meritorious achievements. He set about reviewing the [student] welfare policy K–10 (it has been reviewed three times in the last ten years) to emphasise more of the positive aspects of the school and its students' achievements.'

The Principal of the above school commented:

> 'What we've now got in place is a welfare policy that addresses the whole school needs that the community has had input to, and when you read the document, it is overwhelmingly positive. I think that has been a major change in getting people back on task. The "woe is me" side of things is starting to change ... I noticed in my first year that the main focus of the [full school] assembly ... was to berate ... Even at the end of the year, we only had about five to nine kids achieving gold levels [for good behaviour] ... even the [School] Captains didn't achieve it, so I set about turning that around and last year we had 120 on gold and we had a big celebration.'

A site team from another school reported:

> 'The school holds timetabled assemblies of recognition for rewarding behaviour and achievement, while the Principal holds presentation BBQs at which every student who has not been referred under the discipline system is presented with a Certificate of Appreciation. This is an innovation of the current Principal.'

'Talking up' also took place beyond the school. One site report for a school identified for exceptional outcomes in English noted:

> 'The Principal ... takes every opportunity to promote the work of the teachers, citing occasions where she has shown English units [of work developed at the school] at meetings of teachers held at country centres.'

It was striking how frequently principals were given credit for school improvement by staff, students and community members, yet how these principals usually attempted to deflect such praise to others. The site report for another school commented:

> 'The Principal was full of praise for her "impressive executive" and the head teachers with whom she works. She said, "dread them going". In fact, they said the same about her.'

Such generosity of spirit and lack of professional jealousy is another aspect of moral or authentic leadership, and was seen to positively influence the climate and culture of the schools concerned.

5 Teacher learning, responsibility and trust

Principals (and other leaders) were found to place a high value on teacher learning and funded staff development inside and outside the school. They modelled professional learning, being prepared to learn from teachers, students and others. They released staff to engage in professional development activities and brought others into the school to provide assistance. Principals said they 'never' turned down a legitimate and reasonable request for teacher development assistance. These principals were prepared to invest school funds to promote teachers' professional learning. This connects with the whole school focus on students and their learning mentioned later. A site report team noted:

> 'Professional development is considered to be an important component in improving the skills and knowledge of all school staff. The Principal has increased the budget for training and development across the school ... to ensure that many more teachers can be offered a chance to improve their teaching.'

The research team at another site reported:

> 'The Principal gives considerable encouragement to staff to participate in professional development and several people commented on how adept she was at identifying and utilising sources of funding to enable staff to participate in professional development activity.'

While these principals rarely said no to any reasonable request for professional development, there was an expectation that those taking up these opportunities would in-service staff so that the benefits were maximised. Staff development days and meetings were often given over to providing teachers with new skills and knowledge and the confidence to try different teaching approaches. Through empowering, encouraging and supporting teachers to become learners, these leaders acknowledged and fostered the leadership of others. They respected and recognised others' capacities and achievements. They identified talent and potential and encouraged, 'coached' and supported these people, sometimes at the risk of being accused of favouritism.

They recognised that if change and improvement were to take root in the school culture, they needed to distribute responsibility and leadership capacity throughout the school and to trust people. Sharing of responsibility—distributing leadership as opposed to delegation—also assisted in successful leadership succession. A number of principals joked about making themselves redundant through the development of others.

A site report at a school identified for success with literacy across the curriculum noted:

> 'The Principal has created the context in which these programs operate. There is widespread agreement that the Principal "allows" people to take the lead with ideas.
>
> [A staff member said:] 'We are given "permission to play here by the Principal—always encouraged to try things out".'
>
> 'One English teacher told us that "the Principal does a lot of allowing" and she saw the Principal as having created the "productive environment" for her to grow as a teacher.

The issue of trust and giving people 'space' was seen as an important factor in teacher development. A teacher in a school identified for outstanding outcomes in English as a Second Language commented:

> 'The Principal is very supportive in that he is a good leader but he knows we are doing our job, he doesn't interfere, but he's always there if need be. The last Principal was terrific too.'

Another aspect of trust and shared responsibility is that of 'blame' when something goes wrong. These principals showed a propensity to give and share credit, but to also shoulder responsibility.

6 Student support, common purpose and collaboration

Whether the focus of the site visit was on a curriculum area or a program, it was found that student support in all its guises was central to the exceptional outcomes being achieved.

Student support was seen as broader than formal 'welfare' and 'discipline' policies and programs and was perceived as every teacher's responsibility. Student support was found to have a predominantly academic focus of 'getting students back into learning', rather than being about 'warm fuzzies', or 'enhancing self-concept', to use the words of a number of teachers interviewed. Thus, student support and academic achievement are not seen as mutually exclusive, but mutually reinforcing.[57]

Principals and other leaders facilitated the centrality of student welfare through supporting welfare teams and ensuring a common approach and commitment. Students understood and supported student welfare policies and procedures and perceived student welfare as something done for them, rather than to them. Clear communication, understanding, and consistent and 'fair' application lie at the heart of successful school welfare programs and procedures. One site team noted:

> 'In terms of the alignment between *The Adelaide Goals*, welfare is seen as the basis of everything in the school. "Welfare allows learning to happen [Principal]. There is a lot of PD [personal development] on welfare, behaviour management/welfare systems. For many of the kids, we are the family and we talk about that considerably" ... 70 per cent of [the Principal's] time is welfare, though much is picked up by the two DPs. The background of the kids is often horrific, e.g., teachers have recently supplied heaters and mattresses for a family whose income and savings were gambled away. "Every kid is valued", [the Principal] emphasises, and THAT drives the emphasis on literacy, welfare, numeracy, ICT. Her core philosophy is that "the needs of the kids drive the curriculum", and not the other way around.'

While these schools were not Utopian nor free of discipline and behaviour problems, a common view expressed by staff, students and community members was that student behaviour had improved over time, with commensurate positive effects on school success and reputation.[k] The clear consensus was that 'students cannot learn until their welfare needs have been met'. Improved student behaviour creates an environment where learning can occur.

In a high percentage of schools—both faculty and program sites—it was observed that principals had identified and utilised a central focus, for example, ICT,

---

k   As noted earlier, a mistake that some teachers and schools make is to try and get 'control' of the students before they are taught anything. Good teaching obviates the need to gain control over students, with good behaviour a product, and not necessarily a precursor, of good teaching and learning. In reality, it is a mutually reinforcing cycle.

assessment, literacy, pedagogy, student welfare. Programs to support and develop such areas brought members and parts of the school together, leading to better understanding and commitment and improved efficiencies and outcomes.

However, these leaders were also pragmatic. They knew it is impossible to gain unanimous support, approval and commitment from staff. Rather than attempting to move all staff simultaneously, they concentrated on those who were talented and committed and provided them with support (encouragement, time, resources, and professional development). These pockets of staff might be within faculties or across the school. They were empowered and encouraged by the Principal, who facilitated bringing like-minded staff together. There is a danger in this, in that some staff may be left behind or be resentful and obstructive if they are not included. However, it is equally true that 'if you wait for everyone to get on the bus, the bus will never leave'.

As part of their risk-taking approach, principals gambled that the 'contagion effects' of committed staff and demonstrated success would bring some—but probably not all—negative or reluctant people 'on-side'.

7 Focus on students, learning and teaching: the core category

The overarching theme emerging from analysis of data pertaining to leadership in the schools where exceptional outcomes were found to be occurring in Years 7 to 10 was the belief that the central purpose and focus of the school—its 'core business'—was teaching and learning. These principals and their staff recognised that every effort must be made to provide an environment where each student can experience success and academic, personal and social growth. Even where schools had been identified for success in cross-school programs, it was apparent that there was a central focus on assisting and equipping the individual student so that he or she could succeed academically. 'Knowing' each student as both a learner and as a person was of fundamental importance. A site team noted:

> 'The Head Teacher of English mentioned the support for teaching and learning provided by the Executive when she was asked why she thought [...] High School was selected for the AESOP project. She considered that an important factor was having a "principal who values core business and is enthusiastic about it".'

This view held by the head teacher was confirmed by the site visit team:

> 'The current Principal has headed [the school] for two-and-a-half years ... As Principal she has been concerned with putting "good structures and systems" in place to support the "core business of learning and teaching" in the classroom. The Principal reflected that she has been able to take her "eye off the curriculum" and put in place "frameworks for systems, so teachers are able to meet the demands of learning and teaching".'

A site report from another school noted:

> 'The arrival of the current Principal ... resulted in improvements in the school's success. Since [then] there has been a school-wide focus on teaching and learning. The Principal has undoubtedly contributed to a revival of the school's reputation and an increased focus on academic achievement.'

Principals were found to be relentless in their quest for enhanced student achievement. They did not become distracted and 'bogged down' by the administrative demands of the principalship, finding ways to concentrate their energies on instructional leadership.

They constantly reminded students, staff and the community that the core purpose of the school was teaching and learning. Their external awareness and engagement; their bias towards innovation; their personal qualities; their vision and expectations and the climate of success that results from this; their emphasis on teacher learning; their trust of staff, and their focus on student support, common purpose and collaboration—were all geared to the facilitation of student achievement. Their focus on students, their welfare and learning, acted as a touchstone for all that happened in the school.

In schools of lower socio-economic background it was observed that principals and other leaders placed a high priority on the 'personal' and 'social' aspects of education, with a view to creating an environment where students could experience academic success to improve their life chances. This was consistent with their social justice agenda and high expectations for all mentioned previously.

Principals were not directly responsible for the exceptional educational outcomes observed, but their leadership was found to be a crucial factor in creating and sustaining an environment where teachers can teach, students can learn, and such outcomes can occur. Their influence on school climate and culture, teachers' professional learning and successful teaching was significant.

Comment of the AESOP findings

The set of personal qualities, professional attributes, values, philosophies, approaches and actions listed above might appear idealistic or prescriptive. I realise that this sounds like the job description and person specifications for a 'super principal', but this is what we found.

There is a danger when attributes or factors such as those outlined above are regarded as 'quick fixes' or 'recipes' for success and the importance of school history, context and change are not recognised.

The fact that some of the principals and their staff had spent years reaching present levels of performance and achievement refutes the notion of easy solutions or quick responses to big challenges and problems. It was apparent, however, that it is possible to set up an upward cycle of improvement. The worrying point is that without adequate leadership succession, these hard-fought-for gains can quickly be dissipated. Going up is harder than going down.

Further, the attributes, actions or qualities of principals outlined in this chapter need to be considered as both product (output) and process (input) variables, in that they contribute to future change and improvement. For example, it takes time and effort to develop effective communication methods in a school but once this occurs, effective communication becomes an asset or resource for further improvement. In the majority, if not all of the outstanding sites, it was clear that further improvement was taking place in the context of an 'upward cycle' of success mentioned previously.

One of my favourite quotes from AESOP that speaks to the processes outlined above came from a deputy principal:

'In this school we make plans now, not excuses.'

In other words, changing mindsets is just as important as changing structures or what people know and can do—if not more important.

Finally, as noted previously, the degree of influence of principals was somewhat surprising, given that the project aim was to identify and investigate faculties and teams producing outstanding educational outcomes in Years 7 to 10, rather than effective schools as a whole, or effective principals. This finding could partly call into question the current concentration on the individual teacher as the major within-school factor in student accomplishment. While there is little doubt as to the importance of the individual teacher, based on these findings and the literature in general, principals can, as noted, play key roles in creating and maintaining the conditions and environment where teachers can teach effectively and students can learn.

Concluding remarks

Underestimating and re-estimating educational leadership[58]

Research findings on school-based influences on student achievement, especially the importance of the teacher, have led some to conclude that leadership has very little influence on teaching, and little effect on student achievement.[59]

This view is partly a methodological artefact arising from inappropriate and varying methods being utilised in attempts to reveal the effects—direct, indirect, antecedents, and recursive—of leadership on teaching and student achievement.[60] There is also the related problem of definition, with there being literally hundreds of definitions and conceptions of leadership.[61] Loose and varying definition makes accurate measurement of leadership effectiveness problematic.[62]

W. Edwards Deming, the 'father' or 'guru' of total quality management, consistently put the view that 'the most important measures are both unknown and unknowable'.[63] Albert Einstein is reputed to have said something similar: 'Not everything that counts can be counted, and not everything that can be counted counts'.[1] We know that teaching is important yet teacher effectiveness and performance are equally difficult to define and measure, as evident in the current debates over teacher performance and 'merit' pay. The concept of rewarding teachers on merit is simple and has wide appeal, yet once performance is defined and 'unpacked', the issue becomes far from simple.[64] It follows that if defining and measuring teacher performance is difficult, measuring the influence that leadership might have on teacher and then student performance is even more so. However, this is not a reason to avoid establishing these links or effects.

Additional issues with the measurement of leadership effectiveness include the fact that at any time, any leader will be perceived differently by those he or she works with: some will welcome a new approach, others will cling to the past; some will want decisiveness, others collaboration; what is needed in one situation or part of the organisation may be unsuitable in others. Thus, opinion on any facet of leadership can be different and/or polarised.[65] In turn, leadership has been found to be the major predictor of teachers' satisfaction with school-based phenomena such as supervision, communication and decision-making[66], for better or worse.

As noted, studies of school leadership traditionally focused on the Principal, but today it is recognised that there can be many leaders in a school, including deputy principals, heads of department, program and committee chairs and teachers; it is agreed and seen as desirable that leadership is distributed. The roles of student and community leadership also need to be recognised.

Put simply, in assigning a value to the contribution leadership can make to teacher effectiveness and student achievement, we need to ask what leader or leaders, and what aspects of leadership—managerial, administrative, instructional, developmental, relational, transformational, school climate and culture, or integrated—we are attempting to quantify.

There is thus a complex dynamic underpinning what happens in classrooms and schools that is both difficult to untangle and which can vary within and between schools and over time.

Despite these difficulties of definition and measurement, I believe that the influence of educational leadership on teacher and student performance has generally been underestimated, and that measured direct effects of leadership, which some researchers have found to be very low, are outweighed by indirect and antecedent

---

1 Although some have attributed this to William Bruce Cameron: http://quoteinvestigator.com/2010/05/26/everything-counts-einstein/

effects such as school history, context and organisation, with school climate acting as an intermediate variable between leadership and classroom achievement.[67]

Another aspect of the influence of leadership is that while it is difficult for leaders and those they lead to lift a school's performance—those 'turnaround' schools in the AESOP project had taken six to seven years to recover—it is remarkable how quickly and far a school's climate and performance can fall under bad leadership.

The three research case studies above, as well as the findings from other research projects cited, have confirmed just how powerful an influence leadership can have on school and teaching effectiveness and on student outcomes.

It is true that quality teaching lies at the heart of attempts to raise student outcomes overall, and to close achievement gaps associated with factors such as SES, family background, geographic isolation, non-English speaking background and Aboriginality, but the role that leaders can play in the achievement of these goals is significant.

In the 21st century, educational leaders need to be able to 'talk the talk', and more importantly, 'walk the walk', on approaches that place the individual student and his or her advancement at the centre of the school within a context of evidence-based professional practice by teachers.[68]

In order to make best teaching practice common practice, preparation for and the enactment of instructional leadership, connected with teachers' initial and ongoing professional learning for evidence-based practice, are essential.

Endnotes

1 Barber, M., Whelan, F., & Clark, M. (2010). *Capturing the leadership premium: How the world's top school systems are building leadership capacity for the future.* New York, NY: McKinsey & Company; Day, C., Sammons, P., Hopkins, D. et al. (2009). *The impact of school leadership on pupil outcomes.* Nottingham, England: University of Nottingham; Leithwood, K., Patten, S., & Jantzi, D. (2010). Testing a conception of how school leadership influences student learning. *Educational Administration Quarterly, 46*(5), 671–706; Schleicher, A. (2012). (Ed.). *Preparing teachers and developing school leaders for the 21st century: Lessons from around the world.* Paris, France: OECD Publishing; Wahlstrom, K. (2008). Leadership and learning: What these articles tell us. *Educational Administration Quarterly, 44*(4), 593–597.

2 AITSL [Australian Institute for Teaching and School Leadership]. (2014). *Australian professional standard for principals and the leadership profiles.* Melbourne, Victoria: Author.

3 Leithwood, K., Jantzi, D., & Steinbach, R. (2002). Leadership practices for accountable schools. In K. Leithwood, & P. Hallinger (Eds.). *Second international handbook of educational leadership and administration.* Dordrecht, Netherlands: Kluwer (pp. 849–879); Dinham, S., Collarbone, P., Evans, M., & Mackay, A. (2013). The development and proposed use of a national standard for principals in Australia. *Educational Management, Administration and Leadership, 41*(4), 466–482.

4 Harris, A. (2009). (Ed.). *Distributed school leadership: Different perspectives.* London, England: Springer Press.

5 AITSL [Australian Institute for Teaching and School Leadership]. (2011). *National [Australian] Professional Standards for Teachers.* Melbourne, Victoria: Author.

6   Hattie, J. (2009). *Visible learning—A synthesis of over 800 meta-analyses relating to achievement*. London, England: Routledge. (p. 83)
7   Wright, S., Horn, S., & Sanders, W. (1997). Teacher and classroom context effects on student achievement: Implications for teacher evaluation. *Journal of Personnel Evaluation in Education, 11*, 57–67.
8   Wahlstrom, K., & Seashore Louis, K. (2008). How teachers experience principal leadership: The roles of professional community, trust, efficacy, and shared responsibility. *Educational Administration Quarterly, 44*(4), 458–495. (p. 459)
9   Hattie, J. (2012). *Visible learning for teachers*. London, England: Routledge. (p. 252)
10 Dinham, S. (2008). *How to get your school moving and improving: An evidence-based approach*. Melbourne, Victoria: ACER Press. (p. 15)
11 Marzano, R., Waters, T., & McNulty, B. (2005). *School leadership that works: From research to results*. Alexandria: ASCD. (pp. 10–12)
12 Robinson, V., Lloyd, C., & Rowe, K. (2008). The impact of leadership on student outcomes: An analysis of the differential effects of leadership types. *Educational Administration Quarterly, 44*, 635–674. (p. 638). Copyright © 2008 by V. Robinson, C. Lloyd and K. Rowe. All text extracts from this article are reprinted by Permission of Sage Publications, Inc.
13 Hallinger, P. (2005). Instructional leadership and the school principal: A passing fancy that refuses to fade away. *Leadership and Policy in Schools, 4*, 221–239.
14 Hallinger, P. (2005). (p. 228)
15 Robinson, V., Lloyd, C., & Rowe, K. (2008). (p. 639)
16 See Dinham, S. (1998). Restructuring: The myths, the realities—and survival. *The Practising Administrator, 20*(3), 4–5, 51.
17 Dinham, S., & Rowe, K. (2007). *Teaching and learning in middle schooling: A review of the literature—A report to the New Zealand Ministry of Education*. Melbourne, Victoria: ACER; Hattie, J. (2009).
18 Robinson, V., Lloyd, C., & Rowe, K. (2008). (p. 666)
19 See also Chase, G., & Kane, M. (1983). *The principal as instructional leader: How much more time before we act?* Denver: Education Commission of the States.
20 See Barber, M., & Mourshed, M. (2007). *How the world's best-performing school systems come out on top*. New York, NY: McKinsey & Company.
21 MCEETYA. (2008). Melbourne Declaration on Educational Goals for Young Australians. Canberra, Australia: Author.
22 Barber, M., & Mourshed, M. (2007). (p. 7)
23 Barber, M., & Mourshed, M. (2007). (p. 28)
24 Dinham, S. (2009). The relationship between distributed leadership and action learning in schools: A case study. In A. Harris (Ed.), *Distributed school leadership: Different perspectives*. Dordrecht, Netherlands: Springer Press.
25 Robinson, V., Lloyd, C., & Rowe, K. (2008). (p. 669)
26 Leithwood, K., Louis, K., Anderson, S., & Wahlstrom, K. (2004). *Review of research—how leadership influences student learning*. New York, NY: The Wallace Foundation. (p. 5)
27 Robinson, V., Hohepa, M., & Lloyd, C. (2009). *School leadership and student outcomes: Identifying what works and why*. Wellington, New Zealand: New Zealand Ministry of Education. All extracts from this publication have been reproduced with permission. See https://creativecommons.org/licenses/by/4.0/legalcode
28 See also Robinson, V., Lloyd, C., & Rowe, K. (2008).
29 Robinson, V., Hohepa, M., & Lloyd, C. (2009). (p. 40)
30 Robinson, V., Hohepa, M., & Lloyd, C. (2009). (p. 39)

31   Robinson, V., Hohepa, M., & Lloyd, C. (2009). (p. 40)
32   Robinson, V., Hohepa, M., & Lloyd, C. (2009). (p. 41)
33   Australian Government. (2011). *Review of funding for schooling—Final report.* Canberra: Department of Education, Employment and Workplace Relations.
34   Robinson, V., Hohepa, M., & Lloyd, C. (2009). (pp. 41–42)
35   Robinson, V., Hohepa, M., & Lloyd, C. (2009). (p. 42)
36   Robinson, V., Hohepa, M., & Lloyd, C. (2009). (pp. 42–43)
37   Ayres, P., Dinham, S., & Sawyer, W. (1999). *Successful teaching in the NSW Higher School Certificate.* Sydney: NSW Department of Education and Training.
38   Robinson, V., Hohepa, M., & Lloyd, C. (2009). (pp. 43–47)
39   Aubusson, P., Brady, L., & Dinham, S. (2005). *Action learning: What works?* A research report prepared for the New South Wales Department of Education and Training. Sydney, New South Wales: University of Technology Sydney.
40   Day, C., Sammons, P., Hopkins, D., Harris, A., Leithwood, K., Qing, G., Brown, E., Ahtaridou, E., & Kington, A. (2009). *The impact of school leadership on pupil outcomes.* Nottingham, England: University of Nottingham.
41   Day, C. et al. (2009). (p. 1)
42   Day, C. et al. (2009) (pp. x–xvii)
43   Robinson, V., Hohepa, M., & Lloyd, C. (2009).
44   For more details on the project and its findings see: Dinham, S. (2007). *Leadership for exceptional educational outcomes.* Teneriffe, Qld: Post Pressed.
45   Ayres, P., Dinham, S., & Sawyer, W. (1999). *Successful teaching in the NSW Higher School Certificate.* Sydney: NSW Department of Education and Training. See also Ayres, P., Dinham, S., & Sawyer, W. (2004). Effective teaching in the context of a Grade 12 high stakes external examination in New South Wales, Australia. *British Educational Research Journal, 30*(1), 141–165.
46   Dinham, S., & Rowe, K. (2007).
47   MCEETYA. (1999). *The Adelaide Declaration on National Goals for Schooling in the Twenty-first Century.* Canberra, Australia: Ministerial Council on Education, Employment, Training and Youth Affairs.
48   Dinham, S. (2007b). *Leadership for exceptional educational outcomes.* Teneriffe, Qld: Post Pressed. (p. 15)
49   QSR. (2002). *NUD*IST 6.* Melbourne, Victoria: QSR International.
50   Strauss, A., & Corbin, J. (1990). *Basics of qualitative research: Grounded theory procedures and techniques.* Newbury Park, CA: Sage.
51   Dinham, S. (2007a). The secondary head of department and the achievement of exceptional student outcomes. *Journal of Educational Administration, 45*(1), 62–79; Dinham, S. (2005). Principal leadership for outstanding educational outcomes. *Journal of Educational Administration, 43*(4), 338–356.
52   Dinham, S. (2007a).
53   Dinham, S. (2007b). *Leadership for exceptional educational outcomes.* Teneriffe, Qld: Post Pressed; Dinham, S. (2007a).
54   Dinham, S., & Scott, C. (2000). Moving into the third, outer domain of teacher satisfaction. *Journal of Educational Administration, 38*(4), 379–396.
55   Duignan, P., & Bhindi, N. (1997). Leadership for a new century: Authenticity, intentionality, spirituality, and sensibility. *Educational Management and Administration, 25*(2), 117–132.
56   Hargreaves, A., & Fink, D. (2004). The seven principles of sustainable leadership. *Educational Leadership, 61*(7), 8–13.

57 Scott, C., & Dinham, S. (2005). Parenting, teaching and self-esteem. *The Australian Educational Leader, 27*(1), 28–30; Dinham, S., & Scott, C. (2007). Parenting, teaching and leadership styles. *The Australian Educational Leader, 29*(1), 30–32; 45.

58 This section draws upon Dinham, S. (2007). How schools get moving and keep improving: Leadership for teacher learning, student success and school renewal. *Australian Journal of Education, 51*(3), 263–275.

59 See Opdenakker, M-C., & Van Damme, J. (2007). Do school context, student composition and school leadership affect school practice and outcomes in secondary education? *British Educational Research Journal, 33*(2), 179–206.

60 De Maeyer, S., Rymenans, R., Van Petegem, P., van den Bergh, H., & Rijlaarsdam, G. (2007). Educational leadership and pupil achievement: The choice of a valid conceptual model to test effects in school effectiveness research. *School Effectiveness and School Improvement, 18*(2), 125–145.

61 Northouse, P. (2007). (pp. 1–13)

62 Bennett, N., Crawford, M., & Cartwright, M. (Eds.). (2003). *Effective educational leadership*. London: Paul Chapman. (pp. ix–x)

63 See, for example, Deming, W. E. (1982). *Out of the crisis*. Cambridge, MA: Massachusetts Institute of Technology.

64 Dinham, S. (2006). The merits of merit pay for teachers. *Education Review, 16*(07), October, 12–13.

65 See Scott, C., & Dinham, S. (2003). The development of scales to measure teacher and school executive occupational satisfaction. *Journal of Educational Administration, 41*(1), 74–86.

66 Dinham, S., & Scott, C. (2000). Moving into the third, outer domain of teacher satisfaction. *Journal of Educational Administration, 38*(4), 379–396.

67 De Maeyer et al. (2007). (pp. 140–142)

68 Dinham, S. (2013). Connecting instructional leadership with clinical teaching practice. *Australian Journal of Education, 57*(3), 220–231.

CHAPTER 11

What are the features and benefits of distributed and teacher leadership?

INTRODUCTION

As noted previously, there have been changes in conceptions of educational leadership over recent decades. An earlier focus on educational administration and later management has turned more to leadership for enhanced teaching and learning, that is, instructional leadership. There had been concern with an over-emphasis of the supposed attributes of the charismatic, heroic, transformational, 'super leader' and the finding that such leaders can be negatively associated with leadership sustainability called into question the wisdom of seeking out and appointing such leaders.[1]

Additionally, an earlier focus on formal leadership—especially the Principal—had broadened to consider the influence of others in formal school leadership positions and of teachers, distributed (or distributive) leadership.[2] Although the concept of distributed leadership can be traced back to social psychology in the 1950s, it is only in the last few decades that the concept has received widespread prominence and attention[3], although problems of loose definition and debates over impact remain.[4]

These changes in how educational leadership has been conceived and enacted reflect a number of current realities: that teaching and learning should be the prime focus of the school; that principals cannot bear all the burden of school leadership due to the increasing pressures and demands being placed upon them and the schools they lead; that others in formal leadership positions in schools are also under pressure[5], and that the contribution to educational outcomes of distributed leadership has tended to be overlooked or undervalued.[6]

There is also the issue of leadership succession, especially when leaders who have attempted to keep leadership largely to themselves depart.[7] Overall, there is growing

> recognition that there is much unrealised and unreleased leadership potential and capacity for improvement residing in educational organisations[8], and that distributed leadership, including teacher leadership, is important in growing organisational and individual capacity.

Meanings of distributed leadership

Peter Gronn has considered the multiple meanings of distributed leadership, which fundamentally fall into two groups: the first sees distributed leadership as essentially additive (more leaders, spread leadership); the second sees it as more holistic, including all forms of collaboration and participation. Rather than spreading existing leadership responsibilities and power across more people, a holistic view of distributed leadership is concerned more with the synergies that can occur when people come together to work, plan, learn and act, thus generating further leadership capacity within the individual and the organisation.[9]

Distributed leadership, including teacher leadership (see also delegated leadership, democratic leadership, shared leadership, collective leadership, dispersed leadership[10]) is now a major aspect of, and influence upon, constructs of educational leadership[11], although as Harris has noted that as well as enthusiasm for the perceived benefits of the concept:

> ... we urgently need contemporary, fine-grained studies of distributed leadership practice ... without the associated empirical base it is in danger of becoming yet another abstract leadership theory.[12]

York-Barr and Duke concur: 'there is little empirical evidence to support [teacher leadership's effects]'.[13] However, York-Barr and Duke are optimistic about the potential for educational improvement through teacher leadership 'despite being thwarted by centuries-old structures and conditions of schools that resist change'.[14] This chapter will examine some of this needed evidence.

The nature and effects of distributed leadership

It is important to note that at any time in any school, and indeed within any educational organisation, leadership is *already* distributed. Any new leader appointed to a position therefore needs to consider where formal and informal power, responsibility and influence reside. Over time, he or she might want to foster the leadership of others and even establish new leadership roles and responsibilities—new structures—but it needs to be recognised that fostering and distributing leadership capacity is more organic in nature, rather than being simply a technical response to a challenge.

Harris and Spillane have noted:

> In a practical or normative sense, the chief concern is how leadership is distributed, by whom and with what effect ... It is concerned with how we maximise the potential of distributed leadership for organisational improvement and transformation. The key questions are whether, how and in what form distributed leadership contributes to school improvement. Do we have evidence to show that lateral, less hierarchical staff structures result in notable gains in student performance?[15]

As to whether distributed leadership is a 'good' or 'bad' thing, Harris and Spillane offer the view that:

> It depends on the context within which leadership is distributed and the prime aim of the distribution. Flattening the hierarchy or delegation of leadership does not necessarily equate with distributed leadership, nor does it automatically improve performance. It is the nature and quality of *leadership practice* that matters.[16]

In other words, simply redistributing responsibilities within an organisation without commensurate work in staff mentoring and development is unlikely to have any positive influence on either school effectiveness or student outcomes. The real meaning of distributed leadership is about recognising and developing staff expertise that might otherwise be left undeveloped and unreleased within existing organisational structures. As Harris and Spillane have noted:

> Distributed leadership is not a panacea or a blueprint or a recipe. It is a way of getting under the skin of leadership practice, of seeing leadership practice differently and illuminating the possibilities for organisational transformation. This is not without its risks, as it inevitably means holding up the looking glass to schools and being prepared to abandon leadership practices. For those genuinely seeking transformation and self-renewal, this is a risk well worth taking.[17]

Leithwood and Mascall have considered the literature on what they term 'collective leadership' and have commented upon its benefits:

> The overwhelming disposition of the contemporary literature on distributed leadership ... is that of enthusiastic optimism about its anticipated benefits. As compared with exclusively hierarchical, or focused, forms of leadership, distributed leadership is thought to (a) more accurately reflect the division of labour that is experienced in organizations from day to day and (b) reduce

> the chances of error arising from decisions based on the limited information available to a single leader. Distributed leadership also enhances opportunities for the organization to benefit from the capacities of more of its members; it permits members to capitalise on the range of their individual strengths; and it develops among organizational members a fuller appreciation of interdependence and how one's behaviour [effects] the organization as a whole ... Such leadership allows members to better anticipate and respond to the demands of the organization's environment. Solutions to organizational challenges may develop through distributed leadership that would unlikely emerge from individual sources.[18]

Leithwood and Mascall went on to conduct their own detailed study, and concluded:

> [Our] Results suggest that collective leadership does explain significant variation in student achievement across schools. The influence of collective leadership was most strongly linked to student achievement through teacher motivation. Finally, patterns of leadership influence differed among schools with different levels of student achievement. As compared with schools whose students achieved in the lowest 20% of our sample, schools whose students achieved in the highest 20% attributed considerably more influence to most sources of collective leadership. Furthermore, parents and students were perceived to be relatively influential in those schools[a], as compared with the lower-performing schools.[19]

Teacher leadership

Apart from those occupying formal leadership positions, a remaining part of the set of educators possessing and exercising distributed leadership is that of teachers[b]. (As I have noted previously, I consider every teacher to be a leader. Teachers lead the classes they teach, and they serve in various capacities within schools, including on committees and working groups, through their involvement with groups and performances, sporting teams, in various professional associations outside the school, and so forth.)

Childs-Bowen, Moller and Scrivner have provided a definition of teacher leadership:

---

a The potential positive influences of student and parent leadership tend to be largely ignored in the general literature on distributed leadership.

b The potential leadership influences of administrative staff working in schools, also tends to be under-recognised and researched.

> Teachers are leaders when they function in professional communities to affect student learning; contribute to school improvement; inspire excellence in practice; and empower stakeholders to participate in educational improvement.[20]

The National Comprehensive Center for Teacher Quality in the United States of America reviewed the research literature on enhancing teacher leadership and noted the following benefits:

> Enhancing teacher leadership can help schools and districts reach the following goals:
> - Improve teacher quality ...
> - Improve student learning ...
> - Ensure that education reform efforts work ...
> - Recruit, retain, motivate, and reward accomplished teachers ...
> - Provide opportunities for professional growth ...
> - Extend principal capacity ...
> - Create a more democratic school environment.[21]

The special case of middle leaders: caught in the middle?

We now turn to a crucial level and type of formal leadership, that of middle leaders in schools. This section draws upon two studies of department (faculty) heads in secondary schools in Australia[22], as well as a study of teacher satisfaction, motivation and mental health carried out in primary and secondary schools in Australia, New Zealand, the USA and Canada, and later in other nations.[23]

Pressure for educational change has increased greatly over the past few decades. These pressures and demands are often contradictory, with schools expected to take on a raft of social responsibilities, that is 'extras', while lifting student academic performance and meeting new accountabilities in the 'basics'. Calls for continuous improvement, transformation and data-driven/evidence-based decision-making have become constants for schools.[24]

Educational change needs to be considered in its wider socio-political context, where teacher status is tending to decline, social criticisms and expectations are rising, and there are concerns with both attracting and retaining quality teachers and with leadership succession and sustainability.[25]

Although much change is imposed from above and outside, there is also desire within schools for self-initiated change and improvement to teaching and learning. Often, principals have responsibility for driving change and teachers have responsibility for implementing it. Middle leaders such as secondary heads of department—the term 'Head of Department' (HoD) is used here to avoid confusion, rather than Head Teacher or Faculty Head—occupy key linking positions between principals and classroom teachers.

HODs have formal responsibilities and accountabilities and exert influence horizontally—across their own department and with other departments—and vertically within school hierarchies and beyond the school.[26]

With the trend towards greater school autonomy in certain areas such as management[27], yet greater centralisation, accountability and control through means such as standardised testing and reporting of student and school performance, it can be argued that the workload of the secondary HoD has become more complex, intensive and challenging.

In addition, the HoD usually has a significant teaching load and in larger secondary schools, he or she can be responsible for 10 or more staff and the teaching and learning of hundreds of students.

As a result of these and other responsibilities, which as noted can be countervailing, the secondary HoD has been found to be a high pressure position. Dinham, Scott and colleagues who undertook the overseas replications found that those those in the 'middle' recording higher levels of mental stress and lower levels of occupational satisfaction[28] than others such as principals, deputies and classroom teachers.

Despite the importance of the role, the secondary HoD has continued to be under-researched, when compared with others such as principals and classroom teachers.[29] The importance of principal leadership has long been accepted in school effectiveness research and the individual teacher has been found to be the greatest contributor to student achievement, apart from students themselves.[30] However, it has been increasingly recognised that subject leadership is important in facilitating quality teaching and learning and school improvement.[31] HoDs can have significant influence on the quality of teaching and learning within their departments and individual classrooms.[32] The challenge for HoDs is to move beyond the managerial aspects of the role to engage more with teaching and learning, although to accomplish this, professional learning may be required in both the management and educational leadership areas.[33]

As Goodson and Marsh observed:

> The subject department provides the most common organisational vehicle for school subject knowledge, certainly in secondary schools, but unlike 'the curriculum' it has not been widely researched or much noted in our studies of schools.[34]

Yet life and learning in secondary schools are commonly organised according to subject matter, and the secondary school subject department remains the preferred focus of teaching and learning and the preferred form of curriculum realisation for many, despite attempts to adopt whole-school approaches to teaching and learning.[35]

Research by Stodolsky and Grossman[36] and Grossman and Stodolsky[37] has emphasised the importance of a 'comparative approach toward understanding subject-matter differences among secondary school teachers'. Likewise, due attention needs to be addressed to 'school subjects as specific contexts within which secondary teachers teach'.[38]

Whereas school effectiveness research in the past was concerned more with the macro school level, increasingly, there has been focus on the sub-units within schools such as departments.[39] Research evidence concerned with school improvement emphasises the importance of focusing on efforts to change practices at different levels within an organisation. The largest study of differential school effectiveness in the United Kingdom highlighted the importance of differences between departments in explaining differences in school performance.[40] As Hannay and Ross have concluded, 'we need far more research on the micro-processes involved in secondary schools'.[41]

One study of the secondary head of department

As a result of Dinham and Scott's findings about middle level primary and secondary teachers reporting lower comparative levels of satisfaction and higher levels of mental stress[42], an interview study involving 26 secondary HoDs at four government and non-government high schools[43] was carried out in New South Wales, Australia by Dinham, Brennan, Collier, Deece and Mulford[c]. In summary, the study found that:
- HoDs took on the role for a variety of reasons.
- Only half of HoDs reported the role was what they had expected it to be.
- HoDs were underprepared for the interpersonal aspects of the role, which are heavily dependent upon relationships.
- HoD preparation was largely ad hoc, with formal preparation little utilised and poorly regarded.
- HoDs reported that lack of time to perform the various aspects of the role was the worst aspect of the position.
- Much of the role of the HoD was reactive with little room for discretionary action.
- HoDs felt the quality of their own teaching was compromised by the role.
- HoDs had a wide range of professional learning needs with only half reporting that these were being met.
- The HoD position was poorly rewarded for the breadth and depth of the tasks involved.
- The opportunity to have an influence and to lead other professionals was highly prized by HoDs, some of whom regarded the HoD as the 'best position in the school'.

The secondary head of department: findings from AESOP

Findings from the AESOP study in respect of principal leadership were outlined in the previous chapter. However, the prime focus of the project was actually secondary

---

c   Brennan, Collier, Deece and Mulford were secondary principals enrolled in the ed program at the University of Western Sydney.

subject departments (80 per cent of the 50 sites) and cross-school programs (20 per cent of sites).

As a result of the analysis of data explained previously, secondary faculty heads were found to influence students and their learning through a core category and seven contributing categories:

Core category
- Focus on students and their learning

Contributing categories
- Personal qualities, relationships
- Professional capacity, strategy
- Promotion and advocacy, external relations
- Department planning, organisation
- Common purpose, collaboration, team building
- Teacher learning, responsibility, trust
- Vision, expectations and culture of success

Full results are detailed elsewhere[44], but the following summary captures how the secondary HoDs—the people in the middle—influenced those they worked with to improve teaching and learning in their subject departments and, to a degree, their schools, and in some cases the wider profession. As with the data and findings on principals in the AESOP study, once again there was a high degree of commonality in the attributes, actions, personal qualities and values of these people. I realise that on reading these profiles there might be a feeling that these are idealistic properties, but to reiterate, these findings came from real, impressive, practising, professional people.

1 Personal qualities and relationships
Site reports revealed how the personal qualities of the HoDs were an important aspect of their leadership. These highly effective leaders were people who were dedicated to the profession. Their commitment, energy and enthusiasm for teaching motivated those around them, and was infectious. They had a strong commitment and passion for their teaching subject(s). They were easy to get on with, consistent yet flexible, non-dogmatic, and prepared to admit to their mistakes, taking responsibility for department-based decisions. They carefully considered options although they could be decisive when necessary.

These HoDs demonstrated empathy. They showed care and consideration for others and made themselves available to help when needed. They were inclusive in their dealings with people.

The HoDs had effective interpersonal skills. They had a good way of dealing with students, even the recalcitrant. In this, they are able to distinguish between 'the sin and the sinner'.

One of their most important attributes was that they served as role models for others, setting a 'good example'. They modelled humanity and professionalism, thus exercising both moral and professional leadership and authority. They tended to have a strong influence on less experienced staff.

As part of their positive attitude, they were open to new ideas. They were receptive to the suggestions of others and prepared to try new approaches. They were politically aware and astute in their dealings with other faculties and groups and had a strong presence and reputation in the school. They were effective advocates for their area.

These HoDs let their staff know they cared for them and showed appreciation for what staff do. They frequently gave praise and provided feedback, both positive and constructive.

Over time, they had earned respect from staff, students, parents and the community. In turn, they demonstrated respect for others. They tended to be recognised as exceptional by deputy principals and principals. They elicited loyalty. Staff said they didn't want to let their HOD or faculty down.

A site report for a school identified for achieving exceptional outcomes in English (Years 7–10) noted:

> 'The HoD is held in high regard by her colleagues ... An experienced English teacher described her HoD's leadership as "politically aware" and the woman herself as a "fabulous people-person who is good at negotiating". Further praise came from a young English teacher on staff who enthusiastically stated, "I have one of the best bosses. She treats you as a person, with respect, and I can talk to her about everything. She keeps the whole staff happy".'

2 *Professional capacity, strategy*

These leaders of successful departments were experienced and effective teachers. They possessed depth and breadth of knowledge, had a sound understanding of curricula, and kept themselves and others informed of current developments. The site report for a school identified for English noted:

> 'The HoD has successfully taken the lead in understanding the new [syllabus] concepts, familiarising the staff with them and initiating policies in implementation. All teachers acknowledged her as someone whose subject knowledge was extensive and preeminent and to whom they could turn immediately and unhesitatingly for guidance or explanation. Far from being intimidated by curriculum change, the HoD had embraced it, thus making the transition period much less threatening for her staff.'

These HoDs sought out best practice from outside their department and school. In turn, they were able to model this in teaching, planning, programming and behaviour management. They were open to new ideas and approaches and able to integrate these into their practice. They were good listeners and respected the experience and views of other department members. Their approach was to build upon what is there. It was clear from many site reports that these people took over departments that were operating effectively, but were able to use their professional and personal capacities to take these departments to a higher level. A key aspect to accomplishing this was to release teacher potential through collaboration and team building.

These HoDs were prepared to share resources and encouraged others to do the same. They regularly reported back to staff. They were prepared to share the credit for good ideas, and encouraged, rather than controlled, the 'high fliers' in the department.

They were hardworking, well organised and thorough. They paid attention to detail. They tended to work harder than anyone else in the faculty and stepped in to fill gaps when needed. A key aim was to remove or overcome obstacles to change and higher levels of achievement.

Some HoDs set an example by allocating themselves to lower-ability classes. They were also strategic about the allocation of more capable teachers to where they could best be used, and allocated less experienced and/or less able teachers to facilitate their professional growth.

A site report for an English department noted:

'The HoD herself says that she is a "spoon-feeder" of her staff: "I give them the folders, the material and I think it's important to model for the staff. I won't ask them to do what I wouldn't do myself". Her leadership style is to "work hard and people don't want to let you down. I try to maintain credibility—I'm the one who has no home room and I take the bottom Year 10. I can't switch off. I mark everything and get it back the next day ... instant feedback. More of the others are doing it now as well ... I encourage the staff to write their own comments. Negativity doesn't exist ... I think leadership is about removing obstacles."'

3 *Promotion, advocacy and external relations*

These HoDs were effective advocates for their department, and respected members of their school community. They tended to be active in school 'politics' and were able to secure resources and support for their area. They facilitated networking across the school and with the wider community and profession. They took on other commitments outside their immediate responsibility and had the capacity to mediate between department and school policies, practices and priorities.

A site report for a school identified for Personal Development, Health and Physical Education noted:

'... the HoD PDHPE is able to articulate the needs of the department at the executive level, and make strong representations on the department's behalf. Staff indicated that she consistently presented her case well, and was clear on the outcomes she wanted to achieve ... the HoD's communication skills were manifest in her management of resources. This was brought into sharp focus through her ability to attract outside funding to the department (specifically, through the Parents and Citizens Association). The President of the P&C enthused that the HoD not only made substantive cases for the allocation of funds to the PDHPE department, but was particularly vigilant in reporting back the outcomes of the funding allocation.'

These HoDs raised the profile of and promoted their subject areas with students, parents, the rest of the school, and 'feeder' primary schools. A site report for an English department noted:

'The HoD provides the staff with written weekly "English updates". Moreover, every weekly edition of the [School] Newsletter has an English column. No other department does this regularly and most have no entries. The entries are written by the HoD and are always about what is going on in classrooms, especially in terms of assessment, writing competitions, excursions, HSC study series, opportunities.'

A site report for another school selected for English also highlighted the importance of promoting the subject area:

'The HoD ... [described] English as "the poor cousin of Maths" in the school. She talked about having to "sell" English to the parents as being equally as important as Maths and Science. She maintained that Asian and Middle Eastern parents often felt that whereas they could help their children with the latter subjects, this was not the case with English. Indeed, she felt that English had to be presented in a manner that would lead students to value English highly, focusing on a "step by step" method of explicit teaching, which, to some extent, is not unlike that associated with Maths.'

Their commitments did not prevent the HoDs from engaging in professional activities outside their faculty and school. They participated in and contributed to professional development and in-service across the school and through their active membership of professional associations and other bodies outside the school.

4 Department planning and organisation

These HoDs had a major influence upon department planning and organisation. They oversaw the development and centralisation of teaching resources and took a leading role in programming.

They facilitated with staff the development and implementation of clear policies and procedures and effective communication.

Department meetings were held regularly and tended to be focused on dealing with one or more key issues rather than administration. Decision-making was collaborative with an implicit understanding that there would be universal and uniform application of group decisions.

Detailed and effective evaluation, documentation and reporting were important aspects of department organisation overseen by the HoDs.

Effective student discipline and welfare strategies were developed and instigated and there was thorough follow-up on student matters. HoDs fostered a consistent approach to behaviour management, with students and staff knowing precisely what was involved and what were the processes and consequences.

A site report for a Science department noted:

'Discipline within the department is good ... This is due, to a considerable degree, to the effectiveness of the HoD as a disciplinarian. A number of staff members commented on the reluctance of students to be sent to him for discipline infringements and on his thoroughness in following up students who are referred to him. The HoD commented that, while he likes to take one of the more capable classes in Year 7, he prefers to take the lower ability classes, where discipline problems are more likely to occur, in Years 8 to 10. He commented, not entirely in jest, that "it saves time by cutting out the middle man".'

5 Common purpose, collaboration, team building

As noted, in many cases the 'seeds for success' were present when these HoDs were appointed, but they were able to bring these elements together to take their department to another level of performance. One way this was achieved was through developing a common purpose and commitment among department members, fostering collaboration and building a productive team.

A site report for an English department noted:

'English has a high profile ... It is a "magnet" among the kids ... [The] HoD is the centre orchestrating it all. [The HoD] is central to the success of the department. Good leadership from the HoD is important ... The Principal argues that the HoD is the primary factor in the department's success. English had a poor history before [the HoD] arrived and was a very split staff. She had been on the staff and was occasionally relieving HoD. She gained the position on merit and "set about rebuilding the department. The staff has rallied around her and see themselves as a team ..." For the Deputy Principal, as with the Principal, leadership is an issue: "[the HoD] is able to embrace a whole lot of individual personalities and styles with no cliques".'

These HoDs were adept at drawing out the ideas and opinions of their faculty members. In this way, common agreed goals were developed, which were binding on the department.

A site report for a school selected for Science commented:

'[The HoD's] leadership style is very democratic, a style which is well suited to this particular context. Given the age and experience of the department members, and the fact that they have their own well-tested ideas about educational theory, an autocratic leadership style would not be appropriate. He is sensitive to the views of the department members and is very successful in welding them into a cooperative and effective team. "I'm easy to get on with and I'm prepared to listen to people ... and take on board their ideas" [HoD Science]. Newer members of the department are drawn into a collegial team, which exhibits friendliness and professionalism.'

Department members had a feeling of ownership of their area and felt confident and secure. In this way, high morale and a feeling of common purpose was facilitated. Despite what might be mandated, there was a feeling of joint control.

6 Teacher learning, responsibility, trust

These HoDs modelled and placed a high value on professional learning. They helped staff identify their professional strengths and weaknesses and assisted and encouraged them to address these. They facilitated department-based professional development as well as supporting and encouraging staff to engage in school-wide and out-of-school professional learning.

There was a culture of professional sharing whereby staff assisted each other to share best practice and with staff providing workshops and feedback from their professional learning to their colleagues.

There tended to be 'professional talk' in the staffroom, with the HoD often providing current journals, papers and examples for staff. There was a sharing of latest developments, approaches and ideas.

A site report for a school identified for Mathematics noted how the HoD had subtly and persistently directed the professional learning of staff:

'The HoD is particularly keen to introduce technology to assist students with their learning. He has been responsible for the setting up of the Mathematics computer laboratory and the purchase of additional sets of graphics calculators. He has also supported the introduction of this hardware by ensuring that teachers are trained in the use of this equipment. As well, one of the Mathematics teachers has been allocated one of the compulsory technology classes in Year 7. [The HoD commented]: "Graphics calculators ... we are using a lot more now we have three sets of graphics calculators ... We go to as many inservice courses on them as we can. One by one I have convinced them that [the courses] are a good thing. On faculty meeting afternoons occasionally we sit down and do, say, something on the statistics module or I drag them into the computer room and we'll have a look at this new geometry thing I found or new graphing thing I've found."'

Less experienced teachers were given close attention and given support to help them adjust. There was subtle pressure through role modelling for new teachers to rise to the level of the rest of the department. Through such measures HoDs helped to generate a culture where teachers shared responsibility and contributed for their mutual benefit and for the benefit of their students.

7 *Vision, expectations, culture of success*

These leaders of successful departments possessed a clear vision for what they wanted to achieve. They also had a clear view of the importance and relevance of their subject areas in students' lives.

They sought and accepted input from others to formulate this vision and set high standards and expectations for all.

The HoDs possessed clear personal goals and set high standards for themselves. They modelled professionalism. They believed in working hard and expected the same of students and fellow staff.

A site report for an English Department noted the observations of one teacher:

> '[The HoD] works on your strengths but doesn't let you get away with your weaknesses. She encourages you, suggests new approaches, directs you to resources and to others who might help ... she encourages collaborative and workshop marking. [She] loves and fosters creative writing across all levels. Entry in competitions is encouraged. It starts with in-class work and local competitions through to the *Herald* Young Writers [awards].'

Another teacher from the same English Department commented:

> 'The big issue for success here is the HoD—everyone rises to the team level. She creates a very positive, powerful culture. A weak teacher would not work here—there is an expectation that you pull your weight. [She] leads by consensus. She is part of the group and works hardest by far, we don't want to let her down. She gets kudos as a HoD with us by representing the department and winning. She argues aggressively for our interests and that's how you get support. Helping becomes infectious—there is a 'clan-like' mentality here.'

Casual or replacement teachers were well supported and were expected to teach rather than 'baby sit' students. Casual teachers who did not meet expectations were not normally used again and permanent teachers who do not fit the culture sometimes ended up transferring to another school. When new appointments were made, the HoD made an effort to ensure a good fit with the needs and ethos of the department.

8 *Core category: focus on students and their learning*

As was found to be the case with principals in the AESOP study[45], HoDs had as their prime consideration students and their learning. Rather than academic achievement alone, HoDs and their staff recognised the need to attend to the personal and social needs of students, as this underpinned academic success.

They possessed a genuine concern for students as people. They were aware of the varied backgrounds of their students and had a commitment to students' intellectual and social development.

They and their staff 'knew' their students academically through assessment and tracking of performance from year to year, a process that began in many cases in 'feeder' primary schools. So that students can get the best possible start, there was a focus in many of these departments on the Years 6–7 primary to secondary transition.

Within the department, there was a strong emphasis on monitoring and feedback. There was also recognition of the importance of assessment *for* learning, rather than assessment *of* learning. Assessment tended to be regular and thorough and informed planning and approaches within the department.

The HoD and the department encouraged independence in student learning and found ways to give responsibility and leadership to students. There was an emphasis and expectation that students would take a degree of responsibility for their learning.

These HoDs found ways to reduce administrative demands on teachers, including taking on much of this themselves, so that teachers could concentrate their efforts on teaching and learning.

They also maintained close contact with all classes and were prepared to negotiate with students. What resulted from this focus on students and their learning could be termed a 'teacher-directed, student-centred' culture, something identified in a previous study of successful senior secondary teaching.[46]

A site report for a school where Special Education was investigated noted:

> 'An important aspect of the HoD's leadership was the development of a student-centred culture incorporating high expectations of students, a culture in which roles, responsibilities and procedures for staff and students was mutually understood even if not documented ... [W]hile it was clear that the HoD was an exceptional leader, the features of effective leadership can be found in other individuals [within the department].'

Concluding remarks

Although there was considerable variation across the sample of AESOP study sites in terms of geographic location, socio-economic background, staff experience, subject areas, and programs, there was strong commonality among the heads of department involved with the study.

Male or female, young or old, and regardless of specialisation, HoDs were found to possess and exhibit similar personal qualities, attributes and actions. They could be accurately described as 'authentic' leaders.[47]

The HoDs had their own personalities and foibles, yet the impression they projected was one of professionalism underpinned by humanity. While their actions were an expression of who they were as people, there was evidence that these leaders of successful departments and teams had grown into the role, often under the influence of others and were thus less 'born', and more 'made' as leaders. The implication here is that while not everyone is cut out to be a leader, those with potential can develop and be mentored into the role—leadership can be learnt. A key aspect of the HoDs was how they actively encouraged the leadership capacity of others, thus facilitating distributed leadership and leadership sustainability in their departments.

In considering the known pressures and contradictions of the role of the secondary head of department, the HoDs leading the successful departments and teams studied in the AESOP project had been able to deal with these, and even use them to their advantage. Rather than just surviving, these leaders and the teams they led were thriving, often in difficult circumstances. In many cases, schools and departments had been in decline until principals and heads of department had been appointed.

A challenge for educational employers and systems is to utilise people such as the HoDs encountered in the AESOP study to assist in the development of future leaders, other departments and schools. One negative finding from the study was that these HoDs tended to be neither recognised nor utilised to any great degree outside their school and were in some respects, 'hidden treasures'.[48]

The various studies cited in this chapter all point to the existence and importance of distributed leadership and of the roles leaders can play in facilitating this powerful professional phenomenon and force for change and improvement in schooling.

Endnotes

1. Fullan, M. (2005). *Leadership and sustainability*. Thousand Oaks, CA: Corwin. (pp. 30–31)
2. Harris, A. (2004). Teacher leadership and distributed leadership: An exploration of the literature. *Leading and Managing, 10*(2), 1–9; Dinham, S. (2007). The waves of leadership. *The Australian Educational Leader, 29*(3), 20–27. (p. 27)
3. Gronn, P. (2002). Distributed leadership. In K. Leithwood & P. Hallinger (Eds.), *Second international handbook of educational leadership and administration* (pp. 653–696). Dordrecht, Netherlands: Kluwer.
4. Harris, A. (2008). Distributed leadership: According to the evidence. *Journal of Educational Administration, 46*(2), 173–175.
5. Dinham, S., & Scott, C. (2002). Pressure points: School executive and educational change. *Journal of Educational Enquiry, 3*(2), 35–52; Dinham, S., & Scott, C. (1998). A three domain model of teacher and school executive satisfaction. *Journal of Educational Administration, 36*(4), 362–378; Dinham, S. (1997). Societal expectations, pressures and teaching. *Teaching and Teachers' Work, 5*(3), 1–8.
6. Spillane, J., Halverson, R., & Diamond, J. (2001). Investigating school leadership practice: A distributed perspective. *Educational Researcher, 30*(3), 23–28; Gronn, P. (2002). (p. 654)

7   Lambert, L. (1998). *Building leadership capacity in schools*. Alexandria, VA: ASCD. (p. 10); Hargreaves, A., & Fink, D. (2004). The seven principles of sustainable leadership. *Educational Leadership, 61*(7), 8–13. (p. 8)

8   Crowther, F., Kaagan, S., Ferguson, M., & Hann, L. (2002). *Developing teacher leaders*. Thousand Oaks, CA: Corwin. (pp. 3–16); York-Barr, J., & Duke, K. (2004). What do we know about teacher leadership? Findings from two decades of scholarship. *Review of Educational Research, 74*(3), 255–316.

9   Gronn, P. (2002). (pp. 654–660)

10 Bennett, N., Wise, C., Woods, P., & Harvey, J. (2003). *Distributed leadership*. Nottingham, England: National College for School Leadership. (p. 4)

11 Duignan, P., & Bezzina, M. (2006). *Building leadership capacity for shared leadership in schools—Teachers as leaders of educational change*. Keynote address, Australian Centre for Educational Leadership International Conference, University of Wollongong, New South Wales, February.

12 Harris, A. (2005). Distributed leadership. In B. Davies (Ed.), *The essentials of school leadership* (pp. 160–172). London, England: Paul Chapman. (p. 170)

13 York-Barr, J., & Duke, K. (2004). (p. 292)

14 York-Barr, J., & Duke, K. (2004). (p. 292)

15 Harris, A., & Spillane, J. (2008). Distributed leadership through the looking glass. *Management in Education, 22*(1), 31–34. (p. 32). Copyright © 2008 by A. Harris and J. Spillane. All text extracts from this article are reprinted by Permission of Sage Publications, Inc.

16 Harris, A., & Spillane, J. (2008). (p. 33)

17 Harris, A., & Spillane, J. (2008). (p. 33)

18 Leithwood, K., & Mascall, B. (2008). Collective leadership effects on student achievement. *Educational Administration Quarterly, 44*(4), 529–561. (pp. 530–531). Copyright © 2008 by K. Leithwood and B. Mascall. All text extracts from this article are reprinted by Permission of Sage Publications, Inc.

19 Leithwood, K., & Mascall, B. (2008). (pp. 554–555). Copyright © 2008 by K. Leithwood and B. Mascall. All text extracts from this article are reprinted by Permission of Sage Publications, Inc.

20 Childs-Bowen, D., Moller, G., & Scrivner, J. (2000). Principals: Leaders of leaders. *National Association of Secondary School Principals (NASSP) Bulletin, 84*(616), 27–34. (p. 28)

21 National Comprehensive Center for Teacher Quality. (2007). *Key issue: Enhancing teacher leadership*. Washington DC: Author. (no page)

22 See Dinham, S., Brennan, K., Collier, J., Deece, A., & Mulford, D. (2000), *The secondary head of department: Key link in the quality teaching and learning chain—Quality Teaching Series*, No 2. Deakin, ACT: Australian College of Education; Dinham, S. (2007). *Leadership for exceptional educational outcomes*. Teneriffe, Qld: Post Pressed.

23 See Dinham, S., & Scott, C. (1998). A three domain model of teacher and school executive satisfaction. *Journal of Educational Administration, 36*(4), 362–378; Dinham, S., & Scott, C. (2002). Pressure points: School executive and educational change. *Journal of Educational Enquiry, 3*(2), 35–52; Dinham, S., & Scott, C. (2000). Moving into the third, outer domain of teacher satisfaction. *Journal of Educational Administration, 38*(4), 379–396.

24 Zmuda, A., Kuklis, R., & Kline, E. (2004). *Transforming schools creating a culture of continuous improvement*. Alexandria, VA: ASCD.

25 Dinham, S., & Scott, C. (2000); Scott, C., & Dinham, S. (2002). The beatings will continue until quality improves: Carrots and sticks in the search for educational improvement. *Teacher Development, 6*(1), 15–31; Dinham, S. (2013). The quality teaching movement in Australia encounters difficult terrain: A personal perspective. *Australian Journal of Education, 57*(2), 91–106.

26 Duke, D. (1987). *School leadership and instructional improvement*. New York: Random House; Koehler, M. (1993). *Department head's survival guide*. Upper Saddle River, New Jersey: Prentice-Hall; Dinham, S., Brennan, K., Collier, J., Deece, A., & Mulford, D. (2000); Busher, H., & Harris, A. (2000). *Subject leadership and school improvement*. London, England: Paul Chapman; Gunter, H. (2001). *Leaders and leadership in education*, London, England: Paul Chapman.

27 Beare, H., Caldwell, B., & Millikan, R. (1989). *Creating an excellent school*. London, England: Routledge; Hopkins, D. (2013). *Exploding the myths of school reform*. Melbourne, Victoria: ACER Press.

28 Dinham, S., & Scott, C. (2002).

29 See Goodson, I., & Marsh, C. (1996). *Studying school subjects*. London, England: Falmer Press. (p. 54)

30 Hattie, J. (2009). *Visible learning: A synthesis of over 800 meta-analyses relating to achievement*. London, England: Routledge.

31 Busher, H., & Harris, A. (2000).

32 Ayres, P., Dinham, S., & Sawyer, W. (2000). Successful senior secondary teaching. *Quality Teaching Series*, No. 1, Australian College of Education, September, 1–20; Ayres, P., Dinham, S., & Sawyer, W. (2004). Effective teaching in the context of a Grade 12 high stakes external examination in New South Wales, Australia. *British Educational Research Journal*, $30(1)$, 141–165.

33 Brown, M., Boyle, B., & Boyle, T. (2002). Professional development and management training needs for heads of department in UK secondary schools. *Journal of Educational Administration*, $40(1)$, 31–43.

34 Goodson, I., & Marsh, C. (1996). (p. 54)

35 Siskin, L. S., & Little, J. W. (1995). (Eds.), *The subjects in question: The department organization of the high school*. New York, NY: Teachers College Press.

36 Stodolsky, S., & Grossman, P. (1995). The impact of subject matter on curricular activity: An analysis of five academic subjects. *American Educational Research Journal*, 32, 227–249; Stodolsky, S., & Grossman, P. (2000). Changing students, changing teachers. *Teachers College Record*, $102(1)$, 125–172.

37 Grossman, P., & Stodolsky, S. (1995). Content as context: The role of school subjects in secondary school teaching. *Educational Researcher*, $24(8)$, 5–11, 23.

38 Grossman, P., & Stodolsky, S. (1995). (p. 5)

39 See Busher, H., & Harris, A. (2000); Busher, H., & Harris, A. (1999). Leadership of school subject areas: tensions and dimensions of managing in the middle. *School Leadership and Management*, 19, 305–317.

40 Sammons, P., Thomas, S., & Mortimore, P. (1997). *Forging links: Effective schools and effective departments*. London, England: Paul Chapman.

41 Hannay, L. M., & Ross, J. A. (1999). Department heads as middle managers? Questioning the black box. *School Leadership and Management*, 19, 345–358.

42 Dinham, S., & Scott, C. (2002).

43 Dinham, S., Brennan, K., Collier, J., Deece, A., & Mulford, D. (2000).

44 Dinham, S. (2007). *Leadership for exceptional educational outcomes*. Teneriffe, Qld: Post Pressed; Dinham, S. (2007). The secondary head of department and the achievement of exceptional student outcomes. *Journal of Educational Administration*, $45(1)$, 62–79.

45 Dinham, S. (2007). *Leadership for exceptional educational outcomes*. Teneriffe, Qld: Post Pressed; Dinham, S. (2005). Principal leadership for outstanding educational outcomes. *Journal of Educational Administration*, $43(4)$, 338–356.

46 Ayres, P., Dinham, S., & Sawyer, W. (2000); Ayres, P., Dinham, S., & Sawyer, W. (2004).

47 Duignan, P., & Bhindi, N. (1997). Authenticity in leadership: an emerging perspective. *Journal of Educational Administration*, $35(3)$, 195–209.

48 Dinham, S. (2002). NSW Quality Teaching Awards—Research, rigour and transparency. *Unicorn*, $28(1)$, 5–9.

PART C

Professional learning in education

CHAPTER 12

What forms of professional learning are most effective?

INTRODUCTION

Teachers' professional learning has been shown to be central to successful teaching, student learning and effective schools. In the 'four fundamentals of student achievement' presented in Chapter 2 derived from my earlier work, professional learning was one of the 'big levers' for improving teaching and learning.[1]

John Hattie found from his meta-analyses that professional development had an effect size of 0.51, teachers engaging in micro-teaching had an effect size of 0.88, and providing teachers with formative evaluation on their performance had an effect size of 0.90 in respect of student learning.[2]

While professional learning is often thought of as in-service or formal courses, professional learning frequently occurs through teachers simply talking about their teaching and working together in various ways at department, grade or school level.

In their review of the research literature on teacher professional learning and development, Timperley, Wilson, Barrar and Fung found:

> Opportunities for teachers to engage in professional learning and development can have a substantial impact on student learning. For example, in literacy studies, substantial effect sizes were reported by Phillips, McNaughton, and MacDonald (2001) (ES = 0.48) and by Timperley (2006) (ES = 0.89). These gains equate to more than two years' progress in one year. In writing, English and Bareta (2006) reported an overall effect size of 1.3 over two years, which similarly equates to about two years' progress in one year. More important was the progress made by the 20% of lowest-achieving students. Their progress equated to average achievement gains of an extra three to four years for every one year of schooling (ES = 2.1). In numeracy, the effect sizes reported by Bishop and colleagues (ES

= 0.76) represent a shift from the 50th percentile to between the 66th and 77th percentiles, equivalent to 1–2 stanines.[3]

This chapter reviews traditional and emerging approaches to teachers' ongoing professional learning[a] before presenting a framework for developing and maintaining a learning community in education. This is derived from research studies described to date and additional projects with which I have been involved. While none of the projects was about teachers' professional learning per se, each project added to an overall understanding of the role and nature of building learning communities for fostering quality teaching and student achievement.

Traditional and emerging approaches to teacher professional learning

Traditional approaches to teachers' professional learning tend to be linear, reflecting the typical stages of a teacher's career:
- Formal pre-service teacher education
- On the job, ad hoc professional experience
- Involvement with professional associations
- Informal self-directed professional reading and learning
- Formal in-service courses provided by employers (in school, out of school)
- Formal postgraduate study
- Other short courses.

More recent approaches to teacher professional learning to augment these earlier approaches have included the following. Running across these is greater use of online learning, including the use of social media, learning 'blogs'[b] and the development of online learning communities. It also needs to be noted that various commercial interests, including of both large international publishers and private consulting firms, have become much more active in the provision of 'for profit' professional learning:
- Action research
- Action learning
- Formal mentoring and coaching
- Professional standards and certification (mandatory, voluntary)
- University accredited professional learning modules

---

a Teachers' pre-service learning has been addressed previously, particularly in Chapter 7. The focus of this chapter is on teachers' continued professional development and the role of professional learning communities. Professional development for leaders is addressed in Part E later.

b See http://onlinepracticeandpedagogy.blogspot.com.au/ for example.

- Learning communities
- MOOCs.[c]

In Australia, the widespread provision of professional in-service learning for teachers really only dates back to the early 1970s, when Commonwealth funding for professional learning became available. In the early stages, the focus of professional learning in Australia was more on inputs—dollars spent, courses offered, number of teachers participating. More recently, the emphasis has shifted to measurable outcomes and, in particular, to the impacts of professional learning on student learning and development.

Table 12.1 provides a general overview of the major characteristics of professional development for teachers in the 1970s, contrasted with current trends.

Table 12.1: Trends in teacher professional learning since the 1970s[4]

FROM	TO
Centralised	Decentralised professional learning
System responsibility	Individual, collective responsibility
Off the shelf ('one size')	Tailored learning
Generalised	Contextualised
Off site, apart	On site, embedded
Inputs	Emphasis on outcomes
Passive	Interactive learning
External expert	External partners, advisers
Individual learning	Community learning
Theory based	Problem based
Transactional	Relational
Changing things	Changing people
Learning by seeing, hearing	Action learning
University degrees	Learning modules and short courses
Using research	Doing research
Paper based	Online learning
Broad focus	Student learning focus

---

c   Massive Open Online Courses. See https://www.coursera.org/learn/teaching for example.

This chapter is mainly concerned with the concept of *building learning communities* and *action learning*, the latter a particular type of professional learning and research that has been found to be very effective in the right circumstances.

Background: the individual teacher, school effectiveness and learning communities

Over many decades, films, books and television have portrayed the heroic, individual 'born' teacher battling against the odds to rein in unruly, uncaring students and fire within them a love of learning, often coming up against equally uncaring fellow teachers and inept principals in the process (see *To Sir With Love*, *Stand and Deliver*, *Dead Poets Society*, and *Freedom Writers* for examples of this genre). In the same schools where these teachers work their magic, students of other teachers are stultified and demoralised. Toole and Seashore Louis see this ongoing media fascination reinforcing an educational research tradition focusing on the attributes or traits of individual teachers.[5]

In her book *Powerful Teacher Education*, Linda Darling-Hammond describes the belief that 'good teachers are born and not made' as one of education's 'most damaging myths'; one that has gained the standing of a 'superstition', with harmful consequences for teacher education and schooling.[6] Obviously, if teachers are born and not made, there would be no need for or point to teachers' professional learning. Research evidence, however, points conclusively to the fact that teaching expertise is not a matter of innate qualities, but of learning and growth.[7]

The somewhat romantic, melodramatic view of teaching has persisted, while behind the scenes in education the attention of researchers turned as early as the mid-1960s to the issue of school effectiveness, as detailed in Chapter 1. The question of why some schools seemed to achieve superior results compared with other similar schools began to exercise minds. Up until this time, as noted previously, the prevailing view was that schools made almost no difference to children's development or achievement, which was largely pre-determined by heredity, family background and socio-economic context.[8]

There had been a related focus on the role that leadership can play in school effectiveness in terms of administration and management and later, instructional leadership and its influence on student achievement, as we have seen in previous chapters. An early concentration on principal leadership broadened to include other leaders such as deputy principals, faculty or department heads and teachers themselves. The focus of attention has thus moved from the leader to leadership, with the importance of delegation, trust and empowerment being increasingly recognised. There has been a realisation that leadership has both formal and distributed/distributive aspects, with every teacher a potential leader, as noted in the previous chapter.[9]

Notwithstanding such large-scale work on school effectiveness and educational leadership, the general and unassailable view now is that it is the classroom teacher who adds most to the learning equation, with the exception of that which each student 'brings to the table' (see Chapter 1).[10]

Thus, while there has been ongoing interest in effective schools and effective school leadership from the mid-1960s; since the late 1980s there has been major emphasis placed upon researching, understanding and facilitating quality teaching in schools, because of the growing recognition, supported by many empirical studies, that teachers make the major in-school difference to student achievement. At the same time, the notion of organisations as learning systems or communities has come to the fore[11], along with related concepts such as lifelong learning, collaboration, partnerships, mentoring, synergies, change and renewal.

In reviewing these developments, Kilpatrick, Barrett and Jones proposed the following definition:

> Learning communities are made up of people who share a common purpose. They collaborate to draw on individual strengths, respect a variety of perspectives, and actively promote learning opportunities. The outcomes are the creation of a vibrant, synergistic environment, enhanced potential for all members, and the possibility that new knowledge will be created.[12]

In education, research into the performance of individual teachers has revealed the importance of learning communities in influencing individual teacher effectiveness. Building collaboration and community among teachers has been found to be effective both in promoting teacher professional development and enhancing educational outcomes for students.[13]

Voulalas and Sharpe noted that the concept of the school as a learning community, while almost universally accepted as desirable, is still vague and ambiguous, as is the case with the concept of learning communities more generally. This lack of clarity can make attempts to develop learning communities in education and elsewhere problematic. Following a review of the literature on school learning communities and interviews with principals, Voulalas and Sharpe found that:

> When all the definitions were pieced together the school as a learning community was perceived as a place where life-long learning takes place for all stakeholders for their own continuous growth and development, teachers act as exemplary learners, students are prepared adequately for the future, and mistakes become agents for further learning and improvement. Furthermore, it is a place where collaboration and mutual support is nurtured, clear shared visions for the future are built, and the physical environment contributes to learning.[14]

However, while we now have a workable understanding of what an educational learning community looks like, operationalising the concept can be challenging. A key weakness to date has been the failure to address the 'how' aspects of establishing and maintaining learning communities.

What follows is an attempt to address this weakness. The discussion draws upon a series of research studies that reveal aspects, conditions and dynamics of creating and maintaining learning communities in educational settings, so that individual teachers can be engaged in professional learning with their colleagues to improve both their practice and the achievement of their students.

Case studies of learning communities in practice

As I have recounted, over the past decades I have been involved in a range of research projects that have examined aspects of quality or successful teaching. Below is a brief examination of four of these studies, two of which have been described in earlier chapters, with particular reference to the notion of learning communities and how these may improve teacher learning and performance and student achievement. Once again, the interested reader is referred to the references cited at the end of this chapter for a full explanation of methodological matters and lengthier treatment of the studies.

Following these case studies, commonalities with respect to educational learning communities are outlined and implications and conclusions explored.

1   Senior secondary teaching success

This study of successful senior secondary teaching was described in Chapter 6.[15] Briefly, while the study focused on individual teachers, a key finding, apart from the commonalities in personal qualities, attributes and actions of these teachers, was the view they commonly expressed that their success and that of their students was attributable in large measure to their colleagues in faculties and teaching teams. This was more than just a case of false modesty and was confirmed by other data. Faculties and teams were found to have placed a major emphasis on collaborative, problem-based professional learning.

2   AESOP

Some of the findings from this project have been described in Chapters 10 and 11. In considering the factors responsible for faculties and teams being able to achieve exceptional educational outcomes with their students, teachers' collaborative approaches to professional learning were found to be important.

Faculty/department staff and cross-school team members were ongoing learners and demonstrated an interest in and passion for their area that was contagious. Faculty heads and teachers shared latest approaches and knowledge with each other and were often linked with external bodies such as professional associations and colleagues at other schools. Faculty responsibilities for professional learning were shared and teachers took the lead on learning about various issues.

3 Evaluation of the Australian Government Quality Teaching Program

In 2004–05, a team from the University of Technology Sydney (Peter Aubusson and Laurie Brady) and the University of Wollongong (Dinham) conducted an evaluation of a program, *Quality Teaching Action Learning [QTAL] in New South Wales [NSW] Public Schools*, on behalf of the then NSW Department of Education and Training (DET).

QTAL projects took place in 2004–05 and were funded through the Australian Government Quality Teaching Program (AGQTP). The evaluation brief from the DET was to investigate conditions influencing teachers' implementation of an enquiry-based approach to action learning.

Action learning was defined for the purposes of the project and the evaluation as follows:

> Action learning is a process by which teachers meet together, whether spontaneously or deliberately, to share their experiences and thereby learn from each other. While this has always occurred in school staff rooms on an ad hoc basis, action learning is typically regarded as more systematic: as teams of teachers approaching a common task. There may be at times a 'critical friend', 'mentor', or facilitator. Action learning is commonly viewed as a less formal and less structured approach to addressing the problem than action research. The two terms have become increasingly fused and are now often used interchangeably ...
>
> The following are noteworthy characteristics that apply equally to action research and action learning. They have been previously reported in Brady, Aubusson and Dinham[16]:
> - It is an approach to improving practice by changing it through self-reflective enquiry.
> - It is participatory in that it involves teams of teachers working towards the improvement of their own practices. It is typically generated by individual or collective practitioner interest, so it is not 'done' to other people.
> - It involves the learning/research operating within the context in which the learning/research is to occur. Rather than seeking a panacea, it seeks to investigate what is effective in a particular classroom or school.
> - It is a systematic learning process in which the participants act responsibly. The collaborative and systematic nature of the process differentiates it from the more common thinking teachers experience when they think about their teaching.

- It operates through cycles of action and reflection that are typically repeated, that is, action, reflection, review, and action. Each step is informed by preceding steps to produce a continuing cycle of improvement.
- It is methodologically eclectic, yet typically involves collecting compelling evidence to be used as a basis for improving practice. LaBoskey describes it as improvement-oriented, interactive, using multiple methods, and viewed as constructing, testing, sharing and retesting exemplars of teaching.[17]

The evaluation encompassed 50 individual projects[d] involving 82 NSW public (government) primary and secondary schools that had successfully tendered for grants to investigate school-based and school-driven action learning research, utilising the framework of the NSW DET 'model of pedagogy'.[18]

Within the overarching QTAL activity, each school or group of schools had pursued an individual project (e.g., gifted and talented programs, literacy, quality teaching in science).

The evaluation took in all 50 Quality Teaching Action Learning projects involving the 82 schools, and nine projects were selected and researched as case studies by members of the evaluation team.[19]

The approach usually taken by schools was to use the funding provided under the AGQTP to release small teams from some of their teaching duties to enable them to work together on an approved QTAL project with the assistance of a designated university adviser. Teams were typically volunteers and comprised a mixture of classroom teachers and those in formal leadership positions, although in some cases principals had encouraged the membership of certain individuals.

The evaluation found that the QTAL projects undertaken by school teams as part of the AGQTP were very successful overall, both in promoting and utilising action learning, and in achieving individual project aims.

It was found that being part of such teams led to the professional growth of those involved and that this was manifested in increased leadership activity and influence in the school and sometimes beyond. Recognising individual teachers and empowering them to be involved within the project teams was an important symbolic and practical act of distributing leadership in the project schools, and the process of being involved in the projects facilitated further leadership capacity and potential.

Overall, the evaluation found that:
1. Successful projects were built upon a genuine, recognised need in the school.
2. Successful projects had clear, agreed, achievable and suitable goals.
3. Support from the principal (and other leaders) was essential.
4. A credible, suitable leader for the project was also vital.

---

d   See http://www.curriculumsupport.education.nsw.gov.au/policies/gats/programs/case/agqtp.htm

5. Successful projects were characterised by effective teams and team building.
6. Schools found it difficult to start and to build momentum.
7. It is important to maintain communication with all school staff about the school's project and its progress.
8. Academic partners provided valuable conceptual and theoretical background and assisted with framing, implementing and evaluating project proposals.
9. Teacher release time was a major factor in project success.
10. Schools found the Quality Teaching model a useful conceptual tool and vocabulary for discussion about pedagogy.
11. The most successful schools considered long-term sustainability of the project from the start.
12. Distributive leadership was both a factor in the success and an outcome of action learning.[20]
13. While there were initial indications that programs were successful, evidence of enhanced student outcomes was lacking due to the time frame.
14. There was limited sharing of the successes of school-based initiatives with other schools.
15. Schools and individuals valued and benefited from the sharing conferences held during the project period where project teams from across the state came together to learn, share and report.

Research data (derived from teachers, school project reports and journals, university academic partners and the researchers' site visits) demonstrated that the school-based Quality Teaching Action Learning projects had stimulated and enhanced teacher professional learning in the schools concerned, and in some cases, beyond the schools immediately involved with the projects. The use of teams of interested and committed teachers was fundamental to this process.

Team members were encouraged, empowered and grew in the course of the action learning projects. Important factors in the operation of teams and their projects included the time, focus and support for professional learning, the teamwork and collaboration of team members, and the work of team leaders. The willingness of principals to share power and responsibility and to respect and foster the capacity of others was also crucial.

While the time frame for the QTAL projects was less than a year, there was sufficient evidence to suggest that distributive leadership has the capacity, when aligned with teacher learning, to foster the phenomenon of the learning community. In many of the schools, work had already been undertaken on the project issue or problem, and sustainability of the projects was built in from the start to keep the learning process going beyond the project time frame.

4 NSW Quality Teaching Awards—learning communities and distributed leadership

As detailed in Chapter 6, the New South Wales (NSW) Minister for Education and Training Quality Teaching Awards (QTA) were instigated by the then NSW Minister for Education and Training in 2000 to recognise *and* research quality teaching in that state. From its inception in 2001 until its final year in 2011, the QTA had been developed and administered by the NSW Branch of the Australian College of Educators (ACE).[21] (I chaired the NSW QTA from their inception in 2000 until mid-2007 when I left NSW to take up a position at ACER.)

The QTA was open to teachers from all sectors and levels of education in NSW and was built upon a set of agreed professional teaching standards.[22] The award process involved referees' reports, development of a professional learning portfolio, and site assessment visits conducted by two external 'experts' in the field where teaching was observed and structured interviews with key people took place (i.e., with the candidate, fellow teachers, senior staff, students, community members, etc.).

Between 2001 and 2011, 473 government and non-government teachers from early childhood, primary, secondary, TAFE and university education in NSW received Quality Teaching Awards. As part of the QTA agenda on researching quality teaching, a series of research projects were conducted with QTA recipients resulting in various publications.[23]

Despite the QTA being awarded for individual teaching excellence, as with the HSC study reported previously, it became apparent from the portfolio assessment and site visit processes that in many cases there was a group of people within the particular organisation or workplace committed to enhancing teaching and learning, that is, the QTA recipient was not acting alone, but was part of an active professional learning community.

We decided to conduct a pilot study at two university sites where a QTA recipient had been identified through the assessment process as being an important member of such a group. We were particularly interested in the ecology of learning communities—how and why learning communities arise and how they are sustained.[24]

The method was for two researchers to visit each site to interview the QTA recipient and other key staff. Study questions included:
1. Why and how did discussion on quality teaching arise within the group?
2. What was the process? What people and factors influenced the process? What assisted and constrained the process?
3. What have been the outcomes of the process to date? What is the evidence for these outcomes?
4. How sustainable are the changes? How dependent is the process on one person?
5. Are there wider implications for quality teaching and teacher learning?
6. What role, if any, did the QTA play in the process?

Overall, the findings of the pilot study indicated that a concerted effort had been made to focus on quality teaching and learning within the contemporary context of Australian higher education.

The study showed how leadership, direction and pressure for quality teaching were being exerted on four fronts:

1. By the Commonwealth [federal] Government in asserting the status of quality teaching and learning alongside that of research in university funding and in auditing or quality assurance arrangements such as AUQA (Australian Universities Quality Agency).
2. By the [then] Carrick Institute for Learning and Teaching in Higher Education with its support for quality teaching, specifically in this study through its award programs as a means by which university teachers could demonstrate excellence in teaching and be recognised and rewarded for this.
3. Through universities placing greater emphasis on teaching and learning through formal structures and support; for example, teaching and learning centres and staff development for teaching and learning; a greater emphasis on teaching capacity in appointment, tenure and promotion, and through utilising awards for quality teaching such as the Carrick awards and the NSW QTA to both encourage and demonstrate excellence in teaching in that university.
4. Through the distributive leadership exhibited by individuals and groups of educators within the university, such as the QTA recipients studied here.

In respect of the fourth point above, the study gave insights into the complexities and uncertainties of the change process as groups of like-minded people coalesce, collaborate and act around a quality teaching agenda. It also underscored the value of peer-assessed processes carried out in a voluntary way that enabled collegial reflection on teaching practice.

While there were outside pressures and assistance to improve teaching and learning such as those outlined above in 1–3 above, it was apparent that the two university groups concerned had taken charge of a quality teaching agenda within this context. Concern for students, passion for the particular discipline, and wanting to improve teaching and learning created the impetus for conversation, reflection, learning and change. Those involved had taken action; participation was voluntary and based on perceived needs. Others in the organisation were being involved with and influenced by the quality teaching initiatives to varying degrees through a ripple or contagion effect.

On a cautionary note, the study suggested that there may be a point of disjunction between the leadership, pressure and support that is exhibited by the university in support of quality teaching—that is, 'top-down' pressure for change—and the on-the-ground, day-to-day distributive leadership that is exhibited by the academics themselves working with colleagues through conversations and work in small circles on matters important to them—that is, 'bottom-up' initiatives for change. The extent to which community learning and change around quality teaching can be stimulated, forced or mandated without such on-the-ground commitment and agreement is questionable, particularly in a large organisation like a university where pressure for change can be avoided or minimal, tokenistic compliance can occur.

In both QTA university case studies, the individual preparing for and receiving a QTA had added value to the learning of the group concerned, and the QTA process had become part of the conversation around quality teaching.

The award to one of their number of a QTA was seen as warranted by the rest of the group and a source of group recognition and pride. However, advancing quality teaching was not seen as being mainly about rewards or recognition. That said, it is an inescapable fact that awards for quality teaching are being seen and used increasingly by universities and governments as indicators or proxies for the quality of teaching, with such successes communicated to the wider environment.

Drawing from the case studies: How does a learning community develop and sustain itself?

In considering the findings of the four studies, common key principles, conditions and dynamics were identified in respect of learning communities.

It should be noted that the issue of loose definition remains. It is apparent that organisations can act as learning communities at all levels from the organisation as an overall formal entity, to formal sub-groupings, to cross-functional groups down to smaller and less formal learning teams. This range of operation can make definition problematic, yet in no way diminishes the potential of the phenomenon.

What then can we conclude about learning communities from the various research studies? What works? To answer these questions, the following commonalities were identified from the four studies:

Focus on teaching and learning
- Learning communities have a focus on learning and a desire to learn about learning and teaching; there is use of pedagogic terminology, models and theory, coupled with a conscious effort to de-prioritise administration and management, and prioritise learning within the group.
- Members of learning communities see themselves and their students as going somewhere, with learning being an ongoing process; learning becomes contagious, with others catching the 'bug'.
- Within the group there is recognition that it is necessary to change the way people think if there is to be change in how they act, and thus learning, reflection and questioning are important.
- Members of the group are concerned with establishing and maintaining upward, continuous cycles of improvement; they are not satisfied with the status quo.

Individual and collective belief and support
- Group members possess and demonstrate belief and respect for their profession and discipline; they believe in, even love their area and communicate this to others.
- Members of the group pay attention to social maintenance, trying to make their school, department, or faculty a 'good place'[25]; members respect and care for each other and their students as people, and social and professional relationships are important to group performance.

Problem solving
- There is an emphasis on problem- or issue-based learning and recognition of what is important, with dialogue around identified issues and potential solutions.
- Experimentation, risk-taking and innovation in teaching and learning are encouraged and are a feature of learning communities; there is questioning rather than acceptance of constraints or problems.
- Teaching and learning are context and person specific, with efforts to contextualise and modify as necessary externally derived solutions or approaches.
- There is ongoing reflection on and evaluation of existing and new measures within the learning community, coupled with data-informed decision-making.

Internal expectations and accountability
- The group creates a climate of high expectations and professionalism which members rise to, not wanting to let anyone down, not least their students.
- Members of the group empower each other to take the lead in learning, in turn enhancing individual and group leadership capacity and effectiveness.
- Accountability is to the group, more than to externally imposed accountability measures; group accountability and self-accountability are powerful influences on the learning community's ethos, and action.[e]

Leadership and outside influence
- Leadership outside and inside the group is important in stimulating and facilitating the learning community.
- While learning communities can develop without stimulus or action from above or outside, assistance, guidance, resources and encouragement from others within and in some cases outside the organisation can facilitate the learning process.

---

e   As noted previously, external forms of accountability are weaker drivers for improvement, as these tend to engender minimal, 'get-by', 'satisficing' performance. With internal accountability, however, the group is more empowered, self-governing and aspirational, being less likely to settle for a minimum level of performance.

Overall dynamics
- Time, place, space and language are important elements in creating a learning community.
- Overall, what seems to work most effectively is a combination of external understanding, advice, assistance and recognition ('top-down'), coupled with a focus on internal issues and solutions, with teacher and group learning to address these through empowerment and with internal action and accountability ('bottom-up').

Concluding remarks

The research evidence on learning communities and how these can support teachers' professional learning and improve student achievement is encouraging.

Not surprisingly, there are many who advocate the development of learning communities as means of lifting educational performance. In this age, we have grown accustomed to demanding quick fixes and solutions to problems, what could be termed the '24-hour help desk mentality'. However, learning communities cannot be mandated, imposed, built or operated in a technical, mechanistic sense. Rather, these need to be encouraged, nourished and sustained in the manner of an organic system, hence the interest in ecological approaches.

Building a learning community is more like agriculture or gardening than engineering or chemistry. While agriculture is underpinned by both engineering and chemistry, it is a far more inexact and varied undertaking, heavily dependent on the local and wider environment and reliant on knowledge, learning and judgement.

Some organisations and groups appear to suffer from learning disabilities.[26] These disabilities need to be diagnosed, assessed and addressed through suitable interventions in the same ways in which we would help a student.

As noted, educational leaders cannot, nor should they, attempt to mandate or force the development of learning communities. As Andy Hargreaves has noted, collegiality should not and cannot be contrived or forced.[27] Leaders can, however, assist organisational members to come together, focus and collaborate on issues of importance. Educational leaders need to ensure that teaching and learning are central concerns of the educational organisation and do all in their power to ensure that nothing is allowed to obstruct or distort this central focus.

There is a challenge for educational leaders to deal with situations where learning has atrophied. As McBeath has noted:

> It is hard for teachers to shed an outer skin which has calcified over many years in the classroom where dialogue is a rare commodity no matter how hard teachers strive for it, and in which 'instruction' is the norm.[28]

Educational leaders within and outside the group need to act judiciously to wear away this 'outer skin' so that learning can once again flourish. However, building a learning community should not be construed or seen by others as being about 'fixing' teachers. Educational leaders should look to themselves, their strengths, weaknesses and actions, as well as to others, for problems and solutions.

The voluntary and empowering nature of learning communities is important. In our evaluation of the AGQTP, while we were very positive about the outcomes of the projects and the overall program, our strong recommendation to the Department of Education and Training in NSW was that the program should retain its voluntary status. To make it compulsory would almost guarantee failure or 'lip-service' in many schools, while being very costly if the current model of teacher release was continued.

One of the most encouraging outcomes of these and other related studies has been the extent to which dialogue about and focus on quality teaching have emerged and been seen to reinvigorate jaded, mid-to-late career teachers who are now active participants in learning communities. Other teachers, of course, have never stopped learning.

Another important outcome of the case studies is the degree to which latent leadership potential has been released through the development of the learning communities, in turn providing both a stimulus and resource for further change and improvement.

Finally, to complete the circle, what the various studies and work by others have confirmed is that teachers and groups of teachers can learn, and are more 'made' than 'born', although the 'making' needs to continue career-long. It seems that it is never too late to nourish the learning community if the right conditions are provided.

Endnotes

1. Dinham, S. (2008). *How to get your school moving and improving: An evidence-based approach*. Melbourne, Victoria: ACER Press. (p. 140)
2. Hattie, J. (2012). *Visible learning for teachers*. London: Routledge. (pp. 251–252)
3. Timperley, H., Wilson, A., Barrar, H., & Fung, I. (2007). *Teacher professional learning and development: Best evidence synthesis iteration*. Wellington, New Zealand: Ministry of Education. (p. xxv). Reproduced with permission. See https://creativecommons.org/licenses/by/4.0/legalcode
4. After Dinham, S. (2008). (p. 102)
5. Toole, J. C., & Seashore Louis, K. S. (2002). The role of professional learning communities in international education (pp. 245–279). In K. Leithwood, & P. Hallinger (Eds.), *Second international handbook of educational leadership and administration*. Dordrecht, Netherlands: Kluwer.
6. Darling-Hammond, L. (2006). *Powerful teacher education*. San Francisco: Jossey-Bass. (p. ix)
7. Scott, C., & Dinham, S. (2008). Born not made: The nativist myth and teachers' thinking. *Teacher Development, 12*(2), 115–124.
8. Reynolds. D., Teddlie, C., Creemers, B., Scheerens, J., & Townsend, T. (2000). An introduction to school effectiveness research. In C. Teddlie & D. Reynolds (Eds.), *The international handbook of school effectiveness research* (pp. 3–25). London, England: Falmer Press.

9   Busher, H., & Harris, A. (2000). *Subject leadership and school improvement*. London, England: Paul Chapman; Gronn, P. (2002). Distributed leadership. In K. Leithwood & P. Hallinger (Eds.), *Second international handbook of educational leadership and administration* (pp. 653–696). Dordrecht, Netherlands: Kluwer; Spillane, J., Halverson, R., & Diamond, J. (2001). Investigating school leadership practice: A distributed perspective. *Educational Researcher, 30*(3), 23–28; York-Barr, J., & Duke, K. (2004). What do we know about teacher leadership? Findings from two decades of scholarship. *Review of Educational Research, 74*(3), 255–316; Dinham, S. (2007). The secondary head of department and the achievement of exceptional student outcomes. *Journal of Educational Administration, 45*(1), 62–79; see also (2008). *Journal of Educational Administration, 46*(2), thematic edition on distributed leadership.

10 Hattie, J. (2009). *Visible learning: A synthesis of over 800 meta-analyses relating to achievement*. London, England: Routledge.

11 Senge, P. M. (1990). *The fifth discipline*. Sydney, New South Wales: Random House.

12 Kilpatrick, S., Barrett, M., & Jones, T. (2003). *Defining learning communities*. Paper presented at NZARE/AARE international conference, Auckland, 30 November–3 December.

13 Watson, K., & Steele, F. (2006). Building a teacher education community: Recognising the ecological reality of sustainable collaboration. *Asia-Pacific Forum on Science Learning and Teaching, 7*(1).

14 Voulalas, Z. D., & Sharpe, F. (2005). Creating schools as learning communities: Obstacles and processes. *Journal of Educational Administration, 43*(2), 187–208.

15 Ayres, P., Dinham, S., & Sawyer, W. (1999). *Successful teaching in the NSW Higher School Certificate*. Sydney: NSW Department of Education and Training; Ayres, P., Dinham, S., & Sawyer, W. (1998). *The identification of successful teaching methodologies in the NSW Higher School Certificate: A research report for the NSW Department of Education and Training*. Penrith: University of Western Sydney, Nepean; Ayres, P., Dinham, S., & Sawyer, W. (2000). Successful senior secondary teaching. *Quality Teaching Series*, No. 1, Australian College of Education, September, 1–20; Ayres, P., Dinham, S., & Sawyer, W. (2004). Effective teaching in the context of a Grade 12 high stakes external examination in New South Wales, Australia. *British Educational Research Journal, 30*(1), 141–165; Ayres, P., Dinham, S., & Sawyer, W. (1997). *The identification of successful teaching methodologies in the NSW Higher School Certificate: Identifying the successful teachers*. Penrith: University of Western Sydney, Nepean; Sawyer, W., Ayres, P., & Dinham, S. (2001). What does an effective Year 12 English teacher look like? *English in Australia, 129*(30), 51–63.

16 Brady, L., Aubusson, P., & Dinham, S. (2008a). Teachers as researchers: Action learning for professional development. *Learning and Teaching, 1*(1), 5–16.

17 Brady, L., Aubusson, P., & Dinham, S. (2008b). Action learning: Contemporary professional development. *Curriculum and Teaching, 23*(1), 5–19. (pp. 6–7). Reprinted with permission.

18 NSW Department of Education and Training. (2003). *Quality teaching in NSW public schools: Discussion paper*. Sydney: Professional Support and Curriculum Directorate, NSW DET.

19 See Aubusson, P., Brady, L., & Dinham, S. (2005). *Action learning: What works? A research report prepared for the New South Wales Department of Education and Training*. Sydney: University of Technology Sydney; Brady, L., Aubusson, P., & Dinham, S. (2006). Action learning for school improvement. *Educational Practice and Theory, 28*(2), 27–39; Dinham, S., Aubusson, P., & Brady, L. (2008). Distributed leadership as a factor in and outcome of teacher action learning. *International Electronic Journal for Leadership in Learning, 12*(4). http://www.ucalgary.ca/~iejll/volume12/dinham.htm; Aubusson, P., Steele, F., Dinham, S., & Brady, L. (2007). Action learning in teacher

learning community formation: Informative or transformative? *Teacher Development, 11*(2), 133–148; Brady, L., Aubusson, P., & Dinham, S. (2008b); Brady, L., Aubusson, P., & Dinham, S. (2008b).

20 Dinham, S., Aubusson, P., & Brady, L. (2008). Distributed leadership as a factor in and outcome of teacher action learning. *International Electronic Journal for Leadership in Learning, 12*(4), http://www.ucalgary.ca/~iejll/volume12/dinham.htm

21 Dinham, S. (2002). NSW Quality Teaching Awards—Research, rigour and transparency. *Unicorn, 28*(1), 5–9.

22 Brock, P. (2000). *Standards of professional practice for accomplished teaching in Australian classrooms.* Canberra: Australian College of Educators/Australian Association for Research in Education/Australian Curriculum Studies Association.

23 Bergin, M., Dinham, S., Scott, C., & Brock, P. (2002). *The heart of teaching: Report on the 2001 Quality Teaching Awards Project.* Sydney: Australian College of Educators, NSW Chapter; Dinham, S. (2002); Dinham, S., & Scott, C. (2003). Benefits to teachers of the professional learning portfolio: A case study. *Teacher Development, 7*(3), 187–202; Dinham, S., & Scott, C. (2003). Awards for teaching excellence: Intentions and realities. *Unicorn Online Refereed Article*, No. 24, 1–25; Scott, C., McCulla, N., & Dinham, S. (2007). *The ecology of quality teaching.* Paper presented at the British Educational Research Association Annual Conference, Institute of Education, University of London, September; McCulla, N., Dinham, S., & Scott, C. (2007). Stepping out from the crowd: Some findings from the NSW Quality Teaching awards on seeking recognition for professional accomplishment. *Unicorn Online Refereed Article*, ORA 51, 3–32.

24 See McCulla, N., Scott, C., & Dinham, S. (2009). Quiet conversations in small circles: The role of voluntary awards and distributive leadership in promoting teaching excellence in universities. *Unicorn Online Refereed Article*, ORA 57, 3–22.

25 MacBeath, J. (2006). *Leadership as a subversive activity*, ACEL Monograph Series, No. 39.

26 Senge, P. M. (1990). *The fifth discipline.* Sydney, Australia: Random House; Bhindi, N. (2007). *Why workplaces resist learning.* Paper presented at the Sixth International Conference on Educational Leadership, Australian Centre for Educational Leadership, University of Wollongong, 15 February.

27 Hargreaves, A. (1994). *Changing teachers, changing times.* London, England: Cassell.

28 MacBeath, J. (2006). (p. 19)

CHAPTER 13

What role can leaders play in promoting professional learning and development? What role can professional standards for teachers play?

INTRODUCTION

Andreas Schleicher from the OECD has noted:
> In many countries, the role and functioning of schools are changing—and so is what is expected of teachers. They are asked to teach in increasingly multicultural classrooms. They must place greater emphasis on integrating students with special learning needs, both special difficulties and special talents, in their classes. They need to make more effective use of information and communication technologies for teaching. They are required to engage more in planning within evaluative and accountability frameworks. And they are asked to do more to involve parents in schools. *No matter how good the pre-service education for teachers is, it is cannot be expected to prepare teachers for all the challenges they will face throughout their careers.*[1] [Emphasis added]

There is obviously a clear role for leaders in facilitating the professional learning and development of teachers, both in respect of the individual teacher concerned, and in terms of building a learning community for the betterment of the school and the students and community it serves.

Schleicher has elaborated upon some of the different purposes of such professional learning:
- updating individuals' knowledge of a subject in light of recent advances in the area;
- updating individuals' skills and approaches in light of the development of new teaching techniques and objectives, new circumstances, and new educational research;
- enabling individuals to apply changes made to curricula or other aspects of teaching practice;
- enabling schools to develop and apply new strategies concerning the curriculum and other aspects of teaching practice;
- exchanging information and expertise among teachers and others, e.g., academics and industrialists; or
- helping teachers become more effective.[2]

One of the challenges for educational leaders in achieving the above and other objectives is encouraging and supporting school staff to willingly participate in professional learning. In speaking with sometimes frustrated school leaders in Australia and overseas[3], I frequently hear of the responses these leaders receive to requests for change: 'I'm a good teacher and I get good results, so why should I be involved in professional learning?'; 'Professional learning will stifle my creativity'; 'We are a high-performing school'; 'What I do in my classroom is my business', and the old chestnut mentioned previously, 'We tried that in 1975 and it didn't work'. Other common questions in addition to 'Why?' concern 'When?' and 'Who pays?' When speaking with principals in Germany in 2014–15, for example, they expressed frustration with the situation whereby teachers who have undergone lengthy training—up to seven years—and have obtained permanent 'public servant' status with a 'job for life', are reluctant to engage in further professional learning, especially out of school time and at their own expense. Both professional learning and the use of professional teaching standards are opposed strongly by many teachers and their unions in Germany.[4]

What can leaders do to promote involvement in professional learning and development?

Schleicher has noted the need for policymakers, leaders and practitioners:

> ... to consider both how to support and encourage participation and how to ensure that opportunities match teachers' needs. This needs to be balanced with the cost in terms of both finance and teachers' time. OECD research identifies several aspects as central to successfully bridging the gap between the ideal learning environment and day-to-day practice:
> - well-structured and well-resourced induction programs can support new teachers in their transition to full teaching responsibilities before they

obtain all the rights and responsibilities of full-time professional teachers. In some countries, once teachers have completed their pre-service education and began their teaching, they begin one or two years of heavily supervised teaching. During this period, the beginning teacher typically receives a reduced workload, mentoring by master teachers, and continued formal instruction.
- effective professional development needs to be ongoing, include training, practice and feedback, and provide adequate time and follow-up support. Successful programs involve teachers in learning activities that are similar to those they will use with their students, and encourage the development of teachers' learning communities.
- teacher development needs to be linked with wider goals of school and system development, and with appraisal and feedback practices and school evaluation.
- there is often a need to re-examine structures and practices that inhibit interdisciplinary practice and to give more room for teachers to take time to learn deeply, and employ both inquiry and group based approaches, especially in the core areas of curriculum and assessment.[5]

There is, however, considerable variation in the provision of and requirement for professional development across nations, as the OECD report indicates. The nature and quality of professional development offerings are other key issues. For example, much personal development (PD) is essentially about administration and compliance, rather than growth and development.

Thus, a key question lies in determining the nature of professional learning needed by individuals and groups. In their 'best evidence synthesis' for the New Zealand Ministry of Education, Timperley, Wilson, Barrar and Fung advocated that the source of teachers' learning needs are the learning needs of their students, as indicated in Figure 13.1 on the following page.

This approach is consistent with the MGSE cycle for clinical judgement noted in Chapter 7, which also begins with assessing the learning needs of the student.

Both models or cycles emphasise the primacy of initially focusing on the learner and his or her individual learning needs.

Timperley et al. also emphasise the importance of leaders' influence and actions in assisting and working with teachers in identifying and meeting these professional learning needs:

> Much of the responsibility for promoting the professional development of teachers rests with school leaders ... There is also increasing international recognition of the importance of the role of leaders in organising and promoting the learning of those they lead.

How leaders can best fulfil this role depends on how leadership itself is understood. We have identified four models of leadership and suggest that all contribute to an understanding of what leaders need to know and do in order to promote the learning of their people.[6]

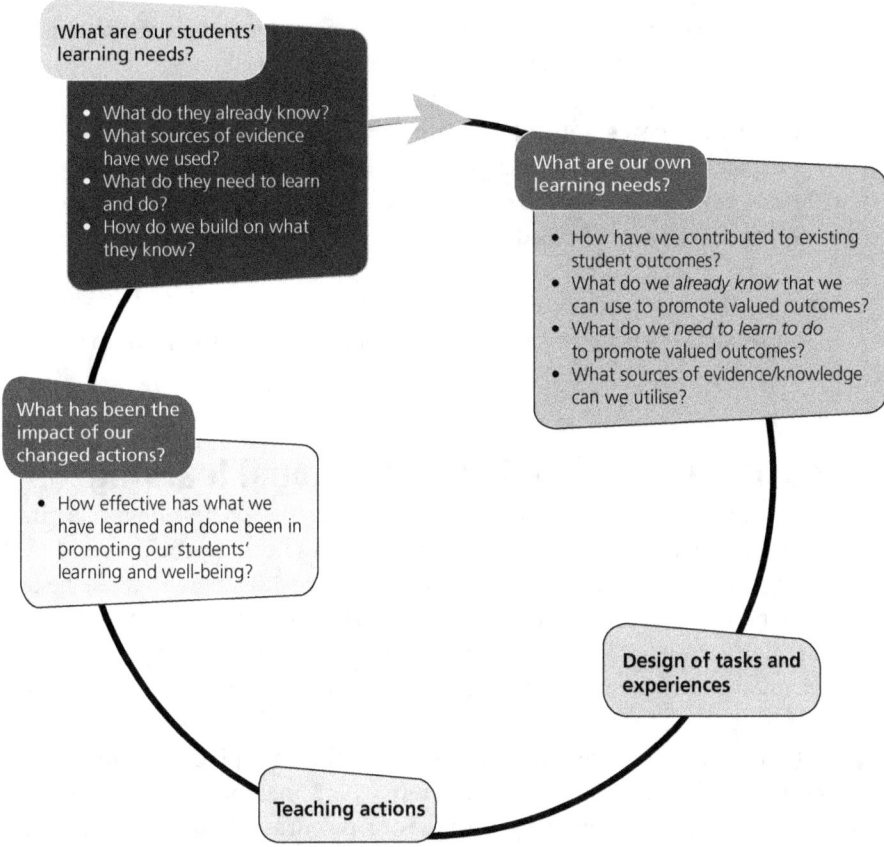

Figure 13.1: Teacher enquiry and knowledge-building cycle to promote valued student outcomes[7]

The four leadership roles derived by Timperley et al. from studies with 'substantive positive outcomes for students' were as follows:

Developing a vision
- The vision encompassed an alternative reality for student outcomes and possibilities for curriculum content and pedagogy.
- The vision was coherent with wider environmental and school policies.

Managing and organising
- Establish priorities and reduce competing demands.
- Engage reluctant participants by putting forward compelling reasons to do so, providing effective content, and engaging teacher theories.
- Ensure focused and productive opportunities to learn.
- Engage appropriate expertise.
- Promote participation in professional communities focused on promoting the teaching–learning relationship in evidence-informed ways.

Leading the professional learning
- Promote a challenging learning culture.
- Know what content and learning activities are likely to be of benefit.
- Promote evidence-informed, self-regulated learning for sustainability.

Developing the leadership of others
- Distribute leadership by developing teacher leaders with specific areas of focus.[8]

The importance of planning professional learning

Of the four leadership roles outlined above, 'leading the professional learning' is most relevant to this discussion. The AESOP study and other projects cited in this book emphasised the importance of the leader being a co-learner with those he or she works with, and of modelling learning for others. However, it is important that there is a professional learning plan, based, as noted, on the learning needs of students, and then the resultant learning needs of teachers, congruent with the broader aims and priorities of the school.

The alternative to a reasoned professional learning plan is some form of smorgasbord or 'shotgun' approach, whereby staff members are exposed to a random raft of professional learning activities or resources without any underlying plan, themes or principles for what is being undertaken. Teaching staff members I've spoken with are critical of such random ad hoc approaches where, for example, every week there is a new article to read that is disconnected from anything that has come before, or what might follow later. In other words, staff members can't see the point or utility of what they are being exposed to, which, at best, is surface learning; this, in turn, tends to breed cynicism and disengagement.

In a report for the Business Council of Australia, we noted:

> There are many professional learning courses, seminars and workshops for teachers, but in total the pattern of provision is brief, localised, fragmented and rarely sequential. They do not amount to a system with a capacity to

engage most teachers in the professional learning experiences that will have a significant effect on student learning.⁹

On the other hand, where teachers have been involved in identifying issues of concern or problems in their school, and have been involved in canvassing and formulating solutions and approaches to deal with these, they are more likely to see the relevance and feel involved with resultant learning.

With action learning approaches, as noted in the previous chapter, staff can implement various interventions and activities and see and measure the impact of these. Modifications can then occur for later interventions. This is deeper, more impactful, involved and lasting learning that can lead to improvement and sustainability.

When school staff members are able to see the impact of what they have attempted, this can act as a spur for further learning. Seeing that a particular strategy has worked, even partially, can motivate further learning and action for improvement.

As noted, teachers' conversations are an important aspect of professional learning. In the AGQTP evaluation, for example, teachers reported, and we observed, that the topics of conversation in staffrooms had changed from 'gardening, golf and superannuation', to teaching and learning. Rather than complaining about certain students, teachers were now discussing methods of teaching them. Models and frameworks of and for quality teaching were important vehicles to facilitate such discussions, providing a language for the participants.[10]

However, engaging staff meaningfully in such planning can be problematic. Douglas Reeves has pointed out that poor engagement with professional learning is often associated with 'initiative fatigue', particularly that which arises from externally imposed changes and requirements impacting on teachers and schools:

> Initiative fatigue does not occur by either accident or malice. Teachers and school leaders do not deliberately overload their task lists with more items than they can conceivably accomplish. Neither do state, provincial, or national policymakers intend the inevitable results of the *Law of Initiative Fatigue* ... Each document request has a well-intended purpose, and each element of a required plan is a response to a perceived need. Nevertheless, despite overwhelming evidence that limited time is a source of dissatisfaction among teachers ... the burdens associated with mandatory planning requirements are proliferating at an alarming rate.[11]

When speaking with teachers in Germany, one of their stated reasons for resisting involvement with professional learning was that many of them saw the in-service learning opportunities provided by the state to be about meeting mandated change agendas, and not about what they felt they needed to improve their practice. On the other hand, I saw some impressive, collaborative professional learning in schools where the staff were working together on issues of importance to them, their students and their school.[12]

Reeves identified from his research nine characteristics of professional development plans that had 'measurable and significant effect on gains in student achievement':

1. **Comprehensive needs assessment**—the plans contained evidence of school leadership decisions regarding the use of time, assignment of staff, and allocation of resources that were directly related to student needs.
2. **Enquiry process**—the plans identified causal relationships between teaching and leadership practices and student results.
3. **Prioritisation**—the plans had six or fewer clearly established priorities.
4. **Specificity**—the plan goals were directly related to academic expectations for students, including specific focus on grade levels, skills and individual students.
5. **Measurability**—a learning community could make an objective statement about the progress or lack of it in their school with regard to the achievement of goals.
6. **Achievability**—the goals were sufficiently challenging to close learning gaps within 3 to 5 years.
7. **Relevance**—the goals represented urgent, critical needs and were clearly aligned with a needs-analysis process.
8. **Timeliness**—the goals had specific dates—season, month, or day—for assessment, data collection and analysis.
9. **Monitoring**—the plans include a specific date to be monitored, along with frequent intervals for examining and reporting progress. Monitoring included not only student results but also professional practices of teachers and school leaders.[13]

The above 'ring true' and are authentic, useful guidelines, based upon my experience with turnaround and effective schools in various projects, including current work with the University of Melbourne network of schools[a], although I would argue for fewer priorities, say three or four at most. It is better to concentrate on a narrower range of high importance priorities rather than trying to concentrate on everything at once. Some successes in areas with 'spill-over' or 'bang for your buck' potential will provide both a foundation and motivation for further professional learning and improvement.

(We will take up some of these points in more detail when we examine school improvement and educational change in Part D.)

---

[a] See http://education.unimelb.edu.au/community/university_of_melbourne_network_of_schools

The role of professional standards for teachers and teaching in professional learning[14]

Ingvarson, Kleinhenz and I have noted:

> The quality of teaching is the main driver of successful student learning outcomes.
>
> Australia's teaching profession and its schools constitute an infrastructure that is critical to its survival in an increasingly global economy.
>
> Every student deserves teachers who are suited to teaching, well trained and qualified, highly skilled, caring and committed to moving forward the learning of their students.[15]

Previous attempts to drive improvement in teacher quality and to attract, retain, recognise and reward accomplished teachers have largely failed.[16] One of the key reasons is that such schemes—of which there have been many in Australia—have never been mainstreamed to form a common or consistent, effective salary and career structure:

> Present arrangements in teaching do not encourage, reward or indeed require advanced professional learning ...
>
> It is clear that there is a broad consensus that action is needed to radically strengthen procedures for recognising and rewarding teachers who reach high teaching standards.[17]

Extensive international and national experience has shown that seemingly simplistic measures such as paying teachers on 'merit' or by 'results' are doomed to fail. Bonus schemes for teachers don't work in driving improvement in the quality of teaching. Rewarding and punishing schools on the basis of 'results' makes little sense when we know that teacher quality varies more within than between schools.[18]

While commencing salaries for teachers are comparable to those in similar professions, present lock-step annual incremental salary and career structures for teachers are 19th-century industrial artefacts that see teachers' salaries peak too soon and at too low a level.

At present, more than three-quarters of Australia's teachers are at the top of such salary scales, where they earn less than 1.5 times the salary of a beginning teacher. This difference is too small and smaller than that in comparable, higher-performing countries, where the differentiation is typically of the order of 1.75 to 2.25 times or even higher.[19]

While too high a proportion of beginning teachers resign in their first three years—25 per cent or more according to some estimates—there is also a hidden resignation spike associated with teachers reaching the top of such salary scales after eight to ten years of teaching, a time at which salaries are rising steeply for the most able practitioners in other professions.[20]

As noted previously, David Berliner[21] has suggested that moving from novice status to achieving competence as a teacher takes around two to three years. The development of a high level of skill, however, takes five to seven years and a great deal of work. The Australian Professional Standards for Teachers introduced in 2011 reflect this reality.[22]

Other 'one shot' strategies to address teacher quality (e.g., higher entry scores, pre-service exit testing) won't work when used in isolation. As I have commented previously in this book and elsewhere, we need to address teacher quality at every step of the teacher career progression from entry onwards, that is, at every key point of leverage.[23]

Caution is needed, however. Rather than simply assessing teachers and making judgements on their capabilities at various career points in the hope that this will somehow lead to improvement, we need to use the concept of assessment *for* learning and development, something now widely advocated for student learning and equally applicable in this context. A concern with the Australian Professional Standards for Teachers (APST) expressed by various parties was that the main use of the standards was going to be more about judgement than development. However, a current evaluation of the implementation of the APST has shown this fear to be unfounded.[24]

The role of professional teaching standards in a new teacher career salary structure

The solution to the complex situation outlined to this point lies in combining two present agendas: the introduction of Australian professional standards, and the calls for 'bonus', 'merit' or 'performance' pay to reward the most able teachers. Together, these can systematically inform, drive and reward improvement in teacher effectiveness.

Professional standards are now seen as crucial in promoting quality teaching and much work has been done in Australia over the past 25 years by professional associations, employers and jurisdictions, work that produced a vast array of standards, frameworks and approaches designed to articulate, engender and, in some cases, recognise and reward quality teaching.[25] Although many of these standards were never actually operationalised, this has been important work, which has not been wasted. The involvement of the profession in thinking about and articulating what teachers need to know, do and understand, has been an important precursor to what we have now and what we need to do now.

For the first time, Australia has a set of national teaching standards for teachers at four levels—*Graduate*, *Proficient* (both mandatory) and *Highly Accomplished* and *Lead* (both optional). The introduction and adoption of these standards—and accompanying standards for teacher education course development and accreditation[26]—provides an ideal opportunity and vehicle to move from the present ramshackle approach to teachers' career structures to a nationally consistent model of professional learning, recognition and reward fit for a profession.[b]

In a report in 2008 for the Business Council of Australia (BCA)[27] prior to the release in 2011 of the current Australian standards, we suggested that equilibrium in a national certification system for Australia's teachers might see around 30 per cent of teachers at the *Highly Accomplished* level and 10% at the *Lead* (Teacher) level. The remaining 60 per cent of teachers would be seeking or have gained certification at the mandatory *Proficient* [registered] level.[c]

In our report we suggested that the top of the *Proficient* salary scale should be around twice the salary of a beginning teacher. Those who achieved *Highly Accomplished* teacher status would have access to a salary scale that would enable them to earn up to 2.5 times the salary of a beginning teacher, while those who achieved *Lead* teacher status could earn more. Teachers would not need to reach the top of salary scales in their particular level before seeking higher level certification.

We recognised that the issue of requiring a certain level of certification for a particular position was a decision best left to employers, given the diversity of Australian schools. It was our hope that eventually all teacher industrial award agreements would incorporate a salary-career structure that was consistent with the proposed framework we outlined.

We now have the Australian Professional Standards for Teachers, but as yet we don't have the framework. While the development, endorsement and acceptance of the APST is a great achievement, the standards represent a beginning and a means, rather than an end. It is what happens after the introduction of the standards that is important.

It has been pleasing to see—at the time of writing—that certification at the higher optional *Highly Accomplished* and *Lead* levels is being piloted and in some cases introduced into various Australian jurisdictions (and that Principals Australia Institute is piloting the certification of principals against the Australian Professional Standard for Principals). Once use of the teaching standards becomes more common and is incorporated into salary and career structures, the impact of the standards on teachers' professional learning and teaching performance, and ultimately on student learning, is likely to both increase and accelerate.

---

b Universities have had such a broadly consistent and (inter)nationally recognised model for decades, with five levels (Tutor [A] to Professor [E]) and around 25 salary steps, along with systems of allowances and rewards for higher duties and positions of responsibility. A Professor typically earns 2.75 times the salary of a first step Level A Tutor, a ratio consistent with the differentiation between a first year teacher and Lead level teacher mentioned previously.

c These proportions are indicative. We did not advocate the use of quotas for the higher levels but rather a criterion-based approach.

Concluding remarks

Some key issues and areas for caution

However, there are a number of key issues that need to be addressed to achieve a true standards-based career structure for Australia's teachers.

Firstly, there is a need for effective performance standards that have authenticity and utility and add value.[28] Performance indicators have yet to be fully developed for the various levels of the APST, although the AITSL website highlights progress in this area, with resources such as 'Illustrations of Practice' against the four levels of the standards.[d]

Secondly, *how* teachers are assessed and *who* conducts these processes are crucial questions. The profession *must* be meaningfully involved and feel ownership of the processes. A weakness in past efforts to operationalise professional standards has been in the training of assessors. More than just 'professional judgement' is required if the process is to have validity, reliability and credibility within and outside the profession.

Thirdly, professional learning opportunities, programs and resources must be developed and provided to accompany and support the standards and these need to be consistent with broader issues such as the emerging national curriculum being developed by the Australian Curriculum, Assessment and Reporting Authority (ACARA).[29] Employers will need to ensure their processes for appointment, induction, supervision, professional development, appraisal and promotion are consistent with and supportive of assessment and certification of teachers at the various levels of the APST[30], and with the Australian Teacher Performance and Development Framework.[31]

Portability, currency and maintenance of certification are also significant issues. Most important, however, as noted, is the question of whether certification of teachers at the voluntary *Highly Accomplished* and *Lead* levels will be rewarded financially through integration into existing and future salary and career structures. If this fails to occur, then the APST will have little traction in driving improvement in the quality teaching. They will be decorative rather than generative.

As noted, it is essential that the assessment processes for teacher certification are—and are seen to be—valid, reliable and credible within and across the profession, and more broadly. The assessment processes must be based upon and congruent with the APST and include observation of teaching and school visitations as well as 'off-site' assessment and validation across schools and systems. Assessors/observers must be fully trained, and over time, should have been certified as *Highly Accomplished* or *Lead*

---

d   See http://www.aitsl.edu.au/australian-professional-standards-for-teachers/illustrations-of-practice/find-by-career-stage teachers themselves. This involvement is essential in both recognising and utilising the expertise of the profession and involving and empowering it in the process.[32]

The goal of advancing quality teaching is best achieved by eventually having all Australian teachers certified at some point of the teacher career continuum from *Graduate*, to *Proficient*, to *Highly Accomplished* and to *Lead* teacher level (and possibly beyond in the case of aspiring and practising principals, although the Australian Professional Standard for Principals was not intended to be used, at least directly, as a performance standard[33]).

While the lower *Graduate* and *Proficient* levels could be assessed by the existing teacher registration authorities within states and territories[34] on a nationally consistent basis; because of the prestige and importance of the *Lead* teacher level, this should be truly national and conducted through or on behalf of AITSL. The *Highly Accomplished* level, being potentially far larger, could follow piloting of the *Lead* level procedures. Ideally, certification at the *Highly Accomplished* level would also be conducted nationally for reasons of consistency and credibility rather than being left to states and territories or individual schools and employers.

However, there are a number of additional issues. A poor 'rubber stamp' process with too many 'unworthy' teachers gaining certification at the higher levels could lead to a salary blow-out, with little credibility or gain from the exercise.

Worthy teachers failing to be recognised would also undermine credibility, take-up and possibly morale. Experience tells us quotas won't work either. The process must be fair and criterion-referenced.

The standards are intended to guide and drive professional learning and not just provide a frame to judge teachers. It will be necessary to measure teacher *performance* and *growth* against the standards at each level. Assessment for each level must be linked to evidence of student learning, the intended impact and outcome of teaching. Multiple measures of student learning will be required, including, class, year and school-based assessments, teacher portfolios (these need careful consideration[35]), NAPLAN results (only where relevant as NAPLAN is a poor proxy for individual teacher quality) and use of other standardised measures and data sources. Key documents such as the Melbourne Declaration[36] and the *Australian Charter for the Professional Learning of Teachers and School Leaders*[37] should be used as frames for the type of evidence of student learning and development that will be required. This goes far beyond a 'scrapbook' approach.

Joan Baratz-Snowden, a key figure in the field, has noted that:

> The most valid assessment processes engage teachers in the activities of teaching—activities that require the display and use of teaching knowledge and skill and allow teachers the opportunity to explain and justify their actions.[38]

As well as the standards for the various levels of certification, protocols and frameworks will need to be developed to guide teachers, their mentors, supervisors and assessors in the gathering and presentation of suitable evidence of performance and achievement across areas such as student learning, contributions to the development of peers and to the school community, involvement in extra-curricular activities, student support, and leadership and service to the profession.

Research and evaluation need to be built into the processes of teacher development, assessment and certification from the start. As noted, professional learning will be essential to the application and outcomes of this overall process.

The scale of the undertaking is daunting given the number of teachers currently practising in Australia and the level of rigour required, yet it can and must be done.

Time for action

After many years of false starts the key pieces of the quality teaching and learning puzzle—including associated areas such as national testing, national accreditation of teacher education programs and the national curriculum—are finally coming together. The Australian Professional Standards for Teachers have the potential to drive, recognise and reward teachers' professional learning and development from the graduate through to the 'expert' or *Lead* level of teaching.

We are on the cusp of a new era of teacher professionalism and the APST and their application are integral to that development.

With the increased expectations placed upon schools, teachers and principals it is vital we have a clear understanding of the sorts of qualities and capabilities needed to meet these and to determine whether they are in fact being developed and demonstrated.

However, to reiterate, it is vital that the APST and the associated measures for teacher professional learning, assessment and certification are integrated into salary and career structures across the profession. This can't be mandated centrally and will be a matter for negotiation within each industrial award. This will not be easy and it won't be cost-neutral, but if it doesn't occur, we will be left with the current loosely connected, ramshackle, outdated, increasingly unattractive and weak system for attracting, developing, retaining, recognising and rewarding teachers, and we can expect to continue to slide down the ranks on international measures such as PISA.

Preliminary results from an evaluation of the implementation of the Australian Professional Standards for Teachers undertaken on behalf of AITSL in 2013–15 are, however, encouraging in that they are revealing increasing engagement of teachers and principals with the standards, with resultant reported benefits.[39]

Without further labouring the point, there is clear evidence from the various studies and reports cited that professional learning and development and the facilitation of a professional learning culture, are essential to enhanced teacher effectiveness and student learning.

Endnotes

1. Schleicher, A. (2011). Teacher development, support: Employment conditions and careers. In OECD, *Building a high-quality teaching profession: Lessons from around the world*. International Summit on the Teaching Profession. Paris, France: OECD Publishing. (p. 24). DOI: http://dx.doi.org/10.1787/9789264113046-en
2. Schleicher, A. (2011). (p. 24)
3. See Dinham, S. (2015). Regulation or deregulation? Observations on education in Germany and Australia. In *Educators on the edge: Big ideas for change and innovation* (pp. 3–15). Refereed Conference Proceedings, ACE 2015 National Conference. Carlton South, Victoria: Australian College of Educators.
4. Dinham, S. (2015).
5. Schleicher, A. (2011). (pp. 24–25)
6. Timperley, H., Wilson, A., Barrar, H., & Fung, I. (2007). *Teacher Professional Learning and Development: Best Evidence Synthesis Iteration*. Wellington, New Zealand: Ministry of Education. (p. xliii). All extracts from this publication have been reproduced with permission. See https://creativecommons.org/licenses/by/4.0/legalcode
7. Timperley, H. et al. (2007). (p. 192)
8. Timperley, H. et al. (2007). (p. 193)
9. Dinham, S., Ingvarson, L., & Kleinhenz, E. (2008). Investing in teacher quality: Doing what matters most. In *Teaching talent: The best teachers for Australia's classrooms* (pp. 5–53). Melbourne, Victoria: Business Council of Australia. (p. 27). All extracts reprinted with permission.
10. Aubusson, P., Brady, L., & Dinham, S. (2005). *Action learning: What works? A research report prepared for the New South Wales Department of Education and Training*. Sydney, New South Wales: University of Technology Sydney.
11. Reeves, D. (2010). *Transforming professional development into student results*. Alexandria, VA: ASCD. (p. 33)
12. Dinham, S. (2015).
13. Reeves, D. (2010). (pp. 34–35)
14. This section is drawn in part from Dinham, S. (2011). *Let's get serious about teacher quality: The need for a new career architecture for Australia's teachers*. Dean's Lecture Series, University of Melbourne, MGSE, 27 September. http://web.education.unimelb.edu.au/news/lectures/pdf/S Dinham PowerPoint 27.9.11.pdf
15. Dinham, S. et al. (2008). (p. 7)
16. See Dinham, S., & Scott, C. (1997). The advanced skills teacher: An opportunity missed? *Unicorn*, 23(3), 36–49.
17. Dinham, S. et al. (2008). (p. 7)
18. Dinham, S. (2013). The quality teaching movement in Australia encounters difficult terrain: A personal perspective. *Australian Journal of Education*, 57(2), 91–106.
19. Dinham, S. et al. (2008). (p. 33)
20. Committee for the Review of Teaching and Teacher Education. (2003). *Australia's teachers: Australia's future advancing innovation, science, technology and mathematics main report*. Canberra: DEST; Dinham, S. (1992). Human perspectives on the resignation of teachers from the New South Wales Department of School Education: Towards a model of teacher persistence. (Doctor of Philosophy thesis). University of New England, Armidale.
21. Berliner, D. (2004). Describing the behaviour and documenting the accomplishments of expert teachers. *Bulletin of Science, Technology and Society*, 24, 200–212.

22. AITSL [Australian Institute for Teaching and School Leadership]. (2011). *National [Australian] Professional Standards for Teachers*. Melbourne, Victoria: Author.
23. Dinham, S. (2008). *Driving improvement in the quality of Australian education: Points of leverage*. Australian College of Educators, Victorian Branch Oration, University of Melbourne, 15 August; Dinham, S. (2015). *Issues and perspectives relevant to the development of an approach to the accreditation of initial teacher education in Australia based on evidence of impact*. Melbourne, Victoria: AITSL.
24. Clinton, J., Hattie, J., Dinham, S., Lingard, R., Gullickson, A., Savage, G., Aston, R., & Brookes, I. (2014). *InSights: Evaluation of the implementation of the Australian professional standards for teachers—Interim report*. Melbourne, Victoria: AITSL; Clinton, J., Dinham, S., Lingard, R., Gullickson, A., Savage, G., Calnin, G; Aston, R., & Dabrowski, A. (2015). *InSights: Evaluation of the implementation of the Australian Professional Standards for Teachers—Interim report 2—2014 key findings*. Melbourne, Victoria: AITSL.
25. Ingvarson, L., Dinham, S., Kleinhenz, E., & Anderson, M. (2009). *An analysis and review of state and territory standards for competent, accomplished and leading teacher levels and school leaders*. Camberwell, Victoria: ACER.
26. AITSL [Australian Institute for Teaching and School Leadership]. (2011). *Accreditation of initial teacher education programs in Australia*. Melbourne, Victoria: Author. Teacher Education Ministerial Advisory Group. (2014). *Action now: Classroom ready teachers*. Canberra, Australia: Department of Education.
27. Dinham, S. et al. (2008).
28. Dinham, S. (2011) *Pilot study to test the exposure draft of the national professional standard for principals—Analysis of interim reports*. Melbourne, Victoria: AITSL.
29. See http://www.acara.edu.au/default.asp
30. AITSL [Australian Institute for Teaching and School Leadership]. (2012). *Certification of highly accomplished and lead teachers principles and processes*. Melbourne, Victoria: Author.
31. AITSL [Australian Institute for Teaching and School Leadership]. (2012). *Australian Teacher Performance and Development Framework*. Melbourne, Victoria: Author.
32. Dinham, S. (2002). NSW Quality Teaching Awards—Research, rigour and transparency. *Unicorn, 28(1),* 5–9.
33. AITSL [Australian Institute for Teaching and School Leadership]. (2014). *Australian professional standard for principals and the leadership profiles*. Melbourne, Victoria: Author.
34. See http://www.atra.edu.au/
35. Dinham, S., & Scott, C. (2003). Benefits to teachers of the professional learning portfolio: A case study. *Teacher Development, 7*(2), 187–202.
36. Ministerial Council on Education, Employment, Training and Youth Affairs. (2008). *Melbourne Declaration on Educational Goals for Young Australians*. Canberra, Australia: Australian Government.
37. AITSL [Australian Institute for Teaching and School Leadership]. (2012). *Australian Charter for the Professional Learning of Teachers and School Leaders*. Melbourne, Victoria: Author.
38. Baratz-Snowden, J. (1990). The NBPTS begins its research and development program. *Educational Researcher, 19*(6), 19–24.
39. Clinton, J. et al. (2015).

PART D

School improvement and educational change

CHAPTER 14

What are the forces, contexts and features of educational change? What role can leaders play?

INTRODUCTION

The purpose of this chapter is to provide an introduction to the issue of organisational change, as well as background to educational change. Leaders have a major role in changing and improving organisations and this role is considered, once again generally, and specifically in respect of education.

We will examine organisational and school culture and climate and the nature of and implications of these for school change. We will also examine why change sometimes goes wrong, and how to prevent and deal with this.

We also consider organisational conflict, its causes and manifestations, and ways of dealing with divergent views. The related phenomena of groupthink and Balkanisation will be examined.

Later chapters in Part D will provide more detail on effecting change in educational organisations and in particular, schools.

The nature of change

Some basic definitions

Duke has provided some simple yet useful definitions to act as an introduction to change and change management:

- **Change:** a difference or departure from the *status quo.*
- **Change process:** the process by which an individual, group, or organisation attempts to achieve change.
- **Effects of change:** the impact or consequences of achieved change.[1]

Forces for change

Many of the forces for change experienced by schools and other organisations are largely external, although one of the challenges for educational leaders is to move beyond *reactive* change to *school-initiated* change. Some of the key external forces for change are[2]:

- economic
- social
- political
- ideological
- technological
- environmental.

People and organisations can react in a variety of ways to such change pressures, depending upon the nature of the particular change and their general predisposition towards change. For example, some people will:

- see change as a threat to their power base, responsibilities and autonomy
- feel uneasy about the risk and possible failure associated with the change
- be deterred by the pressure to do 'more with less', with the same resources
- feel undervalued or devalued by what is being proposed
- find potential disruptions to established procedures and even traditions threatening.

The culture and climate of the organisation[a] and the experience and views towards change of individuals and groups within it will be important in determining reactions and responses to change, responses that can be both emotional and behavioural.

One thing that decades of pressure for change and rising external criticisms have done to some schools and individuals is to create a climate of mistrust and avoidance

---

a   We will consider organisational culture and climate later.

of change through 'change fatigue'. I have interviewed and spoken with a number of principals who had taken over risk- and change-averse schools. Previous principals, some no doubt because they knew they would be retiring soon, had kept change at bay as much as possible, such that when these new principals took over they were faced with a situation where some fairly substantial and unsettling changes had to be instituted immediately if the school was to fulfil its responsibilities and meet various accountabilities. This situation got these principals 'offside' with their new staff as the roadblocks to change were hurriedly removed and their 'new broom' raised a cloud of dust. By their own admission, these principals would have preferred to take their time before engaging in substantive change, but had no choice.

Another aspect is that when so much change is externally mandated and driven, this can act to erode initiative and disempower people. A finding from the AGQTP evaluation considered earlier was that being voluntarily involved in an action learning project addressing a need of the school, despite the fact that the project was externally initiated and supported, had the effect of motivating and energising otherwise jaded and change-averse staff.[3]

It was seen in the AESOP study sites how successful faculties, teams and schools had positive attitudes towards change, and that rather than perceiving change as a threat, leaders looked for the benefits available to them from being associated with new programs and initiatives.[4]

Another key aspect, already noted, is that change is not just about changing procedures or structures, but is often about changing people—what they know, what they can do and their outlook and approach.

A consistent theme in this book is that leadership and professional learning—two of the big levers—play important roles in changing people, and in changing matters such as policies, structures, processes, programs and, ultimately, in re-culturing schools.

Groupthink

Group dynamics play an important role in how individuals and organisations respond to change. One concept that I have found useful in understanding group behaviour and reactions to change is that of 'groupthink'. The term was first coined by William Whyte in the early 1950s and refined and popularised by Irving Janis in the early 1970s in his book *Victims of Groupthink* and in other work.[5]

Groupthink involves 'in-groups' and 'out-groups', and those who are in the in-group exhibit a high degree of unanimity, with the group's decision-making and behaviour being dysfunctional or sub-optimal in its relationships with the rest of the organisation. The group tends to police its members in various ways and filters or distorts information coming into the group. As a result, while the group may appear on some levels to be operating rationally in terms of its own norms and internal rules, its decision-making and performance are faulty and often irrational, as the group does not consider all information and alternative courses of action rationally and objectively because of its various biases.

It should be noted that groupthink can occur within existing formal groups where all or some of the group exhibit groupthink symptoms. Alternatively, the members can be drawn from different formal groups across the organisation because of what members have in common. Levels of an organisation such as an executive made up of senior staff can also exhibit and be afflicted by groupthink. It is possible for whole organisations, even governments, to be under the influence of groupthink. For example, one could classify the 'Cold War' as groupthink on a global scale.

Janis noted that members' cohesion is an important precondition of groupthink, although obviously not all cohesive groups are dysfunctional. History also plays a part in the development of groupthink and some of the examples of groupthink I have encountered in my career had histories to rival the Middle East or Ireland. No one could remember how the group came to be, or why it was so opposed to others in the organisation, but there was clearly a defined group membership and identity recognised by those inside and outside the group.

When new people join an organisation, there is often an auditioning or interviewing process to determine whether the new person 'fits' the group(s) or not. This new arrival might be taken for coffee or drinks—I've seen this happen many times—and told a particular version of the organisation's history, in the hope of 'sussing' them out, getting them 'on side' or even neutralising them. My advice to anyone in this situation is to take your time before committing—if you feel you must—to a particular position or group.

There are a variety of possible causes of groupthink, some of which may operate conjointly:

- There was possibly a lack of 'objective' or 'authoritative' leadership in the past.
- The group may have formed in response to (real or perceived) external threats or conflict.
- Perhaps members of the group shared similar social backgrounds or interests.
- Members of the group may have been geographically isolated from the rest of the organisation (in a particular building, part of the school, campus).
- Perhaps there was an ideological split in the organisation.
- Members of the group were kept isolated or bypassed by those 'in charge'.

Whatever the causes, small initial differences can become larger under groupthink, so that divisions between groups can become wider, deeper, more clearly defined and harder to bridge over time as a 'history' of conflict develops.

To help you identify groupthink, Whyte, Janis and other researchers have noted the following 'symptoms' or groupthink behaviours:

- Filtering and distorting information coming into the group.
- Self-belief in the group's righteousness and 'morality'.

- Exerting pressure on those within the group to conform and not speak out.
- Use of 'mindguards' to protect the group from outside information that might threaten or harm the group and its cohesiveness.
- Failure to consider all alternatives and consequences objectively and rationally.
- Rationalising group dysfunctionality and poor decision-making.
- Seeing and portraying other individuals and groups in stereotypical ways; deriding and attacking the views and positions of others.
- Members suppressing true feelings; don't question ideas of other members openly; may be in awe or fear of influential group leaders.
- Group seeing itself in a struggle for survival; may see itself as invulnerable.
- 'Escalation of commitment' in that the group continues to pursue an increasingly destructive, harmful path or conflict, and even increases its commitment, despite evidence that it is failing; adopting a 'crash or crash through', 'win–lose' approach.[6]
- Projecting an image of unity to outside world; votes as a 'bloc' in meetings and decision-making; 'hunts as a pack'.

Dealing with groupthink

I'll have a wager that you have had experience of groupthink, maybe even as part of a group. The key question is how to deal with it.

Most researchers and writers advocate some form of outside intervention to break open the solidarity of the group and to let light and air into the situation when dealing with groupthink. For example:

- Form some type of matrix structure within the organisation so that group members become members of other groups to work on issues, tasks or problems and in doing so, widen their understanding of the organisation.
- Where there is a formal group such as a faculty experiencing groupthink, appointing an external evaluator or facilitator to speak with all members confidentially, conduct 'reality testing', and report back to group.
- Confront the ideas of the group rationally and without personalities; emphasise use of evidence.
- Meet with group members individually; seek their input, ideas and reactions and test these with the group membership without 'naming names'.
- Commend members of the group publicly for their achievements, even (and especially) if the group culture and norms reject recognition for its members.
- Refuse to take sides or listen to accounts of past 'disasters' or 'war stories'; be scrupulously fair in dealing with the group and its members.
- Use external experts to provide information, alternatives and assistance.
- Break up some of the social 'glue' of the group; invite members selectively to social occasions with other staff; invite members to join with other staff on projects as above.
- If all else fails: issue an ultimatum; break up the group operationally/geographically; appoint a new leader; restructure; transfer some staff.

(In my experience, it's easier to utilise these strategies if you are new or external to the organisation. You can ask 'dumb', seemingly naïve questions as an outsider without any 'baggage'.)

It should be noted that groupthink is a continuum, with elements present in all organisations. It is useful if you can be attuned to the history of the organisation and sensitive to the symptoms of groupthink. Forming productive, professional relationships with all group members may be difficult, especially the case-hardened 'blockers' (see later), but you need to make the effort. Unresolved groupthink can lead to a 'toxic', dysfunctional organisational culture, and no leader wants that.

Balkanisation

Balkanisation can be defined as the breakdown or fragmentation of a region, division or organisation into smaller formal and informal units. It owes its name to the political fragmentation and reformation of the Balkan states that occurred over several centuries.

Various researchers and commentators have written on the fact that fragmentation is a phenomenon found in many schools, especially secondary schools with their traditional divisions or 'silos' based on subject specialisation. Andy Hargreaves applied the term 'balkanisation' in his book *Changing Teachers, Changing Times* in 1994. He noted that in schools there were identifiable patterns of teachers' relationships and that:

> In balkanised cultures, these patterns mainly consist of teachers working neither in isolation, nor with most of their colleagues as a whole school, but in smaller sub-groups within the school community, such as secondary school subject departments, special needs units, or junior and senior primary divisions within the elementary school.[7]

As with cohesion—a feature or precondition of groupthink, but desirable outside that context—there is nothing inherently wrong with teachers working together in small groups. In fact, it is desirable. The problem arises when teachers working in these small groups are isolated and insulated from those in other groups, whom they might see as competitors, and it is in this situation where groupthink can develop and take hold, with members' main loyalties and efforts directed towards the group and its goals, rather than to the organisation as a whole and those it is meant to serve.

Overcoming resistance to change

The organisational and educational change literatures emphasise that participation, information, education, communication, involvement, support and agreement are all necessary means for overcoming resistance to change.

McLagen offers five strategies for success with change:

- Be sure the change will add value.
- Match change process with the change.
- Provide management support.
- Prepare the system for change.
- Help people align.[8]

It is commonly agreed that working with and through people is the key to successful change. Smith has noted:

> It is people who make up organisations and it is they who are the real source of, and vehicle for, change. They are the ones who will either embrace or resist change. If organisational change is to take hold and succeed then organisations and the people who work in them must be readied for such transformation. Change readiness is not automatic and it cannot be assumed. A failure to assess organisational and individual change readiness may result in managers spending significant time and energy dealing with resistance to change.[9]

Smith has identified three key steps in creating readiness for change:

- creating a sense of need and urgency for change;
- communicating the change message and ensuring participation and involvement in the change process, and
- providing anchoring points and a base for the achievement of change.[10]

Pennington suggests that proposed changes can be placed along two scales: radical–incremental, and core–peripheral (see Figure 14.1 below). Plotting the character of a proposed change along these scales can provide a sense of how difficult the introduction of any particular initiative might be and how much 'disturbance' to the status quo it might both require and generate.

- **Radical changes** to an institution's or department's core business will normally generate higher levels of disturbance and be associated with higher levels of risk;
- **Incremental changes** to peripheral activities are often considered to be unexceptional ('fine tuning') with low disturbance and low risk and can be accommodated as a matter of course, especially if the group involved has a successful past record of continuous improvement.

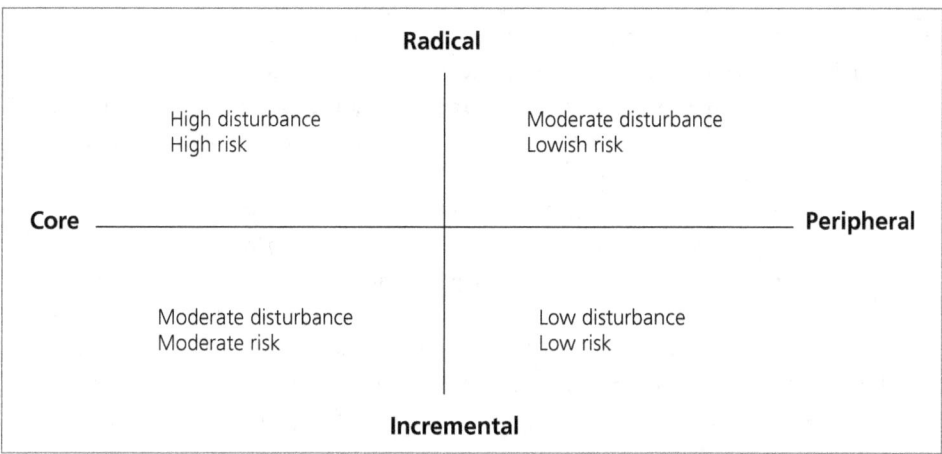

Figure 14.1: Radical and incremental change[11]

Pennington notes that, as a general rule, professionals and technical staff will tend to resist changes that are perceived to threaten their core values and practices, that is, changes that have a negative impact on individuals, and those which diminish group autonomy.[12]

Counting the numbers in educational change[13]

In politics, having 'the numbers' or the support of the membership for any initiative is essential. In educational change, the numbers are equally important.

In considering the likely success of any desired change, it is useful for educational leaders to consider the membership of three broad groups:

1 **The Enthusiasts**—supporters for the change who will be prepared to commit time and effort to the initiative. Enthusiasts range from the informed and 'hard headed' to the naïve. Enthusiasts may have experience and expertise in the area or may be prepared to 'give it a go' if such familiarity is lacking. Enthusiasts tend to be early adopters and risk-takers, although sometimes they let their heart rule their head. There are two sub-groups of enthusiasts: those who will cheerfully support almost anything, and those who will provide support for a particular issue. Enthusiasts can also be initiators of change.

2 **The Watchers**—as the name implies, these people are more calculative and are open to persuasion. They are generally compliant. Watchers are prepared to consider a change on its merits. As with enthusiasts, they will go along with a leader who has won their respect and trust, suspending judgement until later. Watchers can go either way on an issue. Over time, they can become increasingly involved and supportive if they are exposed to convincing evidence and argument. Small successes can bring

> watchers on side. However, if the change process is handled badly, watchers can withdraw their support and involvement and may even join the third group.
>
> 3. **The Blockers**—blockers may be opposed to a particular change, or change in general. They can be active or passive in their opposition. They will not be swayed by rational argument or evidence and can be counted on to resist change. Even if their opposition is muted, members of this group may use their influence with others to obstruct and 'white ant' (eat away at or undermine) the change. Alternatively, they may say little but will studiously ignore the change, waiting for it, and you, to go away. Blockers may have been in the school or system for some time, their views having hardened over the years. 'Balkanisation' and 'groupthink' can govern the thinking and actions of blockers. Blockers tend to police each other and filter out and distort unwelcome information. In some cases, there may be different groups of blockers who oppose each other, which can make life interesting.

Both the composition of the above groups ('who') and the number of people each contains ('how many') can be significant in the success of educational change. For example, if the blockers comprise a small number of highly influential people, the desired change could be doomed before it starts or undermined once it begins.

In an overall group of 20, 5 enthusiasts and 10 watchers could be enough of a critical mass to see a change through. However, 8 enthusiasts and 8 blockers would indicate polarisation of staff, with conflict and failure likely.

As an educational leader, it is instructive to reflect on the composition and numbers of each group for any proposed change. Knowledge of the organisation's history, culture and group dynamics are also important. Past failed attempts at change need to be understood and considered as some blockers act as 'keepers of the nightmare' (see Deal and Peterson later[14])—'we tried that and it didn't work'; '... was a disaster', and so forth. Of course, blockers ignore their own roles in such failures.

Schools and other educational institutions are not democracies, however, and leaders have to make unpopular decisions at times for the overall good of the organisation. Additionally, much change is mandated and the real issue is how to accommodate change of this nature and use it to the organisation's advantage. When it comes to decision-making, the most effective educational leaders possess each of these capacities, being both courageous and strategic, as we have seen in discussion of the AESOP study findings.[15]

The evaluation of the Australian Government Quality Teaching Program (AGQTP) mentioned previously highlighted the importance of leaders carefully considering the composition and influence of groups.[16] In forming AGQTP action learning teams, many principals thoughtfully and strategically selected project team leaders and encouraged and 'massaged' team membership. In several cases, principals admitted to having induced key watchers and potential blockers to join project teams, operating on the Lyndon B. Johnson theory that it would be better to have these people 'inside the tent', than outside.[b]

These principals reasoned that once such people had become involved and had developed a personal stake in the projects, they would influence others to provide support or at least to give the projects 'a go'; that is, their commitment would escalate, this time with positive consequences.

In the AESOP study, some principals of successful and/or turnaround schools had made the decision to bypass the blockers altogether. They concentrated on encouraging, professionally developing and empowering groups of enthusiasts and watchers, hoping to achieve contagion effects from successful change across the wider school. As noted previously, there is a danger in this, in that the leader can be accused of 'playing favourites', but the bigger danger is that nothing happens of a positive nature.[17]

A key aspect in all of this, is knowing one's fellow staff—and, where relevant students and community members—and how people might react to any change in the status quo. Over time, successfully managed change (and retirements and transfers) can see the weakening of the blockers' power base and the overcoming of a culture of negativity and resistance.[18]

A final point for educational leaders to consider: don't take the opposition of the blockers too personally. Their behaviour is frequently irrational and the result of personal, group and organisational history. Applying rational thinking to irrational behaviour doesn't always work, and their opposition is almost a vote of confidence in and a character reference for you.

Why does change go wrong?

One of the fundamental errors in perception is that change is about management. The term 'change management' is misleading. The various studies cited in this book, including the AESOP study and the AGQTP evaluation, showed that successful change is much more about active *leadership of people* than *management of systems*.

Particularly where change is in the high disturbance/high risk and moderate disturbance/moderate risk quadrants identified by Pennington[19], a number of things are likely to happen that can compromise the change effort and progress. Each was evident to some degree in the AGQTP evaluation described previously:

- Getting started is difficult.
- Maintaining momentum takes effort.
- Progress is slower than expected.
- Goals and targets need revision (usually downwards).

---

b US President Lyndon B. Johnson is reputed to have said in respect of the Director of the FBI, J. Edgar Hoover: 'It's probably better to have him inside the tent pissing out, than outside the tent pissing in'. Source: *New York Times*, 31 October, 1971.

- Direction changes.
- Setbacks occur.
- Evidence to judge progress and improved performance is lacking.
- Criticism and doubt emerge.

To help us understand why these problems occur, Kotter, who studied the change experiences of over 100 companies, noted a number of common errors:

1. Not establishing a great enough sense of urgency.
2. Not creating a powerful enough guiding coalition.
3. Lacking a vision.
4. Under-communicating the vision by a factor of ten.
5. Not removing obstacles to the new vision.
6. Not systematically planning for and creating short-term wins.
7. Declaring victory too soon.
8. Not anchoring changes in the corporation's culture.[20]

Kotter found:

> In the final analysis, change sticks when it becomes 'the way we do things around here', when it seeps into the bloodstream of the corporate body. Until new behaviours are rooted in social norms and shared values, they are subject to degradation as soon as the pressure for change is removed.
>
> Two factors are particularly important in institutionalizing change in corporate culture. The first is a conscious attempt to show people how the new approaches, behaviors, and attitudes have helped improve performance. When people are left on their own to make the connections, they sometimes create very inaccurate links ...
>
> The second factor is taking sufficient time to make sure that the next generation of top management really does personify the new approach ... One bad succession decision at the top of an organization can undermine a decade of hard work.[21]

The above observations on where change goes wrong and what is needed to make it 'stick' ring true in the light of the research with which I've been involved. The key aspects appear to centre on:
- getting people engaged and empowered to tackle the change
- communicating and selling the change
- providing the necessary professional learning and development
- leading, encouraging and defending the change
- using evidence to monitor, evaluate and modify the change effort
- celebrating and communicating successes along the way.

The importance of organisational climate and culture

You can't hope to work in, or change schools, without coming up against school culture.

I have visited many schools in a variety of states, systems and countries over the years. As experienced educators, when we go into a school we quickly make a series of judgements based on a range of evidence, observations and cues that give us a 'feel' for the school. The problem for people who have spent a long time in a school is that these cues may no longer be seen—they develop organisational myopia, unseeingly stepping over or around the 'dead dogs' in the corridor and failing to recognise the 'elephant in the room' or the 'wood from the trees'.

The implication here is that we need to stand back periodically and view our organisation from the eyes of a stranger or visitor. What we see, hear and feel will be important indicators of the culture and health of our organisation. I suggest to my postgraduate students who are school leaders that they visit each other's schools and give feedback on what they see as an outsider. I also suggest that they telephone their own school—disguising their voice—and ask for help. The reception they receive may be instructive.

There are a variety of definitions of organisational climate and culture. Climate is basically the day-to-day 'feel' of the organisation, and our judgement of climate is based largely on observable features, events and behaviours. Climate can change fairly readily, for good or bad, under the influence of leadership. Climate is almost the collective 'morale' of the organisation.

Culture, on the other hand, is deeper, harder to read, and harder to change. It is usually considered to comprise the behavioural norms, assumptions and beliefs of an organisation, developed over longer periods of time, sometimes generations, and even centuries in the case of some long-established schools and other organisations.

These norms, values and beliefs may be unspoken, largely unquestioned and constantly reinforced for people both consciously and unconsciously.

McBrien and Brandt have offered the following, slightly different, definitions and explanations:

> School culture and climate refers to the sum of the values, cultures, safety practices, and organizational structures within a school that cause it to function and react in particular ways ... Although the two terms are somewhat interchangeable, school climate refers mostly to the school's effects on students, while school culture refers more to the way teachers and other staff members work together.[22]

The work of Schein has been important in our understanding of organisational culture, which he has defined as:

> A pattern of shared basic assumptions that the group learned as it solved its problems of external adaptation and internal integration, that has worked well

enough to be considered valid and, therefore, to be taught to new members as the correct way to perceive, think, and feel in relation to those problems.[23]

Schein discerned three levels of organisational culture, resembling an iceberg:

Level 1: Tangible Elements (artifacts and creations); includes verbal, visual, behavioral manifestations. *[the tip of the iceberg]*
Level 2: Values and Beliefs; mission statements, philosophy, credo. *[above the water line and partly visible below the surface]*
Level 3: Underlying assumptions, taken for granted assumptions; invisible, deep-seated, subconscious assumptions about human nature, relationships, reality. *[under the water and out of sight]*

As a new leader, it takes time to tune into, dig down, and understand the culture of a school, particularly in coming to an understanding of Level 3 above, which those who have been at the school longer than you may be unable to articulate beyond the simple observation that 'it's the way we do things around here'.[24] New arrivals may not be taught about the culture in any overt way but rather, slowly tune into and become aware of it. On the other hand, what they or you might be told, may not fit with contemporary reality. Regardless, people tend to absorb and later to enact and reinforce the culture as they interact with others and take part in day-to-day school life.

Where schools have control over hiring of staff, there may be a conscious effort to select and screen applicants for positions based upon their perceived 'fit' with the school's culture. Those employed who don't fit the culture and who can't or won't change their views may feel that they don't belong, which could lead to conflict or resignation.

In their book *Transforming Schools*, Zmuda, Kuklis and Kline offer six steps of continuous improvement in schools that begin with recognition of school culture:

1. Identify and clarify the core beliefs that define the school's culture.
2. Create a shared vision by explicitly defining what these core beliefs will look like in practice.
3. Collect accurate, detailed data and use analysis of the data to define where the school is now and to determine the gaps between the current reality and the shared vision.
4. Identify the innovation(s) that will most likely close the gaps between the current reality and the shared vision.
5. Develop and implement an action plan that supports teachers through the change process and integrates the innovation within each classroom and throughout the school.

6. Embrace collective autonomy as the only way to close the gaps and embrace collective accountability in establishing responsibility for closing the gaps.[25]

Similarly, Deal and Peterson, in their book *Shaping School Culture*, have identified eight major symbolic roles for leaders seeking to build strong and cohesive school cultures:

1. **Historian:** seeks to understand the social and normative past of the school.
2. **Anthropological sleuth:** analyses and probes for the current set of norms, values and beliefs that define the current culture.
3. **Visionary:** works with other leaders and the community to define a deeply value-focused picture of the future for the school; has a constantly evolving vision.
4. **Symbol:** affirms values through dress, behavior, attention, routines.
5. **Potter:** shapes and is shaped by the school's heroes, rituals, traditions, ceremonies, symbols; brings in staff who share core values.
6. **Poet:** uses language to reinforce values and sustains the school's best image of itself.
7. **Actor:** improvises in the school's inevitable dramas, comedies, and tragedies.
8. **Healer:** oversees transitions and change in the life of the school; heals the wounds of conflict and loss.[26]

Deal and Peterson conceptualise schools as 'tribes' and note that many school leaders inherit a dysfunctional, divided, intertribal mess. They come up against and must engage with 'toxic' school cultures and sub-cultures.

Characteristics of toxic school cultures include staff and the school as a whole being focused on negative values (making the school better for staff; serving only an elite group of students; focusing on unimportant/less important outcomes). Meaning for members of the 'tribe' is derived from sub-culture membership, e.g., anti-student, anti-system and anti-community sentiments, or life outside work (fishing, golf, gardening, sport, food and wine—anything except teaching). People soaked in toxic school cultures may behave quite differently out of school, being seemingly different people.

In toxic schools:

- The elements of culture reinforce negativity.
- Values and beliefs are negative.
- The culture works against anything that is positive.
- Rituals and traditions are phony, joyless, counter-productive.[27]

Powerful sub-culture members become:

- Negaholics. [a great label]
- Saboteurs.
- Pessimistic story tellers.
- 'Keepers of the nightmare'. [I love that]
- Prima donnas.
- Space cadets.
- Martyrs.
- Driftwood, deadwood and ballast.[28]

Deal and Peterson's 'antidotes for negativism' include:

- Confront the negativity head on—give people a chance to vent their venom in a public forum (listen, challenge, wait for more positive elements to emerge).
- Shield and support positive cultural elements and staff.
- Focus attention on the recruitment, selection and retention of effective, positive staff—replace chronic negaholics.
- Rabidly celebrate the positive and the possible.
- Consciously and directly focus on eradicating the negative and rebuilding around positive norms and beliefs.
- Develop new stories of success, renewal and accomplishment.
- Help those who might succeed and thrive in a new school to make the move.[29]

As a leader, coming to an appreciation of your school's culture is vital. You need to understand where it's been, and where it's at, if you are to take your school to where you want it to go. Likewise, you need to understand where people are coming from if you hope to lead them somewhere else.

The successful leaders profiled previously in this book attended to all three of Schein's levels, ranging from their attention to school vision, down to management of daily events, and everything in between. They were also able to recognise the symptoms and causes of 'negativism' identified by Deal and Peterson, seeking to drive out negative attitudes and behaviours and modelling a positive approach and mindset. They were relentless in 'talking up' the school, its students and staff.

Managing conflict and change

It would be misleading and unrealistic to suggest that change doesn't involve conflict. Any time people are put together on a common task, there is the potential for conflict.

Conflict is usually defined as some form of incompatibility of views between individuals or groups who then engage in a process to accommodate these differences. (There can also be internal conflict over the course of action on an issue, where an individual is faced with choice.) Where one side attempts to see its view or position triumph, this can result in a 'win–lose' situation (see below), which can sow the seeds for later and continuing conflict, with groupthink and Balkanisation possible outcomes, and, if severe enough, a toxic culture resulting.

It should also be stated that some people seem to thrive on drama and conflict. When one conflict subsides, they go in search of another, or even start their own. Some people I've worked with were capable of starting a fight in an empty room.

The bureaucratic view of conflict as espoused by Max Weber—the German political economist and sociologist who published numerous influential papers in the late 19th and early 20th centuries—was that organisational conflict could be overcome, or better still avoided, by rules and procedures—bureaucratic systems—that impersonally and objectively govern the behaviour of all employees.[30]

However, other writers such as Mary Parker Follett—an American social worker, consultant and writer whose career overlapped with that of Weber and who introduced the term 'conflict resolution'—have seen conflict as a necessary accompaniment to change and the development of new ideas and approaches.[31] Under this view, leaders should not strive to eliminate or keep a lid on conflict, but rather to use it productively to question accepted practices and find innovative solutions.

'Win–win', 'win–lose', and 'lose–lose' strategies

The origins of 'win–win', 'win–lose' and 'lose–lose' strategies lie in game theory. Today, they are also associated with situations where different approaches to conflict resolution can result in differing outcomes.

With a 'win–win' approach, each side emerges with 'face' intact, largely because the conflict has been depersonalised, and with each party demonstrating flexibility, honesty and communicating openly in seeking creative solutions to the conflict. The good of the organisation and those it serves are usually the most important considerations in this situation.

With a 'win–lose' situation, however, each side defines and sees the matter in those terms, and pursues its own goals, rather than higher organisational goals. It becomes a contest of wills and force, with each side seeking to damage the other's case and emerge victorious. Objectivity and the consideration of evidence and alternatives can go out the window. 'Might' is not always 'right', but in 'win–lose' conflicts, might frequently prevails.

Aside from coming to the wrong decision, an outcome of 'win-lose' conflict can be that the 'winner' has their power enhanced and the 'loser' is diminished in some way. The resultant ill feeling and hostility can mean that the two individuals or groups will find it difficult to trust each other or to work together in the future.

In some cases, the contest can be so intense and damaging that there are no winners, that is 'lose–lose', the classic pyrrhic victory, named for King Pyrrhus of Epirus whose army suffered terrible casualties in defeating the Romans during the Pyrrhic War.

The role of the leader

Authoritative leaders[c] don't ignore conflict, nor do they seek to suppress it. Following the advice of Mary Parker Follett, they seek to resolve it. They don't leave it to the parties concerned to 'sort it out amongst themselves', an example of uninvolved leadership that I've seen at close quarters, and a 'cop-out'. Hopefully, the approach and actions of the authoritative leader will go a long way towards preventing conflict but as has been pointed out, conflict can represent a healthy airing of differing views, and thus the role of the leader is to see the conflict resolved in a 'win–win' fashion for the greater benefit of the people and organisation concerned.

There are a number of approaches or roles for leaders I've observed that parallel the 'win–win' approach to conflict resolution:
- Keep personalities, 'previous records' or history out of discussions.
- Encourage the parties to consider all evidence and options.
- Don't let one party bully the other—give each equal standing and opportunity to express their views; you need to be both coach and referee.
- Be even-handed and open yourself, and be prepared to listen (some people just need to 'vent'); encourage the individuals or parties concerned to do likewise.
- Focus on the issues and alternatives, encouraging the parties to devise and test a solution, while keeping in mind that a compromise is often not the best means to accomplish this, but the third-best alternative.
- Be firm and decisive if necessary.
- Adopt a trial period and agree to review any decisions openly after a suitable time.
- Thank the parties for their passion and their contribution.

Flanagan and Finger have offered some simple and helpful advice for coping with irate people[d], advice that is consistent with 'win–win' approaches and

---

c We will consider authoritative leadership later in Part D.

d We will examine working with difficult people in more detail later in Part D.

authoritative leadership. I've used this approach successfully in my own work as an educational leader.

As Flanagan and Finger note, letting someone put their case is often half the solution to resolving the problem. Sometimes people just want someone to listen:

- Get the person seated and comfortable [in a suitable location].
- Listen to what the person has to say.
- Summarise the situation as you see it.
- Identify the options.
- Explore the options and settle on a fair solution.
- Apportion any blame fairly.
- Express appreciation.[32]

Finally, let me share a few lessons learned from observing a masterful Deputy Principal of the 'old school' I encountered early in my career. As a 'year adviser' at a large secondary school, I was often able to observe 'Fred' in action in the DP's office.

Deputy principals tend to have many people sent to them for various problems, alleged crimes and atrocities, and 'Fred' dealt with all sorts respectfully, giving every student the chance to put their case. He was a 'bushy' by upbringing, and alert to the ways of the 'bush lawyer'. He was fair and firm, and 'guilty' students often thanked him when he gave his judgement because of the way he handled the situation. He had a way of leading people to the truth.

The lessons I learned were simple yet powerful; that there are always two sides to every story, sometimes more, and you won't find out the truth by making snap judgements. The worst thing you can say is 'I don't want to hear about …'. Another reason for listening is that those students who are 'spinning a yarn' often trip themselves up in their explanations. A final lesson I learned was to distinguish the 'sin from the sinner'; that is, 'You have done a bad thing', rather than 'You are a bad person'. Above all, be fair and respectful, even if you don't particularly admire the person concerned or you find them obnoxious. Keep your cool and keep these matters at a professional level. Take pride in your professionalism.[e]

This also applies to dealing with parents. On occasion, my professionalism has been sorely tested by abusive and in a few cases, drunken parents, including one man who fell off his chair, lay on the floor and wanted to continue the 'interview' from that position. It helps to remember that some people (and their children) have tough lives.

---

e   And try not to take conflict home with you.

Concluding remarks

A final comment on conflict

Occasionally you will encounter outright hostility, verbal and even physical attacks on persons and total intransigence—what some writers on organisational behaviour have quaintly called 'nefarious attacks'.[33] This is different to what might be called productive conflict caused by a difference of views. There may be hurtful language, public denigration, defamation, bullying and harassment. People can suffer dreadfully under such attacks.

These situations require a different approach utilising authoritative leadership. Such cases are intolerable and have to be dealt with under the law and according to the regulations and procedures of your school or system. You must act quickly and decisively. An important role for the leader is to protect and defend their staff in such situations. You will earn a lot of respect through doing so.

Endnotes

1. Duke, D. (2004). *The challenges of educational change*. Boston, MA: Pearson. (p. 16)
2. See Glass, G. (2008). *Fertilizers, pills, and magnetic strips: The fate of public education in America*. Charlotte, NC: Information Age Publishing.
3. Aubusson, P., Brady, L., & Dinham, S. (2005). *Action learning: What works?* A research report prepared for the New South Wales Department of Education and Training. Sydney, New South Wales: University of Technology Sydney; Dinham, S. (2009). The relationship between distributed leadership and action learning in schools: A case study. In A. Harris (Ed.). *Distributed school leadership: Different perspectives* (pp. 139–154). Dordrecht, Netherlands: Springer Press.
4. Dinham, S. (2007). *Leadership for exceptional educational outcomes*. Teneriffe, Qld: Post Pressed.
5. Janis, I. (1972). *Victims of groupthink*. Boston, MA: Houghton Mifflin.
6. Staw, B. (1976). Knee-deep in the big muddy: A study of escalating commitment to a chosen course of action. *Organizational behavior and human performance, 16*(1), 27–44.
7. Hargreaves, A. (1994). *Changing teachers, changing times*. London, England: Cassell. (p. 213)
8. McLagen, P. (2002). Success with change. *T + D, December*, 44–45.
9. Smith, I. (2005). Achieving readiness for organisational change. *Library Management, 26*(6/7), 408–412. (p. 408). All extracts from this publication have been reproduced with permission from Emerald Group Publishing Limited.
10. Smith, I. (2005). (p. 409)
11. Pennington, G. (2003). *Guidelines for promoting and facilitating change*. York, England: LTSN Generic Centre. (p. 6). Reproduced with permission.
12. Pennington, G. (2003).
13. This section is drawn from Dinham, S. (2008). Counting the numbers in educational change. *The Australian Educational Leader, 30*(1), 56–57.
14. Deal, T., & Peterson, K. (1999). *Shaping school culture*. San Francisco, CA: Jossey-Bass.
15. Dinham, S. (2007).
16. Aubusson, P., Brady, L., & Dinham, S. (2005).

17 Dinham, S. (2005). Principal leadership for outstanding educational outcomes. *Journal of Educational Administration, 43*(4), 338–356.
18 Dinham, S. (2007). How schools get moving and keep improving: Leadership for teacher learning, student success and school renewal. *Australian Journal of Education, 51*(3), 263–275.
19 Pennington, G. (2003).
20 Kotter, J. (1995). Leading change: Why transformation efforts fail. *Harvard Business Review, 73*(2), March–April, 59–67. Text extracts from this publication have been adapted and reprinted with permission.
21 Kotter, J. (1995). (p. 67)
22 McBrien, J., & Brandt, S. (1997). *The language of learning: A guide to education terms.* Alexandria, VA: ASCD. (p. 89)
23 Schein, E. H. (1992). *Organizational culture and leadership.* (2nd ed.). San Francisco, CA: Jossey-Bass.
24 Deal T. E. (1985). The symbolism of effective schools. *Elementary School Journal, 85*(5), 601–620.
25 Zmuda, A., Kuklis, R., & Kline, E. (2004). *Transforming schools.* Alexandria, VA: ASCD. (pp. 18–19)
26 Deal, T., & Peterson, K. (1999). (pp. 87–88)
27 Deal, T., & Peterson, K. (1999). (pp. 119–122)
28 Deal, T., & Peterson, K. (1999). (pp. 119–122)
29 Deal, T., & Peterson, K. (1999). (pp. 127–128)
30 Weber, M. (1905). *The Protestant ethic and the spirit of capitalism.* In German *Die protestantische Ethik und der Geist des Kapitalismus.*
31 See Follett, M. P. (1941). *Dynamic administration: The collected papers of Mary Parker Follett.* H. Metcalf & L. Urwick, (Eds.). London, England: Pitman.
32 Flanagan, N., & Finger, J. (1989). *Management in a minute.* Brisbane, Qld: Plumb Press. (pp. 36–37)
33 Wynn, R. (1972). *Administrative response to conflict.* Pittsburgh, PA: Tri-State Area School Study Council. (pp. 7–8).

CHAPTER 15

What does it mean to be an authoritative leader?

INTRODUCTION

The successful senior secondary teachers described in Chapter 6[1] and the leaders of schools achieving exceptional student outcomes in Chapter 10[2] shared a number of attributes. Members of each study had high-level interpersonal skills and personal qualities that were admired. They had earned a high degree of credibility, and their relations with others were characterised by mutual respect and trust. Their expectations for staff and students were high, but so too were their expectations for themselves. They set a good example through moral authority, strongly believed in what they were doing and regularly articulated and demonstrated these values and beliefs to others. Each group made teaching and learning their main priority, with students and student learning their central focus.

The above philosophy of 'give a lot, expect a lot' was particularly marked in schools from areas of lower socio-economic status. There is a tendency to dichotomise schools as being either of 'welfare' or 'academic' types. In welfare (usually low SES) schools, there are frequently lower expectations, with an emphasis on inculcating 'social' and 'living' skills and boosting student self-esteem at the expense of academic achievement, yet in the two projects if was evident that the function of student welfare in the disadvantaged or lower SES schools was more about 'getting students back into learning' for their future benefit, than making students feel better about themselves.

In helping to understand this situation, Catherine Scott and I used the work of Diana Baumrind[3] to provide a conceptual framework for analysis. We believe that Baumrind's work on parenting styles has strong resonance and utility for understanding both quality teaching and effective leadership.

Parenting styles

Intuitively, parenting and teaching appear to have a lot in common. Each involves attempting to meet children's needs and providing guidance for their development. Both parents and teachers have a high level of duty of care as older, wiser adults in positions of responsibility and authority. Each has a nurturing aspect, coupled with control and guidance, hopefully leading to maturity of thought and action, self-confidence and autonomy for the young people concerned, so that they can make a place for themselves in society and lead fulfilling lives.

Equally apparent is the fact that there are different approaches to parenting and teaching. A key question then, is whether some approaches are more effective than others in meeting the needs and expectations of children and society.

The consequences for children of what have been called different styles of parenting have been the subject of considerable research since the late 1960s, beginning with the work of Diana Baumrind. According to Baumrind, two dimensions underlie parenting: *responsiveness* and *demandingness*. Each considers the nature of the parent–child relationship.

Responsiveness, also described as warmth or supportiveness, is defined as 'the extent to which parents intentionally foster individuality, self-regulation and assertion by being attuned, supportive, and acquiescent to children's special needs and demands'.

Demandingness (or behavioural control) refers to 'the claims parents make on children to become integrated into the family whole, by their maturity demands, supervision, disciplinary efforts and willingness to confront the child who disobeys'.[4]

By considering the two dimensions of responsiveness and demandingness and whether each is low or high, four parenting styles have been proposed:
1. **Uninvolved**—low responsiveness, low demandingness
2. **Authoritarian**—low responsiveness, high demandingness
3. **Permissive**—high responsiveness, low demandingness
4. **Authoritative**—high responsiveness, high demandingness.

Based upon the research of Baumrind and later work by others, the following profiles for each of the four types are provided.

1 Uninvolved parenting

Uninvolved parents are low on both demandingness and responsiveness. They may feed and clothe their children but show little interest in them, either to display warmth and affection or to discipline them and provide structure and consistent expectations. Uninvolved parents are frequently living in difficult circumstances that overwhelm their capacity to be sensitive and supportive towards their children. Children from uninvolved parenting and homes tend to fare poorly in all domains of development. Extreme forms of uninvolved parenting are neglect and abandonment or 'failing to provide the necessities of life', as it is termed in some jurisdictions.

2 Authoritarian parenting

Authoritarian parents are high on demandingness and expect obedience from children 'because I say so'. They may inflict punishment when compliance is not forthcoming. They attempt to instil traditional values, such as obedience and respect for authority. They are also low on responsiveness and do not consult or negotiate with children about expectations, nor display much warmth towards them.

This style of parenting is regarded these days as 'old-fashioned' and when people wish to make unflattering comparisons between old and new style teaching it is an authoritarian style that is generally claimed to characterise teachers from the 'bad old days' of 'chalk and talk'.

Children from authoritarian homes tend to perform well at school and not to become involved in problem behaviour. However, they also tend to have poorer social skills, lower self-esteem, and to be more prone to emotional problems, including depression. Not surprisingly, some children of authoritarian parenting will later rebel or 'break free'.

3 Permissive parenting

In direct contrast to authoritarian parents are permissive parents, who are low on demandingness and high on responsiveness. Permissive parents are accepting and affirming of the child's impulses, desires, and actions. They consult with the child about family decisions and give explanations for rules while making few demands for household responsibility and orderly behaviour. The permissive parent is a resource for the child but not an active agent responsible for shaping or altering ongoing or future behaviour. The permissive parent allows the child to regulate their own activities as much as possible, avoids exercising control, and does not encourage them to obey externally defined standards. Permissive parents attempt to use reason and even pleading, but not overt power or sanctions, to accomplish parental ends.

Children reared permissively tend to have high self-esteem, are generally cheerful and positive in outlook, and are more creative than their peers. So far, so good. However, they also tend to do poorly at school, to lack persistence at challenging tasks, to be unpopular with their peers because of poor social skills and to be spontaneously rebellious and dependent in their relations with parents and other adults. They are also much more likely than their peers raised by authoritarian parents to be involved in antisocial and/or illegal acts.

4 Authoritative parenting

In contrast to both the permissive and the authoritarian styles, authoritative parents are high on both responsiveness and demandingness. They are warm and supportive of their children, aware of their current developmental needs and sensitive to meeting these needs. They also have high expectations and set appropriate limits while providing structure and consistent rules, the reasons for which they explain to their child, rather than simply expecting unthinking obedience. While they maintain adult authority, they are also willing to listen to their child and to negotiate about rules and situations.

This combination of sensitivity, caring, high expectations and structure has been shown to have the best consequence for children, who commonly display high academic achievement, good social skills, moral maturity, autonomy and high self-esteem.

Teaching and parenting styles

In our original paper on parenting and teaching styles we stated how we believed this typology had relevance to understanding teaching today.[5]

Not surprisingly, because of the numerous parallels evident between parenting and teaching, we were advocating for an authoritative teaching style. This was based upon findings from various research projects with which we had been involved, including those cited previously, and our experience with beginning teachers, many of whom appeared to subscribe to a permissive model of teaching (see below).

Among other lessons from application of Baumrind's typology to teaching, we were interested in the notion of building student self-esteem. There is a popular view that boosting student self-esteem can lead to a range of desirable outcomes. Conversely, self-esteem that is too low is believed to lead to problematic outcomes for the individual concerned. The argument also goes that students from minority and lower socio-economic backgrounds will tend to have lower self-esteem and need to feel better about themselves if they are to be successful. Boosting or increasing their self-esteem is thus desirable.[a]

Catherine Scott and I have each been involved with teacher pre-service education over many years and at several universities. The bulk of our pre-service teachers came to us with a strong interest in children and a desire to help them grow and thrive. Along with this 'caring for kids' ethos, they frequently expressed a strong aversion to being in a position of authority over children.

The general social distrust of anyone in a position of authority has made its way into students' value systems, as has the idea of the teacher as the 'guide by the side' who facilitates children's learning and their 'self-actualisation'.[6] Our student teachers also articulated the view that the supreme duty of the teacher is to foster self-esteem, which they believe will inevitably lead to other desirable outcomes such as academic achievement and kind and considerate behaviour. This desire is accompanied by fear that higher demands, competition, 'failure', criticism and expectations that challenge children may damage their self-esteem, because not all will be able to meet these expectations. Instead, learning must be 'fun' and relevant, and so effortless that children 'hardly feel it happening', to quote one of our pre-service students.

---

a   We considered self-concept or self-esteem in Chapter 2.

Our teacher pre-service students then, would like their future students to be confident and independent learners ('lifelong learners', to use the popular term), with high self-esteem, but to also work cooperatively with others. Can what we know about parenting help to decide the best way to aid students to become the best people that they can? Is a teaching style that aims to facilitate learning and development while avoiding asserting searching authority over children, likely to result in future citizens who display all the virtues listed above?

To respond to these questions, the comparison between permissive and authoritative parenting suggests that self-esteem is not the cause of anything; rather it is the consequence of having warm and responsive parents and presumably teachers. It can co-occur with either the desirable traits of the authoritatively reared child or with the less desirable attributes of the permissively parented young person.

What makes the difference for good and not so good outcomes is the level of demandingness that the child has also experienced. High expectations, clear rules, appropriately enforced adult authority and consistent structure make the difference between the autonomous, mature, responsible young person and the rebellious, whining, socially inept 'spoilt' child.

Those who have seen the television series *Brat Camp*[b] will recognise the problems associated with a permissive style of parenting. In the series, rebellious, 'spoilt' adolescents from the United Kingdom are sent to a desert in the United States of America for a period of months where the aim is to provide the demandingness that has been lacking in their upbringing to this point.

Totally unused to compliance with authority, structure and direction, these young people find the going hard, coming up against staff who are well-trained and unbending in their demands for discipline and acceptable, responsible behaviour.

In their home situations, the parents of these children had been unable or unwilling to institute any form of guidance or control and had resorted in many cases to buying their son's or daughter's compliance. These young people responded to this permissive, indulgent parenting style by being verbally, and in some cases physically, abusive to their parents and engaging in various forms of anti-social, self-destructive and illegal behaviour.

Not surprisingly, many had experienced problems at school and were basically dysfunctional young people. The 'tough love' approach demonstrated in *Brat Camp* is shown to be successful with the majority of these young people, with the transformation in their relationship with others, and their feelings about themselves quite pronounced, at least for the duration of the program. For some, however, the process fails and they revert to their previous patterns of behaviour. Obviously, such remedies are expensive, time-consuming and beyond the means of most families.

---

b   Available on YouTube. See https://www.youtube.com/watch?v=IwT4cIF6yzg

Sometimes there is a feeling in schools that a choice has to be made between concentrating on student welfare—responsiveness—and a focus on behaviour and achievement—demandingness. Lessons drawn from research literature on school and teacher effectiveness and parenting styles suggest that the best outcomes are achieved where both responsiveness and demandingness are the focus of school policies and procedures.

Research from the AESOP study detailed earlier confirmed the existence of a belief in—yet refuted the truth of this dichotomy—between perceptions of welfare and academic schools. Schools where exceptional academic or subject outcomes were being achieved were found to have highly effective student welfare practices and programs underpinning this academic success. On the other hand, at schools where the existence of exceptional outcomes in cross-school programs was identified, the main function of these programs was to 'get students back into learning', 'we are not interested in "warm fuzzies" or self-concept', as a number of teachers involved with 'welfare' programs noted.

The AESOP study confirmed that it should not be a matter of circumstances or choice whether a school is a 'welfare' school, or one where academic achievement is prized. Both aspects are vital to student success. What tends to happen in practice, however, is that certain students (Indigenous, low SES, non-English-speaking background) are categorised and stigmatised. Teachers have lower expectations for these students, and in some cases for whole schools. It is thought that the best thing for these students is to keep them off the streets, teach them the 'basics' and boost their self-esteem.

In the best schools, however, there is a focus on students *and* their learning, and all students can experience success, self-efficacy and achievement being the best builders of self-esteem and confidence.

Applying the typology to educational leadership

After applying Baumrind's typology of parenting styles to what we know about teaching, we then turned out attention to educational leadership.[7] In considering the findings of a range of research projects focusing to various degrees on quality teaching, educational leadership (including distributive leadership and instructional leadership) and teachers' professional learning (cited in this book), we found that the four types of parenting and teaching can be productively applied to educational leadership, given the central, 'high-impact' role relationships play in the practice of leadership. As with any typology, the four prototypes are 'extremes', unlikely to be found in an ideal or 'pure' form, but helpful in our understanding of reality. No one is totally demanding or totally responsive, and not even a single-celled organism is totally lacking in either responsiveness or demandingness towards its environment.

What then might each broad type of leadership look like, based upon the findings of the above research projects? It should be noted that these types of leadership have been observed at all levels within schools and in educational hierarchies. My guess is that as you read the profile of each, you won't be able to resist mentally allocating people of your acquaintance to each type.[c]

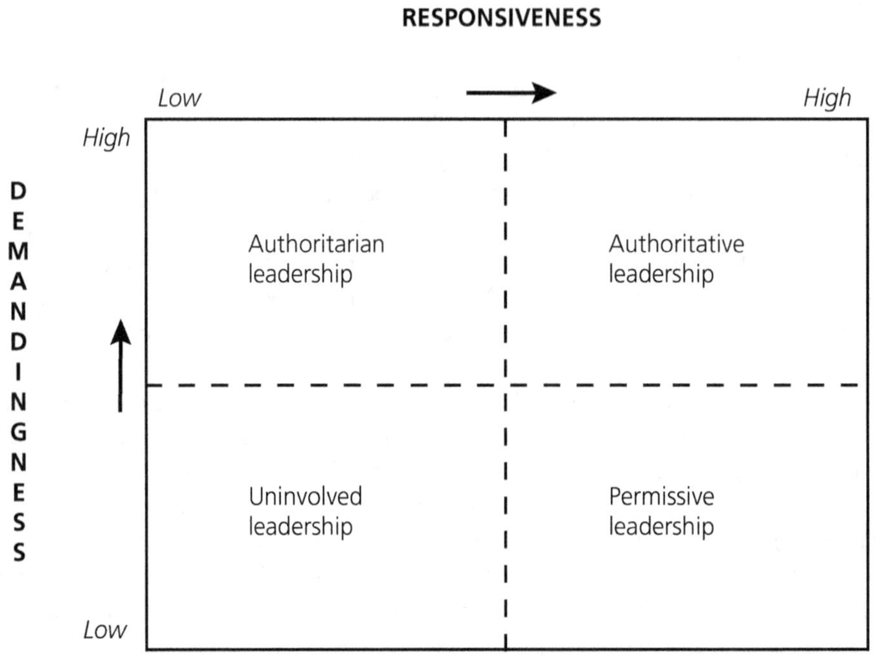

RESPONSIVENESS

	Low	High
High DEMANDINGNESS Low	Authoritarian leadership	Authoritative leadership
	Uninvolved leadership	Permissive leadership

Figure 15.1: Four prototypes of leadership (Dinham & Scott, after Baumrind)[8]

1 Uninvolved leadership

The uninvolved leader is low in both responsiveness and demandingness towards others, and practises leadership by abrogation or neglect. They make little impact of a positive nature on the school, its performance or its culture. The uninvolved leader can be an effective administrator and may rationalise their lack of educational leadership through the piles of papers they deal with. Alternatively, the uninvolved leader may be overwhelmed by their situation.

Under uninvolved leadership, staff are left to their own devices with few demands made upon them, and they receive little direction or support. Positive and negative feedback and recognition tend to be lacking. Students and staff perceive such leaders

---

c   The term 'organisation' is sometimes used in the following discussion to cover the various domains of the leader (faculty, department or team, school, and so forth).

as remote, and uninvolved leaders tend to have a low profile in the community and wider profession. Few know them well.

Standards and expectations from the uninvolved leader are not clearly articulated and are possibly too low. The resultant inconsistency and uncertainty can lead to confusion, conflict and poor organisational performance.

Insufficient attention and direction may be given to key organisational functions such as planning, policies, recruitment and induction, systems, communication and evaluation. The values and norms of the organisation may be unclear.[9]

Under uninvolved leadership, the school or department is reactive, drifting and possibly sinking. 'Balkanisation' and 'groupthink' (see Chapter 14) can flourish in this leadership vacuum and sub-groups can push the organisation into dangerous areas. Other leaders and groups may attempt to keep the organisation afloat and on course, but this is difficult without support from the 'top'.

While good things can happen in individual classes and within teams of teachers, the organisation is neither a true learning community, nor close to reaching its potential. Schools and departments operating under uninvolved educational leadership are thus sub-optimal in their performance.

2 Authoritarian leadership

Authoritarian leaders are high on demandingness and expect compliance from all concerned. They have a traditional conception of leadership based on obedience and respect for positional authority and status. They tend not to negotiate or consult with staff, students or the community, but expect their orders to be obeyed without question.

Reflecting their low responsiveness, authoritarian leaders focus on procedures rather than people. Because of their use of rules, punishments and sanctions, they may be feared or resented, rather than respected or liked. Recognition and positive feedback from the authoritative leader are lacking, although people may occasionally receive a blast from the leader as the leader reinforces control and authority by pulling people back into line and reminding them who is the boss.

Standards and expectations of the authoritarian leader may be high and are reinforced by extrinsic mechanisms. Control, consistency and order are emphasised at the expense of flexibility and compassion. Rules, 'going by the book' and equal treatment for all override flexibility.

Schools and departments of authoritarian leaders may be orderly and well run, with delegation, reporting and accountability systems utilised to facilitate this. There tends to be a high degree of dependency on the authoritarian leader, who has the final say on everything. Organisations led by authoritarian leaders can be characterised by low risk taking and innovation.

There may be considerable untapped potential in organisations led by authoritarian leaders. Staff and students can be infantilised under such leadership.

Some will appreciate the uncompromising stance and strength of the authoritarian leader (including novice or less able teachers who need structure), while others will feel stifled and frustrated by their lack of input to the organisation and their lack of opportunities to exercise leadership (including expert teachers who desire greater autonomy).[10]

There may be a leadership vacuum with the departure of the authoritarian leader because of staff dependency and his or her failure to practise distributive leadership and develop staff capacity.

3   Permissive leadership

Permissive leaders are by definition the opposite of the authoritarian leader. They are more responsive than demanding. Permissive leaders may have good people skills and be open and responsive to the needs and wishes of others. Permissive leaders may spend much of their time being available.

As permissive leaders value the input of others, planning and decision-making can take quite some time. Permissive leaders tend to use reason and consensus building rather than direction and authority, and the permissive leader may find it difficult to be decisive.

Permissive leaders allow staff and students a high degree of discretion and even indulgence, but a lack of direction and accountability can prove counterproductive. The trust and leeway permissive leaders extend to others can be exploited. The permissive leader may demonstrate a reluctance or incapacity to intervene or confront, leaving it to others to work out a solution.

Standards and expectations can be unclear, contradictory and too low. The permissive leader is undemanding and may make allowances for those who transgress or fail to deliver. Again, some will exploit this. Small problems can become bigger under permissive leadership because of a lack of willingness to intervene and make 'hard' decisions.

Schools led by permissive leaders can be characterised by organisational looseness and a lack of clarity and consistency in the application of systems and procedures.

There may be a lack of individual and collective responsibility, resulting in a degree of disorder and even disobedience and chaos as people 'do their own thing'. The permissive leader may frequently change their mind, depending upon the last person they have spoken with. Permissive leaders often use covert, 'special' deals to obtain or 'buy' cooperation from certain individuals or groups. Lack of transparency and consistency in decision-making can thus be a problem with permissive leadership.

Some self-directed teachers and groups of teachers will flourish under a permissive leadership regime, while others will drift through lack of direction or worse, avoid responsibility. Others will take the opportunity to build a power base.

While schools led by permissive leaders can be happy, sociable places, this may be at the expense of progress and achievement as the permissive leader attempts to keep everyone happy.

4   Authoritative leadership

Authoritative leaders share the positive attributes of permissive and authoritarian types. They are responsive, warm and supportive. They are sensitive to a diversity of individual and collective needs and are inclusive. They are good listeners and collaboratively build consensus and commitment. They tend to be good networkers, with a high profile beyond the school. They are aware of and responsive to the environment within and outside the school.

Authoritative leaders are also demanding. They are clear in their expectations of themselves, staff and students. They communicate high standards and set an example that others seek to emulate. They are assertive, without over-reliance on the rules and sanctions of the authoritarian leader. Authoritative leaders 'give a lot and expect a lot'. People say they don't want to let the authoritative leader down. The personal qualities of the authoritative leader are admired by most, but not always by all. They rely more on moral and personal than positional or formal authority.

Authoritative leaders exercise their authority appropriately and in a timely fashion. They know when to consult and when to be decisive. They have the skills to work with others and the courage to act alone.

Authoritative leaders put students and their learning at the centre of the school. They seek ways for every student to experience success and to achieve. They see student welfare as essential to academic success and oversee clear and effective welfare policies and procedures.

Authoritative leaders give timely and appropriate feedback, both positive and negative. People know where they stand with the authoritative leader.

Authoritative leaders place a strong emphasis on professional learning and are prepared to invest in this inside and outside the school. They model professional learning for others. People have the opportunity and encouragement to flourish under authoritative leadership. The authoritative leader seeks to develop competent, assertive, self-regulated staff and students.

These leaders possess a vision for the future development of the school, which they communicate clearly. They tend to have a bias towards innovation and action, and practise distributive leadership rather than line management delegation. Other staff are encouraged, entrusted and supported to develop new programs, policies and practices. The professionalism and capabilities of others are recognised and the authoritative leader is able to release untapped potential in individuals and the organisation as a whole.

Authoritative leaders are strategic and realise the impossibility of moving a whole staff forward simultaneously—as noted, if one 'waits for everyone to get aboard the bus, it will never leave'. They thus empower individuals and groups, hoping for a contagion or groundswell effect. Through influence and action, the authoritative leader moves people out of their comfort zones.

Schools led by authoritative leaders tend to move and improve through an emphasis on continual evaluation, evidence, planning and action. Even when change is externally imposed, authoritative leaders find ways to use this to the school's advantage.

Overall, authoritative leaders have a positive influence on school climate and culture. Authoritative leaders build leadership capacity and provide for leadership sustainability and effective leadership succession when they depart.

An important point to note is that the authoritative leader may well vary the 'mix' of responsiveness and demandingness depending on the situation. They may, for example, be more or less demanding or responsive with certain groups or at certain stages of the organisation's development.

The vast majority of leaders encountered in the AESOP study and teachers in the successful senior teaching study could be readily classified as being of the authoritative type, based on the findings of the two projects.

Educational leaders and relationships

The above analysis, arising from the findings of a range of recent research projects, is premised on the notion that educational leadership is heavily dependent upon relationships.

Michael Fullan, a prolific writer on educational change, has noted:

> [w]e have found that the single factor common to every successful change initiative is that relationships improve. If relationships improve, things get better. If they remain the same or get worse, ground is lost. Thus leaders must be consummate relationship builders with diverse people and groups—especially with people different than themselves.[11]

Authoritative leaders and teachers are 'relationship' people, able to 'read' and respond to others. They understand people and they understand change, which they help others to appreciate and come to grips with. They are authentic leaders, in that they model those qualities, attributes and behaviour they expect of others.

Authoritative leaders rely more on moral than positional authority, and influence more than overt control. In their relationships with teachers and students, authoritative leaders balance a high degree of responsiveness with a high degree of demandingness.

As noted, these leaders place a high priority on professional learning, which they perceive as key to changing people, practices and performance.

In many of the schools visited as part of the research projects cited previously, the most telling indicator of the power of authoritative leadership—exhibiting both high responsiveness and high demandingness—was that departments and whole schools had been turned around with commensurate improvement in student performance indicators. Schools and faculties formerly in decline were now thriving, with school leaders having to cope with a new problem of excessive demand for limited student places. In other cases, new leaders took schools and faculties that had plateaued at an acceptable level of performance to higher levels of achievement.

To offer a cautionary comment, as noted previously, the AESOP study found that the 'turning around' and 'lifting up' processes can take around six to seven years to accomplish, although some improvements can occur almost immediately.[12]

Those looking for and advocating quick fixes for struggling schools need to consider the intense, coordinated effort and teamwork, and professional learning under authoritative forms of leadership that such improvement requires. However, the evidence is clear that it can be done. As noted, one research participant commented in the AESOP study, 'in this school we make plans now, not excuses'.

Education from the early 1960s to today: where we went wrong

I want at this point to introduce an analysis and argument that some of you may find challenging.

In the early 1960s, I think it is accurate to say that 'traditional' education in much of the 'western' world was characterised by high demandingness and low responsiveness, that is an authoritarian relationship existed between schools and students. This was certainly the case where and when I went to school.

There was a major emphasis on discipline, to the extent that corporal punishment and expulsion were not uncommon. There was little attempt to differentiate curricula, which were largely fixed with little flexibility for teachers and students and accompanied by a range of public and internal examinations. Post-compulsory retention rates were lower than now and students who didn't perform or conform were 'encouraged' or forced to leave school. Homes and the community generally were also more 'traditional' or authoritarian, and parents generally 'backed' the school and its teachers without questioning too much how the school operated, indicative of a general respect for institutions and authority.

During the 1960s, however, a wave of questioning of tradition, accepted practices and authority swept the western world. This was an era of protest and far-reaching social change. This change was reflected in, and in turn influenced by, changing thinking in teacher preparation and schooling, which came more under the influence of 'progressivism'.

Quite rightly, there was a feeling at this time that schools needed to respond more to students as people and to better cater for their individual backgrounds and needs. We recognised that we increasingly lived in a multicultural, diverse and changing society.

Education academics, system officials and teachers questioned established school organisational and teaching practices, and over the following decades curriculum prescription and testing gave way to school-based curriculum development. Some external and internal examinations were removed and replaced with other forms of assessment. Students, like many members of society, began to speak up and engage in various forms of questioning, protest and activism.

Social concerns such as pollution and environmental degradation, racism, sexism, drugs, sexual health and awareness, nuclear warfare, militarism and multinationalism found their place in school curricula. Values education became prominent.

As noted, many of these developments were desirable and even overdue and were part of schools becoming more responsive to students.

However, I believe that *a fundamental error of perception occurred at this time that has ramifications to this day.*

Concluding remarks

Using the benefit of hindsight and applying the typology developed by Baumrind retrospectively, I believe that *demandingness and responsiveness were falsely dichotomised.*

Ideologically, it was thought that any increase in responsiveness towards students must be accompanied by, and in fact required, a decrease in demandingness: to be responsive was to be progressive; to be demanding was to be traditional.

Over time, some schools and schooling as a whole became more responsive to, *and less demanding of* students; that is, they became more permissive, with commensurate effects on matters such as standards, behaviour, expectations, teaching methods and the balance of the curriculum. Other false dichotomies have also reflected the polarisation of ideologies in education over this period: knowledge versus skills; learning processes versus subject content; competition versus collaboration; progressivism versus conservatism; subjects versus thematic approaches; 'guide by the side' versus 'sage on the stage' teaching, and so forth.[13]

I believe that the false dichotomisation of demandingness with responsiveness has contributed to many of the problems we see in schools today, problems that include:
- Student disengagement due to lower expectations and failure to challenge and extend students.
- Behavioural problems through lack of, or inconsistent guidance, standards and discipline; general lack of self-discipline.
- Teacher role conflict and ambiguity.
- Downgrading of teacher expertise and status and de-professionalisation of teaching.
- Denigration of 'teacher direction' of students and forms of more explicit teaching.
- Overuse of student discovery and enquiry-based learning approaches.[14]
- Fear of harm to students arising from 'competition' and failure; lack of honesty in assessment.

- Learning must be 'relevant' and 'fun'; 'dumbing-down', and grade inflation.
- Self-esteem boosting in isolation from achievement.

These phenomena need to be considered in the context of societal changes, including families and society being generally less authoritarian and more permissive, and adolescence and young adulthood being spread over a longer period.

When problems such as those cited above occur, there is a tendency to conclude that responsiveness has not gone far enough and is still being hindered by demandingness that is too high. Thus, problems are further exacerbated as 'more fuel is put on the fire' in the efforts of schools to be more responsive and less demanding.

There has been something of a reaction to this situation in recent times, with recognition by some that things have gone too far, but the false dichotomisation of responsiveness and demandingness remains problematic. It is difficult to re-introduce higher levels of demandingness when students and teachers have become accustomed to a different regime. (See previous references to *Brat Camp*.)

In Australia, there has been a steady drift of students to the non-government sector over recent decades. In some cases, this is because parents are looking for certain values they perceive to be lacking or insufficiently emphasised in government schools. Non-government schools are thought to provide greater discipline (demandingness), while being more attuned to students' needs (responsiveness). There are no doubt other reasons for this shift, but the crux of the matter appears to be that many in the community *perceive* non-government schools to be more 'authoritative' than their government school counterparts, which are perceived as more 'permissive', or even verging on the 'uninvolved'.

As a result, it is apparent that many government schools in Australia are attempting to emulate what some believe they see in the private sector: greater emphasis on discipline, wearing of school uniform, greater respect for teachers and other adults, higher standards of self-discipline and behaviour and a better quality peer group. This argument is yet another dichotomy and is, of course, grossly unfair. It is just as dangerous and fallacious to generalise about all government schools as it is to stereotype all non-government schools. The schools in the AESOP study were all government schools and the vast majority were of the authoritative type, as we have observed.

Some who speak out about this situation of lesser demandingness and greater responsiveness in schools (and society) are painted as traditionalists who are part of a 'back to basics' movement, that is, seeking more authoritarianism as per the early 1960s.

However, *the best teachers, educational leaders and schools today exhibit both high demandingness and high responsiveness*; that is, the relationship between schools, teachers, leaders and students is authoritative. In fact, this has probably always been the case, as it has been with parenting.

In this respect, more authoritative approaches to teaching and leadership actually represent a move towards a more desirable status quo, authoritative schooling, rather than a step backwards to authoritarianism.

In Chapter 16 we consider the role of leadership in turnaround schools, those school improvement strategies that are most effective, and the contentious issue of school autonomy.

> **Acknowledgement:** Catherine Scott provided the insight to apply Baumrind's typology of parenting styles to teaching. We then developed this thinking to apply the typology to educational leadership and leadership generally.[15] This chapter is based mainly on two of our papers, along with findings from the various studies cited.[16] The final section came from my further thinking using the typology.

Endnotes

1. Ayres, P., Dinham, S., & Sawyer, W. (1999). *Successful teaching in the NSW Higher School Certificate*. Sydney: NSW Department of Education and Training; Ayres, P., Dinham, S., & Sawyer, W. (2000). *Successful senior secondary teaching. Quality Teaching Series, No 1*, Australian College of Education, September, 1–20; Ayres, P., Dinham, S., & Sawyer, W. (2004). Effective teaching in the context of a Grade 12 high stakes external examination in New South Wales, Australia. *British Educational Research Journal, 30*(1), 141–165.
2. Dinham, S. (2007). *Leadership for exceptional educational outcomes*. Teneriffe, Qld: Post Pressed.
3. See, for example, Baumrind, D. (1989). Rearing competent children. In W. Damon (Ed.), *Child development today and tomorrow* (pp. 349–378). San Francisco, CA: Jossey-Bass; Baumrind, D. (1991). The influence of parenting style on adolescent competence and substance abuse. *Journal of Early Adolescence, 11*(1), 56–95.
4. Baumrind, D. (1991). (p. 62)
5. Scott, C., & Dinham, S. (2005). Parenting, teaching and self esteem. *The Australian Educational Leader, 27*(1), 28–30.
6. See Maslow, A. H. (1943). A Theory of Human Motivation. *Psychological Review, 50*(4), 370–96.
7. Dinham, S., & Scott, C. (2007). Parenting, teaching and leadership styles. *The Australian Educational Leader, 29*(1), 30–32, 45.
8. Dinham, S., & Scott, C. (2008). Responsive and demanding leadership, *Synergy, 6*(2), 19-21. http://www.slav.schools.net.au/synergy/vol6num2/dinhamscott.pdf (p. 19). Reproduced with permission.
9. Schlechty, P. (2005). *Creating great schools: Six critical systems at the heart of educational innovation*. San Francisco, CA: Jossey-Bass.
10. Dreyfus, S., & Dreyfus, H. (1980). *A five-stage model of the mental activities involved in directed skills acquisition*. Berkeley: Operations Research Center, University of California.
11. Fullan M. (2001). *Leading in a culture of change*. San Francisco, CA: Jossey-Bass. (p. 5)
12. Dinham, S. (2007). How schools get moving and keep improving: Leadership for teacher learning, student success and school renewal. *Australian Journal of Education, 51*(3), 263–275.

13 Dinham, S. (2006). Teaching and teacher education: Some observations, reflections and possible solutions. *ED Ventures, 2,* 3–20.
14 Mayer, R. (2004). Should there be a three-strikes rule against pure discovery learning? *American Psychologist, 59*(1), 14–19.
15 Dinham, S. (2007). Authoritative leadership, action learning and student accomplishment. *Conference Proceedings* (pp. 33–39), Australian Council for Educational Research, 2007 Research Conference; Dinham, S., & Scott, C. (2008). Responsive, demanding leadership. *Management Today,* April, 32–35.
16 Scott, C., & Dinham, S. (2005); Dinham, S., & Scott, C. (2007).

CHAPTER 16

What role does leadership play in turnaround schools? What school improvement strategies are most effective?

INTRODUCTION

The notion of a turnaround school means different things in different places, but essentially, it is about addressing the issue of 'failing' schools. Some of the thinking behind turnaround in education has been borrowed from other sectors, both public (e.g., hospitals), and corporate (e.g., firms). In the United States of America it is more of an external formal process and movement[1], while in countries such as Australia turning around schools is more of a self-initiated process undertaken by school leaders, sometimes with systemic support.

The issue of school improvement, a legitimate concern, has to some degree become entangled with ideological debates and trends concerning the supposed failings of (public) education, and the need to expose education to external market forces, resulting in a greater presence in education of commercial interests and initiatives such as charter schools, academies, government-funded independent schools, 'free schools', and for-profit schools.[2]

This chapter examines the issue of turnaround schools and, in particular, the role that leaders and leadership can play in this process.

We have already considered some aspects of school change and improvement in previous chapters; in this chapter we focus more directly on reversing decline in school performance and the school improvement strategies that have been found to be most effective.

The turnaround school phenomenon: an overview

Joseph Murphy has reviewed the literature on the turnaround school phenomenon:

> Over the last decade, the notion of turning around failing schools has burst onto the educational landscape in various countries throughout the world. Powered by government accountability systems and a growing body of knowledge about productive schooling for all youngsters, educators, policymakers, and actors in the general community have been calling for dramatic action to turnaround schools that fail to effectively educate large numbers of students.[3]

In attempting to define turnaround, Murphy has noted that there are three, overlapping ways that 'turnaround' can be conceptualised:

1. **As a condition or situation**—requiring action
2. **As a process**—reversing decline and returning to a 'healthy' state
3. **As a consequence**—the end state of successful action.[4]

As a result of his extensive review of the literature on turnaround in respect of schools and more generally, Murphy came to a number of conclusions:

> I was able to cull out three extremely visible leadership patterns in the mosaic of organizational rejuvenation. Specifically, I reported that leadership is the most critical element in the narrative of organizational recovery. I also observed that for a variety of reasons a change in top-level leadership is often-to-generally required for organizations to recover. Finally, I reported that certain dimensions of leadership, but not styles, consistently define turnaround managers ...
>
> ... the adoption of strategies that do not pay explicit attention to leadership in their designs would appear to be questionable.
>
> ... recovery efforts that attempt to prop up the existing leaders of failing schools merit scrutiny. Indeed, 'inspection' strategies designed to lay visible the facts of school problems and 'leader helper' strategies intended to support principals/heads may prove too weak to produce the aggressive changes needed in failing schools. Reading of the turnaround literature outside of education tells us that the recovery plan should begin with the assumption of leadership change.
>
> ... it is possible that more than one change in top leadership may be required in school turnarounds. Specifically, the efficiency stage of recovery may necessitate one type of administrator while the entrepreneurial phase may call for another type of leader. Similarly, there is a period in the timeline of decline and failure after which leadership replacement will likely be ineffective ...

> Finally, while being sensitive to the warning about the appropriateness of a single, context free model of turnaround leadership, there are patterns of skills and dispositions that should be privileged in the search for agents of school recovery. In particular, since failing organizations are marked by a plethora of organizational dysfunctions and often characterized by a prevailing sense of gloom, it is helpful for turnaround leaders to have unusual supplies of optimism and persistence and a penchant for enjoying the risks needed to break a school's pernicious cycle of decline.[5]

Thus, while Murphy rightly champions the importance of leadership in turning around poorly performing, declining schools, he is blunt about the need to change the leader or leaders at the top of the organisation if the desired change is to occur. He is also clear on the fact that a different approach to leadership might be needed during the change, and before the change and improvement process is 'bedded down', or in other words, those driving the change might need to adopt a contingency approach to leadership.

This is certainly in accord with my experience. I have rarely seen a school that has been able to arrest decline and embark on an improvement process without a change of leadership at or near the 'top'. Around one-third of the 38 AESOP study schools could have been classified as 'failing' and in decline prior to the appointment of a new principal, and in some cases other leaders. On average, completing the turnaround process took some six to seven years, with some quite stunning results.[6]

The US approach

As mentioned previously, the USA has adopted a more interventionist approach to the issue of 'failing' schools. The 'No Child Left Behind' Act of 2001 (NCLB)[7], or to give it the full title: 'An act to close the achievement gap with accountability, flexibility, and choice, so that no child is left behind', was legislated to set standards for schooling (state and not national), with measurable goals, and to development assessments in basic skills. Schools not meeting these accountability standards can face financial and other punishments.

The 'official blog' of the US Department of Education quotes President Obama:

> Because we know that about 12% of America's schools produce 50% of America's dropouts, we're going to focus on helping states and school districts turn around their 5,000 lowest-performing schools in the next five years.[8]

The US Department of Education blog goes on to outline the 'helping' strategy to be employed:

Turning around the nation's 5,000 lowest-performing schools, Secretary Duncan has said, is 'part of our overall strategy for dramatically reducing the drop-out rate, improving high school graduation rates and increasing the number of students who graduate prepared for success in college and the workplace.'

The Obama administration is making an historic commitment to support state and local education leaders in turning around the nation's lowest-achieving schools.

The U.S. Department of Education is providing $4 billion for this effort. To qualify for this funding under the Title 1 School Improvement Grant program[a], states must identify their lowest-performing schools in economically challenged communities and transform those schools using one of the four following intervention models:

- **Turnaround model:** Replace the principal and rehire no more than 50% of the staff, and grant the principal sufficient operational flexibility (including in staffing, calendars/time and budgeting) to fully implement a comprehensive approach to substantially improve student outcomes.
- **Restart model:** Convert a school or close and reopen it under a charter school operator, a charter management organization, or an education management organization that has been selected through a rigorous review process.
- **School closure:** Close a school and enrol the students who attended that school in other schools in the district that are higher achieving.
- **Transformation model:** Implement each of the following strategies: (1) replace the principal and take steps to increase teacher and school leader effectiveness; (2) institute comprehensive instructional reforms; (3) increase learning time and create community-oriented schools; and (4) provide operational flexibility and sustained support.[9]

The above can be seen to be a menu of strong, external, interventionist practices that include closing schools and removing principals and teachers. Implicit in the above measures are support for Murphy's findings on leadership and some form of external 'circuit-breaker', but the measures obviously go far further than those Murphy advocates.[10]

Which school improvement strategies are most effective?

The importance and impact of school leadership have been examined in previous chapters. Here, our focus is more on substantive improvement of under-performing schools going through a turnaround process.

---

a   See http://www2.ed.gov/programs/sif/index.html

David Hopkins, in a paper for the National College for School Leadership, has noted:

> Our own work in supporting a variety of school improvement initiatives suggests that the focus of instructional leadership needs to be on two key skill clusters ... These are:
> - strategies for effective teaching and learning
> - the conditions that support implementation, in particular staff development and planning.[11]

Hopkins goes on to link student outcomes and school improvement:

> ... school improvement is a distinct approach to educational change that enhances student outcomes as well as strengthening the school's capacity for managing change. School improvement is about raising student achievement through focusing on the teaching-learning process and the conditions that support it. It is about strategies for improving the school's capacity for providing quality education in times of change.
>
> This definition is consistent with the research on effective school improvement initiatives. Those strategies that enhance student outcomes tend to:
> - focus on specific outcomes which can be related to student learning, rather than succumbing to external pressure to identify non-specific goals such as 'improve exam results'
> - when formulating strategies, draw on theory and on research into practice and the teachers' own experiences, so that the rationale for the required changes is established in the minds of those expected to bring them about
> - recognize the importance of staff development, since it is unlikely that developments in student learning will occur without developments in teachers' practice
> - provide for monitoring the impact of policy and strategy on teacher practice and student learning early and regularly, rather than rely on post hoc evaluations.[12]

The above, while consistent to some degree with the US approach outlined previously, has a much greater emphasis on initiative for change rather than external pressure to lift 'results'. Hopkins goes on to expand on aspects of this school-initiated improvement strategy:

Our experience of facilitating leadership within the IQEA [Improving the Quality of Education for All] school improvement project suggests that instructional leaders display the following characteristics:
- an ability to articulate values and vision around student learning and achievement, and to make the connections to principles and behaviours and the necessary structures to promote and sustain them
- an understanding of a range of pedagogic structures and their ability to impact on student achievement and learning
- an ability to distinguish between development and maintenance structures, activities and cultures
- a strategic orientation, the ability to plan at least into the medium term, and an entrepreneurial bent that facilitates the exploitation of external change
- an understanding of the nature of organisational capacity, its role in sustaining change, and how to enhance it
- a commitment to promoting enquiry, particularly into the 'how' rather than the 'what'
- a similar commitment to continuing professional development and the managing of the teacher's life cycle
- an ability to engender trust and provide positive reinforcement.[13]

Once again, the strategies and approaches identified by Hopkins and his colleagues are congruent with the findings of the AESOP study. A dual focus on improving teaching and learning, coupled with building overall capacity in the school[14], has resulted in the arrest of decline, consolidation and then improvement in both teaching and learning, and in overall efficiency.

A valuable resource on school improvement are the conference proceedings of the Australian Council for Educational Research 2012 research conference *School Improvement: What does research tell us about effective strategies?*.[15] In his paper delivered to the conference, Geoff Masters provides a 'framework for continual improvement' that considers areas for action at a student, teacher, school and system level[16]: See Table 16.1 on the following page for a summary of this framework.

Table 16.1: A framework for continual improvement (Masters)[17]

	STUDENTS	TEACHERS	SCHOOLS	SYSTEMS
Commitment to improvement	a commitment to, and belief in, every student's ability to learn successfully	a commitment to the continual development of every teacher's effectiveness	a commitment to the continual development of every school's practices and programs	a commitment to continually improve the effectiveness of system initiatives and support
Improvement framework	a framework that describes increasing levels of student learning and achievement	a framework that describes increasing levels of teacher expertise and effectiveness	a framework that describes increasing levels of school practice and performance	a framework that describes increasing levels of system practice and performance
Assessment processes	processes for establishing where students are up to in their learning	processes for establishing current teacher expertise and effectiveness	processes for evaluating current school practices and performance	processes for evaluating current system practices and performance
Improvement strategies	evidence-based teaching strategies tailored to students' current levels of progress and learning needs	evidence-based, differentiated strategies for developing teacher expertise and effectiveness	evidence-based, differentiated strategies for improving school practices and programs	evidence-based, differentiated strategies for enhancing system effectiveness and support
Feedback and monitoring	a process for monitoring learning and providing feedback to guide student action	a process for monitoring and recognising increasing teacher expertise and effectiveness	a process for monitoring and reflecting on progress in improving school practices and programs	a process for monitoring and reflecting on progress in improving system initiatives and support

Masters notes that:

> Effective classroom teaching and distributed instructional leadership are keys to improving student outcomes. Almost all school systems understand this, but not all systems take the logical next step of making the improvement of day-to-day teaching and the development of effective instructional leadership the primary focus of their reform efforts. Instead, priority is given to secondary considerations such as redesigning school curricula, measuring performance levels, increasing local autonomy[b] and holding schools publicly accountable. Improvements in student outcomes depend on an alignment of effort—by students, teachers, school leaders, systems and governments—to enhance the quality and effectiveness of day-to-day teaching and learning.
>
> For all these groups, improvement depends on a commitment and belief that performance can be further improved; a clear understanding of what improvement would look like; a way of establishing current levels of performance as starting points for action; a familiarity with evidence-based, differentiated improvement strategies; and ongoing processes for monitoring progress and evaluating improvement efforts.[18]

Once again, the above findings and views are strongly consistent with the research evidence presented in this book.

What about the issue of school autonomy?

The theory that greater school autonomy will lead to greater flexibility, innovation and therefore student attainment is intuitively appealing, persuasive and pervasive. School autonomy has become something of an article of faith. However, establishing correlation and causation is not so easy.

The Department for Education in the United Kingdom states:

> There is evidence that giving heads and teachers greater freedom over their curriculum, budget and staff can help improve the quality of the education they provide and reduce the attainment gap. We also believe giving parents, teachers and charities the ability to open schools in response to the needs of the local community will help to raise standards.[19]

The 'evidence', however, is not referenced. Similarly, the Australian Government Department of Education has stated:

---

b   School autonomy as a means to improvement will be considered shortly.

Both internationally and in Australia, evidence emphasises the advantages of school autonomy as part of a comprehensive strategy for school improvement.

In Australia, schools in all states and territories have been moving towards more autonomous and independent models to improve education outcomes.

The Australian Government also recognises that giving schools and school leaders greater autonomy can help improve student results.

Great schools have leaders and teachers who have the independence to make the decisions and develop the courses that best meet the needs of their students.[20]

David Hopkins reviewed the evidence for school autonomy and found:

The myth of autonomy is currently centre stage given the increasing prevalence of 'right of centre' governments to embrace the trend towards devolution of school management. The rhetoric is that if we let schools be free—release them from bureaucratic control and encourage independence, self-governance and making one's own decisions—then they will flourish. This is an attractive and populist image.

However we know from the evidence of PISA ... that there is no correlation between decentralisation and achievement.[21]

Thus, if correlation between school autonomy and student achievement can't be established, causation would seem to be out of the question. Hopkins[22] cites the findings of the McKinsey report *Capturing the Leadership Premium*:

... differences in what leaders do are not directly related to the level of autonomy they are given. Internationally, there is no relationship between the degree of autonomy enjoyed by a school principal and their relative focus on administrative or instructional leadership.[23]

The OECD has provided a helpful disaggregation of aspects of autonomy:

In countries where schools have greater autonomy over what is taught and how students are assessed, students tend to perform better.

In countries where schools *account for their results* by posting achievement data publicly, schools that *enjoy greater autonomy in resource allocation tend to show better student performance* than those with less autonomy.

In countries where there are *no such accountability* arrangements, *schools with greater autonomy in resource allocation tend to perform worse.*[24] [Emphasis added, see Figure 16.1]

What role does leadership play in turnaround schools?

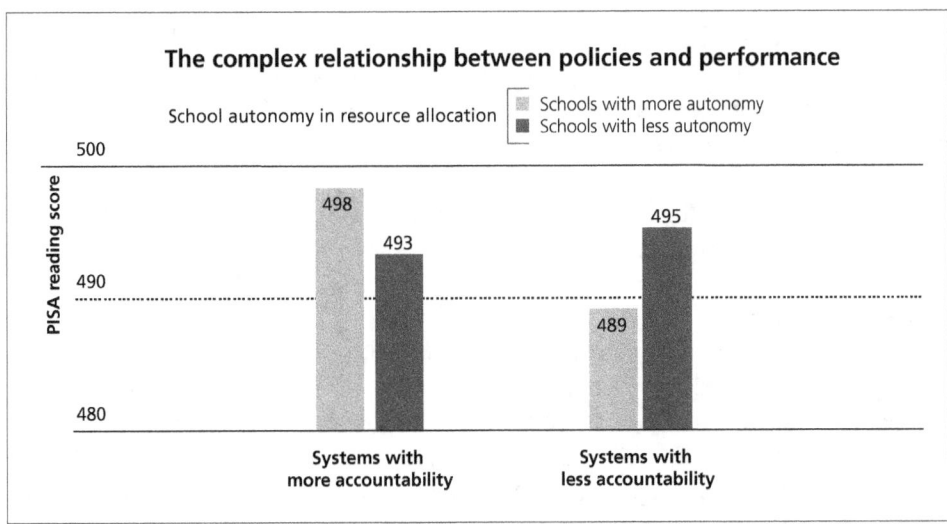

Figure 16.1: The complex relationship between policies and performance[25]

Thus, the key question is 'autonomy over what'? Public schools that have greater autonomy—which usually means greater responsibility for certain functions—often have more accountability in other areas, accompanied by less funding and less systemic support. In the 1970s, Karl Weick described schools as loosely coupled organisations, yet with certain aspects being tightly coupled.[26] While some aspects of (public) school operation may have become 'looser' under the guise of autonomy (use of resources, hiring and utilisation of staff, raising funds), others have become more tightly coupled or controlled (accountability for student achievement, curricula, teacher standards, teacher appraisal, external testing, school reporting).

Another aspect lies with school leaders' preparedness and willingness to adopt more responsibility and greater autonomy. Some school leaders and their communities may well be enthusiastic about greater autonomy, others ambivalent, and some should probably have less and not more autonomy. A telling point is that there may well be two very similar schools in the same system with ostensibly the same amount of autonomy, yet one is performing at a higher level than the other. In other words, it is how the individual leader and their leadership team utilise the opportunities and powers available to them that is the most important factor, rather than the relative notional amount of accountability and responsibility they enjoy.

Thus, there is likely to be a spectrum of capability and motivation for greater school autonomy. Ironically, some schools will need greater support to become more autonomous.[27]

What is needed above all, however, is clear research evidence that the initiative of greater school autonomy works, and if so, under what conditions.

Concluding remarks

We have seen in this and other chapters that genuine turnaround in schools *is* possible. It takes a certain strategic approach, driven by leadership—and some would argue new leaders—that focuses both on improving teaching and learning, and overall school organisation and performance.

It is clear that such turnaround and improvement often requires external support and even pressure for change.

It is also necessary to form a 'coalition of the willing', as leaders can't accomplish this task on their own.

Various remedies or 'quick fixes' to the problem of poorly performing and declining schools have been proposed, including moving out senior staff, parachuting in 'super principals', renaming, restructuring and re-opening schools, 'selling off' schools to private providers, and punishing and rewarding schools (e.g., *No Child Left Behind*[28] and *Race to the Top*[c] in the USA), yet the research evidence on the impact of such measures is inconclusive or not convincing. What is convincing, however, is the number of schools that have been able to halt the slide, turn things around, and begin the upward process of improvement, and we have the research findings and frameworks to guide us in this process.

Endnotes

1. See US Department of Education. (2010). *What's possible: Turning around America's lowest-achieving schools*. http://www.ed.gov/blog/2010/03/whats-possible-turning around-americas-lowest-achieving-schools/
2. See Dinham, S. (2015). The worst of both worlds: How US and UK models are influencing education in Australia. *Educational Policy Analysis Archives, 23*(49), http://dx.doi.org/10.14507/epaa.v23.1865; Ravitch, D. (2010). *The death and life of the great American school system*. New York, NY: Basic Books; Ravitch, D. (2014). *Reign of error: The hoax of the privatization movement and the danger to America's public schools*. New York, NY: Knopf; Berliner, D. C., Glass, G. V., & Associates. (2014). *50 myths & lies that threaten America's public schools*. New York, NY: Teachers College Press.
3. Murphy, J. (2008). The place of leadership in turnaround schools. *Journal of Educational Administration, 46*(1), 74–98. (p. 74). Copyright © Emerald Group Publishing Limited, all rights reserved.
4. Murphy, J. (2008). (pp. 76–78)
5. Murphy, J. (2008). (pp. 90–91)
6. Dinham, S. (2007). *Leadership for exceptional educational outcomes*. Teneriffe, Qld: Post Pressed; Dinham, S. (2005). Principal leadership for outstanding educational outcomes. *Journal of Educational Administration, 43*(4), 338–356.
7. US Department of Education. (2001). *No Child Left Behind Elementary and Secondary Education Act* (ESEA). http://www2.ed.gov/nclb/landing.jhtml
8. US Department of Education. (2010). (no page reference)

---

c   See www.ed.gov/blog/2009/06/higher-standards-better-tests-race-to-the-top

9   US Department of Education. (2010). (no page reference)
10 Murphy, J. (2008).
11 Hopkins, D. (n.d.). *Instructional leadership and school improvement*. Nottingham, England: National College for School Leadership. www3.nccu.edu.tw/~mujinc/teaching/9-101principal/refer8-2(kpool-evidence-hopkins).pdf (p. 3). All extracts from this publication have been reproduced with permission. See http://www.nationalarchives.gov.uk/doc/open-government-licence/version/3/
12 Hopkins, D. (n.d.). (pp. 4–5)
13 Hopkins, D. (n.d.). (pp. 5–6)
14 Dinham, S., & Crowther, F. (2011). Sustainable school capacity-building—one step back, two steps forward? *Journal of Educational Administration, 49*(6), 1–8; Dinham, S., & Crowther, F. (2011). (Eds.). Building organisational capacity in school education. *Journal of Educational Administration, 49*(6), 614–738.
15 Australian Council for Educational Research. (2012). *School improvement: What does research tell us about effective strategies?* 2012 Research Conference. Melbourne, Victoria: Author.
16 Masters, G. (2012). Continual Improvement through aligned effort. In *School Improvement: What does research tell us about effective strategies?* (pp. 3–7) 2012 Research Conference. Melbourne, Victoria: ACER.
17 Masters, G. (2012). (p. 6)
18 Masters, G. (2012). (p. 3)
19 Department for Education (UK). (2013). *Increasing the number of academies and free schools to create a better and more diverse school system*. https://www.gov.uk/government/policies/increasing-the-number-of-academies-and-free-schools-to-create-a-better-and-more-diverse-school-system. (no page reference)
20 Australian Government. (2014). *School autonomy—Independent public schools*. Canberra, Australia: Department of Education. http://www.studentsfirst.gov.au/school-autonomy. (no page reference)
21 Hopkins, D. (2013). *Exploding the myths of school reform*. Melbourne, Victoria: ACER Press. (p. 29)
22 Hopkins, D. (2013). (p. 30)
23 Barber, M., Whelan, F., & Clark, M. (2010). *Capturing the leadership premium: How the world's top school systems are building leadership capacity for the future*. McKinsey & Company. http://mckinseyonsociety.com/capturing-the-leadership-premium/. (no page reference)
24 OECD. (2011). School autonomy and accountability: Are they related to student performance? *PISA in focus*, No. 9, 1–4, OECD Publishing. DOI: http://dx.doi.org/10.1787/5k9h362kcx9w-en
25 OECD. (2011). (p. 4)
26 Weick, K. (1976). Educational organizations as loosely coupled systems. *The Administrative Science Quarterly, 21*, 1–19.
27 Dinham, S. (2007); Dinham, S. (2008). *How to get your school moving and improving: An evidence-based approach*. Melbourne, Victoria: ACER Press.
28 US Department of Education. (2001).

CHAPTER 17

What strategies for leading teachers and teams are most effective? What are effective processes for teacher assessment and evaluation?

INTRODUCTION

In previous chapters we examined both the importance of classroom teaching and the importance of leadership in creating the conditions where teachers can teach and students can learn. However, we now want to consider how teachers, both as individuals, but importantly, in teams, view and respond to leadership, and the leadership approaches that are most effective in motivating and moving staff. The issue of working with difficult people is also considered.

We also consider processes that have been found to be effective for both assessing and developing teachers, as well as weaknesses of many present approaches.

Teachers' views on leadership: the importance of leadership to teacher satisfaction

I have conducted and been involved with a range of projects that have examined aspects of teacher satisfaction, dissatisfaction and stress. These include my doctoral research into teacher resignation, a study of teachers' partners, and the Teacher 2000 Project, an international study of teacher and school executive satisfaction, motivation and mental health coordinated by Catherine Scott and myself.[1]

A study and comparison of teacher and school executive (leader) satisfaction in Australia (n = 892), England (n = 609) and New Zealand (n = 600) undertaken as part of the Teacher 2000 Project found:

> ... teachers in all three countries reported highest satisfaction with items and scales concerned with their 'core business'. This 'first domain' covered the areas of facilitating student achievement, their own growth, and pastoral care aspects of teaching such as working with students and assisting them to become better people.
>
> Teachers and school executive across the three samples were dissatisfied with aspects of teaching outside their control, such as those associated with imposed workload, change and change management, and promotion opportunities and procedures. They were most dissatisfied with aspects of their standing in society such as their status, perceptions of this work (open-ended comments mentioned 'long holidays', 'short days', 'women's work', 'not a real job') and criticism from the media, employer, politicians and community generally.
>
> However, the study also revealed a 'third domain' of teacher satisfaction. While teachers reported high satisfaction with their 'core business' and were simultaneously highly dissatisfied with matters in the broader community and profession over which they had little control, there was also a 'third domain' of occupational satisfaction revealed by the research findings. *School-based factors outside the classroom such as items to do with school leadership, school reputation and school infrastructure were rated as neither highly satisfying nor highly dissatisfying overall, and it was here that there appeared most variation from school to school, with school leadership being the most important influence on participants' reported satisfaction with school-based items.*[2] [Emphasis added]

Thus, the powerful influence of school leadership, and in particular the principal, was revealed by the study findings, not only in the three countries under study above, but in later replications of the study in the United States of America, Canada, Malta, Cyprus and subsequent locations.

To go further, I noted:

> The teacher satisfaction research clearly showed that teachers want to teach and school leaders want to support teaching and learning. However attempts in recent times to make schools responsible for a raft of what were formerly community and family roles, to introduce more and more into school curricula to meet a range of disparate needs and agendas, to make schools more accountable for funding and to 'do more with less', to try to lift school performance through measuring and publicising student and school achievement, to criticise teachers and schools for being 'out of touch' with society, when every day they deal with it first hand through contact with its children—all these factors and more have been found to drive teacher status down and have made teaching a less attractive career for both practising and prospective teachers.
>
> There are a number of imperatives arising from these findings. Teachers and schools cannot reasonably be expected to solve problems over which they have little control nor capacity to deal with. Educational systems, governments, and society need to acknowledge their collective responsibility for the current extrinsic factors giving rise to worrying levels of teacher dissatisfaction and the erosion of teachers' intrinsic satisfaction. The increasing pace and scope of educational change has exacerbated this problem, rather than solving it, although clearly change is needed in many instances. It is ironic that in some schools, continual pressure for change seems to have induced a 'victim', reactive, disempowered mentality, hindering school-based change and discouraging initiative.
>
> While it is encouraging to find that leadership can make a difference to teacher and executive satisfaction at the school level, school leaders and teachers are largely at the mercy of a generally unsympathetic, increasingly demanding set of external forces, and need understanding, support and assistance to deal with this situation, rather than criticism and blame for failure to deliver what society is demanding of them.[3]

Team leadership

We have seen previously the slow and complex processes that can result in schools turning around and improving. Leaders cannot do this important work on their own; they need to work with and through others, and thus the influences of leaders on student outcomes tend to be indirect. We also noted how quickly these hard-fought gains can be eroded under poor leadership.

Wahlstrom and Seashore Louis drew upon the findings of a national (US) research project in a paper for the *Educational Administration Quarterly*. They noted firstly:

> Ask anyone who has had [one] or more years working in a school whether leadership has made a difference in their work and the answer will be an

unhesitating 'Yes.' No matter who the respondent is—teacher, custodian, education assistant, specialist, office support staff—they all seem to know good (and bad) leadership when they experience it. Furthermore, most people can identify particular behaviours of school leaders that they remember as being effective.[4]

In reviewing the literature, the authors commented:

> ... leadership in a school is a phenomenon that is both practiced and experienced. Our review suggests that leadership practices that share power are credited with creating greater motivation, increased trust and risk taking, and building a sense of community and efficacy among its members. However, peer relationships established among adults may have an equal or greater impact on classroom practice. Confounding the notion of schools as arenas of shared leadership for instruction is the hierarchical nature of school organizations that continues to permeate the perceptions and expectations that teachers and principals have about one another.[5]

In summarising their own research findings, Wahlstrom and Seashore Louis noted:

> Three types of instructional behaviors—*Standard Contemporary Practice, Focused Instruction,* and *Flexible Grouping Practices*—emerged as strong factors which operationally described effective teacher practice. The presence of shared leadership and professional community explain much of the strength among the three instructional variables. Furthermore, the effect of teachers' trust in the principal becomes less important when shared leadership and professional community are present. Self-efficacy strongly predicts Focused Instruction, but it has less predictive value for the other measures of instructional behavior ... there are no discernible patterns that suggest that the level of the principal (elementary vs. secondary) have more or less influence on teacher instructional behaviors.[6] [Emphasis added]

In a report for the National College for School Leadership[a], Matthews drew upon data derived from Ofsted inspections, case studies and other empirical sources to profile highly effective headteachers (i.e., principals) who work through others, including teams of teachers in their schools. These actions and approaches resonate strongly with the AESOP study[7] and other findings cited in this book:

---

a   Office for Standards in Education, Children's Services and Skills. See https://www.gov.uk/government/organisations/ofsted/about

Clear pupil-centred vision and purpose ensured pupils reached their potential. Maximising young people's well-being and achievements was at the heart of these schools.

Getting the best or most out of people was related to the philosophy, leadership approach and personal skills of the headteacher, including:
- Motivating, encouraging, trusting and valuing colleagues to do well
- Modelling, leading by example, especially in teaching
- Providing an opportunity to undertake greater responsibility and undergo development programmes from the second year of teaching
- Promoting professional development focused on teaching, learning and leadership, and keeping abreast of change; coaching is much in evidence
- Encouraging initiative and allowing people—students and staff—to experiment, confident they will be supported
- Showing interest and being generous with praise, encouragement and help in moving forward
- Knowing the names of a very high proportion of learners; valuing and respecting them
- Being community-minded, involving, consulting and being engaged within the local community
- Building teams and empowering them.[8]

Matthews went on to conclude:

> The most effective leadership provides for CPD[b] of all staff, including structured opportunities for leadership development ...
>
> As far as possible, effective leaders of learning apply the same principles, values and expectations to staff as to student learning, building a community of learners ...
>
> The development of pedagogical leadership relies on effective modelling and shared approaches to planning, teaching, assessment, evaluation, support and intervention ... Pedagogical leadership development has a strong practice-based element. It has to be locally centred in schools of sufficient quality to host programmes.[9]

The Wallace Foundation, in its review of leadership impact, also stressed the key role of the principal in bringing together staff and the essential elements for success that might otherwise remain fragmented and lacking in impact in the school:

---

b   Continuing Professional Development.

Education research shows that most school variables, considered separately, have at most small effects on learning. The real payoff comes when individual variables combine to reach critical mass. Creating the conditions under which that can occur is the job of the principal.[10]

The Wallace Foundation identified 'five key functions' effective principals perform, all of which are achieved by working with and through individuals and teams in schools:

- *Shaping a vision of academic success for all students*, one based on high standards.
- *Creating a climate hospitable to education*, in order that safety, a cooperative spirit and other foundations of fruitful interaction prevail.
- *Cultivating leadership in others* so that teachers and other adults assume their part in realising the school vision.
- *Improving instruction* to enable teachers to teach at their best and students to learn at their utmost.
- *Managing people, data and processes* to foster school improvement.

Each of these five tasks needs to interact with the other four for any part to succeed ... When all five tasks are well carried out, however, leadership is at work.[11]

If anything, the above findings from the various projects and studies cited only serve to further emphasise the crucial role that school leadership structures and leaders have in working with others to create the environment where teachers can teach, students can learn and develop, and the needs and expectations of the community and broader society can be met.

Dealing with difficult people

When the findings from the various teacher and executive satisfaction projects were compared, apart from general workload and imposed change, one of the most commonly reported sources of dissatisfaction and stress for principals and others in formal leadership positions was that of dealing with difficult people, that is, adults rather than students.

Earlier I explained my simple observed typology of people in schools, comprised of 'enthusiasts', 'watchers', and 'blockers', and the desirability of considering the number and influence of those in each group when change is considered.[12] Obviously, some blockers can be difficult and/or under-performing people to deal with as individuals, and as part of groups when Balkanisation and groupthink hold sway, but there are others who can also be difficult to deal with, including both high performing teachers, and those we seek to improve or even move on.

There is something termed the 8–15–5 principle that has been used both in the general field of organisational behaviour and more specifically in classroom management.[13] According to this principle, there are three groups of students in a typical classroom: about 80 per cent of students consistently follow the rules, 15 per cent occasionally break the rules, and 5 per cent often break the rules.

According to Curwin and Mendler:

> The trick of a good discipline plan is to control the 15 per cent without alienating the 80 per cent and without backing the 5 per cent into a corner. Plans that are heavily punitive tend to control the 15 per cent, this giving the illusion that they are successful. However, the seeds are sown for the out-of-control students to explode or for some of the 80 per cent to lose interest in learning.[14]

W. Edwards Deming, the 'father' of 'total quality management', said something similar about adult workers, in that designing rules and procedures to control the 5 per cent or so of dysfunctional employees that will be applied to all workers is ultimately counter-productive.[15] Dreyfus and Dreyfus also noted from their work on expertise that it is a mistake to treat an expert like a novice, and vice versa.[16]

Whitaker is in general agreement, and makes the point that:

> ... the *least* important people in your school [are] the difficult teachers. One of the faults in education and educational leadership is that we give too much power to these difficult people. This must stop. It is important that principals consistently remind themselves that the essential people on a faculty are the positive and productive people. Too often we make decisions based on our least important people.[17]

In dealing with teachers, then, it also seems inappropriate to devise rules and practices to cater for the 'lowest common denominator'. Rather, the answer seems to lie with knowing every teacher as a learner and a person, as with students, and in applying both responsive and demanding—that is, authoritative—leadership. Individualised feedback, both positive and negative, and having those difficult conversations with difficult and/or under-performing people appear key, based upon the research cited in this book.[18] One of the most challenging, yet important things in dealing with such people is to continue to model professionalism in the face of unprofessional behaviour and performance:

> Make sure that you do not treat them in the manner that they treat others. Never raise your voice, use sarcasm, or treat them rudely. It is also critical that we do not take a confrontational or argumentative approach. A simple guideline for working with difficult students in classroom discipline is always

to treat students as though their parents were in the room. This same idea applies to working with difficult teachers. Always treat them as though the entire staff were in the room. Realise that your positive and productive teachers want these negative staff members dealt with, but they want it done in a professional manner.

One final piece of advice is to never argue with difficult persons ... they have much more practice at it than you do.[19]

Whitaker goes on to make a number of suggestions concerning dealing with difficult teachers that appear to be congruent with both my research findings and my experience as an educational leader over many years. Space precludes a full explanation but as a guide to overcoming and dealing with difficult people, the following 'menu' of strategies can be helpful:

- Look for the good part—catch them doing something right.
- Give difficult teachers responsibility.
- Praise in front of a superior.
- Raising discomfort levels.
- Empower the good guys.
- Accepting responsibility—they can't pass the buck.
- Using faculty meetings effectively.
- Use peers—but use caution.
- Always assume that they want to do what is right.
- Approach them when you are ready—when you are comfortable and when they are most uncomfortable.
- Be a broken record.
- Focus on eliminating behaviours.
- Focus on our own behaviours.
- Understand the dynamics—deal with the negative leaders.
- Break up the group.
- Sometimes you have to shuffle the deck—moving people (room, grade).[20]

A not entirely unexpected bonus is when a difficult teacher begins to 'feel the heat' from such strategies and pressure to lift their performance, and decides to seek a transfer, resign or retire. An alternative is when the school is still in decline and the option of a 'forced transfer' due to lower student enrolments means someone has to go. It's important here to be brave, as the difficult teacher may well have his or her supporters and a power base inside and even outside the school.

One principal I interviewed as part of a project on a turnaround school maintained that she was in danger of 'going under' until such time as a difficult staff member was forced to leave the school. Declining enrolments meant that a teacher needed to be transferred. The Principal chose an experienced teacher with an established power base who was very popular inside and outside the school, and whom she knew to be undermining her authority and her efforts at change. Making this teacher leave the school was a very 'brave', contentious decision but ultimately, the correct one, in that the Principal was only then able to begin effective planning and action for change.[21]

However, in the absence of voluntary transfers, retirements, or forced transfers, it may be necessary to go down the path of dismissal, and this can take quite some time, depending on the systems in place within the school and/or sector. Sometimes this is a matter of non-renewal or certification/registration of probationary teachers, but in other cases it involves the dismissal of permanent or tenured teachers. Following established procedure is essential, as is thorough documentation to establish that you have done everything in your power to remedy the situation short of dismissal, which now appears as the only option.

(Whitaker and Fiore have written a book entitled *Dealing with Difficult Parents and with Parents in Difficult Situations* that is outside the scope of this book, but worth consulting.[22])

Teacher assessment and evaluation: issues and problems

It is generally agreed that effective teacher assessment and evaluation, coupled with developmental feedback, is desirable if teachers are to be developed and teaching is to be improved. The problem lies with coming up with the right system.

Linda Darling-Hammond has summarised some of the problems with current teacher evaluation systems:

- lack of consistent, clear standards of good practice
- no focus on improving practice
- inadequate time and staff for effective evaluations
- little or no consideration of student outcomes
- cookie-cutter procedures that don't consider teacher needs
- detachment of evaluations from professional development.

... criteria and methods for evaluating teachers vary substantially across schools and districts, and these are typically disconnected from the ways teachers are evaluated at key career milestones—when they complete pre-service teacher education, when they become initially licenced, and when they are tenured.[23]

In many cases, teacher evaluation is an annual, largely meaningless ritual to satisfy some form of external accountability. It might be traumatic or it might be low-level, that is, a 'rubber stamp' virtually everyone receives. What is needed is a move to a more regular, focused assessment regime, coupled with expert constructive feedback. What has worked particularly well in some of the studies cited in this book is where there is an opening up of classrooms, trust, and peer collaboration, learning and discussion. In the study of senior secondary teaching success, for example, it was clear that teachers were almost constantly moving in and out of their colleagues' classrooms, offering advice, giving feedback and contributing to lessons.[24] As noted previously, Hattie found that providing teachers with formative feedback on their performance had a (very large) effect size of 0.90.[25]

Marshall has advocated changing the formal teacher assessment process to something more ongoing, where classroom visits are unannounced, frequent and short in duration, with a face-to-face discussion between the person conducting the assessment and the teacher as soon as possible after the event, and with the assessor demonstrating humility and honesty. Marshall also recommends that systematic records be kept and, importantly, attempts are made to link the performance of the individual teacher to teaching teams and teamwork, which is the reality of how many teachers learn, plan, work and develop. Such observations and follow-up can then feed into more formal annual appraisals.[26]

Marzano has highlighted one of the tensions and contradictions with many teacher evaluation systems: that of confusing judgement with development.[27] As mentioned previously, at the time of writing this book, I was a member of a team conducting an evaluation of the Australian Professional Standards for Teachers (APST)[28] for the Australian Institute for Teaching and School Leadership (AITSL). One of the concerns held by various stakeholders concerning the use of the APST was that the standards would be used primarily for judgement of a teacher's performance at a point in time, with little emphasis on or benefit for further development. However, findings from the evaluation have been encouraging, with developmental use of the standards predominating, and with the standards providing both a framework and a language for teachers to have professional conversations about teaching and learning.[29]

In Marzano's view, teacher evaluation systems that focus on development have three major characteristics:

1. The system is comprehensive and specific.
2. The system includes a developmental scale.
3. The system acknowledges and rewards growth.[30]

Moore Johnson and Fiarman are in broad agreement with Marzano, but also consider the potential of peer review, both for judgement of performance, but more importantly, for developmental purposes. Examining Peer Assistance and Review (PAR) programs in the USA, they offered some guidance in the design and implementation of peer review systems:

- **Select stars**—advertise and conduct rigorous selection of PAR panel members who need to be expert teachers and who will guide consulting [assessing] teachers.
- **Establish clear guidelines**—makes the work of PARs more predictable and less stressful for teachers.

- **Rely on teaching standards and rubrics.**
- **Offer rich training and support.**
- **Provide supervision by the PAR panel**—for the consulting teachers conducting the observations.
- **Focus on both evaluation and assistance.**[31]

Charlotte Danielson is a pre-eminent researcher in the field of observation of classroom practice. She adds a number of key considerations to the above discussion:

> ... for a system of teacher evaluation to be defensible (either professionally or legally) it must be fair—that is, the judgements that are made about a teacher's practice must accurately reflect the teacher's true level of performance. And because the quintessential skill of teaching is *teaching*, and it can be observed, we should conduct those observations with integrity and skill ...
>
> It's true that teaching is supported by a lot of behind-the-scenes work, but nevertheless, we *can* observe the interactive work with students, and this is the heart of teaching. Therefore, classroom observation is a crucial aspect of any system of teacher evaluation. No matter how skilled a teacher is in other aspects of teaching—such as careful planning, working well with colleagues, and communicating with parents—if classroom practice is deficient, an individual cannot be considered a good teacher.[32]

An important issue to note at this point is that student test scores are frequently advocated, especially by non-educators, as appropriate proxies for teacher quality and effectiveness. There are many reasons why this is simplistic, flawed thinking. Measures such as the National Assessment Program—Literacy and Numeracy (NAPLAN)[c] in Australia have their uses, including providing measures of individual student performance, and overall and relative school performance and growth, but such results are not adequate indicators of the effectiveness of individual teachers, given the timing, scope and nature of the tests.

Another simplistic solution is simply to get rid of 'bad' teachers, but to do so, even presuming they could be replaced by 'better' teachers[33], would require fair and defensible processes, as Danielson has advocated above, and the assessment of many thousands of teachers, not to mention the adequate training of assessors. Appeals against such dismissals might clog up tribunals and courts for years.

There is a third matter of concern, in that where states in the USA have introduced mandatory assessments of teachers, virtually everyone 'passes', and more than that, there is 'grade inflation', such that large numbers of teachers are rated to be performing at the highest levels, the so-called 'widget effect'.[34]

---

c http://www.nap.edu.au/naplan/naplan.html

Concluding remarks

Teacher assessment and evaluation: What works and what is needed?

In an informative YouTube presentation entitled *Making Teacher Evaluations Meaningful* and in other work[35], Charlotte Danielson makes a powerful case for assessing teacher effectiveness. She notes the two key dimensions of rigour and stakes, and how, in many teacher evaluation systems, there is a lack of congruence and/or positive impact. This means systems that are *high stakes yet have low rigour* (dangerous and to be avoided), or systems that have *high rigour yet are low stakes* (e.g., structured mentoring programs that don't lead to anything), and systems that have both *low rigour and low stakes* (e.g., informal mentoring programs that don't mean anything, have low impact, yet could be argued to be congruent). Systems that are both *high stakes and have high rigour* are advocated for potentially having the greatest impact of the four on assessing and improving teaching (uncommon, yet desirable, e.g., National Board certification[d] in the USA).[36]

Danielson's framework begins, as it must, by defining what teachers actually *do*, in terms of four domains, which then provide a framework for assessing teaching:

Domain 1: Planning and Preparation
- Demonstrating knowledge of content and pedagogy
- Demonstrating knowledge of students
- Setting instructional outcomes
- Demonstrating knowledge of resources
- Designing coherent instruction
- Designing student assessments

Domain 2: The Classroom Environment
- Creating an environment of respect and rapport
- Establishing a culture for learning
- Managing classroom procedures
- Managing student behaviour
- Organising physical space

Domain 3: Instruction
- Communicating with students
- Using questioning and discussion techniques
- Engaging students in learning
- Using assessment in instruction
- Demonstrating flexibility and responsiveness

Domain 4: Professional Responsibilities
- Reflecting on teaching

---

d   http://www.nbpts.org/

- Maintaining accurate records
- Communicating with families
- Participating in a professional community
- Growing and developing professionally
- Showing professionalism.

In devising frameworks to assess teaching, there is always the issue of themes or issues that tend to run across any framework. Danielson recognises some of these 'common themes':

- Equity
- Cultural sensitivity
- Higher expectations
- Developmental appropriateness
- Accommodating individual needs
- Appropriate use of technology
- Student assumption of responsibility.[37]

Danielson uses the four domains and framework to create rubrics for each area under consideration, with four levels of performance: 'unsatisfactory', 'basic', 'proficient', and 'distinguished', with descriptors for each element and level of performance.

When using any such framework for performance assessment purposes, one of the most important steps lies with the training of assessors and in standards setting to ensure consistency of judgement. A common failure in implementing performance and development frameworks is underestimating the need for such training and the requisite performance standards to be applied. As well as being fair and defensible, any such system needs to meet the criteria of validity, reliability and credibility. Poor decision-making can undermine confidence and 'buy-in' to any teacher performance and development assessment system, no matter how well designed.

A further key consideration lies with what happens following the observation and assessment. Findings need to be worked through, discussed, and implications and follow-up or changes to practice determined and agreed upon.

Finally, most assessment protocols for the observation of teaching, either 'home-grown' or 'off-the-shelf', lack psychometric soundness, with the exception of a few instruments such as the Classroom Assessment Scoring System (CLASS)[e] and the Framework for Teaching (FFT) developed by Danielson.[f] This represents both a weakness and a challenge in developing more effective assessment systems.

---

e   CLASS: http://teachstone.com/classroom-assessment-scoring-system/

f   FFT: https://www.danielsongroup.org/framework/ (contains free downloads of the evaluation instrument and other very valuable resources.

Australian Teacher Performance and Development Framework

The Australian Institute for Teaching and School Leadership (AITSL) has released the *Australian Teacher Performance and Development Framework* for national implementation.[g][38] This framework is underpinned by the Australian Charter for the Professional Learning of Teachers and School Leaders[39], the Australian Professional Standards for Teachers[40], and the Australian Professional Standard for Principals.[41] It is intended that every teacher in Australia will, in collaboration with other teachers and supervisors, use the framework for performance assessment and developmental purposes, on an ongoing basis.

The Framework is also supported by valuable resources provided by AITSL such as *Classroom Observation Strategies*[h], *Certification Evidence*[i] and *Illustrations of Practice*.[j]

Endnotes

1 See Dinham, S. (2008). *How to get your school moving and improving: An evidence-based approach.* Melbourne, Victoria: ACER Press. (Chapter 5); Dinham, S. (1992). Human perspectives on the resignation of teachers from the New South Wales Department of School Education: Towards a model of teacher persistence. (Doctor of Philosophy thesis). University of New England, Armidale, New South Wales; Dinham, S. (1993). Teachers under stress. *Australian Educational Researcher, 20*(3), December, 1–16; Dinham, S. (1995). Time to focus on teacher satisfaction. *Unicorn, 21*(3), 64–75; Dinham, S., & Scott, C. (1996). *The Teacher 2000 Project: A study of teacher satisfaction, motivation and health.* Penrith, New South Wales: University of Western Sydney, Nepean; Dinham, S., & Scott, C. (1997). The advanced skills teacher: An opportunity missed? *Unicorn, 23*(3), 36–49; Dinham, S., & Scott, C. (1998). A three domain model of teacher and school executive satisfaction. *Journal of Educational Administration, 36*(4), 362–378; Scott, C., Cox, S., & Dinham, S. (1999). The occupational motivation, satisfaction and health of English school teachers. *Educational Psychology, 19*(3), 287–308; Dinham, S., & Scott, C. (2000). Moving into the third, outer domain of teacher satisfaction. *Journal of Educational Administration, 38*(4), 379–396; Scott, C., Stone, B., & Dinham, S. (2001). 'I love teaching but ...' International patterns of teacher discontent. *Education Policy Analysis Archives, 9*(28), 1–7; Dinham, S., & Scott, C. (2002). Pressure points: School executive and educational change. *Journal of Educational Enquiry, 3*(2), 35–52; Scott, C., & Dinham, S. (2002). The beatings will continue until quality improves: Carrots and sticks in the search for educational improvement. *Teacher Development, 6*(1), 15–31; Scott, C., & Dinham, S. (2003). The development of scales to measure teacher and school executive occupational satisfaction. *Journal of Educational Administration, 41*(1), 74–86.

2 Dinham, S. (2008). (pp. 86–87)

g http://www.aitsl.edu.au/docs/default-source/professional-growth-resources/professional-learning-resources/australian_teacher_performance_and_development_framework.pdf?sfvrsn=2

h http://www.aitsl.edu.au/professional-growth/support/classroom-observation-strategies

i http://www.aitsl.edu.au/certification/certification-evidence

j http://www.aitsl.edu.au/australian-professional-standards-for-teachers/illustrations-of-practice/find-by-career-stage

3   Dinham, S. (2008). (pp. 90–91)
4   Wahlstrom, K., & Seashore Louis, K. (2008). How teachers experience principal leadership: The roles of professional community, trust, efficacy, and shared responsibility. *Educational Administration Quarterly, 44*(4), 458–495. (p. 459). Copyright © 2008 by K. Wahlstrom and K. Seashore Louis. All text extracts from this article are reprinted by Permission of Sage Publications, Inc.
5   Wahlstrom, K., & Seashore Louis, K. (2008). (p. 467)
6   Wahlstrom, K., & Seashore Louis, K. (2008). (p. 458)
7   Ayres, P., Dinham, S., & Sawyer, W. (1999). *Successful teaching in the NSW Higher School Certificate.* Sydney, New South Wales: NSW Department of Education and Training.
8   Matthews, P. (n.d.). *How do school leaders successfully lead learning?* Nottingham: National College for School Leadership. http://dera.ioe.ac.uk/254/1/download%3Fid%3D23637%26filename%3Dhow-do-school-leaders-successfully-lead-learning.pdf (p. 9). All extracts from this publication have been reproduced with permission. See https://www.nationalcollege.org.uk/
9   Matthews, P. (n.d.). (p. 38)
10 The Wallace Foundation. (2011). *The school principal as leader: Guiding schools to better teaching and learning.* New York, NY: The Wallace Foundation. http://www.wallacefoundation.org/knowledge-center/school-leadership/effective-principal-leadership/Documents/The-School-Principal-as-Leader-Guiding-Schools-to-Better-Teaching-and-Learning.pdf (p. 2)
11 The Wallace Foundation. (2011). (pp. 4–5)
12 Dinham, S. (2008). Counting the numbers in educational change. *The Australian Educational Leader, 30*(1), 56–57.
13 See, for example, Curwin, R., & Mendler, A. (1988). Packaged discipline programs: Let the buyer beware. *Educational Leadership,* October, 68–71.
14 Curwin, R., & Mendler, A. (1988). (p. 70)
15 Deming, W. E. (1982). *Out of the crisis.* Cambridge, MA: Massachusetts Institute of Technology.
16 See Dreyfus, S., & Dreyfus, H. (1980). *A five-stage model of the mental activities involved in directed skills acquisition.* Berkeley: Operations Research Center, University of California.
17 Whitaker, T. (2002). *Dealing with difficult teachers.* Larchmont, NY: Eye on Education. (p. 19). All extracts from this publication are reproduced with permission by Taylor and Francis (US).
18 See Dinham, S., & Scott, C. (2008). Responsive, demanding leadership. *Management Today,* April, 32–35.
19 Whitaker, T. (2002). (p. 27)
20 Whitaker, T. (2002). (pp. 23–152)
21 Dinham, S., Buckland, C., Callingham, R., & Mays, H. (2008). Factors responsible for the superior performance of male students in Years 3 and 5 standardised testing at one Australian primary school. *Learning and Teaching, 23*(1), 51–70.
22 Whitaker, T., & Fiore, D. (2001). *Dealing with difficult parents and with parents in difficult situations.* Larchmont, NY: Eye on Education.
23 Darling-Hammond, L. (2013). *Getting teacher evaluation right.* New York, NY: Teachers College Press. (pp. 4–5)
24 Ayres, P., Dinham, S., & Sawyer, W. (1999).
25 Hattie, J. (2012). *Visible learning for teachers.* London, England: Routledge. (p. 251)
26 Marshall, K. (2012). Let's cancel the dog-and-pony show. *Phi Delta Kappan, 94*(3), 19–23.

27 Marzano, R. (2012). The two purposes of teacher evaluation. *Educational Leadership, 70*(3), 14–19.
28 AITSL [Australian Institute for Teaching and School Leadership]. (2011). *Australian Professional Standards for Teachers*. Melbourne, Victoria: Author.
29 Clinton, J., Dinham, S., Lingard, R., Gullickson, A., Savage, G., Calnin, G., Aston, R., & Dabrowski, A. (2015). *InSights: Evaluation of the implementation of the Australian Professional Standards for Teachers—Interim report 2—2014 Key findings*. Melbourne, Victoria: AITSL.
30 Marzano, R. (2012). The two purposes of teacher evaluation. *Educational Leadership, 70*(3), 14–19.
31 Moore Johnson, S., & Fiarman, S. (2012). The potential of peer review. *Educational Leadership, 70*(3), 20–25.
32 Danielson, C. (2012). Observing classroom practice. *Educational Leadership, 70*(3), 32–37.
33 See Wiener, R., & Jacobs, A. (2011). *Designing and implementing teacher performance management systems: Pitfalls and possibilities*. Washington DC: The Aspen Institute—Education and Society Program. http://www.newsroom.aitsl.edu.au/sites/www.newsroom.aitsl.edu.au/files/field/pdf/designing_and_implementing_teacher_performance_management_systems_-_pitfalls_and_possibilities_-_the_aspen_institute.pdf (p. 4)
34 Wiener, R., & Jacobs, A. (2011). (p. 7)
35 See The Danielson Group (2013). *The framework for teaching*. https://www.danielsongroup.org/framework/
36 Danielson, C. (n.d.). *Making teacher evaluations meaningful*. http://www.youtube.com/watch?v=KzDcYuSsU2E
37 The Danielson Group. (2013).
38 AITSL [Australian Institute for Teaching and School Leadership]. (2012). *Australian Teacher Performance and Development Framework*. Melbourne, Victoria: Author.
39 AITSL [Australian Institute for Teaching and School Leadership]. (2012). *Australian Charter for the Professional Learning of Teachers and School Leaders*. Melbourne, Victoria: Author.
40 AITSL [Australian Institute for Teaching and School Leadership]. (2011). *Australian Professional Standards for Teachers*. Melbourne, Victoria: Author.
41 AITSL [Australian Institute for Teaching and School Leadership]. (2014). *Australian Professional Standard for Principals and the Leadership Profiles*. Melbourne, Victoria: Author.

PART E

Leadership preparation and development

CHAPTER 18

What are current, effective approaches to school leadership preparation?

INTRODUCTION

The importance of school education for national development and prosperity has increasingly been recognised. As we commented in a review of leadership preparation in Australia:

> Mulford notes that the context of educational leadership and management has been pictured 'as involving large-scale, if not global, cultural, technological, economic, and political forces for change'.[1] Contextual issues include the transition of Western economies from manufacturing to service and information, the rise of new communication technologies, environmental concerns and sustainable living, and social changes such as the fragmentation of family and community settings.[2]
>
> The role of the principal 'is seen as one of increasing change, complexity, diversity, and intensity'.[3] There is both centralisation, with greater emphasis on national standards, national testing and a national curriculum, and decentralisation, with greater management and legal responsibilities resting on the principal.[4] Recent Commonwealth (federal) initiatives, including 'National Partnership Agreements', have closely connected Australia's educational performance with national productivity.[5]
>
> A broader, changed conception of educational leadership has also emerged, shifting from administration, to management, to instructional leadership—leadership for teaching and learning—and including others in formal leadership positions in schools and teacher leadership, the latter two categories being grouped under the umbrella of 'distributed leadership'.[6],[7]

As I have noted previously, in my work with turnaround schools, it is very rare in my experience to see a school turned around without the influence of leadership, and, in particular, new leadership, when previous methods have not worked and a school has either declined or plateaued. Leithwood and colleagues agree:

> ... there are virtually no documented instances of troubled schools being turned around without intervention by a powerful leader. Many other factors may contribute to such turnarounds, but leadership is the catalyst.[8]

In a report entitled *Preparing Future Leaders: Effective Preparation for Aspiring School Principals*, AITSL has noted[9]:

> Excellent school leaders are fundamental to a high-quality education system. A sustained focus on the professional growth of school leaders will support the achievement of the vision for all young Australians to become successful learners, confident and creative individuals, and active and informed citizens. Successful schools provide their students and communities with a solid foundation in a rapidly changing world and this requires leaders with strength and substance.
>
> The role of the school principal, as defined in the Australian Professional Standard for Principals (the Standard), is complex and evolving. With increasing principal autonomy, there are greater opportunities for and demands on principals to make good decisions at the local level and this has implications for the development of a corresponding leadership skill set. If every school leader is to create a culture where teachers and students thrive, they require effective preparation that builds this leadership capability and supports high performance in increasingly decentralised settings.
>
> In many Australian jurisdictions, there is increasing concern about the ageing demographic profile of school leaders, the decline of the appeal of the job, and the implications of this for matching supply to demand. The increasing demands of the job and a perception of high stress levels and poor wellbeing appear to be acting as deterrents to those who might otherwise be interested in the role. This is supported by survey results that show approximately half of current deputy principals do not intend to apply for a principal position in the next three years.[10]

Given the greater expectations being placed upon principals and other school leaders, both as educational instructional leaders and more generally, it is hardly surprising that the identification, preparation and development of aspiring and practising educational leaders has assumed such importance and prominence. This has been underlined by evidence that it is becoming harder to attract people to the principalship, in particular[11], and recognised in such initiatives as the Australian National Standard for Principals introduced in 2011[12], associated work by AITSL on leadership profiles[a], a 360° reflection

---

a   http://www.aitsl.edu.au/leadership-profiles

tool[b] and a school leadership clearing house[c], as well as current work by Principals Australia Institute on certification of principals against the APSP.[d]

There is also a raft of leadership preparation programs offered by educational systems, professional associations, universities, private providers and other bodies.

Perceived weaknesses of leadership preparation programs

Earlier in this book I described many educational leadership preparation programs as being like 'doughnuts', in that the missing centrepiece to these management-based courses was student learning and effective teaching. More recent programs have, however, addressed this shortcoming. The final chapter of this book will examine the findings from one instructional leadership program with which I have been involved.

Some of the perceived weaknesses with many university-based educational leadership preparation courses that have been identified include:

- Admission standards that allow leadership preparation participants to essentially 'self-select' themselves without having to demonstrate either the potential or the intention to assume school leadership positions;
- Curricula and knowledge base that may not adequately take into account the needs of schools, districts and increasingly diverse student bodies;
- Weak connections between theory and practice;
- Faculty who may have little field experience as leaders; and
- Shallow or poorly designed internships and field-based experiences that are not sufficiently connected to the rest of the program.[13]

However, one of the most serious shortcomings of many leadership preparation programs is a failure to adequately prepare educational leaders to work with evidence and, in particular, to consider and measure the effects or impacts of their actions on teacher effectiveness and student outcomes. We have already seen that a failure of teachers to consider the impact of their teaching on student outcomes can result in the situation where one could say 'I taught them but they didn't learn'. Similarly, for leaders, this can result in a situation where a leader could say 'I led them but they didn't respond to my leadership', or in medical parlance, 'The operation was a success, but the patient died'.

---

b   http://www.aitsl.edu.au/australian-professional-standard-for-principals/360-reflection-tool
c   http://www.aitsl.edu.au/school-leadership-ecollection
d   http://www.pai.edu.au/

Approaches to educational leadership preparation

The Australian Institute for Teaching and School Leadership has, as noted, developed a range of resources, tools and frameworks to support school leadership development and school leaders' professional practice. AITSL has made five major recommendations for preparing school leaders:

1. **Take a systematic, standards-based and coherent approach**—
   To be effective, principal preparation must be systematic and coherent, based on clearly articulated professional standards. It should include the following elements:
   - a thorough appreciation of leadership demographics and trends
   - clear and shared understandings of the principal role, underpinned by professional standards
   - a focus on the attractiveness of the principal role so that teachers are eager to make the move into leadership
   - responsibility for identifying and preparing future leaders shared between employers, system leaders and the profession
   - structured professional development opportunities for aspiring principals that focus on leadership abilities.
2. **Identify and nurture talent**—In the best approaches to principal preparation, potential leaders are identified early in their careers and given a range of opportunities to develop their leadership skills. Successful succession planning requires:
   - structured, transparent career pathways
   - clear selection prerequisites for promotion.
3. **Match learning to an individual's capabilities, career stage and context**—Pathways to advancement should be clear, with professional learning appropriate to each level explicit, well understood and sustained after appointment. To be effective, learning for aspiring leaders should occur in three broad stages:
   - developing deep and comprehensive pedagogical knowledge as the foundation for strong instructional leadership. This learning can be done relatively early in the journey to principalship as it is compatible with a teaching role
   - developing the many higher-order and interpersonal skills required by principals, including strategic thinking, change leadership, and emotional and social intelligence. This learning is best developed over time and should occur well before an aspirant takes on the role of principal
   - developing management skills. This learning is best undertaken immediately prior to assuming a principal role, as it can then be consolidated through immediate practice.

4. **Use evidence-based adult learning techniques**—Highly effective preparation programs reflect an understanding of a range of adult learning techniques that have been shown to be effective and provide a diversity of experiences over time. They include:
   - discriminating application and selection processes matched to the learning opportunity
   - spaced delivery, blended learning and the opportunity to apply new skills and knowledge, collaborate, gain feedback and receive ongoing support
   - a degree of personalisation that takes into account the needs, career stage and context of the individual
   - an emphasis on learning from experts and practitioners
   - recognition for the learning undertaken.
5. **Evaluate programs for impact**—It is critical to engage in rigorous evaluation for purposes of accountability and improvement. Principal preparation programs should:
   - provide evidence of participant readiness to take on the role
   - measure impact upon take-up of role
   - demonstrate growth in the number of well-prepared aspirants available to take up future vacancies.[14]

The importance of working with and through others

We have already considered the notion that leadership, and school leadership, is increasingly seen as a group process, whereby the leader seeks to work with and through others to achieve their agenda and the goals of the organisation. Similarly, there has been a change in the conception of school leadership preparation to reflect this. No longer do we conceptualise the leader as someone issuing orders and edicts from behind a desk, or on the other hand, motivating others through their charismatic personality.

The Wallace Foundation, in a report entitled *Becoming a Leader: Preparing School Principals for Today's Schools*[15], cited Kati Haycock:

> When you meet the leaders in the places that are really getting the job done, they are not the kind of leaders that just turn things around by the sheer force of their personality. They are regular people. They are totally focused. They are totally relentless. They are not big, outsized personalities and they are not the only leaders in their schools. Especially in the larger schools, the principals know that they can't get it all done themselves. Those are the places that improve. Leadership is not about one person, it's about building a shared commitment and building a leadership team.

Effective leadership programs must, therefore, prepare leaders to work with others. It is not sufficient just to have a plan for improvement. Staff must be drawn into the processes of planning, professional learning, implementation, evaluation, and change, because ultimately, it is what happens in individual classrooms and with individual students that is most important.

The Wallace Foundation, drawing upon research at Stanford University, went on to outline 'four action lessons' for better leadership, and in particular, principal preparation. In doing so, it acknowledged the realities that no single program or model 'will fit all' candidates, nor all situations in which principals can find themselves:

- **Lesson One**—Successful principal training programs are significantly different from the majority of programs in existence. They are more selective, more focused on improvement of instruction, more closely tied to the needs of districts, and provide more relevant internships with hands-on leadership experience ...
- **Lesson Two**—Leadership training should not end when principals are hired. It should continue with high-quality mentoring for new principals and with professional development for all principals to promote career-long growth in line with the evolving needs of schools and districts ...
- **Lesson Three**—High-quality leader development can make a real difference, but providing it can involve added costs. Resources therefore should be directed at quality programs with proven benefits ...
- **Lesson Four**—Fixing what's wrong with leadership preparation is essential, but not enough. Addressing the leadership challenge also requires remedying the difficult working conditions that can undermine even the best-trained principals.[16]

The final 'lesson' is an important one. The position of principal is arguably the most important one in a school, as numerous research findings cited in this book have attested. It is a position of great and increasing responsibility, accountability and pressure. It is not for the faint-hearted.

Leadership preparation, selection, evaluation and ongoing support and professional development are therefore crucial, in order to get the right people into these positions and to keep them there for the time needed to do their work of change.

Concluding remarks

We have already considered the benefits that can arise from the formulation and use of professional standards for teachers in articulating the work of teachers and in informing the processes of teacher reflection, appraisal and development.

There are similar benefits that can arise from the use of professional leadership standards. Many of the leadership programs in use across the world utilise professional standards for principals and other leaders. These standards are important for capturing and articulating the work of such leaders, along with the knowledge and values society and employers hold for them. Such professional standards also serve to communicate to others the complexity and importance of the role in question, as well as informing the processes of self-reflection, professional learning, professional dialogue with others, selection, appraisal and ongoing professional development, both self-initiated and provided by others. The following chapter considers the use of such standards in greater detail.

Endnotes

1. Mulford, B. (2002). Leadership development: Introduction. In K. Leithwood, & P. Hallinger (Eds.), Second international handbook of educational leadership and administration (pp. 1025–1030). Dordrecht, Netherlands: Kluwer Academic Publishers, Vol. 2. (p. 1025)
2. Boyd, W. L. (1999). Environmental pressures, management imperatives, and competing paradigms in educational administration. *Educational Management & Administration*, 27(3), 283–297; Wyn, J. (2009). *Touching the future: Building skills for life and work.* Melbourne, Victoria: ACER.
3. Mulford, B. (2002). (p. 1025)
4. Caldwell, B. J., Calnin, G., & Cahill, W. (2002). Mission possible? An international analysis of headteacher/principal training. In M. Tucker & J. Codding (Eds.), *The principal challenge: Leading and managing schools in an era of accountability* (pp. 111–130). San Francisco, CA: Jossey-Bass; Anderson, M., Gronn, P., Ingvarson, L., Jackson, A., Kleinhenz, E., McKenzie, P., Mulford, B., & Thornton, N. (2007). *OECD improving school leadership activity: Australia: Country background report.* Canberra, Australia: DEEWR.
5. See http://www.federalfinancialrelations.gov.au/content/npa/education/smarter_schools/improving_teacher/national_partnership.pdf
6. Harris, A. (2009). *Distributed school leadership: Evidence, issues and future directions.* Penrith, NSW: Australian Council for Educational Leaders.
7. Dinham, S., Anderson, M., Caldwell, B., & Weldon, P. (2011). Breakthroughs in school leadership development in Australia. *School Leadership and Management, 31*(2), 139–154. (pp. 139–140). Reprinted with permission.
8. Leithwood, K., Seashore Louis, K., Anderson, S., & Wahlstrom, K. (2004). *Review of research—How leadership influences student learning.* New York, NY: The Wallace Foundation. (p. 4)
9. AITSL [Australian Institute for Teaching and School Leadership]. (2015). *Preparing future leaders: Effective preparation for aspiring school principals.* Melbourne, Victoria: Author. (p. 4). Copyright © 2015 AITSL. ACER has reproduced an extract from the AITSL publication with permission from the copyright owner. This publication is solely created by ACER and does not represent the views of, and is not endorsed by, AITSL.
10. McKenzie, P., Weldon, P., Rowley, G; Murphy, M., & McMillan, J. (2014). *Staff in Australia's schools 2013: Main report of the survey.* Melbourne, Victoria: ACER.
11. McKenzie, P. et al. (2014).
12. AITSL [Australian Institute for Teaching and School Leadership]. (2014). *Australian Professional Standard for Principals and the leadership profiles.* Melbourne: Author.
13. Darling-Hammond, L., LaPointe, M., Meyerson, D., & Terry Orr, M. (2007). *Preparing school leaders for a changing world.* Stanford, CA: Stanford University and The Finance Project. (pp. 4–6)

14 AITSL [Australian Institute for Teaching and School Leadership]. (n.d.). *Are aspiring principals well prepared for this challenging role?* Melbourne, Victoria: Author. http://www.aitsl.edu.au/principal-preparation. Copyright © AITSL. ACER has reproduced an extract from the AITSL publication with permission from the copyright owner. This publication is solely created by ACER and does not represent the views of, and is not endorsed by, AITSL.

15 The Wallace Foundation. (2008). *Becoming a leader: Preparing school principals for today's schools*. New York, NY: The Wallace Foundation. (p. 2)

16 The Wallace Foundation. (2008). (pp. 5–9)

CHAPTER 19

What are the potential benefits of professional standards for school leaders?

INTRODUCTION

By way of introduction, Dinham, Anderson, Caldwell and Weldon have noted the development of and use of leadership standards in education both generally and in Australia, prior to the introduction of the Australian Professional Standard for Principals (APSP) in 2011[1]:

> The first educational leadership standards—which were intended to capture the essence of educational leaders' 'work' for a variety of purposes such as selection, professional development and appraisal—were developed in the 1990s in the US, the UK and Australia.[2] These generally comprised exhaustive lists of competencies—atomised 'shopping lists'—encapsulating the duties of principals and other leaders. Such standards were positive in that they 'have helped inform the development and improvement of many leadership programs and policies'.[3] However, more recently developed leadership standards have moved away from such competency lists to 'capabilities', the former now generally seen as unrepresentative of leadership roles, inflexible with regard to different occupational positions and career stages, and unable to adequately address ethical, moral and contextual issues in leadership.[4] Competencies have also been criticised for being more about measuring performance 'now' than being aspirational in guiding and encouraging further growth.

With the move from competencies to leadership capabilities, there has been a commensurate shift from use of the term 'standard' to the use of broader 'frameworks', some seeing standards as implying standardisation and with frameworks being conceived as more flexible and applicable to varied contexts and settings.

While many sets of leadership standards and frameworks have been developed independently across Australia by a variety of educational systems and professional associations, there has been considerable work in the last decade around the development of a national standards framework for school leadership.[5]

As Anderson et al. noted, however, despite this flurry of activity in the area of leadership standards and preparation programs in Australia, there are no formal requirements to become a principal. In most jurisdictions:

> ... a four-year teaching qualification and [teacher] registration remain the only formal requirements for school leaders.[6]

However, even the above is not universally true. There are principals in Australia who are not trained or registered teachers and there are some schools that ostensibly don't even have principals, but rather CEOs or managers.

The development, piloting and introduction of the Australian Professional Standard for Principals

An account of the development of the Australian Professional Standard for Principals has been provided by Dinham, Collarbone, Evans and Mackay, each of whom was very much involved with the process[7]:

> One of the challenges in formulating professional standards for principals is to capture the sheer diversity of the contexts in which they can operate: from teaching principals in small schools to those heading multi-campus schools; from low to high SES [Socio-Economic Status] and low to high NESB [Non-English Speaking Background]; from urban to regional to isolated; from struggling, coasting to successful schools, and in government, other systemic and independent schools.
>
> Years of largely discrete work by educational systems, professional associations and other bodies within Australia had resulted in many and varied leadership standards and frameworks being in use across the nation although a uniform national standard was lacking. In 2008, work on national

leadership standards[a] began. This was part of broader work around national professional standards for teachers which had an even longer history[8].

When the Australian Council for Educational Research (ACER) was contracted to conduct a mapping and consolidation of Australian leadership/principal standards for the Commonwealth Department of Education, Employment and Workplace Relations (DEEWR), it examined more than sixty extant leadership/principal standards and frameworks then being used for a variety of purposes across the nation.[9] This set was by no means exhaustive. Like others, ACER concluded that given developments in Australia such as national student standardised testing and a national curriculum, the time was right for a national standard for principals to complement the national standards for teachers (at four career stages) and national accreditation of teacher education courses, developments advocated previously in a report for the Business Council of Australia.[10]

When thoughts turned to developing national standards for leaders/principals there were conflicting views about their intended nature, audience and purpose. Some advocated a generic standard for leadership, while others favoured a standard for principals or multiple sets of standards for aspiring, practising and even exemplary principals. A key point of disagreement was whether a standard for principals should be used for performance appraisal purposes (i.e., a *performance standard*) or as a guide for professional development, self-reflection and to inform processes such as promotion and appraisal (i.e., a *content standard*).

These debates were at times intensely political and some stakeholders were quite passionate about the superiority of 'their' standard(s). It should be noted that while much of education in Australia is funded directly and indirectly through the federal tax system, constitutionally, education is a state and territory responsibility, and thus gaining agreement for national initiatives in education is not easy. 'Whose responsibility?' and 'who pays?' are frequent refrains.

Over time, jurisdictions, employers, systems, professional associations and individual schools had also developed their own processes to guide, select, appoint and appraise school leaders. Some of these were underpinned or informed by leadership and/or principal standards and frameworks, but the terrain was quite muddy overall.

Gaining universal stakeholder agreement for a National [now Australian] Professional Standard for Principals was not an easy task and represented a significant achievement. To compound matters, the timeframe to write the Standard and have it endorsed was extremely challenging.[11]

---

a   The singular 'Standard' was adopted later, as was the designation 'Principal'.

Once agreement was reached across the various jurisdictions, AITSL commenced work on the principal standard in early 2010, with drafting beginning in September that year. Dame Professor Patricia Collarbone from the United Kingdom played a key role in this work as an external expert and 'circuit breaker'. AITSL also established an external expert steering group and an internal expert group drawn from across stakeholders to guide and support this work and there was an intensive and extensive process of research, drafting, critical review and feedback involving organisations and jurisdictions from across Australia.

The drafting of the standard was guided by a set of principles:
- Privilege the skills and knowledge specific to educational leadership
- Reflect the complexity and changing nature of contemporary school leadership
- Recognise the collaborative nature of school leadership
- Encourage a futures focused leadership capacity
- Guide principal preparation, development programs and self-reflection to meet the needs of school leaders in different contexts.

Initial research focused upon current thinking about school leadership and standards for principals and leaders used in other countries, including the UK, Canada, New Zealand and the United States of America, as well as the range of standards already in existence in Australia identified by ACER.

The research into school leadership highlighted at the outset the importance of school context, leadership practices, models of leadership and personal qualities, knowledge and skills. What became apparent was the range of environments and the complexity, critical significance and interrelated nature of the role of Principal. The first exposure draft of the standard[12] was developed to reflect these findings:
- The school context in which the Principal works is unique and of critical importance. The size of the school, the age of students, its traditions, location and other community factors mean that the standard must be applicable to the diverse nature of Australia's schools. 'At the same time though, most of the evidence we have reviewed suggests that good leadership is the same irrespective of context, and that 'what works' is surprisingly consistent'.[13]
- It should be focused on the primary task of the organisation, in this case, learning, teaching and student outcomes.
- The practices and competencies of leaders evolve as they move through their career and their learning and development needs to reflect this as well as being available when and where they need it.
- Leadership is collaborative and distributed among members of school teams; it does not reside in one individual. The role of the leader is to orchestrate and engage with and grow and develop other leaders at all levels of the school.
- New models of leadership within and beyond the school are emerging, with school leaders taking on a range of roles within their community.

- In order to improve the life chances of all students within the community and the nation, principals have a wider responsibility that involves developing the education system as a whole at local and national levels.
- Controversially, research shows that a small handful of personal qualities and skills explain a high proportion of the variation in leadership effectiveness.[14] Successful leaders draw upon the same repertoire of personal qualities and capabilities. This in turn explains a significant amount of the variation in leadership effectiveness.

In addition to this work, there was extensive consultation with principals, parents' associations, academics, state officials, professional associations and other stakeholders. This was an iterative process that took place throughout the development of the standard. The responses supported the key findings from the research. They reinforced the importance of context and the enormous diversity in schools across Australia and the systems in which principals operate as well as the challenges that exist for the Indigenous population and others.

There was consensus that the purpose of the standard needed to be clearly articulated and the language accessible. It required focus on professional development, creativity and risk-taking and should include self-reflection, ethics and values. The importance of relationships and working with others was also stressed by respondents.

Following the research and first round of consultation, the conceptual model was refined and tested for completeness and clarity. It was critical that the model reflected the systemic nature of the role of Principal and was clear and unambiguous. It was only then that this could be built upon and turned into an accessible and useable standard.

At this stage the international panel of experts reviewed a draft of the standard.[b] Their feedback centred upon the need to make even more explicit the purpose of the standard—what is it for and what difference will it make. What would be needed to increase its take up and impact were also important questions. There were helpful suggestions related to leadership requirements, professional practices and language from the external panel.

A small but significant change took place as the conceptual model was developed and tested with stakeholders. The name changed from 'National Standards for Principals' to 'The National Professional Standard for Principals', and later still, 'Australian' was substituted for 'National'. The use of standard, singular, was in response to the overwhelming consensus that the power of the model lies in the way it reflects the integrated and interrelated nature of the role of the principal. Everything

---

b Professor Phil Hallinger, Hong Kong Institute of Education; Professor Kenneth Leithwood, University of Toronto; Professor Viviane Robinson, University of Auckland; Dr Sandra Stein, New York City Leadership Academy; Associate Professor David Ng Foo Seong, Nanyang Technological University, Singapore; Steve Munby, Chief Executive of the National College for School Leadership, UK.

that principals do in their professional practice is underpinned by their vision and values, their knowledge, and their personal qualities, requirements common to all leaders: 'There are statistically empirical and qualitatively robust associations between heads' educational values, qualities and their strategic actions and improvements in school conditions leading to improvements in student outcomes'.[15] The name change reflected the systemic or holistic nature of the role and the fact that it is not simply a list of attributes, duties or activities. See Figure 19.1 for the final version of the model.

Together, the leadership requirements and the practices principals undertake to enact these requirements are far more than a list of 'person specifications' or a role description. For a principal, they go right to the heart of what it means to be responsible for the life chances of young people in their school, community and society.

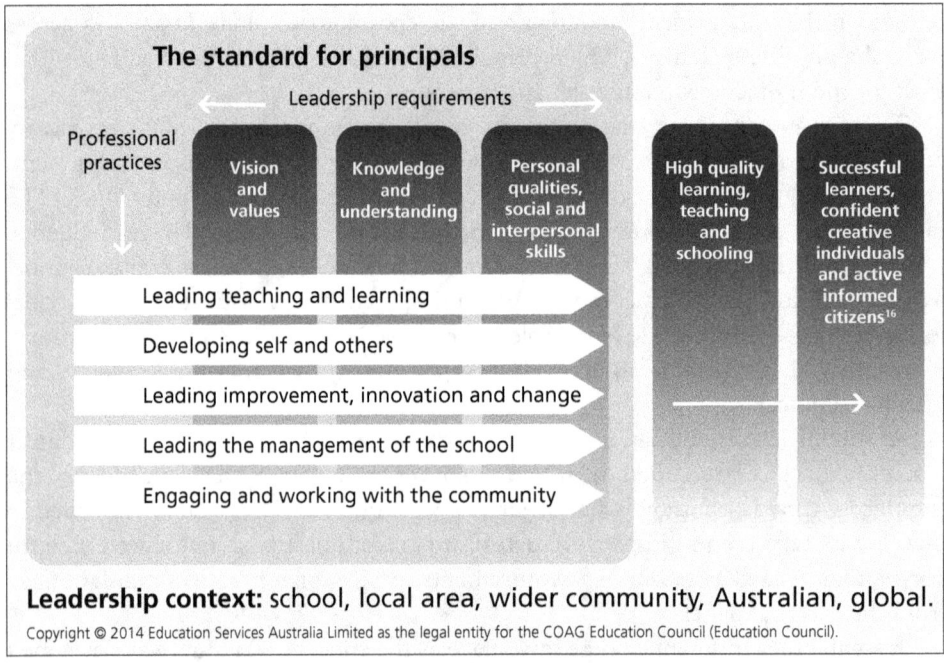

Figure 19.1: The Australian Professional Standard for Principals [17]

Piloting the exposure draft of the National Standard for Principals

The exposure draft of the Standard noted that:

> The National Professional Standard for Principals (the Standard) sets out what principals are expected to know, understand and do to achieve excellence in their work. It takes full account of the crucial contribution made by principals in:
> • raising student achievement at all levels and all stages

- promoting equity and excellence
- creating and sustaining the conditions under which quality teaching and learning thrive
- influencing, developing and delivering community expectations and government policy
- contributing to the development of a 21st century education system at local, national and international levels.[18]

It is important to note that it was determined by AITSL through consultation with stakeholders that the Principal Standard would be a *content*, rather than a *performance* standard; that is, the standard was not intended to be used directly to select principals, assess or certify principals against the standard nor to appraise principal performance. If the standard was to be used for performance purposes, it would need to be designed quite differently, with prescribed levels of performance and validated psychometrically to ensure the standard was fit for purpose.[c]

Because of the above distinction, it was decided that rather than go through a lengthy process of validation—as was deemed necessary and occurred with the national teacher standards[19]—it would be more beneficial to engage the profession nationally in piloting or 'road-testing' the Standard in 'real-world' situations.[d]

It was determined that pilot projects (under the umbrella of the overall piloting) should take place in a variety of contexts and that the exposure draft of the principal standard be applied to a range of its intended purposes, the core and common feature of which was to be active *use* of the standard with principals, aspiring principals and other stakeholders.

To the above end, tenders were called for in late 2010, with projects to commence early in 2011 for completion by early June 2011.

Nine organisations were selected by AITSL to undertake ten pilot studies. While each project had a particular focus and context, each was required to specifically address three key research questions within a common research approach[20]:

1. **Authenticity**—Is the Standard authentic? To what extent does the Standard accurately define the leadership requirements and professional practice of effective principals? Does the Standard describe *effective* school leadership? Does the Standard provide a framework of the knowledge and skills of effective principals, regardless of context?

---

c However, as noted, Principals Australia Institute subsequently decided to use the APSP for assessment and certification purposes and at the time of writing was in the process of developing methods and indicators to enable the APSP to be used for this purpose. Additionally, it has also been noted how AITSL has developed leadership profiles to again enable the use of the standard for performance purposes. The rapid take-up of the APSP and its use for performance purposes was somewhat surprising.

d This piloting project occurred under the direction of Stephen Dinham.

2. **Usefulness**—Is the Standard useable? How well does it provide an effective framework for professional learning? How useful would the Standard be for planning professional development and reflecting on practice? How effectively could it help to inform strategies to attract, prepare and develop effective principals for leading 21st century schools? How useful is it as a guide to inform the management of self and others?
3. **Value-add**—Does the Standard value-add to the knowledge and skills of effective principals? Is the Standard fair and reasonable? Is it inspirational and aspirational? What evidence supports the Standard? [after Dinham]

Suggested or possible approaches outlined in the tender document included but were not limited to:

   a. mapping existing professional learning approaches/programs for current and aspiring principals against the Standard
   b. developing a reflection tool/activity/program for individual self-reflection, self-assessment and development using the Standard
   c. developing and evaluating a new professional leadership activity/program based on the Standard
   d. integrating the Standard into existing or purpose-designed leadership development activities
   e. using the Standard to inform the development of mentoring, coaching program/course
   f. mapping the Standard against existing purpose-designed management policies and procedures and resources.

Concluding remarks

General findings from the 10 pilot studies

Space precludes detailed examination of the 10 pilot studies[21] but what follows is an overview of the general findings and recommendations.

Principals, other educators and stakeholders overwhelmingly welcomed the development of the National [Australian] Professional Standard for Principals, which was seen as overdue and meeting a need:

> 'We applaud the work of the Australian Institute for Teaching and School Leadership in developing the National Professional Standard for Principals.' Rural Education Forum Australia [REFA]

> 'The draft Standard is viewed as a positive initiative by the representatives of the business, parent and teacher groups that were consulted. The AITSL document provided an opportunity for clarity and authority in a potentially confusing area.' Australian Council for Educational Research [ACER]

'There was significant evidence from principals in the pilot study that the Standard accurately defined the leadership requirements and professional practices of effective principals and that the Standard described effective leadership.' New South Wales Department of Education and Communities [DECS]

'This project focused on the use of the Principal Professional Standard as a professional learning tool and it is clear that the Standard has met our expectations of what a good framework could do for principals' thinking, knowledge and understanding.' Tasmanian Department of Education and Training [Tas DET]

There was general agreement as to the appropriateness of the content of the Standard in capturing what principals need to be able to know, understand and do. It was found that the correct balance has been struck between prescription or detail and generality within the Standard.

The potential role of the standard in promoting reflection and informing professional learning was one of the most common strengths identified in the pilot studies.

In terms of the central study questions of *authenticity*, *utility* and *value add*, once again the views of practising and aspiring principals as well as stakeholders were positive:

'The Standard is perceived as achievable through a wide range of professional learning strategies. Its comprehensiveness and balance as a professional learning mechanism are notable ... The Standard is particularly useful for experienced principals involved in mentoring, coaching or training aspirants to the principal position.' Australian Council for Educational Leaders [ACEL]

'The Standard has been received positively by the participants of this pilot study. The authenticity of the Standard was positively attested to in all areas with over 80% of responses indicating the opinion that accurate interpretation of the Standard encourages innovation and provides the system with a direction for the development of capable leaders. The standard was considered a valuable tool for the design of professional learning and as a tool for self-reflection. There was also overwhelmingly positive feedback in terms of the value-add capacity of the standard in the form of adding to the skills and knowledge of existing leaders and as an inspirational target for aspirants.' Western Australian Department of Education [WA DE]

'The Standard enables principals to reflect on their practice in specific circumstances and over time ... The Standard promotes an holistic approach to self-reflection, encouraging principals to consider the interaction between leadership requirements and professional practices ... The Standard provides a guide for principal self-assessment and planning of further professional learning ... The Standard adequately describes the role of principal

> ... The Standard is a useful guide/reference especially for aspiring and new leaders. The Standard could be used widely with the school community, Governing Council, staff and leadership teams ... The Standard is clearly written in accessible language.' South Australian Department of Education and Children's Services [SA DECS]

> 'Generally the Standard was considered to be credible and reflect the work of school principals in regional and remote locations. It was considered to be sufficiently broad to take account of all the different types of responsibilities with which they deal.' Centre for School Leadership, Learning and Development, Charles Darwin University [CDU]

> 'In relation to the use of the Standard as a framework for professional learning there was substantial evidence from principals in the New South Wales government school survey and focus group that the Standard provides a framework for planning professional learning and reflecting on practice and that the Standard provides a framework for professional learning.' [NSW DEC]

Some stakeholders however, more so than principals, had a perception that the Standard will, should or could be used to judge principals' performance. As far as principals were concerned, there was a clear preference for the Standard to be used for *developmental* and not *judgemental* or performance measurement purposes. Thus, there existed and no doubt still exists some confusion over the purpose(s) of the standard.[e]

> 'Most groups of school principals who participated in this study thought the document would be of value to them and their staff, however most found it difficult to see how it was a "professional learning" document. Some expressed concern that it was difficult to make the distinction between a 'performance standard' and 'professional learning' standard.' [CDU]

> '[The Standard] Could inform professional performance and development discussions but participants were unsure of the value of the Standard as a performance assessment tool.'[f] [PA]

Generally, practising principals were more likely to identify with and profess to understand the Standard than aspiring principals. This is hardly surprising and

---

e   The view was expressed by some that the Standard needs 'indicators of performance' if it was to be successfully applied for the purpose of judging performance, but as noted, this runs counter to the stated purpose and uses of the Standard, although as noted, such indicators are now being developed to meet this demand.

f   Principals Australia (PA) [now Principals Australia Institute], conducted two pilot studies.

points to an important aspect of the standard—articulating the role of the principal to those not in the position. Research has shown that many principals do not fully appreciate the complexity and demands of the role until the full responsibility is placed upon their shoulders[22]:

'There was some constructive feedback. However, these responses were of two kinds: personalised responses and cautionary responses. The personalised responses came from inexperienced leaders in the form of comments such as "I don't understand". The more cautionary responses emanated from senior leaders who understood and applauded the Standard themselves.' [WA DE]

While the value of the standard to aspiring and practising principals was uniformly recognised, there was a view that the standard was of lesser value to other stakeholders in engendering understanding of the role and work of the principal.

'The authenticity and use of The Standard by parents and school communities was seen to be less obviously of benefit to them.' [CDU]

A challenge for the standard is of capturing and accommodating the myriad contexts in which Australian principals operate. This was a recurring theme in the various reports, most of which were supportive of the degree to which the standard does in fact allow for context.

A matter raised in a number of reports was the question of what comes next: the need for an adequate communication strategy; a 'launch'; means to engage the profession and professional development opportunities were all advocated.

'A National Launch [is needed that] heralds the release of the Standard to highlight the importance of the work of school leaders, rather than a gradual leaking of the document as an optional framework ... Attention is focussed on the implementation of the Standard by principals ... Jurisdictions could be supported in developing appropriate resources to be shared with a national audience.' [SA DECS]

'The next step in developing the Standard should be profession led and driven by a strong "user" perspective ... The next step in developing the Standard should be open and transparent, and engage parents, students and the general public as "consumers". This will contribute to raising the status of the principalship as a high standing profession in Australian society, and ensure greater public understanding of the link between quality school leadership and improved student outcomes ... AITSL should engage with the profession's leaders on how the profession itself intends to relate to the proposed AITSL Standard ... The implementation of the Standard must be accompanied by an effective Marketing and Communications Strategy resourced by AITSL ... The implementation of the Standard must be accompanied by an effective professional education and training strategy with the aim of ensuring that all principals have a deep understanding and awareness of the Standard.' [PA]

As noted, the APSP has now been in use since 2011, and AITSL in particular has developed a world-class set of support materials to accompany the APSP. Various jurisdictions are increasingly utilising the standard for a variety of purposes, including some performance uses not initially envisaged.

As we observed in our paper outlining the development of the APSP:

> Australia now has for the first time a ... Professional Standard for Principals. This in itself is a remarkable achievement, given the context and history of Australian education. However ultimately, the Standard is a means and not an end. It will be some time before there is evidence emerging of the impact of the Standard on school leadership, the quality of teaching, and student learning and development in Australian schools. More broadly, it will be fascinating to observe the degree to which the Standard has contributed to a more informed view of the principalship within the profession and wider community and the degree to which the various uses of the Standard have served to attract high calibre people to the key role of principal.[23]

Early signs of acceptance, take-up, and use are encouraging, and the APSP appears to be fast becoming an integral part and driver for the professional development of aspiring and practising principals in Australia.

Endnotes

1. Dinham, S., Anderson, M., Caldwell, B., & Weldon, P. (2011). Breakthroughs in school leadership development in Australia. *School Leadership and Management, 31*(2), 139–154. (p. 142). Reprinted with permission.
2. Ingvarson, L., Anderson, M., Gronn, P., & Jackson, A. (2006). *Standards for school leadership: A critical review of the literature.* Canberra, Australia: Teaching Australia; ISLLC. (1996). *Interstate school leaders licensure consortium: Standards For School Leaders.* Washington, DC: Council of Chief State School Officers.
3. Christie, K., Thompson, B., & Whiteley, G. (2009). *Strong leaders, strong achievement: Model policy for producing the leaders to drive student success.* Denver, CO: Education Commission of the States. (p. 1)
4. Dempster, N. (2001). *The professional development of school principals: A fine balance*: Professorial Lecture, 24 May, Griffith University Public Lecture Series. (p. 18)
5. Ingvarson, L. et al. (2006); Clarke, S. (2008). Only connect: Australia's recent attempts to forge a national agenda for quality school leadership. In M. Brundrett, & M. Crawford (Eds.), *Developing school leaders: An international perspective* (pp. 138–154). London: Routledge; Dinham, S., Ingvarson, L., & Kleinhenz, E. (2008). Investing in teacher quality: Doing what matters most. In *Teaching talent: The best teachers for Australia's classrooms.* Melbourne: Business Council of Australia.

6   Anderson, M., Gronn, P., Ingvarson, L., Jackson, A., Kleinhenz, E., McKenzie, P., Mulford, B., & Thornton, N. (2007). *OECD improving school leadership activity: Australia: Country background report.* Canberra, Australia: DEEWR. (p. 58)

7   Dinham, S., Collarbone, P., Evans, M., & Mackay, A. (2013). The development and proposed use of a national standard for principals in Australia. *Educational Management, Administration and Leadership, 41*(4), 466–482. All extracts reprinted with permission.

8   Dinham, S., Ingvarson, L., & Kleinhenz, E. (2008). Dinham, S., Ingvarson, L., & Kleinhenz, E. (2008). *Mapping of the Common Substance of Graduate Teacher Standards Developed and Implemented by ATRA Members Against the MCEETYA Framework for Standards—Development of Graduate Teacher Standards Australia.* Camberwell, Victoria: ACER.

9   Dinham, S., Ingvarson, L., Kleinhenz, E., & Anderson, M. (2009). *The Draft National Professional Standards Framework for Teachers and School Leaders.* Melbourne, Victoria: ACER.

10 Dinham, S., Ingvarson, L., & Kleinhenz, E. (2008).

11 Dinham, S. et al. (2013). (p. 469)

12 AITSL [Australian Institute for Teaching and School Leadership]. (2010). *National [Australian] Professional Standard for Principals exposure draft.* Melbourne, Victoria: Author.

13 Barber, M., Whelan, F., & Clark, M. (2010). *Capturing the leadership premium: How the world's top school systems are building leadership capacity for the future.* New York, NY: McKinsey & Company. (p. 3)

14 Leithwood, K., Day, C., Sammons, P., Harris, A. and Hopkins, D. (2006). *Seven strong claims about successful school leadership.* Nottingham, England: National College for School Leadership.

15 Day, C., Sammons, P., Hopkins, D., Harris, A., Leithwood, K., Gu, Q., Brown, E., Ahtaridou, E., & Kington, A. (2009) *The Impact of School Leadership on Pupil Outcomes.* Nottingham, England: University of Nottingham, p. 1.

16 Ministerial Council on Education, Employment, Training and Youth Affairs (MCEETYA). (2008) *Melbourne Declaration on Educational Goals for Young Australians.* Canberra, Australia: MCEETYA.

17 AITSL [Australian Institute for Teaching and School Leadership]. (2014). *The Australian Professional Standard for Principals and Leadership Profiles.* Melbourne, Victoria: Author. (p. 11). ACER has reproduced an extract of the Australian Professional Standard for Principals (2014) (Standard) with permission from the copyright owner. The Standard was developed by AITSL and endorsed by the Education Council. This publication is solely created by ACER and does not represent the views of, and is not endorsed by, AITSL or the Education Council.

18 AITSL [Australian Institute for Teaching and School Leadership]. (2010). (p. 3)

19 Pegg, J., McPhan, G., Mowbray, B., & Lynch, T. (2010). *Validation of the Australian Professional Standards for Teachers:* Executive summary. Melbourne, Victoria: AITSL.

20 Dinham, S. (2011). *Pilot study to test the exposure draft of the National Professional Standard for Principals—Analysis of interim reports.* Melbourne, Victoria: AITSL.

21 See Dinham, S. (2011) for details.

22 Dinham, S. (2008). *How to get your school moving and improving: An evidence-based approach.* Melbourne, Victoria: ACER Press.

23 Dinham, S., Collarbone, P., Evans, M., & Mackay, A. (2013). (p. 481)

CHAPTER 20

How can educational leaders be prepared?: A case study of the Master of Instructional Leadership at the University of Melbourne

INTRODUCTION

This chapter considers the impact of involvement for participants and their professional practice, of candidates enrolled in the first 2013 cohort of the Master of Instructional Leadership (MIL) degree in the Melbourne Graduate School of Education at the University of Melbourne.

This evaluation was conducted and reported by Helen Stokes, Warren Marks and me, all of whom have been involved in the development and implementation of the program and, in particular, the subject Leading Learning and Teaching. I would like to thank Helen and Warren, both for their contribution to the MIL and for permission to use part of our evaluation.

This final chapter also serves to bring together some of the threads and key understandings that have been running through this book, and thus is a conclusion and commentary for what has gone before.

Summary of major developments in the fields of learning, teaching and school leadership: recapping the major themes of this book

There are a number of broad and powerful research findings that have shaped conceptions and enactment of teaching, learning and school leadership in recent times. The first and perhaps most significant is that the teacher has been recognised as the biggest *in-school* influence on student achievement.[1] As Wright, Horn and Sanders have noted:

> ... the most important factor affecting student learning is the teacher ... The immediate and clear implication of this finding is that seemingly more can be done to improve education by improving the effectiveness of teachers than by any other single factor.[2]

A second powerful finding lies in the recognition that leadership can have a major influence on both teacher effectiveness and student learning[3], although the effects of leadership on student learning are less direct than those of teaching, and are thus more difficult to measure. Allied to this finding on the significance of leadership is the realisation that leadership in schools not only resides with those in formal positions of leadership, but is in fact shared and 'distributed', with every teacher being a leader in some respects.[4] There has also been recognition that rather than being innate, leadership capabilities can be developed and learned.[5] Thus, it follows that the identification, development and support of leaders, both formal and informal, are important if teacher effectiveness and student learning are to be improved.

A third finding has been the recognition that professional learning is the key to improving teacher effectiveness, leadership capability and student learning.[6] Newer, more effective approaches to professional learning are often site-based, collaborative, problem focused, evidence-based and utilise action learning and cycles of inquiry.[7]

Underpinning and running across the broad developments in thinking and practice outlined above, is the growing recognition that what occurs in schools needs to have a firm basis in evidence.[8] There are two sources or aspects to this evidence. The first is the extant research literature that informs teachers' professional practice, school leadership and organisation. The second source of evidence is that sought and derived by teachers and teams from their professional practice within the school that then informs evaluation of success and impact, further change and future practice.

This chapter draws on the above conceptual, research and development context to showcase a formal professional master's program in instructional leadership, aimed mainly at teachers, leading teachers, assistant/deputy principals and principals from primary and secondary schools, and considers the impacts of program involvement on participants' 'professional knowledge', 'professional practice' and 'professional engagement'[9], in order to bring about significant change in their schools through leading and working with others.

The importance of teacher leadership and instructional leadership

Teacher leadership and student achievement

There has been a shift in conceptions of educational leadership in recent times. An earlier focus on educational administration and later management has turned more to leadership for enhanced teaching and learning.[10] There had been concerns with an over-emphasis on the supposed attributes of the charismatic, heroic, 'transformational leader'[11], and the finding that such leaders can be 'negatively associated with leadership sustainability' has called into question the wisdom of seeking out and appointing such leaders.[12]

Additionally, an earlier focus on formal leadership—especially the principal—has broadened to consider the influence of other school leaders (deputies, other executive) and teachers, that is, distributed (or distributive) leadership.[13] Although the concept of distributed leadership can be traced back to social psychology in the 1950s, it is only in the last two decades or so that the concept has received widespread prominence and attention[14], although problems of loose definition remain.[15]

These changes in how educational leadership is conceived and enacted reflect a number of realities: that teaching and learning *should* be the prime focus of any school; that principals cannot bear all the burden of leadership; that others in formal leadership positions also exercise leadership[16], and that the contribution to educational outcomes of teachers' leadership has tended to be undervalued.[17]

There has been growing recognition that there is much unreleased leadership potential and capacity for improvement residing in educational organisations[18] and that distributed leadership is important in growing organisational and individual capability and performance.

Gronn considered the multiple meanings of distributed leadership, which fundamentally fall into two groups: the first seeing distributed leadership as essentially additive (more leaders, spread leadership) and the second more holistic, including forms of collaboration and participation.[19] Rather than spreading leadership responsibilities across more people, an holistic view of distributed leadership is concerned with the synergies that can occur when people come together to work, plan, learn and act, thus generating further leadership capability and capacity within the individual and the organisation.

Distributed leadership, including teacher leadership, is now a major aspect of constructs of educational leadership, although as Harris noted, as well as enthusiasm for the perceived benefits, 'we urgently need contemporary, fine-grained studies of distributed leadership practice ... without the associated empirical base it is in danger of becoming yet another abstract leadership theory.'[20] However, as noted previously, York-Barr and Duke are optimistic about the potential for educational improvement through teacher leadership 'despite being thwarted by centuries-old structures and conditions of schools that resist change'.[21] Harris noted:

> Contemporary studies of distributed leadership are going beyond the conceptual and empirical descriptions of what distributed leadership *is* to look much more closely at issues of impact and outcome.[22]

The issues of impact and outcomes of teacher leadership on teaching and learning are central concerns of this chapter and of the MIL.

Instructional leadership and student achievement

As noted, the effects of leadership on student learning are less direct than those of teaching and are thus more difficult to measure. However, a meta-analysis of 35 years of research by Marzano, Waters and McNulty concluded:

> A highly effective school leader can have a dramatic influence on the overall academic achievement of students.[23]

The word 'can' above is significant. It is important to distinguish between different approaches to or types of leadership. Effective management of day-to-day school functions involving budgeting, facilities, teacher hiring and evaluation, planning and accountability, can result in a well-run school, but if this is the extent or main focus of leadership, there may be little effect on improving student achievement. This situation has led to calls for what has been termed 'instructional leadership', or as I prefer to call it, leadership for teaching and learning. Robinson et al. noted that:

> Instructional leadership theory has its empirical origins in studies undertaken during the late 1970's and 80's of schools in poor urban communities where students succeeded despite the odds ... these schools typically had strong instructional leadership, including a learning climate free of disruption, a system of clear teaching objectives, and high teacher expectations for students.[24]

Hallinger observed that despite interest in instructional leadership arising from the above research into effective schools going back as far as the late 1970s:

> During the mid-1990s, however, attention shifted somewhat away from effective schools and instructional leadership. Interest in these topics was displaced by concepts such as school restructuring and transformational leadership.[25]

However, the findings from international meta-analytic work comparing the impact of various approaches to educational leadership—including both transformational and instructional—along with wider developments and concerns (e.g., equity and achievement gaps, international and national testing results), caused a re-examination of the worth of instructional leadership. Robinson et al. concluded from their meta-analysis on the impact of various leadership approaches:

> The comparison between instructional and transformational leadership showed that the impact [on student outcomes] of the former is three to four times that of the latter.[26]

Thus while the need for instructional leadership had been recognised for three decades or more, the approach has only re-gained prominence within the past decade[27].

Contemporary research findings are increasingly compelling on the relationship between instructional leadership and student outcomes. Hattie found from his extensive meta-analytic research that:

> School leaders who focus on students' achievement and instructional strategies are the most effective ... It is leaders who place more attention on teaching and focused achievement domains ... who have the higher effects.[28]

Robinson et al. offered a similar view:

> The more leaders focus their influence, their learning, and their relationships with teachers on the core business of teaching and learning, the greater their influence on student outcomes.[29]

An international review for McKinsey & Company by Barber, Whelan and Clark found:

> High-performing ['top' 15%] principals focus more on instructional leadership and developing teachers. They see their biggest challenges as improving teaching and curriculum, and they believe that their ability to coach others and support their development is the most important skill of a good school leader.[30]

Barber, Whelan and Clark also found that a thorough knowledge of teaching and learning on behalf of leaders is essential if teachers are to be developed and supported to be able to move forward the learning of every student in their care:

> Leadership focused on teaching, learning, and people is critical to the current and future success of schools.[31]

However, penetrating the, often closed, classroom door remains a challenge for principals and other leaders. Wahlstrom and Seashore Louis have commented:

> In the current era of accountability, a principal's responsibility for the quality of teachers' work is simply a fact of life. How to achieve influence over work settings (classrooms) in which they rarely participate is a key dilemma.[32]

How instructional leaders can be prepared and how they work collaboratively and effectively with those they lead and work with to influence and improve teaching and student achievement are key concerns of both this book and of the Master of Instructional Leadership at the University of Melbourne.

The course: Master of Instructional Leadership

The Master of Instructional Leadership (MIL) (Melbourne Graduate School, University of Melbourne) was initiated and designed in 2011–12 because of a perceived need for an educational leadership program with a strong central emphasis on understanding and improving teaching and learning, rather than the more typical approaches to educational leadership programs that tend to emphasise administration and management. The program needed to be built upon a strong platform of research and evidence, if it was to achieve its aims. The need for such a program was supported by an externally commissioned market research report that indicated strong potential interest from the profession in such a program.[33]

The seven core units (or subjects) of the MIL (there is an eighth 'open' elective unit) were designed to align with the Australian Professional Standards for Teachers (APST) (*Highly Accomplished* and *Lead* levels)[34], and in particular, with the Australian Professional Standard for Principals (APSP).[35]

The five key 'professional practices' of the APSP provided a framework for the design of the program:
- Leading Teaching and Learning
- Developing Self and Others
- Leading Improvement, Innovation and Change
- Leading the Management of the School
- Engaging and Working with the Community.

The MIL program was also designed to achieve outcomes against the three 'leadership requirements' or domains of the APSP:
- Vision and Values
- Knowledge and Understanding
- Personal Qualities, Social and Interpersonal Skills.

The three domains of the APST above were also important organisational and design constructs for the MIL.

(Figure 19.1 in the previous chapter provides an overview of the APSP.)

The seven core units (subjects) of the MIL comprise:

1. **Evidence for Learning and Teaching** (which focuses on what teaching/learning works best; what criteria can be developed to measure success; and how to evaluate the impacts of leadership decisions on both teachers and students) [developed by John Hattie]
2. **Leading Learning and Teaching** (which critically examines the research evidence linking quality teaching with student outcomes; the role and influence of various leadership approaches; change management and effective teacher professional learning) [developed by Stephen Dinham][a]
3. **Leading Assessment** (which explores assessment and reporting frameworks; teacher, leader, school and system use of data-informed and evidence-based decision and policy formulations) [developed by Patrick Griffin]
4. **Leading Schools through Leading Self** (which explores the concepts that self-leadership is a critical basis for successful school leadership; and the importance of school leaders behaving with integrity and moral purpose) [developed by Lea Waters]
5. **Leading Educational Research** (which focuses on evidence-based research utilising qualitative and quantitative data collection; and the protocols for conducting well-designed, well-analysed and ethical research) [developed by Helen Stokes]
6. **Researching Leadership Practice** (which focuses on the successful design, development, implementation and evaluation of a school-based/work-site based innovation associated with instructional practice aimed to improve student learning) [developed by Helen Stokes]
7. **Understanding Schools** (which critically explores the structure, organisation and culture of schools through the conceptual tool of framing; exploring how schools can be successfully transformed within an instructional leadership orientation) [developed by David Gurr and Lawrie Drysdale].[b]

---

a   *Evidence for Learning and Teaching* (Hattie) and *Leading Learning and Teaching* (Dinham) comprise an embedded, two-unit Professional Certificate in Instructional Leadership, which may be undertaken as a standalone qualification.

b   The MIL is delivered through a combination of 'intensives' (two, two-day face-to-face sessions for each subject) and online activities and learning. Candidates come from across Australia and overseas.

Evaluation of the impact of the MIL on the first cohort: research methodology

A mixed method methodology was adopted for this research. Burke Johnson and Onwuegbuzie define mixed methods research as 'where the researcher mixes or combines quantitative and qualitative research techniques, methods, approaches, concepts or language in a single study'.[36] At the heart of the adoption of a mixed methods approach is finding a method or number of methods (both quantitative and qualitative) that will answer the research questions most fully, or as Cuervo, Crofts and Wyn describe, to 'fill in the gaps from each technique'.[37]

Research sample
Thirty graduates from the first cohort (2013–14) of the MIL formed the potential sample for this research and were invited (by email) to participate in this evaluation of the impact of the MIL program.

Four of this potential sample were not located in schools and could not complete the survey, in that it was not possible for them to answer questions associated with changes in practices and impacts on teaching and learning in a school attributable to the MIL. Twenty of the 26 eligible remaining graduates (77 per cent) completed the survey (see Table 20.1).

Data collection
There were two forms of data collection: a questionnaire (quantitative and qualitative data) and a focus group (qualitative data). Both sources of data were collected six months after graduation from the course as part of a course evaluation and research cycle.

In this research, a within-stage mixed-model design was employed[38] and data collection—questionnaire and focus group—was accomplished within a single stage. The questionnaire and a series of open-ended focus group questions were devised concurrently, with the focus group being conducted following questionnaire implementation.

Survey questionnaire
The questionnaire was based on the Australian Professional Standards for Teachers (*Highly Accomplished* and *Lead* levels)[39], and the focus group questions were based on the Australian Professional Standard for Principals.[40] The questionnaire included questions with a five-point rating scale (with an additional unsure category of response) (quantitative data collection) as well as open-ended questions (qualitative data collection) where respondents could provide examples of school practice and the impact of the program on their 'professional knowledge', 'professional practice', and 'professional engagement', the three domains of the APST.

The judgement of the participants (sample group) was captured by the use of a consistent stem for each question: 'My candidature in the MIL has enhanced my capacity to ...'.

Survey questionnaire cohort

Twenty respondents completed the online survey. The composition of this cohort is displayed in Table 20.1. In brief, there were:
- eight principals
- seven assistant/deputy principals
- one 'leading teacher'
- one classroom teacher
- three (now) non-school based participants.

Table 20.1: MIL graduate survey respondents

LEVEL	MALE	FEMALE	TOTALS
Primary	2	5	7
Secondary	4	5	9
K-12	3	1	4
Sub-totals	**9**	**11**	**20**
POSITION			
Principal	4	4	8
Assistant principal	3	4	7
Leading teacher	0	1	1
Teacher	0	1	1
Other	2	1	3
Sub-totals	**9**	**11**	**20**

The focus group cohort
Nine MIL graduates participated in the focus group. Participation in the focus group was a function of being available to meet with the researchers in Melbourne at a given time.[c] Of these respondents there were:
- two primary principals and one secondary principal
- one primary assistant principal and two secondary assistant principals
- one primary leading teacher
- one secondary classroom teacher
- one education research fellow.

Data analysis
A combination of the Miles and Huberman framework[41] and the Burke Johnson & Onwuegbuzie framework[42] was used to analyse the data from the questionnaire (quantitative and qualitative responses) and the focus group. The Miles and Huberman framework follows a four-step process that includes: *data reduction*; *data display*; *identifying themes*, and *verifying conclusions*. In the data reduction stage, the qualitative statements of each participant from both the questionnaire and the focus group were coded according to the three main APST domains—professional knowledge, professional practice and professional engagement—and the seven standards.

Across these data, display patterns and interrelationships were identified relating to overall impact of the course and significant change in schools. Analysis also drew on Burke Johnson and Onwuegbuzie's framework[43] to add the stage of data comparison in order to compare the quantitative (questions with a five-point scale) and qualitative (open-ended questions and focus group responses) data. Finally, the 'confirmability'[44] of the data was assessed against the emergent theory and multiple sources of data (quantitative and qualitative).

Findings and discussion
The quantitative data is displayed under the three main themes of professional knowledge, professional practice and professional engagement and the seven APST standards (see Table 20.2 on the following page).

---

c   This number was limited by the number of interstate and more remote graduates.

Table 20.2: Survey responses [n = 20] (based on APST) [quantitative questions/data only]

	STRONGLY AGREE	AGREE	DISAGREE	STRONGLY DISAGREE	UNSURE
SECTION A: PROFESSIONAL KNOWLEDGE					
Q2: My candidature in MIL has enhanced my capacity to 'know students and how they learn'	80%	20%			
Q4: My candidature in MIL has enhanced my capacity to 'know the content and how to teach it'	50%	40%	10%		
SECTION B: PROFESSIONAL PRACTICE					
Q6: My candidature in MIL has enhanced my capacity to 'plan for and implement effective teaching and learning'	70%	30%			
Q8: My candidature in MIL has enhanced my capacity to 'create and maintain supportive and safe learning environment'	70%	20%	10%		
Q10: My candidature in MIL has enhanced my capacity to 'assess, provide feedback and report on student learning'	50%	40%			10%
SECTION C: PROFESSIONAL ENGAGEMENT					
Q12: My candidature in MIL has enhanced my capacity to 'engage in professional learning'	80%	10%			10%
Q14: My candidature in MIL has enhanced my capacity to 'engage professionally with colleagues'	90%	10%			
Q16: My candidature in MIL has enhanced my capacity to 'engage professionally with parents/carers and the community'	30%	60%			10%

Discussion from qualitative data analysis (questionnaire, focus group)

Theme 1: Professional knowledge
Under Professional knowledge are the sub-themes of *a) Knowing the students and how they learn*, and *b) Knowing the content and how to teach it*.

a) Knowing the students and how they learn
The respondents identified a range of sources within the program that assisted them to know students and how they learn. At the basis of this was learning how to use data to improve student outcomes and understand what was working in the classroom, including feedback cycles, learning intentions, success criteria, evidence-based judgements and assessment rubrics.

One principal commented:

> 'It helped me work with teachers to develop strategies and practices to identify student point of need. This was used to plan and implement T&L[d] that met the needs of the students.' (Principal Secondary)

A leading teacher found that:

> 'Understanding the factors that have a high effect size in impacting student learning outcomes has helped me to guide learning practices within our school. At my school we used evidence-based research to inform practice. We are focused on strategies that have a high effect size.' (Leading teacher Primary)

b) Knowing the content and how to teach it
The majority of respondents identified that as a leadership course, the MIL was not specifically focused on teaching content. They did, however, reflect on aspects of the course and how these had assisted them to lead teachers in their school in understanding the content they were teaching. Two principals commented:

> 'Understanding the factors influencing student learning outcomes has enabled me to set the direction for literacy across the school. Using evidence-based research and deepening my understanding of subject content and how to teach it has helped me to refine my practice and to coach staff to build their capacity in this area.' (Principal Primary)

> 'Overall the generic approaches to teaching and learning were very useful in providing good specific feedback to teachers about their teaching practices.' (Principal P–12)

---

d   Teaching and Learning

Theme 2: Professional practice

Under Professional practice are the three sub-themes: *a) Plan for and implement effective teaching and learning*, *b) Create and maintain supportive and safe learning environments*, and *c) Assess, provide feedback and report on student learning*.

a) Plan for and implement effective teaching and learning

Respondents identified a range of activities and structures such as developing program logics and rubric design for use in assessment they learnt through the MIL that had assisted them (and those they work with) to learn how to plan for and implement effective teaching. As one principal commented:

> 'The work we did in rubric design has been used by staff to collaboratively develop outstanding rubrics. This made teachers interrogate the curriculum and discuss the learning.' (Principal Secondary)

Another respondent commented on the action research project she implemented in her school in the second year of the course that drew together and allowed her to use the learning from the first year, particularly about professional learning communities:

> 'My action [learning] research project centred around implementing PLTs[e] across the school to look at how this impacted reading instruction across the school. The complaint at school prior to this project was that we completed benchmark assessments in reading on children and did not use this data to inform practice. We now use PLTs for all areas across the school. Student data, work samples and assessments are now firmly placed within the PLT structure.' (Leading teacher Primary)

Another teacher discussed how it wasn't just structures and processes that were important for leading the implementation of effective teaching and learning. He found his learning on how to build a culture of learning was of particular relevance and this then led him to question his own practice, values and beliefs in regard to instructional leadership. He commented:

> 'Leading teaching and learning helped me to identify areas for growth and provided me with a framework to grow. Leading self was a revelation. To understand the actions that drove my leadership I needed to understand my values and beliefs. Only then could I begin to understand my leadership and how I could change to lead teaching and learning more effectively.' (Acting AP Secondary)

---

e   Professional learning teams.

b) Create and maintain supportive and safe learning environments

Respondents outlined frameworks they were exposed to during the course that assisted them with creating safe learning environments. One principal commented:

> 'We have defined our school's vision and mission in relation to Dinham's work under the broad heading and theme: High nurture, high calling, reflecting Dinham's high responsive / high demanding framework.' (Principal P–12)

Respondents also mentioned that awareness of aspects of positive psychology assisted them in understanding how to create supportive learning environments for both students and staff. As one principal commented:

> 'Positive psychology provided a stimulus for ensuring that we make sure the 'goose' is healthy to continue producing the "golden eggs". This subject aligned with the 7 habits of highly effective people and provided many tools that practically assisted me as a leader with staff well-being strategies, as well as my own.' (Principal Primary).

While another commented that learning about positive psychology:

> 'Really made me consider the professional and personal relationships in the workplace and how I, as leader, influenced the climate and the positivity within my school.' (Principal Secondary)

Creating supportive environments, linked to understanding how change works in schools. A number of the MIL units explored the change process and prepared candidates to engage in it. One teacher commented:

> 'By understanding the process of change and learning how to prepare for change I now have more skills to assist schools through this process. This topic helped me to determine more of why the teaching staff at my former school [was] not united in how to address student support in the school. This was affecting student engagement and the support of student behaviour.' (Leading Teacher Primary)

c) Assess, provide feedback and report on student learning

Respondents reported that the work they undertook on providing student feedback had changed practice in their schools. In particular it was about developing an understanding of feedback's importance and factors influencing its effectiveness and then linking it with understanding assessment and the work on 21st-century skills.

As one teacher commented:

'At the end of last year I led the change in our reporting and assessment practices. Formative assessment now informs planning; feedback to move students forward is imbedded in teacher practice across the school. All teams use student learning data to inform planning and decisions are based on Dufour—what are we going to teach, how will we know the students have learnt it, what will we do if they haven't and what will we do if they already know it?' (Leading Teacher Primary)

While another respondent reported that as a result of the MIL and his learning:

'Feedback is a big part of what we do at my school. Every student in our school has a goal for reading, writing, spelling and in maths. They receive feedback in relation to how they are going in achieving their goal through conferences with their teacher and staff have a very strong understanding of the continuum of learning in each of the curriculum areas outlined in order for them to set appropriate goals with their students.' (Principal Primary)

Theme 3: Professional engagement

Under the theme of professional engagement there were three sub themes of: *a) Engage in professional learning*, *b) Engage professionally with colleagues*, and *c) Engage professionally with parents/carers and the community*.

a) Engage in professional learning

Respondents reported that undertaking the MIL program encouraged them to read professionally and that this had changed how they went about their practice in schools. They now see themselves and are seen by others as learners, open to research and willing to apply research. They have achieved one of the intended outcomes of the MIL, that of becoming a 'critical consumer' of research. This new knowledge is often shared with others (see b) below).

One teacher commented:

'I continue to read widely and I do not implement anything without first having read about the topic. For example, we are looking at how we teach reading F–2. I have consulted experts, read widely and lead staff through changes.' (Leading Teacher Primary)

Another found that the course also led to him questioning and looking for evidence. He commented:

'I have continued to be more engaged in professional learning by reading more research articles and taking on more action learning projects. The MIL course has enabled me to question the programs we have introduced at the College and have been prepared to look at the various data that is available.' (Assistant Principal Secondary)

Respondents also commented that they continue to use the resources provided through the program. One principal commented:

> 'The strength of the MIL is the access to the high quality articles and recommended texts. The recommended readings are invaluable and I have recently gone back to three texts to implement a project focused on improving teacher practice through feedback.' (Principal Primary)

While another respondent commented:

> 'I can't express how valuable MIL was for me. Professional learning is crucial for all professionals. The conversations I had with others in my course, the stories, the reflections I listened to, were all valuable. I loved the structure of the MIL—the fact that we weren't in a lecture theatre, we were encouraged to work together as professionals, and learn from each other.' (Classroom Teacher Secondary)

b) Engage professionally with colleagues

Respondents reported that they regularly shared the learning from the course with their staff and colleagues. They reported that they had increased confidence to both engage in professional conversations about teaching and learning and to lead change in the school.

As one principal commented:

> 'I have been able to engage in deep conversation, knowing I have the research base (not just: "gut instinct" to expand and consider options.' (Principal P-12)

Other leaders reported on how the course assisted them to relate to their colleagues. One commented:

> 'I am able to be much more supportive because of what I have learned.' (AP Secondary)

While two other respondents reported on the value of communication and conversations. One found that the course:

> 'Helped me to be more open to feedback and listen before answering.' (AP Secondary)

The other respondent commented:

> 'I think professional conversations are crucial, and this was reinforced during MIL. I have learnt that no matter how difficult the person is to work with (such as one of the teachers I am working with this year), having professional conversations is crucial, and there will always be something you can learn from them.' (Classroom Teacher Secondary)

c) Engage professionally with parents/carers and the community

Respondents reported that using professional feedback tools and gaining a wider understanding of stakeholders had broadened and changed the way they worked across their school communities. One principal commented that using surveys to gather feedback on her leadership:

> '... gave me cause to consider my leadership style(s) when working with parents and other stake holders and I believe this enabled me to make some improvements/adjustments in how I approached this part of my role.' (Principal Secondary)

While an acting assistant principal found that he now has the:

> '... tools and models to view a community through several lenses and how to support people with strong associations to each frame. Instead of reacting to challenging situations I am now able to step back and view a school community from the balcony.' (Acting AP Secondary)

Concluding remarks

Implications from the MIL evaluation

It was apparent from the quantitative and qualitative data provided by respondents and the analysis of these data that involvement with the MIL program had been transformative. The opportunity to acquire new knowledge, engage in guided reflection on current practice, to acquire new frameworks, tools and methods, the social and professional interaction with others and the undertaking of action learning projects within their workplace, with the capability to measure the impact of these, were means to achieve powerful learning, not just for the participants, but in many cases for their colleagues and those they lead in schools. This learning and its application had directly resulted in changes to school focus and organisation, teaching and student learning, although longer-term impacts would need to be verified.

All 20 survey respondents strongly agreed (80%) or agreed (20%) that the course had enhanced their capacity to know students and how they learn, while 90% strongly agreed (50%) or agreed (40%) that the MIL had enhanced their capacity to know content and how to teach it. Not only had the course added to their professional learning, but it had also clearly provided the stimulus for further learning and for the learning of those with whom they work.

In terms of professional practice, all 20 respondents strongly agreed (70%) or agreed (30%) that the MIL had enhanced their capacity to plan for and implement effective teaching and learning. Ninety per cent strongly agreed (70%) or agreed (20%) that they had developed increased capacity to create and maintain supportive and safe learning environments, with 90% of respondents also strongly agreeing (50%) or agreeing (40%) that their involvement with the MIL had enhanced their capacity to assess, provide feedback and report on student learning.

In respect of professional engagement, 90 per cent strongly agreed (80%) or agreed (10%) that the MIL had enhanced their capacity to engage in professional learning. All respondents strongly agreed (90%) or agreed (10%) that they had enhanced their capacity to engage professionally with colleagues through completion of the MIL. This was strongly supported by the qualitative data from the questionnaire and the focus group, which indicated the 'contagion effects' of being involved with the course, in that the MIL provided the knowledge, means and confidence to work more productively with colleagues regardless of whether the respondent was in a formal leadership position or not. These data strongly indicate the enhanced distributed leadership capability and impact of respondents.

Finally, 90 per cent of respondents strongly agreed (30%) or agreed (60%) that their candidature in the MIL had enhanced their capacity to engage professionally with parents/carers and the community, something that was not a major focus of the MIL program, but is nevertheless an important outcome of enhanced professional capabilities.

Overall, the questionnaire and focus group findings indicated a hunger on the part of these experienced educators to be able to improve their professional knowledge, professional practice and professional engagement, in order to facilitate and lead change and improvement in teaching and learning through evidence-based practice. There was a strong view that their professional learning would continue beyond the requirements of the MIL.

Providing greater numbers of aspiring and practising educational leaders with enhanced capabilities to work with others to improve teaching and learning—that is, getting to scale—is thus both an opportunity and a challenge for educational systems.

More generally, the Australian Professional Standard for Principals and the Australian Professional Standards for Teachers were found to be valuable both in shaping the design of the Master of Instructional Leadership and in assessing its impact.

Final comments

Thank you for reading to this point. I won't keep you much longer. I hope that you have found this book to be valuable in adding to your knowledge and understanding of what it means to be a leader of learning and teaching.

For me, the essential messages from all this work can be summed up as follows:
- **Quality teaching** matters.
- **Leadership** is a big enabler and is exercised **with** and **through people**.
- **Professional learning** is essential for change.

- The best classrooms, departments, schools, and even systems have a central focus on **students** as **learners** and **people**.
- Educational systems, leaders and teachers need to plan, proceed, assess, evaluate and modify as necessary **on the basis of evidence**.
- **Data** is not just about compliance—it is about **improvement**.
- **Vision is important** but it must rest on **evidence**.

I hope that you can utilise this knowledge and understanding to improve and transform teaching and learning in the context in which you work, and that you have been motivated in some way to keep learning, as I am, after 40 years as an educator.

Best wishes,
Stephen Dinham
July 2016

Endnotes

1. Wright, S., Horn, S., & Sanders, W. (1997). Teacher and classroom context effects on student achievement: Implications for teacher evaluation. *Journal of Personnel Evaluation in Education, 11*, 57–67; Hattie, J. (2009). *Visible learning: A synthesis of over 800 meta-analyses relating to achievement.* London, England: Routledge; Dinham, S. (2013). The quality teaching movement in Australia encounters difficult terrain: A personal perspective. *Australian Journal of Education, 57*(2), 91–106.
2. Wright, S., Horn, S., & Sanders, W. (1997. (p. 63)
3. Hattie, J. (2009); Dinham, S. (2007). How schools get moving and keep improving: Leadership for teacher learning, student success and school renewal. *Australian Journal of Education, 51*(3), 263–275; Robinson, V., Lloyd, C., & Rowe, K. (2008). The impact of leadership on student outcomes: An analysis of the differential effects of leadership types. *Educational Administration Quarterly, 44*, 635–674. Copyright © 2008 by V. Robinson, C. Lloyd and K. Rowe. All text extracts from this article are reprinted by Permission of Sage Publications, Inc.
4. Spillane, J. (2006). *Distributed leadership.* San Francisco, CA: Jossey-Bass; Harris, A. (2009). (Ed.). *Distributed school leadership: Different perspectives.* Dordrecht, Netherlands: Springer Press.
5. Dinham, S., Anderson, M., Caldwell, B., & Weldon, P. (2011). Breakthroughs in school leadership development in Australia. *School Leadership and Management, 31*(2), 139–154.
6. Dinham, S. (2008); Hattie, J. (2009); Schleicher, A. (2012). (Ed.). *Preparing teachers and developing school leaders for the 21st century.* Paris, France: OECD; Robinson, V., & Timperley, H. (2007). The leadership of the improvement of teaching and learning: Lessons from initiatives with positive outcomes for students. *Australian Journal of Education, 51*, 247–262.
7. Brady, L., Aubusson, P., & Dinham, S. (2006). Action learning for school improvement. *Educational Practice and Theory, 28*(2), 27–39; Aubusson, P., Steele, F., Dinham, S., & Brady, L. (2007). Action learning in teacher learning community formation: informative or transformative? *Teacher Development, 11*(2), 133–148; Timperley, H., Wilson, A., Barrar, H., & Fung, I. (2007). *Teacher professional development: Best evidence synthesis iteration.* Wellington: New Zealand Ministry of Education.

8   Dinham, S. (2015). Pseudo-science, inequality and decline. *Journal of Professional Learning*, Semester 1, http://cpl.asn.au/journal/semester-1-2015/pseudo-science-inequality-and-decline
9   AITSL [Australian Institute for Teaching and School Leadership.] (2011). *Australian Professional Standards for Teachers*. Melbourne, Victoria: Author.
10 Dinham, S. (2007). The waves of leadership. *The Australian Educational Leader*, 29(3), 20–21, 27.
11 Robinson, V. et al. (2008).
12 Fullan, M. (2005). *Leadership and sustainability*. Thousand Oaks, CA: Corwin. (pp. 30–31)
13 Harris, A. (2004). Teacher leadership and distributed leadership: An exploration of the literature. *Leading and Managing*, 10(2), 1–9; Harris, A. (2009); Dinham, S. (2007). How schools get moving and keep improving: Leadership for teacher learning, student success and school renewal. *Australian Journal of Education*, 51(3), 263–275.
14 Gronn, P. (2002). Distributed leadership. In K. Leithwood, & P. Hallinger (Eds.), *Second international handbook of educational leadership and administration* (pp. 653–696). Dordrecht, Netherlands: Kluwer. (p. 653)
15 Harris, A. (2008). Distributed Leadership: According to the evidence. *Journal of Educational Administration*, 46(2), 172–188. (pp. 173–175)
16 Dinham, S., & Scott, C. (2002). Pressure points: School executive and educational change. *Journal of Educational Enquiry*, 3(2), 35–52; Dinham, S., Brennan, K., Collier, J., Deece, A., & Mulford, D. (2000). The Secondary Head of Department: Key link in the quality teaching and learning chain. *Quality Teaching Series*, No. 2, Australian College of Education, 1–35.
17 Spillane, J., Halverson, R., & Diamond, J. (2001). Investigating school leadership practice: A distributed perspective. *Educational Researcher*, 30(3), 23–28; Gronn, P. (2002). (p. 654)
18 Crowther, F., Kaagan, S., Ferguson, M., & Hann, L. (2002). *Developing teacher leaders*. Thousand Oaks, CA: Corwin. (pp. 3–16); York-Barr, J., & Duke, K. (2004). What do we know about teacher leadership? Findings from two decades of scholarship. *Review of Educational Research*, 74(3), 255–316.
19 Gronn, P. (2002). (pp. 654–660)
20 Harris, A. (2005). Distributed leadership. In Davies, B. (Ed.), *The essentials of school leadership*. London, England: Paul Chapman. (p. 70)
21 York-Barr, J., & Duke, K. (2004). (p. 292)
22 Harris, A. (2009). (p. 19)
23 Marzano, R., Waters, T., & McNulty, B. (2005). *School leadership that works: From research to results*. Alexandria, VA: ASCD. (p. 10)
24 Robinson et al., (2008). (p. 638)
25 Hallinger, P. (2005). Instructional leadership and the school principal: A passing fancy that refuses to fade away. *Leadership and Policy in Schools*, 4, 221–239. (p. 228)
26 Robinson et al., (2008). (p. 666)
27 Dinham, S. (2007). The waves of leadership. *The Australian Educational Leader*, 29(3), 20–21, 27.
28 Hattie, J. (2009). (p. 83)
29 Robinson et al. (2008). (p. 636)
30 Barber, M., Whelan, F., & Clark, M. (2010). *Capturing the leadership premium: How the world's top school systems are building leadership capacity for the future*. New York, NY: McKinsey & Company. (p. 7).

31 Barber, M. et al., (2010). (p. 28)
32 Wahlstrom, K., & Seashore Louis, K. (2008). How teachers experience principal leadership: The roles of professional community, trust, efficacy, and shared responsibility. *Educational Administration Quarterly, 44*, 458–495. (p. 459)
33 Coulton, C., & Kirkhope, J. (2012). *University of Melbourne education leadership research*. Melbourne, Victoria: Sweeney Research.
34 AITSL [Australian Institute for Teaching and School Leadership]. (2011). *Australian Professional Standards for Teachers*. Melbourne, Victoria: Author.
35 AITSL [Australian Institute for Teaching and School Leadership]. (2011). *Australian Professional Standard for Principals*. Melbourne, Victoria: Author; Dinham, S. (2011). *Pilot study to test the exposure draft of the National Professional Standard for Principals—Final Report*. Melbourne, Victoria: AITSL; Dinham, S., Collarbone, P., Evans, M., & Mackay, A. (2013). The development and proposed use of a national standard for principals in Australia. *Educational Management, Administration and Leadership, 41*(4), 466–482.
36 Burke Johnson, R., & Onwuegbuzie, J. (2004). Mixed method research: A research paradigm whose time has come. *Educational Researcher, 33*(7), 14–26. (p. 17)
37 Cuervo, H., Crofts, J. & Wyn, J. (2013). *Generational insights into new labour market landscapes for youth, Research Report 42*. Melbourne, Victoria: Youth Research Centre, University of Melbourne. (p. 8)
38 Burke Johnson, R., & Onwuegbuzie, J. (2004).
39 AITSL [Australian Institute for Teaching and School Leadership]. (2011). *Australian Professional Standards for Teachers*. Melbourne: Victoria: Author.
40 AITSL [Australian Institute for Teaching and School Leadership]. (2011). *Australian Professional Standard for Principals*. Melbourne: Victoria: Author.
41 Miles, M., & Huberman, M. (1994). *Qualitative data analysis*. Thousand Oaks, CA: Sage Publications.
42 Burke Johnson, R., & Onwuegbuzie, J. (2004).
43 Burke Johnson, R., & Onwuegbuzie, J. (2004). (p. 22)
44 Miles, M., & Huberman, M. (1994). (p. 11)

References

AACTE. (2012). *Educator preparation: Myths and facts.* Washington, DC: American Association of Colleges for Teacher Education. https://www.aau.edu/WorkArea/DownloadAsset.aspx?id=13450

Alter, J., & Coggshall, J. G. (2009). *Teaching as a clinical practice profession: Implications for teacher preparation and state policy.* New York: National Comprehensive Centre for Teacher Quality.

Anderson, M., Gronn, P., Ingvarson, L., Jackson, A., Kleinhenz, E., McKenzie, P., Mulford, B., & Thornton, N. (2007). *OECD improving school leadership activity: Australia: Country background report.* Canberra, Australia: DEEWR.

Argyris, C. (1982). *Reasoning, learning, and action.* San Francisco, CA: Jossey-Bass.

Aubusson, P., Brady, L., & Dinham, S. (2005). *Action learning: What works? A research report prepared for the New South Wales Department of Education and Training.* Sydney: University of Technology Sydney.

Aubusson, P., Steele, F., Dinham, S., & Brady, L. (2007). Action learning in teacher learning community formation: Informative or transformative? *Teacher Development, 11*(2), 133–148.

Australian Council for Educational Research. (2012). *School improvement: What does research tell us about effective strategies?* 2012 Research Conference. Melbourne, Victoria: Author.

Australian Curriculum, Assessment and Reporting Authority. (2014). *NAPLAN achievement in Reading, Persuasive Writing, Language Conventions and Numeracy: National report for 2014.* Sydney: ACARA.

Australian Education Union. (2009). *New educators survey 2008.* Melbourne, Victoria: Author.

Australian Government. (2011). *Review of funding for schooling—Final report.* Canberra, Australia: Department of Education, Employment and Workplace Relations.

Australian Government. (2014). *School autonomy—Independent public schools.* Canberra, Australia: Department of Education. http://www.studentsfirst.gov.au/school-autonomy

AITSL [Australian Institute for Teaching and School Leadership]. (2010). *National [Australian] Professional Standard for Principals exposure draft.* Melbourne, Victoria: Author.

AITSL [Australian Institute for Teaching and School Leadership]. (2011). *Accreditation of initial teacher education Programs in Australia.* Melbourne, Victoria: Author.

AITSL [Australian Institute for Teaching and School Leadership]. (2011). *National [Australian] Professional Standards for Teachers.* Melbourne, Victoria: Author.

AITSL [Australian Institute for Teaching and School Leadership]. (2011). *National [Australian] Professional Standard for Principals: Final report.* Melbourne, Victoria: Author.

AITSL [Australian Institute for Teaching and School Leadership]. (2012). *Australian Teacher Performance and Development Framework.* Melbourne, Victoria: Author.

AITSL [Australian Institute for Teaching and School Leadership]. (2012). *Australian Charter for the Professional Learning of Teachers and School Leaders.* Melbourne, Victoria: Author.

AITSL [Australian Institute for Teaching and School Leadership]. (2014). *Australian Professional Standard for Principals and the leadership profiles.* Melbourne, Victoria: Author.

AITSL [Australian Institute for Teaching and School Leadership]. (2015). *Preparing future leaders: Effective preparation for aspiring school principals.* Melbourne, Victoria: Author.

References

AITSL [Australian Institute for Teaching and School Leadership]. (n.d.). *Are aspiring principals well prepared for this challenging role?* Melbourne, Victoria: Author. http://www.aitsl.edu.au/principal-preparation

Ayres, P., Dinham, S., & Sawyer, W. (1998). *The identification of successful teaching methodologies in the NSW Higher School Certificate: A research report for the NSW Department of Education and Training.* Penrith: University of Western Sydney, Nepean.

Ayres, P., Dinham, S., & Sawyer, W. (1999). *Successful teaching in the NSW Higher School Certificate.* Sydney: NSW Department of Education and Training.

Ayres, P., Dinham, S., & Sawyer, W. (2000). Successful senior secondary teaching. *Quality Teaching Series*, No. 1, Australian College of Education, September, 1–20.

Ayres, P., Dinham, S., & Sawyer, W. (2004). Effective teaching in the context of a Grade 12 high stakes external examination in New South Wales, Australia. *British Educational Research Journal, 30*(1), 141–165.

Bahou, L. (2011). Rethinking the challenges and possibilities of student voice and agency. *Educate*, Special Issue, January, 2–14.

Baratz-Snowden, J. (1990). The NBPTS begins its research and development program. *Educational Researcher, 19*(6), 19–24.

Barber, M., & Mourshed, M. (2007). *How the world's best-performing school systems come out on top.* New York, NY: McKinsey & Company.

Barber, M., Whelan, F. & Clark, M. (2010). *Capturing the leadership premium: How the world's top school systems are building leadership capacity for the future.* New York, NY: McKinsey & Company. http://mckinseyonsociety.com/capturing-the-leadership-premium/

Baumrind, D. (1989). Rearing competent children. In W. Damon (Ed.), *Child development today and tomorrow* (pp. 349–378). San Francisco, CA: Jossey-Bass.

Baumrind, D. (1991). The influence of parenting style on adolescent competence and substance abuse. *Journal of Early Adolescence, 11*(1), 56–95.

Beare, H., Caldwell, B., & Millikan, R. (1989). *Creating an excellent school.* London, England: Routledge.

Benn, M. (2012). *School wars—The battle for Britain's education.* London, England: Verso.

Bennett, N., Crawford, M., & Cartwright, M. (Eds.). (2003). *Effective educational leadership.* London, England: Paul Chapman.

Bennett, N., Wise, C., Woods, P., & Harvey, J. (2003). *Distributed leadership.* Nottingham, England: National College for School Leadership.

Bennett, T. (2013). *Teacher proof—Why research in education doesn't always mean what it claims, and what you can do about it.* Milton Park, Oxon: Routledge.

Bergin, M., Dinham, S., Scott, C., & Brock, P. (2002). *The heart of teaching: Report on the 2001 quality teaching awards project.* Sydney: Australian College for Educators, NSW Chapter.

Berliner, D. (1988). *The development of expertise in pedagogy.* Washington, DC: AACTE Publications.

Berliner, D. (2004). Describing the behaviour and documenting the accomplishments of expert teachers. *Bulletin of Science, Technology & Society, 24*(3), 200–212.

Berliner, D., & Biddle, B. (1995). *The manufactured crisis: Myths, fraud, and the attack on America's public schools.* Cambridge, MS: Perseus.

Berliner, D. C., Glass, G. V., & Associates. (2014). *50 myths & lies that threaten America's public schools.* New York, NY: Teachers College Press.

Bhindi, N. (2007). *Why workplaces resist learning.* Paper presented at the Sixth International Conference on Educational Leadership, Australian Centre for Educational Leadership, University of Wollongong, 15 February.

Bligh, M., & Meindl, J. (2005). The cultural ecology of leadership: An analysis of popular leadership books. In D. Messick & R. Kramer, *The psychology of leadership.* Mahwah, NJ: Lawrence Erlbaum.

References

Boston, K. (2013, February 16). School results tell the story too well: The funding model has failed. *The Australian*.

Bowles, T., Hattie, J., Dinham, S., Scull, J., & Clinton, J. (2014). Proposing a comprehensive model for identifying teacher candidates. *Australian Educational Researcher, 41*(4), 365–380.

Boyd, W. L. (1999). Environmental pressures, management imperatives, and competing paradigms in educational administration. *Educational Management & Administration, 27*(3), 283–297.

Brady, L. (1987). *Curriculum development*. (2nd ed.). New York, NY: Prentice Hall.

Brady, L., Aubusson, P., & Dinham, S. (2006). Action learning for school improvement. *Educational Practice and Theory, 28*(2), 27–39.

Brady, L., Aubusson, P., & Dinham, S. (2008). Action learning: Contemporary professional development. *Curriculum and Teaching, 23*(1), 5–19.

Brady, L., Aubusson, P., & Dinham, S. (2008). Teachers as researchers: Action learning for professional development. *Learning and Teaching, 1*(1), 5–16.

Bransford, J., Brown, A., & Cocking, R. (Eds.). (2000). *How people learn: Brain, mind, experience, and school*. Washington, DC: National Academy Press.

Brill, S. (2011). *Class warfare—Inside the fight to fix America's schools*. New York, NY: Simon & Schuster.

Brock, P. (2000). *Standards of professional practice for accomplished teaching in Australian classrooms*. Canberra: Australian College of Educators/Australian Association for Research in Education/Australian Curriculum Studies Association.

Brock, P. (2005). The Garth Boomer memorial lecture. Australian Curriculum Studies Conference, University of the Sunshine Coast, 21 September 2005.

Brown, M., Boyle, B., & Boyle, T. (2002). Professional development and management training needs for heads of department in UK secondary schools. *Journal of Educational Administration, 40*(1), 31–43.

Burke Johnson, R., & Onwuegbuzie, J. (2004). Mixed method research: A research paradigm whose time has come. *Educational Researcher, 33*(7), 14–26.

Busher, H., & Harris, A. (1999). Leadership of school subject areas: Tensions and dimensions of managing in the middle. *School Leadership and Management, 19*, 305–317.

Busher, H., & Harris, A. (2000). *Subject leadership and school improvement*. London, England: Paul Chapman.

Caldwell, B. J., Calnin, G., & Cahill, W. (2002). Mission possible? An international analysis of headteacher/principal training. In M. Tucker & J. Codding, (Eds.), *The principal challenge: Leading and managing schools in an era of accountability* (pp. 111–130). San Francisco, CA: Jossey-Bass.

Campbell, C., & Sherington, G. (2013). *The comprehensive public high school: Historical perspectives*. New York, NY: Palgrave Macmillan.

Chase, G., & Kane, M. (1983). *The principal as instructional leader: How much more time before we act?* Denver: Education Commission of the States.

Childs-Bowen, D., Moller, G., & Scrivner, J. (2000). Principals: Leaders of leaders. *National Association of Secondary School Principals (NASSP) Bulletin, 84*(616), 27–34.

Christie, K., Thompson, B., & Whiteley, G. (2009). *Strong leaders strong achievement: Model policy for producing the leaders to drive student success*. Denver, CO: Education Commission of the States.

Christodoulou, D. (2014). *Seven myths about education*. London, England: Routledge.

Clancy, L. (2004). *Culture and customs of Australia*. Westport, CT: Greenwood Press.

Clarke, S. (2008). Only connect: Australia's recent attempts to forge a national agenda for quality school leadership. In M. Brundrett & M. Crawford (Eds.), *Developing school leaders: An international perspective* (pp. 138–154). London, England: Routledge.

References

Clinton, J., Dinham, S., Lingard, R., Gullickson, A., Savage, G., Calnin, G., Aston, R., & Dabrowski, A. (2015). *InSights: Evaluation of the implementation of the Australian Professional Standards for Teachers—Interim report 2—2014 key findings.* Melbourne, Victoria: AITSL.

Clinton, J., Hattie, J., Dinham, S., Lingard, R., Gullickson, A., Savage, G., Aston, R., & Brookes, I. (2014). *InSights: Evaluation of the implementation of the Australian professional standards for teachers—Interim report.* Melbourne, Victoria: AITSL.

Cochran-Smith, M., & Zeichner, K. (Eds.). (2005). *Studying teacher education.* New Jersey: Lawrence Erlbaum.

Coe, R., Aloisi, C., Higgins, S., & Major, L. (2014). *What makes great teaching? Review of the underpinning research.* Durham University: Centre for Evaluation and Monitoring & The Sutton Trust.

Coleman, J. (1966). *Equality of opportunity study.* Ann Arbor, MI: Inter-University Consortium for Political and Social Research.

Committee for the Review of Teaching and Teacher Education. (2003). *Australia's teachers: Australia's future advancing innovation, science, technology and mathematics main report.* Canberra, Australia: DEST.

Cook-Sather, A. (2009). Introduction learning from the student's perspective: Why it's important, what to expect, and important guidelines. In A. Cook-Sather (Ed.), *Learning from the student's perspective: A sourcebook for effective teaching* (pp. 1–20). Boulder, CO: Paradigm Publishers.

Coulton, C., & Kirkhope, J. (2012). *University of Melbourne education leadership research.* Melbourne, Victoria: Sweeney Research.

Council for the Accreditation of Educator Preparation. (2015). *CAEP evidence guide.* Washington, DC: Council for the Accreditation of Educator Preparation.

Crowther, F., Kaagan, S., Ferguson, M., & Hann, L. (2002). *Developing teacher leaders.* Thousand Oaks, CA: Corwin.

Cuervo, H., Crofts, J., & Wyn, J. (2013). *Generational insights into new labour market landscapes for youth, Research report 42.* Melbourne, Victoria: Youth Research Centre, University of Melbourne.

Curtis, K. (2012, 11 September). OECD education report shows what to do. *The Sydney Morning Herald.* http://www.smh.com.au//breaking-news-national/oecd-education-report-shows-work-to-do-20120911-25qou.html

Curwin, R., & Mendler, A. (1988). Packaged discipline programs: Let the buyer beware. *Educational Leadership,* October, 68–71.

Danielson, C. (2012). Observing classroom practice. *Educational Leadership, 70*(3), 32–37.

Danielson, C. (n.d.). *Making teacher evaluations meaningful.* http://www.youtube.com/watch?v=KzDcYuSsU2E

The Danielson Group. (2013). *The framework for teaching.* https://www.danielsongroup.org/framework/

Darling-Hammond, L. (2006). *Powerful teacher education.* San Francisco, CA: Jossey-Bass.

Darling-Hammond, L. (2012). *Creating a comprehensive system for evaluating and supporting effective teaching.* Stanford, CA: Stanford Centre for Opportunity Policy in Education.

Darling-Hammond, L. (2013). *Getting teacher evaluation right.* New York, NY: Teachers College Press.

Darling-Hammond, L., & Baratz-Snowden, J. (2005). (Eds.). *A good teacher in every classroom.* San Francisco, CA: Jossey-Bass.

Darling-Hammond, L., Hammerness, K., with Grossman, P., Rust, F., & Shulman, L. (2005). The design of teacher education programs. In L. Darling-Hammond, & J. Bransford (Eds.), *Preparing teachers for a changing world: What teachers should learn and be able to do* (pp. 390–441). San Francisco, CA: Jossey-Bass.

Darling-Hammond, L., LaPointe, M., Meyerson, D., & Terry Orr, M. (2007). *Preparing school leaders for a changing world*. Stanford University: Stanford University and The Finance Project.

Day, C., Sammons, P., Hopkins, D., Harris, A., Leithwood, K., Qing, G., Brown, E., Ahtaridou, E., & Kington, A. (2009). *The impact of school leadership on pupil outcomes*. Nottingham, England: University of Nottingham.

De Maeyer, S., Rymenans, R., Van Petegem, P., van den Bergh, H., & Rijlaarsdam, G. (2007). Educational leadership and pupil achievement: The choice of a valid conceptual model to test effects in school effectiveness research. *School effectiveness and school improvement*, *18*(2), 125–145.

Deal, T. E. (1985). The symbolism of effective schools. *Elementary School Journal*, *85*(5), 601–620.

Deal, T., & Peterson, K. (1999). *Shaping school culture*. San Francisco, CA: Jossey-Bass.

Deans for Impact. (2015). *The science of learning*. Austin, TX: Author.

Dekker, S., Lee, N., Howard-Jones, P., & Jolles, J. (2012). Neuromyths in education: Prevalence and predictors of misconceptions among teachers. *Frontiers in Psychology*, *3*(429), 1–8.

Deming, W. E. (1982). *Out of the crisis*. Cambridge, MA: Massachusetts Institute of Technology.

Demos. (2004). *About learning: Report of the Learning Working Group*. London, England: Author.

Dempster, N. (2001). *The professional development of school principals: A fine balance*: Professorial Lecture, 24 May, Griffith University Public Lecture Series.

Department for Education (UK). (2013). *Increasing the number of academies and free schools to create a better and more diverse school system*. https://www.gov.uk/government/policies/increasing-the-number-of-academies-and-free-schools-to-create-a-better-and-more-diverse-school-system

Dinham, S. (1992). Human perspectives on the resignation of teachers from the New South Wales department of school education: Towards a model of teacher persistence. (Doctor of Philosophy thesis). University of New England, Armidale.

Dinham, S. (1993). Teachers under stress. *Australian Educational Researcher*, *20*(3), December, 1–16.

Dinham, S. (1995). Time to focus on teacher satisfaction. *Unicorn*, *21*(3), September, 64–75.

Dinham, S. (1997). Societal expectations, pressures and teaching. *Teaching and Teachers' Work*, *5*(3), 1–8.

Dinham, S. (1997). Teaching and teachers' families. *Australian Educational Researcher*, AARE, August, *24*(2), 59–88.

Dinham, S. (1998). Restructuring: The myths, the realities—and survival. *The Practising Administrator*, *20*(3), 4–5, 51.

Dinham, S. (2002). NSW Quality Teaching Awards: Research, rigour and transparency. *Unicorn*, *28*(1), 5–9.

Dinham, S. (2005). Principal leadership for outstanding educational outcomes. *Journal of Educational Administration*, *43*(4), 338–356.

Dinham, S. (2006). Teaching and teacher education: Some observations, reflections and possible solutions. *ED Ventures*, *2*, 3–20.

Dinham, S. (2006). The merits of merit pay for teachers. *Education Review*, *16*(07), October, 12–13.

Dinham, S. (2007). The secondary head of department and the achievement of exceptional student outcomes. *Journal of Educational Administration*, *45*(1), 62–79.

Dinham, S. (2007). How schools get moving and keep improving: Leadership for teacher learning, student success and school renewal. *Australian Journal of Education*, *51*(3), 263–275.

Dinham, S. (2007). *Leadership for exceptional educational outcomes*. Teneriffe, Qld: Post Pressed.

Dinham, S. (2007). The waves of leadership. *The Australian Educational Leader*, *29*(3), 20–21, 27.

Dinham, S. (2007). The lesson of Jonah. *Education Review*, *17*(8), 5.

References

Dinham, S. (2007). Authoritative leadership, action learning and student accomplishment. In Conference proceedings, *Australian Council for Educational Research, 2007 Research Conference* (pp. 33–39). Melbourne, Victoria: ACER.

Dinham, S. (2008). Counting the numbers in educational change. *The Australian Educational Leader, 30*(1), 56–57.

Dinham, S. (2008). Driving improvement in the quality of Australian education: *Points of leverage*. Australian College of Educators, Victorian Branch Oration, University of Melbourne, 15 August.

Dinham, S. (2008). Feedback on feedback. *Teacher*, May, 20–23.

Dinham, S. (2008). *How to get your school moving and improving: An evidence-based approach*. Melbourne, Victoria: ACER Press.

Dinham, S. (2009). The relationship between distributed leadership and action learning in schools: A case study. In A. Harris (Ed.), *Distributed school leadership: Different perspectives* (pp. 139–154). Dordrecht, Netherlands: Springer Press.

Dinham, S. (2010). The perils of self-esteem boosting. *Leadership in Focus*, Summer, 20, 23–25.

Dinham, S. (2011). Improving the quality of teaching in Australia. *Education Canada, 51*(1), 34–38.

Dinham, S. (2011). *Let's get serious about teacher quality*. Melbourne, Victoria: Melbourne Graduate School of Education. [video] https://www.youtube.com/watch?v=hT49plkJ7Ek

Dinham, S. (2011). *Let's get serious about teacher quality: The need for a new career architecture for Australia's teachers*. Dean's Lecture Series, University of Melbourne, MGSE, 27 September. [lecture notes] http://web.education.unimelb.edu.au/news/lectures/pdf/S Dinham PowerPoint 27.9.11.pdf

Dinham, S. (2011). *Pilot study to test the exposure draft of the national professional standard for principals—Final report*. Melbourne, Victoria: AITSL.

Dinham, S. (2012). The hijacking of the quality teaching movement. *Professional Educator, 11*(7), 8–11.

Dinham, S. (2012). A political education: hijacking the quality teaching movement. *The Conversation*, August. http://theconversation.edu.au/a-political-education-hijacking-the-quality-teaching-movement-9017

Dinham, S. (2013). The quality teaching movement in Australia encounters difficult Terrain: A personal perspective. *Australian Journal of Education, 57*(2), 91–106.

Dinham, S. (2013). Connecting Instructional Leadership with Clinical Teaching Practice. *Australian Journal of Education, 57*(3), 220–231.

Dinham, S. (2013). The quality teaching movement in Australia: Losing our confidence, losing our way and getting back on track. Phillip Hughes Oration, Australian College of Educators, ACT Branch, Canberra, 28 February.

Dinham, S. (2014). Primary schooling in Australia: Pseudo-science plus extras times growing inequality equals decline. In *What counts as quality in education?* (pp. 8–15). Carlton South, Victoria: Australian College of Educators.

Dinham, S. (2015). Regulation or deregulation? Observations on education in Germany and Australia. In *Educators on the edge: Big ideas for change and innovation*, Refereed Conference Proceedings ACE 2015 National Conference. Carlton South, Victoria: Australian College of Educators.

Dinham, S. (2015). The worst of both worlds: How US and UK models are influencing education in Australia. *Educational Policy Analysis Archives, 23*(49), 1–20. http://dx.doi.org/10.14507/epaa.v23.1865

Dinham, S. (2015). *Regulation or deregulation? Observations on education in Germany and Australia*. Keynote address, Australian College of Educators National Conference, Brisbane, 24 September.

Dinham, S. (2015). *Issues and perspectives relevant to the development of an approach to the accreditation of initial teacher education in Australia based on evidence of impact*. Melbourne, Victoria: AITSL.

Dinham, S. (2015). Pseudo-science, inequality and decline. *Journal of Professional Learning*, Semester 1, np. http://cpl.asn.au/journal/semester-1-2015/pseudo-science-inequality-and-decline

Dinham, S., Anderson, M., Caldwell, B., & Weldon, P. (2011). Breakthroughs in school leadership development in Australia. *School Leadership and Management, 31*(2), 139–154.

Dinham, S., Aubusson, P., & Brady, L. (2008). Distributed leadership as a factor in and outcome of teacher action learning. *International Electronic Journal for Leadership in Learning, 12*(4), 1–14. http://iejll.journalhosting.ucalgary.ca/index.php/ijll/article/view/548/210

Dinham, S., Brennan, K., Collier, J., Deece, A., & Mulford, D. (2000). *The secondary head of department: Key link in the quality teaching and learning chain—Quality teaching series, No 2*. Deakin, ACT: Australian College of Education.

Dinham, S., Buckland, C., Callingham, R., & Mays, H. (2008). Factors responsible for the superior performance of male students in Years 3 and 5. Standardised testing at one Australian primary school. *Learning and Teaching, 23*(1), 51–70.

Dinham, S., Cairney, T., Craigie, D., & Wilson, S. (1995). School climate and leadership: research into three secondary schools. *Journal of Educational Administration, 33*(4), August, 36–58.

Dinham, S., Collarbone, P., Evans, M., & Mackay, A. (2013). The development and proposed use of a national standard for principals in Australia. *Educational Management, Administration and Leadership, 41*(4), 466–482.

Dinham, S., & Crowther, F. (2011). (Eds.). Building organisational capacity in school education. *Journal of Educational Administration, 49*(6), 614–738.

Dinham, S., & Crowther, F. (2011). Sustainable school capacity-building—One step back, two steps forward? *Journal of Educational Administration, 49*(6), 1–8.

Dinham, S., Ingvarson, L., & Kleinhenz, E. (2008). *Mapping of the common substance of graduate teacher standards developed and implemented by ATRA members against the MCEETYA framework for standards—Development of graduate teacher standards Australia*. Camberwell, Victoria: ACER.

Dinham, S., Ingvarson, L., & Kleinhenz, E. (2008). Investing in teacher quality: Doing what matters most. In *Teaching talent: The best teachers for Australia's classrooms* (pp. 5–53). Melbourne, Victoria: Business Council of Australia.

Dinham, S., Ingvarson, L., Kleinhenz, E., & Anderson, M. (2009). *The draft National Professional Standards Framework for Teachers and School Leaders*. Melbourne, Victoria: ACER.

Dinham, S., & Rowe, K. (2007). *Teaching and learning in middle schooling. A review of the literature—A report to the New Zealand Ministry of Education*. Melbourne, Victoria: ACER.

Dinham, S., & Rowe, K. (2008). *Teaching and learning in middle schooling: A review of the literature*. Wellington, New Zealand: New Zealand Ministry of Education. http://www.educationcounts.govt.nz/__data/assets/pdf_file/0020/36281/913_TL-MidSchool.pdf

Dinham, S., & Scott, C. (1996). *The Teacher 2000 Project: A study of teacher satisfaction, motivation and health*. Penrith: University of Western Sydney, Nepean.

Dinham, S., & Scott, C. (1997). The advanced skills teacher: An opportunity missed? *Unicorn, 23*(3), 36–49.

Dinham, S., & Scott, C. (1998). A three domain model of teacher and school executive satisfaction. *Journal of Educational Administration, 36*(4), 362–378.

Dinham, S., & Scott, C. (2000). Moving into the third, outer domain of teacher satisfaction. *Journal of Educational Administration, 38*(4), 379–396.

Dinham, S., & Scott, C. (2002). Pressure points: School executive and educational change. *Journal of Educational Enquiry, 3*(2), 35–52.

Dinham, S., & Scott, C. (2003). Awards for teaching excellence: Intentions and realities. *Unicorn Online Refereed Article*, No. 24, 1–25.

Dinham, S., & Scott, C. (2003). Benefits to teachers of the professional learning portfolio: A case study, *Teacher Development, 7*(3), 187–202.

References

Dinham, S., & Scott, C. (2007). Parenting, teaching and leadership styles. *The Australian Educational Leader, 29*(1), 30–32; 45.

Dinham, S., & Scott, C. (2008). Responsive and demanding leadership, *Synergy, 6*(2), 19–21. http://www.slav.schools.net.au/synergy/vol6num2/dinhamscott.pdf

Dinham, S., & Scott, C. (2008). Responsive, demanding leadership. *Management Today*, April, 32–35.

Dinham, S., & Scott, C. (2012). Our Asian schooling infatuation: The problem of PISA envy. *The Conversation*, September. https://theconversation.edu.au/our-asian-schooling-infatuation-the-problem-of-pisa-envy-9435

Donovan, M. (2015). Aboriginal student stories, the missing voice, to guide us towards change. *The Australian Educational Researcher*, July, 1–13.

Donovan, M., Bransford, J., & Pellegrino, J. (1999). (Eds.). *How people learn: Bridging research and practice*. Washington, DC: National Academy Press.

Dowling, A. (2008). Unhelpfully complex and exceedingly opaque: Australia's school funding system. *Australian Journal of Education, 52*(2), 129–150.

Dreyfus, S. (2004). The five-stage model of adult skill acquisition. *Bulletin of Science, Technology & Society, 24*(3), 177–181.

Dreyfus, S., & Dreyfus, H. (1980). *A five-stage model of the mental activities involved in directed skills acquisition*. University of California, Berkeley: Operations Research Center.

Duignan, P., & Bezzina, M. (2006). *Building leadership capacity for shared leadership in schools—Teachers as leaders of educational change*. Keynote address, Australian Centre for Educational Leadership International Conference, University of Wollongong, February.

Duignan, P., & Bhindi, N. (1997). Authenticity in leadership: An emerging perspective. *Journal of Educational Administration, 35*(3), 195–209.

Duignan, P., & Bhindi, N. (1997). Leadership for a new century: Authenticity, intentionality, spirituality, and sensibility. *Educational Management and Administration, 25*(2), 117–132.

Duke, D. (1987). *School leadership and instructional improvement*. New York, NY: Random House.

Duke, D. (2004). *The challenges of educational change*. Boston, MA: Pearson.

Dweck, C. (2000). *Self-theories—Their role in motivation, personality and development*. Philadelphia, PA: Psychology Press.

Elmore, R. (1996). Getting to scale with good educational practice. *Harvard Educational Review, 66*(1), 1–26.

English, F. (2005). Introduction—A metadiscursive perspective on the landscape of educational leadership in the 21st century. In F. English (Ed.), *The Sage handbook of educational leadership* (pp. xi–xii). Thousand Oaks, CA: Sage Publications.

Fayol, H. (1916). *Administration industrielle et générale; prévoyance, organisation, commandement, coordination, contrôle*. Paris, France: H. Dunod et E. Pinat.

Fiedler, F. (1965). Engineer the job to fit the manager. *Harvard Business Review, 43*, 115–122.

Flanagan, N., & Finger, J. (1989). *Management in a minute*. Brisbane, Queensland: Plumb Press.

Flynn, J. R. (1984). The mean IQ of Americans: Massive gains 1932 to 1978. *Psychological Bulletin, 95*, 29–51.

Follett, M. P. (1941). *Dynamic administration: The collected papers of Mary Parker Follett*. H. Metcalf & L. Urwick (Eds.). London, England: Pitman.

Fullan M. (2001). *Leading in a culture of change*. San Francisco, CA: Jossey-Bass.

Fullan, M. (2005). *Leadership and sustainability*. Thousand Oaks, CA: Corwin.

Gibson, J., Ivancevich, J., & Donnelly, J. (1994). *Organizations: Behavior, structure, processes* (8th ed.). Burr Ridge, IL: Irwin.

Gladwell, M. (2008). *Outliers: The story of success*. New York, NY: Little, Brown, and Company.

Glass, G. (2008). *Fertilizers, pills, and magnetic strips: The fate of public education in America*. Charlotte, NC: Information Age Publishing.

Glass, G. V. (1976). Primary, secondary, and meta-analysis of research. *Educational Researcher, 5*, 3–8.

Glasson, T. (2009). *Improving student achievement*. Carlton South, Victoria: Curriculum Corporation.

Goe, L., Bell, C., & Little, O. (2008). *Approaches to evaluating teacher effectiveness: A research synthesis*. Washington, DC: National Comprehensive Center for Teacher Quality.

Goodson, I., & Marsh, C. (1996). *Studying school subjects*. London, England: Falmer Press.

Gronn, P. (2002). Distributed leadership. In K. Leithwood & P. Hallinger (Eds.), *Second international handbook of educational leadership and administration* (pp. 653–696). Dordrecht, Netherlands: Kluwer.

Gronn, P., Ingvarson, L., Jackson, A., Kleinhenz, E., McKenzie, P., et al. (2007). *OECD improving school leadership activity: Australia: Country background report*. Canberra, Australia: DEEWR.

Grossman, P., & Stodolsky, S. (1995). Content as context: The role of school subjects in secondary school teaching. *Educational Researcher, 24*(8), 5–11, 23.

Gunter, H. (2001). *Leaders and leadership in education*. London, England: Paul Chapman.

Hallinger, P. (2005). Instructional leadership and the school principal: A passing fancy that refuses to fade away. *Leadership and Policy in Schools, 4*, 221–239.

Hannay, L. M., & Ross, J. A. (1999). Department heads as middle managers? Questioning the black box. *School Leadership and Management, 19*, 345–358.

Hargreaves, A. (1994). *Changing teachers, changing times*. London, England: Cassell.

Hargreaves, A., & Fink, D. (2004). The seven principles of sustainable leadership. *Educational Leadership, 61*(7), 8–13.

Harris, A. (2004). Teacher leadership and distributed leadership: An exploration of the literature. *Leading and Managing, 10*(2), 1–9.

Harris, A. (2005). Distributed leadership. In B. Davies (Ed.), *The essentials of school leadership*. London, England: Paul Chapman.

Harris, A. (2008). Distributed leadership: According to the evidence. *Journal of Educational Administration, 46*(2), 172–188.

Harris, A. (2009). (Ed.). *Distributed school leadership: Different perspectives*. London, England: Springer Press.

Harris, A. (2009). *Distributed school leadership: Evidence, issues and future directions*. Penrith, NSW: Australian Council for Educational Leaders.

Harris, A., & Spillane, J. (2008). Distributed leadership through the looking glass. *Management in Education, 22*(1), 31–34.

Hatano, G., & Inagaki, K. (1986). Two courses of expertise. In H. A. H. Stevenson & K. Hakuta (Eds.), *Child development and education in Japan* (pp. 262–272). New York, NY: Freeman.

Hattie, J. (2003). *Teachers make a difference: What is the research evidence?* Paper presented to ACER Annual Conference, October.

Hattie, J. (2007). *Developing potentials for learning: Evidence, assessment, and progress*. EARLI Biennial Conference, Budapest, Hungary.

Hattie, J. (2009). *Visible learning: A synthesis of over 800 meta-analyses relating to achievement*. London, England: Routledge.

Hattie, J. (2012). *Visible learning for teachers*. London, England: Routledge.

Hopkins, D. (2013). *Exploding the myths of school reform*. Melbourne, Victoria: ACER Press.

Hopkins, D. (n.d.). *Instructional leadership and school improvement*. Nottingham, England: National College for School Leadership. www3.nccu.edu.tw/~mujinc/teaching/9-101principal/refer8-2(kpool-evidence-hopkins).pdf

References

Hopkins, D., Ainscow, M., & West, M. (1994). *School improvement in an era of change*. London, England: Cassell.

Hopkins, D., Harris, A., & Jackson, D. (1997). Understanding the school's capacity for development. *School Leadership and Management, 17*(3), 401-411.

Hopkins, D., Harris, A., Singleton, C., & Watts, R. (2000). *Creating the conditions for teaching and learning*. London, England: David Fulton Publishers.

Ingvarson, L., Anderson, M., Gronn, P., & Jackson, A. (2006). *Standards for school leadership: A critical review of the literature*. Canberra, Australia: Teaching Australia.

Ingvarson, L., Dinham, S., Kleinhenz, E., & Anderson, M. (2009). *An analysis and review of state and territory standards for competent, accomplished and leading teacher levels and school leaders*. Melbourne, Victoria: ACER.

ISLLC. (1996). *Interstate school leaders licensure consortium: Standards for school leaders*. Washington, DC: Council of Chief State School Officers.

Janis, I. (1972). *Victims of groupthink*. Boston, MA: Houghton Mifflin.

Joyce, B., Wolf, J., & Calhoun, E. (1993). *The self renewing school*. Alexandria, VA: ASCD.

Kilpatrick, S., Barrett, M., & Jones, T. (2003). *Defining Learning Communities*. Paper presented at NZARE/AARE international conference, Auckland, 30 November - 3 December.

Kim, K. H. (2012, July 10). Yes, there is a creativity crisis. *The Creativity Post*. http://www.creativitypost.com/education/yes_there_is_a_creativity_crisis

Kirschner, P., Sweller, J., & Clark, R. (2006). Why minimal guidance during instruction does not work: An analysis of the failure of constructivist, discovery, problem-based, experiential, and inquiry-based teaching. *Educational Psychologist, 41*(2), 75-86.

Koehler, M. (1993). *Department head's survival guide*. Upper Saddle River, NJ: Prentice-Hall.

Kotter, J. (1990). *A force for change: How leadership differs from management*. New York, NY: Free Press.

Kotter, J. (1995). Leading change: Why transformation efforts fail. *Harvard Business Review, 73*(2), March-April, 59-67.

Kotterman, J. (2006). Leadership versus management: What's the difference? *The Journal for Quality and Participation, 29*(2), 13-17.

Labaree, D. F. (2004). *The trouble with ED schools*. New Haven, CT: Yale University Press.

Lambert, L. (1998). *Building leadership capacity in schools*. Alexandria, VA: ASCD.

Lawrence, P., & Lorsch, J. (1967). Differentiation and integration in complex organisation. *Administrative Science Quarterly, 12*(1), 1-47.

Leithwood, K., Day, C., Sammons, P., Harris, A., & Hopkins, D. (2006). *Seven strong claims about successful school leadership*. Nottingham, England: National College for School Leadership.

Leithwood, K., & Duke, D. (1999). A century's quest to understand school leadership. In J. Murphy, & K. Louis (Eds.), *Handbook of research on educational administration*. San Francisco, CA: Jossey-Bass.

Leithwood, K., Jantzi, D., & Steinbach, R. (2002). Leadership practices for accountable schools. In K. Leithwood, & P. Hallinger (Eds.), *Second International Handbook of Educational Leadership and Administration* (pp. 849-879). Dordrecht, Netherlands: Kluwer.

Leithwood, K., & Mascall, B. (2008). Collective leadership effects on student achievement. *Educational Administration Quarterly, 44*(4), 529-561.

Leithwood, K., Patten, S., & Jantzi, D. (2010). Testing a conception of how school leadership influences student learning, *Educational Administration Quarterly, 46*(5), 671-706.

Leithwood, K., Seashore Louis, K., Anderson, S., & Wahlstrom, K. (2004). *Review of research—How leadership influences student learning*. New York, NY: The Wallace Foundation.

Lubienski, C., & Lubienski, S. (2013). *The public school advantage: Why public schools outperform private schools*. Chicago, IL: University of Chicago Press.

Lunzer, E., & Gardner, K. (1984). *Learning from the written word*. London, England: Oliver and Boyd.

MacBeath, J. (2006). Leadership as a subversive activity. *ACEL Monograph Series*, No. 39.

McBrien, J., & Brandt, S. (1997). *The language of learning: A guide to education terms*. Alexandria, VA: ASCD.

McCulla, N., Dinham, S., Brock, P., & Scott, C. (2015). Identifying, validating and recognising the work of accomplished teachers: Reflections on a decade of research and experience within the NSW Minister for Education and Training & Australian College of Educators' Quality Teaching Award. *ACE NSW Refereed Research Monograph*, 1-52.

McCulla, N., Dinham, S., & Scott, C. (2007). Stepping out from the crowd: Some findings from the NSW Quality Teaching Awards on seeking recognition for professional accomplishment. *Unicorn Online Refereed Article*, ORA 51, 3-32.

McCulla, N., Scott, C., & Dinham, S. (2009). Quiet conversations in small circles: The role of voluntary awards and distributive leadership in promoting teaching excellence in universities. *Unicorn Online Refereed Articles*, ORA 57, 3-22.

McGaw, B. (2007). Crisis? The real challenges for Australian education. *Independent Education*, 37(2), 21-23.

McGuinness, D. (1997). *Why our children can't read and what we can do about it*. New York, NY: Simon & Schuster.

McKenzie, P., Weldon, P., Rowley, G., Murphy, M., & McMillan, J. (2014). *Staff in Australia's schools 2013: Main report of the survey*. Melbourne, Victoria: ACER.

McLagen, P. (2002). Success with change. *T + D*, December, 44-45.

McLean Davies, L., Anderson, M., Deans, J., Dinham, S., Griffin, P., Kameniar, B., Page, J., Reid, C., Rickards, F., Tayler, C., & Tyler, D. (2013). Masterly preparation: Clinical practice in a graduate pre-service teacher education program. *Journal of Education for Teaching*, 39(1), 93-106.

McLean Davies, L., Dickson, B., Rickards, F., Dinham, S., Conroy, J., & Davis, R. (2015). Teaching as a clinical profession: translational practices in initial teacher education – an international perspective, *Journal of Education for Teaching*, 41(5), 514-528.

Marshall, K. (2012). Let's cancel the dog-and-pony show. *Phi Delta Kappan*, 94(3), 19-23.

Marzano, R. (2003). *What works in schools—Translating research into action*. Alexandria, VA: ASCD.

Marzano, R. (2010). Developing expert teachers. In R. Marzano (Ed.), *On excellence in teaching*. Bloomington, IN: Solution Tree Press.

Marzano, R. (2012). The two purposes of teacher evaluation. *Educational Leadership*, 70(3), 14-19.

Marzano, R., Pickering, D., & Pollock, J. (2005). *Classroom instruction that works—Research-based strategies for increasing student achievement*. Upper Saddle River, NJ: Pearson.

Marzano, R., Waters, T., & McNulty, B. (2005). *School leadership that works: From research to results*. Alexandria, VA: ASCD.

Maslow, A. H. (1943). A theory of human motivation. *Psychological Review*, 50(4), 370-96.

Masters, G. (2012). Continual improvement through aligned effort. In *School improvement: What does research tell us about effective strategies? 2012 Research Conference* (pp. 3-7). Melbourne: ACER.

Matthews, P. (n.d.). *How do school leaders successfully lead learning?* Nottingham: National College for School Leadership. http://dera.ioe.ac.uk/254/1/download%3Fid%3D23637%26filename%3Dhow-do-school-leaders-successfully-lead-learning.pdf

Mayer, R. (2004). Should there be a three-strikes rule against pure Discovery Learning? *American Psychologist*, 59(1), 14-19.

Mayo, E. (1933). *The human problems of an industrial civilisation*. New York, NY: Macmillan.

Miles, M., & Huberman, M. (1994). *Qualitative Data Analysis*. Thousand Oaks, CA: Sage Publications.

References

Ministerial Council on Education, Employment, Training and Youth Affairs [MCEETYA]. (2008). *Melbourne Declaration on Educational Goals for Young Australians*. Canberra, Australia: Australian Government.

Moore Johnson, S., & Fiarman, S. (2012). The potential of peer review. *Educational Leadership, 70*(3), 20–25.

Mulford, B. (2002). Leadership development: Introduction. In K. Leithwood, & P. Hallinger (Eds.), *Second International Handbook of Educational Leadership and Administration* (Vol. 2, pp. 1025–1030). Dordrecht, Netherlands: Kluwer.

Murphy, J. (2008). The place of leadership in turnaround schools. *Journal of Educational Administration, 46*(1), 74–98.

National Comprehensive Center for Teacher Quality. (2007). *Key issue: Enhancing teacher leadership*. Washington DC: Author.

National Council for Accreditation of Teacher Education. (2010). *Transforming teacher education through clinical practice: a national strategy to prepare effective teachers*. Washington, DC: National Council for Accreditation of Teacher Education.

Neisser, U. (1997). Rising scores on intelligence test. *American Scientist, 85,* 440–447.

Northouse, P. (2007). *Leadership*. (4th ed.). Thousand Oaks, CA: Sage.

NSW Department of Education and Training. (2003). *Quality teaching in NSW public schools: Discussion paper*. Sydney: Professional Support and Curriculum Directorate, NSW DET.

NSW Education. (2014). *Great teaching inspired learning*. http://www.dec.nsw.gov.au/our-services/schools/great-teaching-inspired-learning.

Nuthall, G. (2007). *The hidden lives of learners*. Wellington, New Zealand: NZCER.

OECD. (2005). *Teachers matter: Attracting, developing and retaining effective teachers*. Paris, France: OECD.

OECD. (2009). *Creating effective teaching and learning environments: First results from TALIS*. Paris, France: OECD Publishing.

OECD. (2009). *Evaluating and rewarding the quality of teachers—International practices*. Paris, France: OECD Publishing.

OECD. (2009). *What makes a school successful? Resources, policies and practices*. Paris, France: OECD Publishing.

OECD. (2010). *Education at a glance 2010: OECD Indicators*. Paris, France: OECD Publishing.

OECD. (2010). *Making reform happen*. Paris, France: OECD Publishing.

OECD. (2010). *Strong performers and successful reformers—Lessons from PISA for the United States*. Paris, France: OECD Publishing.

OECD. (2011). School autonomy and accountability: Are they related to student performance? *PISA in Focus, 9,* 1–4. http://www.oecd.org/pisa/pisaproducts/pisainfocus/48910490.pdf

OECD. (2011). *Building a high-quality teaching profession: Lessons from around the world*. International Summit on the Teaching Profession. Paris, France: OECD Publishing.

OECD. (2011). *Education at a glance: OECD indicators*. Paris, France: OECD Publishing.

OECD. (2012). *Preparing teachers and developing school leaders for the 21st century*. Paris, France: OECD Publishing.

OECD. (2012). *Connected minds: Technology and today's learners*. Paris, France: OECD Publishing.

OECD. (2013). *Innovative learning environments*. Paris, France: OECD Publishing.

OECD. (2013). *Leadership for 21st century learning*. Paris, France: OECD Publishing.

OECD. (2013). *Measuring improvements in learning outcomes*. Paris, France: OECD Publishing.

OECD. (2013). *Teachers for the 21st century: Using evaluation to improve teaching*. Paris, France: OECD Publishing.

OECD. (2014). *Measuring innovation in education: A new perspective*. Paris, France: OECD Publishing.

OECD. (2014). *Education at a glance 2014: OECD indicators*. Paris, France: OECD Publishing.

OECD. (2014). *New insights from TALIS 2013: Teaching and learning in primary and upper secondary education*. Paris, France: OECD Publishing.

OECD. (2015). *Schools for 21st-century learners: Strong leaders, confident teachers, innovative approaches*. Paris, France: OECD Publishing.

OECD. (2015). *Students, computers and learning: Making the connection*. Paris, France: OECD Publishing.

OECD. (n.d.). *Programme for International Student Assessment (PISA)*. http://www.oecd.org/pisa/aboutpisa/

Opdenakker, M-C., & Van Damme, J. (2007). Do school context, student composition and school leadership affect school practice and outcomes in secondary education? *British Educational Research Journal, 33*(2), 179–206.

Pashler, H., McDaniel, M., Rohrer, D., & Bjork, R. (2008). Learning styles—concepts and evidence. *Psychological Science in the Public Interest, 9*(3), 105–119.

Paul, A. (2004). *The cult of personality: How personality tests are leading us to miseducate our children, mismanage our companies, and misunderstand ourselves*. New York, NY: Free Press.

PDK. (2012). A nation divided: Results of the 44th annual PDK/Gallup poll of the public's attitudes towards the public schools. *Phi Delta Kappan, 94*(1), [special edition].

Pegg, J., McPhan, G., Mowbray, B., & Lynch, T. (2010). *Validation of the Australian professional standards for teachers: Executive summary*. Melbourne, Victoria: AITSL.

Pennington, G. (2003). *Guidelines for promoting and facilitating change*. York, England: LTSN Generic Centre.

Phelan, P., Locke Davidson, A., & Cao, H. (1992). Speaking up: Students' perspectives on school. *Phi Delta Kappan*, May, 695–704.

Preiss, B., & Butt, C. (2013, January 18). Teacher entry ranking tumbles. *The Age*. http://www.theage.com.au/data-point/teacher-entry-ranking-tumbles-20130117-2cwb5.html

Productivity Commission. (2012). *Schools workforce, research report*. Canberra, Australia: Australian Government.

QSR. (2002). *NUD*IST 6*. Melbourne, Victoria: QSR International.

Ravitch, D. (2010). *The death and life of the great American school system*. New York, NY: Basic Books.

Ravitch, D. (2012). Yong Zhou on PISA, *Diane Ravitch's blog*, 11 August. http://dianeravitch.net/2012/08/11/yong-zhao-on-pisa/

Ravitch, D. (2014). *Reign of error: The hoax of the privatization movement and the danger to America's public schools*. New York, NY: Knopf.

Reeves, D. (2010). *Transforming professional development into student results*. Alexandria, VA: ASCD.

Reynolds. D., Teddlie, C., Creemers, B., Scheerens, J., & Townsend, T. (2000). An introduction to school effectiveness research. In C. Teddlie, & Reynolds, D. (Eds.), *The international handbook of school effectiveness research* (pp. 3–15). London, England: Falmer Press.

Richardson, J. (2005). Instruments for obtaining student feedback: A review of the literature. *Assessment & Evaluation in Higher Education, 30*(4), 387–415.

Robinson, V., Hohepa, M., & Lloyd, C. (2009). *School leadership and student outcomes: Identifying what works and why*. Wellington, New Zealand: New Zealand Ministry of Education.

Robinson, V., Lloyd, C., & Rowe, K. (2008). The impact of leadership on student outcomes: An analysis of the differential effects of leadership types. *Educational Administration Quarterly, 44*, 635–674.

Robinson, V., & Timperley, H. (2007). The leadership of the improvement of teaching and learning: Lessons from initiatives with positive outcomes for students. *Australian Journal of Education, 51*, 247–262.

References

Rowe, K. (2003). *The importance of teacher quality as a key determinant of students' experiences and outcomes of schooling*. Discussion paper prepared for the Interim Committee of the NSW Institute of Teachers. Sydney: NSWIT.

Rudduck, J. (2007). Student voice, student engagement, and school reform. In D. Thiessen & A. Cook-Sather (Eds.), *International handbook of student experience in elementary and secondary school* (pp. 587–610). Dordrecht, Netherlands: Springer.

Rudduck, J. & Flutter, J. (2004). *How to improve your school: Giving pupils a voice*. London, England: Continuum.

Sahlberg, P. (2014). *Facts, true facts and research in improving education system*. Paper presented at the British Education Research Association, London, 21 May.

Sammons, P., Thomas, S., & Mortimore, P. (1997). *Forging links: Effective schools and effective departments*. London: Paul Chapman.

Sawyer, W., Ayres, P., & Dinham, S. (2001). What does an effective Year 12 English teacher look like? *English in Australia*, *129*(30), 51–63.

Schein, E. H. (1992). *Organizational culture and leadership*. (2nd ed.). San Francisco, CA: Jossey-Bass.

Schlechty, P. (2005). *Creating great schools: six critical systems at the heart of educational innovation*. San Francisco, CA: Jossey-Bass.

Schleicher, A. (2011). Teacher development, support: Employment conditions and careers. In OECD, *Building a high-quality teaching profession: lessons from around the world*. Paris, France: OECD Publishing.

Schleicher, A. (2012). (Ed.). *Preparing teachers and developing school leaders for the 21st century: Lessons from around the world*. International Summit on the Teaching Profession. Paris, France: OECD.

Scott, C. (2008). No gift for the talented: A lousy label for any child. *Professional Educator*, *7*(1), 4–5.

Scott, C. (2009). How the ghosts of the nineteenth century still haunt education. *Policy Futures in Education*, *7*(1), 75–87.

Scott, C. (2010). The enduring appeal of 'learning styles'. *Australian Journal of Education*, *54*(1), 5–17.

Scott, C. (2015). *Learn to teach, Teach to learn*. Port Melbourne, Victoria: Cambridge University Press.

Scott, C., Cox, S., & Dinham, S. (1999). The occupational motivation, satisfaction and health of English school teachers. *Educational Psychology*, *19*(3), 287–308.

Scott, C., & Dinham, S. (2002). The beatings will continue until quality improves: Carrots and sticks in the search for educational improvement. *Teacher Development*, *6*(1), 15–31.

Scott, C., & Dinham, S. (2003). The development of scales to measure teacher and school executive occupational satisfaction. *Journal of Educational Administration*, *41*(1), 74–86.

Scott, C., & Dinham, S. (2005). Parenting, teaching and self-esteem. *The Australian Educational Leader*, *27*(1), 28–30.

Scott, C., & Dinham, S. (2008). Born not made: The nativist myth and teachers' thinking. *Teacher Development*, *12*(2), 115–124.

Scott, C., & Dinham, S. (2013). A 'battered' profession. *Sheilas*, 14 February. http://sheilas.org.au/2013/02/a-battered-profession/

Scott, C., Kleinhenz, E., Weldon, P., Reid, K., & Dinham, S. (2010). *Master of Teaching MGSE: Evaluation report*. Melbourne, Victoria: ACER.

Scott, C., McCulla, N., & Dinham, S. 2007. *The ecology of quality teaching*. Paper presented at the British Educational Research Association Annual Conference, Institute of Education, University of London, September.

Scott, C., Stone, B., & Dinham, S. (2001). 'I love teaching but ...': International patterns of teacher discontent. *Education Policy Analysis Archives*, *9*(28), 1–7.

Senge, P. M. (1990). *The fifth discipline.* Sydney, New South Wales: Random House.

Shulman, L. (1986). Those who understand: Knowledge growth in teaching. *Educational Researcher, 15*(2), 4–14.

Simon, H., & Chase, W. (1973). Skill in chess. *American Scientist, 61*(4), 394–403.

Siskin, L. S., & Little, J. W. (1995). (Eds.). *The subjects in question: The department organization of the high school.* New York, NY: Teachers College Press.

Smith, I. (2005). Achieving readiness for organisational change. *Library Management, 26*(6/7), 408–412.

Spillane, J. (2006). *Distributed leadership.* San Francisco, CA: Jossey-Bass.

Spillane, J., Halverson, R., & Diamond, J. (2001). Investigating school leadership practice: A distributed perspective. *Educational Researcher, 30*(3), 23–28.

Stahl, S. (1999). Different strokes for different folks? A critique of learning styles. *American Educator,* Fall, 1–5.

Staw, B. (1976). Knee-deep in the big muddy: A study of escalating commitment to a chosen course of action. *Organizational behavior and human performance, 16*(1), 27-44.

Stewart, D., Sun, J., Patterson, C., Lemerle, K., & Hardie, M. (2004). Promoting and building resilience in primary school communities: Evidence from a comprehensive 'health promoting school' approach. *International Journal of Mental Health Promotion, 6*(3), 26–33.

Stodolsky, S., & Grossman, P. (1995). The impact of subject matter on curricular activity: An analysis of five academic subjects. *American Educational Research Journal, 32,* 227–249.

Stodolsky, S., & Grossman, P. (2000). Changing students, changing teachers. *Teachers College Record, 102*(1), 125–172.

Strauss, A., & Corbin, J. (1990). *Basics of qualitative research—Grounded theory procedures and techniques.* Newbury Park, CA: Sage.

Taylor, F. (1911). *The principles of scientific management.* New York, NY: Harper and Brothers.

Teacher Education Ministerial Advisory Group. (2014). *Action now: Classroom ready teachers.* Canberra, Australia: Department of Education.

Thomson, S., De Bortoli, L., & Buckley, S. (2013). *PISA in brief: Highlights from the full Australian report: PISA 2012: How Australia Measures Up.* Melbourne, Victoria: ACER.

Thomson, S., Hillman, K., Wernert, N., Schmid, M., Buckley, S., & Munene, A. (2012). *Highlights from TIMSS & PIRLS 2011 from Australia's perspective.* Melbourne, Victoria: ACER.

Timperley, H., Wilson, A., Barrar, H., & Fung, I. (2007). *Teacher professional learning and development: Best evidence synthesis iteration.* Wellington, New Zealand: Ministry of Education. http://www.oecd.org/edu/school/48727127.pdf

Tomazin, F. (2013, 24 February). Victoria throws education reforms into disarray. *The Age.*

Toole, J. C., & Louis, K. S. (2002). The role of professional learning communities in international education. In K. Leithwood & P. Hallinger (Eds.), *Second international handbook of educational leadership and administration.* Dordrecht, Netherlands: Kluwer.

Tovey, J. (2013, February 19). High marks 'not the key' to better teachers, *The Age.*

US Department of Education. (2001). *No Child Left Behind Elementary and Secondary Education Act* (ESEA). http://www2.ed.gov/nclb/landing.jhtml

US Department of Education. (2010). *What's possible: Turning around America's lowest-achieving schools.* http://www.ed.gov/blog/2010/03/whats-possible-turning-around-americas-lowest-achieving-schools/

US Department of Education. (2011). *Our future, teachers: The Obama administration's plan for teacher education reform and improvement.* Washington, DC: US Department of Education.

Victoria Department of Education and Early Childhood Development. (2012). *New directions for school leadership and teaching profession.* Melbourne, Victoria: DEECD.

References

Voulalas, Z. D. & Sharpe, F. (2005). Creating schools as learning communities: Obstacles and processes. *Journal of Educational Administration, 43*(2), 187–208.

Wahlstrom, K. (2008). Leadership and learning: What these articles tell us. *Educational Administration Quarterly, 44*(4), 593–597.

Wahlstrom, K., & Louis, K. (2008). How teachers experience principal leadership: The roles of professional community, trust, efficacy, and shared responsibility. *Educational Administration Quarterly, 44*(4), 458–495.

Wallace Foundation. (2008). *Becoming a leader: Preparing school principals for today's schools*. New York, NY: The Wallace Foundation.

Wallace Foundation. (2011). *The school principal as leader: Guiding schools to better teaching and learning*. New York, NY: The Wallace Foundation. http://www.wallacefoundation.org/knowledge-center/school-leadership/effective-principal-leadership/Documents/The-School-Principal-as-Leader-Guiding-Schools-to-Better-Teaching-and-Learning.pdf

Watson, K., & Steele, F. (2006). Building a teacher education community: Recognising the ecological reality of sustainable collaboration. *Asia-Pacific Forum on Science Learning and Teaching, 7*(1), n.p.

Weber, M. (1905). *The Protestant ethic and the spirit of capitalism*. In German *Die protestantische Ethik und der Geist des Kapitalismus*. n.p.

Weber, M. (1930). *The Protestant ethic and the spirit of capitalism*. (first translated to English by Talcott Parsons). London, England: Allen & Unwin.

Weick, K. (1976). Educational organizations as loosely coupled systems. *The Administrative Science Quarterly, 21*, 1–19.

Whitaker, T. (2002). *Dealing with difficult teachers*. Larchmont, NY: Eye on Education.

Whitaker, T., & Fiore, D. (2001). *Dealing with difficult parents and with parents in difficult situations*. Larchmont, NY: Eye on Education.

Wiener, R., & Jacobs, A. (2011). *Designing and implementing teacher performance management systems: Pitfalls and possibilities*. Washington DC: The Aspen Institute—Education and Society Program. http://www.newsroom.aitsl.edu.au/sites/www.newsroom.aitsl.edu.au/files/field/pdf/designing_and_implementing_teacher_performance_management_systems_-_pitfalls_and_possibilities_-_the_aspen_institute.pdf

Wilkinson, R., & Pickett, K. (2009). *The spirit level: Why more equal societies almost always do better*. London, England: Allen Lane.

Willingham, D. (2009). *Why students don't like school*. San Francisco, CA: Jossey-Bass.

Wilson, B. (2005). *Unlocking potential*. Paper presented at the 2005 Australian and New Zealand School of Government (ANZSOG) Conference, University of Sydney, 29 September.

Wright, S., Horn, S., & Sanders, W. (1997). Teacher and classroom context effects on student achievement: Implications for teacher evaluation. *Journal of Personnel Evaluation in Education, 11*, 57–67.

Wyn, J. (2009). *Touching the future: Building skills for life and work*. Melbourne, Victoria: ACER.

York-Barr, J., & Duke, K. (2004). What do we know about teacher leadership? Findings from two decades of scholarship. *Review of Educational Research, 74*(3), 255–316.

Zeichner, K., & Tabachnick, B. (1981). Are the effects of university teacher education 'washed out' by school experience? *Journal of Teacher Education, 32*(3), 7–11.

Zhao, Y. (2010). A true wake-up call for Arne Duncan: The real reason behind Chinese students, top PISA performance, *Yong Zhao*, 10 December. (n.p.). http://zhaolearning.com/2010/12/10/a-true-wake-up-call-for-arne-duncan-the-real-reason-behind-chinese-students-top-pisa-performance/

Zmuda, A., Kuklis, R., & Kline, E. (2004). *Transforming schools: Creating a culture of continuous improvement*. Alexandria, VA: ASCD.

Index

Aboriginal and Torres Strait Islander students 127
   see also Indigenous students
accountability 144, 211
accreditation 75–6, 228
action, bias towards 161–3
action learning 147, 202–12
adaptive expertise 90–1
advanced beginner stage 83
AESOP study 204-5
   data analysis 153, 156–8
   findings 173–4, 186–94
   junior secondary education focus 154–5
   perception as 'review' 157
   post-study publications 158
   powerful connections 153
   site teams 157–8
alienation 154
appraisals 88
assessment 107
   assessment (teaching) domains 291–2
   discussing/comparing 37
   formative and summative 20
   of students 107
   using rubrics 36
   valid and reliable criteria 40
auditing 40
Australian Council for Educational Research (ACER)
   MGSE M Teach evaluation 121
   standards mapping/consolidation 306–10
Australian Government Quality Teaching Program (AGQTP) 68
   evaluation, *case study* 205–7
Australian Institute of Teaching and School Leadership (AITSL) 68, 298
   leader preparation recommendations 300–1
Australian Professional Standards for Teachers (APST) 89
Australian Teacher Performance and Development Framework 293
Australian Tertiary Admission Rank (ATAR) 75, 96
   'spending all one's ATAR' 74
authenticity 126
authoritarian leadership 259–60
authoritarian parenting 254
authoritative leaders/leadership 253–66
authoritative parenting 254–5
autonomy 275–7
awareness (mental function) 84

baby boomers 5
balkanisation 237, 259
behaviour
   groupthink behaviours 235–6
   instructional behaviours 283
   professional behaviours 95
   rule or 'maxim'-governed behaviour 84
beliefs 95
Best Evidence Synthesis *case study* 148–53
bias, towards innovation and action 161–3
blame 171
brain exercise 29

categorising 11–12, 31
change 26, 159–61, 166
   forces for 233–4
   group dynamics 234–7
   nature of 233
   overcoming resistance to 237–9
   radical and incremental 238–9
   reasons for going wrong 241–2
   see also educational change
change management 247
classroom management 95
classrooms 125, 128
   climate of 95, 105
   interactions 85–6
   a quality teacher in every 71
   routines in 90
client centrality 116
clinical practice 83, 114–21

Index

Clinical Praxis Examination initiative 119
coeducation 4–17
coercive power 136–7
'cognitive principles' 15–16
Coleman Report 3–4
collaboration 71, 126, 140, 157–8, 171–2, 173
common purpose 171–2
Commonwealth Supported Places (CSP), 'uncapping' 73–4
communication, open and respectful 128
communities 116, 128–30
    learning *see* learning communities
compassion 163
competence/competencies 83, 305–6
comprehensive education 4–17
conflict 250
conflict management 247
conflict resolution 152
constructivism, discovery learning and 28–9
content knowledge 26–7, 94
continual improvement framework 244–5, 273–4
culture of evidence 129
culture of success 165–9
curriculum
    21st century curriculum 29
    'content free' curriculum 26–7
    early curricula 26
    planning, coordinating, and evaluating 150–1
    curriculum documents 31

DARTS (Direct Activities Related to Texts) 106
data analysis/gathering, tools 153
decision (mental function) 84
demandingness 253–4, 258, 264–5
didactic instruction 37, 71
difference 152
difficult people, dealing with 285–8
'digital natives' 29
direct instruction 28, 37, 71
disadvantage 75, 127
discipline 102, 152
discovery learning 28–9
discussion 107, 125
disengagement 154
distributed leadership 320–1
    case study 208–10
    distribution patterns 154
    educational leadership, changed conception of 297
    meanings 181
    nature and effects 181–3
education
    for clinical practice 116
    comprehensive 4–17
    educational administration 139, 140
    effects of disadvantage on 127
    leadership in 138–40
    1960s to current 263–4
    professional learning in 200–13, 217–28
    supposed problems; ineffective solutions 69–71
educational change 232–50, 253–66, 269–78, 281–93
    broad groups 239–40
    forces, contexts and features 232–50
    numbers counting 239–41
    role of leaders in 232–50
educational leaders
    influences on teaching and learning 144
    relationships and 262–3
educational leadership 320
    broad conception 297
    complexity 148
    importance and impact 134–41, 144–76, 181–95
    thinking and approaches changes 134–41
    typology application 257–62
    underestimating and re-estimating 174–6
educational leadership preparation *see* leadership preparation programs
effect size 20–3, 27, 124–5, 144
    of direct instruction 28
    for labelling and categorising 33
    of leadership dimensions 149–52
    for SES 24
    of spaced practice 37
    student achievement effects 8
    student learning influences 9
    of teacher-to-student feedback 38
Effective Leadership and Pupil Outcomes Project, The 153–4
8–15–5 principle 286
emergent leadership 136
emotional intelligence 29
empathy 163
engagement 126, 159–61
    see also disengagement
entity intelligence theory 32, 33–4
environment 15, 152, 291

equity achievement gap 70
essay writing 106
evaluation
    MGSE M Teach evaluation (ACER) 121
    of principle preparation programs 301
    of teachers *see* teacher assessment and evaluation
    of teaching and curriculum 150–1
evidence-based approach/techniques 115, 128, 301
    research evidence use 116, 212–13
    teaching considerations 20–42
Exceptional Schooling Outcomes Project, An 154–74
    AESOP data analysis 156–8
    background 154–5
    case study site selection 155–6
expectations 31, 149–50, 165–9
expert power 136–7
expert teachers 85–90
    from novice to 86, 89
    the 'sage on the stage' 27
expertise 84
    experts – 'naturals' 84–5
    international and national emphasis 66–78
    routine, importance of 89–90
    routine and adaptive 90–1
    skills acquisition 83–4
    teacher 83–91
    time required to reach 89
    see also gifted and talented students
external awareness 159–61

face time 21
family background 64, 202
feedback 38–42, 86, 88, 124
    approaches 40
    negative 40–1
    related to parental feedback 41
    sought by teachers 129, 165
    structured approach 40–2
    students' questions regarding 39–40
    using rubrics 36–7
five-stage skills acquisition model 83–4
'Flynn Effect' 12, 24
fragmentation 237

gifted and talented students 4, 34
goals 48–9, 149–50, 165
group work 107
groupthink 234–7, 259

harmful practice 11–12, 32–3
'Head of Department' (HoD) 184–95
home atmosphere 7–8
How People Learn publications 14–17, 32, 91

inclusion 126
independent student activity 107
Indigenous students 127
    PISA results and 52–3
    see also Aboriginal and Torres Strait Islander students
initial teacher education (ITE) 66
    Action Now: Classroom Ready Teachers 114
    development and support 67
    early teaching experiences (graduates) 117
    engagement in reform 67
    evaluation and compensation 67
    ongoing concerns 114–21
    recruitment and training 66
    teacher oversupply in 73
innovation 161–3, 275
in-school professional development 103
instruction 291
    quality of 94–5
instructional leadership 14, 321–2
    dimensions 145
    emergence, decline, re-emergence 144–8
    emphasis 143
    'instruction' connotations 145
    Master of Instructional Leadership *case study* 318–35
    versus school restructuring and transformational leadership 145–6
intelligence 33–4

judgement (clinical) 116
    MGSE approach – circular process 119–20
junior secondary education 154
    student outcomes and leadership 158–73

knowledge domains 26–7, 116

labels/labelling 31
    dangers and harm 11–12
leaders
    authoritative 253–66
    'contagious' positive attitudes 161–2, 172
    goals establishment and expectations 149–50
    influences 154

Index

planning, coordinating, and evaluating teaching/curriculum 150-1
repertoire 153
roles 245, 248-9
strategic resourcing 150
supportive environments establishment 152
teacher learning and development, promoting and participating in 151
working with evidence 299
leadership 13-14, 22-3
  'action lessons' 302
  assigned *versus* emergent 135-7
  case studies 148-74
  conceptualising 138-40
  contribution to student outcomes 158-73
  defining 134-5, 175
  distributive influence 154
  educational 134-41, 144-76, 181-95
  effective strategies 281-93
  five dimensions – Best Evidence Synthesis 149-52
  framework 148-54
  of learning communities 211
  versus management 137-8
  middle level 184-6
  professional standards 306-16
  prototypes 258
  roles 219-20, 269-78, 298
  school 148-53
  talent identification 300
  targeted resource use 150
  teacher 183-4
  teachers' views on 281-2
  team 282-5
  thinking and approaches changes 134-41
  trait approaches to 135
  see also Master of Instructional Leadership (MIL) *case study*
leadership preparation programs 147
  approaches 300-2
  'doughnut' shortcoming 299
  evidence-based techniques 301
  perceived weaknesses 299
learners
  individual learner; individual person 20-2
  labelling and categorising 11-12, 31
learning
  capabilities, career stage and context matching 300
  clear learning intentions 36

'core business' 172-3
discovery learning 28-9
educational leaders' influences 144
evidence base 23-7
goals for 149-50
guiding through interactions 85-6
harm can be done 32-3
How People Learn publications 14-17, 32, 91
learning community focus 210
major developments 319-20
monitoring 86
no evidence base 28-37
professional learning in education 200-13, 217-28
representations of 85
student perspectives on 35, 125-31
styles 29-31
teacher learning 169-71
learning blogs 200
learning communities 125, 202-4
  case studies in practice 204-10
  collective beliefs and support 211
  development and self-sustainability 210-12
  dynamics 211-12
  research evidence 212-13
learning difficulties 86
legitimate power 136-7
lessons 87, 98, 105, 302
listening 128-30, 165
literacy 50-2
'lose-lose' strategies 247-8

malleable intelligence theory 33-4
management *versus* leadership 137-8
Master of Instructional Leadership (MIL)
  case study 318-35
  core units 324
  course framework 323-4
  impact and implications (first cohort) evaluation 325-35
Master of Teaching (M Teach) 117-21
mathematical literacy
  literacy variations 51-2
  PISA results 50-1
measured 'IQ' 3, 12
Melbourne Declaration 47-9
Melbourne Graduate School of Education (MGSE) 117-21
meta-analysis 6-8, 321-2
middle leaders 184-6

Index

middle school movement 29, 154
'Mozart effect' 29
multiple intelligences (MI) (Gardner) 29, 31
Myers-Briggs 31

National Assessment Program—Literacy and Numeracy (NAPLAN) tests 25, 68, 146, 227
National (Australian) Professional Standard for Principals 305–12
    pilot study findings 312–16
    piloting exposure draft 310–12
networking 103
'neuro-linguistic programming' 29
neuromyths 32
note-making 106
novice stage 83
    from novice to expert 86, 89
    rule or 'maxim'-governed behaviour 84
NSW Department of Education 96–7
NSW Higher School Certificate (HSC) 96
    focus 5, 105
    teaching success 99–108
NSW Quality Teaching Awards, *case study* 208–10

observation 98, 107–8
occupational satisfaction 281
one-to-one conferences 37
open questions 107
order 152
    see also routine
organisational climate and culture 243–6
    iceberg metaphor 244
orientation (of teachers) 101–2
    out-of-school professional development 103–4

parenting styles 253–7
pedagogy 87–8, 139, 206
    'clinical' term 116
    pedagogical content knowledge 94
    pedagogically purposed resources 150
Peer Assistance and Review (PAR) programs 289–90
peer effects 7
people
    change and 234
    dealing with difficult people 285–8
    giving people 'space' 170–1
    learning methods 14–17
    students as both learners and people focus 20–2, 172–3
performance
    appraisals 88
    policy–performance relationship 277
    school performance, investigations 5–6
    permissive leadership 260–1
permissive parenting 254
personal development (PD) 218
personality tests 31
planning 71, 104, 150–1, 220–2, 291, 300
power 126, 136–7
    personal *versus* positional 135–7
    power bases 136–7
    'powerful connections' prominence in AESOP 153
praise 34
principal leadership 129, 159–73
principals 7
    achievement facilitation 158
    personal qualities and relationships 154, 163–5
    Preparing Future Leaders: Effective Preparation for Aspiring School Principals 298
    principal preparation approach 300–1
    roles 297–8
    student focus 172–3
    student support, common purpose and collaboration 171–2
    teacher learning, responsibility and trust 169–71
    vision, expectations and culture of success 165–9
    see also leadership preparation programs
problem solving 211
problem talk 153
professional learning 22
    in education 200–13
    most effective forms 200–13
    planning importance 220–2
    professional standards, role in 223–5
    traditional/emerging approaches 200–2
professional learning and development 217–28
    bridging the gap 217–18
    in-school 103
    out-of-school 103–4
    plan characteristics 222
    promoting and participating in 151, 217–20
    teachers 102–4

professional standards 228
    APST 89
    attention needed 76
    basis for principal preparation approach 300, 302–3
    benefits for leaders 302–3, 306–16
    National (Australian) Professional Standard for Principals 305–12
    new teacher career salary structure 224–5
    roles 217–28
    standards of practice 116
proficiency 84
Programme for International Student Assessment (PISA) 25, 55, 146
    Australian performance 50–4, 58–9
    features 50
    Finnish and Asian performances 54, 65
    PISA envy... 54
Progress in International Reading Literacy Study (PIRLS) 54–8, 146
    Australian performance 58–9
    qualitative data 155–6
    quality teaching 23, 94–111, 139
    Australian movement, view 67–78
    case study 96–9
    defined 94–6
    entry standards 73–4
    international and national emphasis 66–78
    reports and findings 66–7

Quality Teaching Awards (QTA) 110–11
quantitative data 156
questioning 106–7

rational bureaucracy 138
reading literacy 51, 52
recognition and recollection (mental functions) 84
relationships 163–5, 262–3, 277
    teachers–students relationships 102, 125
research
    'missing voice' of student 126
    quality emphasis and value 66–78
    quality teachers/teaching 94–111
    'representative' quality 128
    on school effectiveness 5–6
    student achievement 3–17, 47–61
    student engagement in 126
    teacher expertise 83–91
    teacher preparation 114–22

on teaching for learning 125–31
teaching – what works? 20–42
see also SAR
research methodology (MIL)
    data analysis 327
    data collection 325
    findings and discussion 327–8
    focus group 327
    qualitative data analysis, discussion 329–34
    research sample 325
    survey questionnaires 325–6
resources 104, 161–2
    pedagogically purposed strategic resourcing 150
respect 86, 102, 128, 163
    for difference 152
responsibility 169–71
responsiveness 253–4, 258, 264–5
reward power 136–7
risk-taking 162, 172
routine 89–90, 152
    see also order
routine expertise 90–1
rubrics 36, 292

SAR (students as researchers), activities 126–7
school climate 129
    adversarial 129
school improvement
    authoritative leaders 253–66
    educational change 232–50
    effective processes and strategies 271–5, 281–93
    evidence-based approach 128
    'missing voice' of student 126
school leadership 148–53
    major developments 319–20
schools 7–8
    autonomy issue 275–7
    background 99
    effectiveness 5–6, 202–4
    facilities 167–8
    'failing' schools *see* turnaround school phenomenon
    funding 76–7
    key questions to ask 49
    matriculation schools 4
    policies and programs 162, 277
    school restructuring 145–6

schooling, student perspectives on 35, 125–31
  student achievement and 3–4
  'taking the pulse' 128
  'talking up' 168–9
  toxic schools 245–6
scientific literacy 51, 52
secondary head of department 186–94
self-criticism 36
self-esteem 34–5, 255
self-report grades 35–7
senior secondary teaching
  case study 204
  success factors 99–108
sensitivity 130, 153, 255
social constructivism 28–9
social media 200
socio-economic status (SES) 3, 53, 64, 97, 156, 173, 252
  effects of 24–5
spaced practice (learning strategy) 37–8
stakeholders 160
standards-based career structure 224–5
  key issues 226–8
stereotyping 4, 25, 31
stigmatising 25
student achievement
  achievement gaps 154
  broad conception 47–9
  fundamentals 20–3
  high- and low-achieving students 130–1
  influences on 6–8, 144
  in-school influence on 7–8
  instructional leadership and 321–3
  intelligence and 33–4
  international measures 50–8
  international patterns 47–61
  recognition of 168
  schools, making a difference to 3–4
  teacher leadership and 320–1
  value-adding measures 155
student learning *see* learning
student outcomes
  expert teacher influences 86
  impact of leadership 144–76
  leadership contribution 158–73
  school leadership and 148–53
  school restructuring as weak driver for 145–6
student perspectives
  consideration of 130
  differing perceptions of caring 130–1

feedback provision, quality of 129
on schooling, teaching, learning 35, 125–31
student support 171–2
student surveys 128–29
  acting upon 129
  bi-modal responses 128
student voice
  conflation with other notions 125
  exclusion concerns 127
  key issues 126
students 7–8
  benefits of listening to 125–27
  central focus as learners and people 20–2, 152, 172–3
  gifted and talented 4, 34
  Indigenous *see* Indigenous students
  teachers' relationships with 102
subject departments (faculties) 97–8, 100–1, 155
  group influences (on success) 100–1
successful teaching 139
succession planning 300
surveys, student 128–30

teacher assessment and evaluation
  effective processes 281–93
  issues and problems 288–90
  Making Teacher Evaluations Meaningful 291–2
teacher education
  clinical practice in a graduate entry pre-service program 114–21
  course accreditation 75–6
  program characteristics 115
  see also initial teacher education
teacher expertise, development 83–5
teacher leadership 183–4
  student achievement and 320–1
teacher learning 169–71
  goals for 149–50
  promoting and participating in 151
teacher preparation
  clinical approaches 114–22
  traditional approaches, shortcomings 114–22
teacher satisfaction 71–3
  importance of leadership to 281–2
teachers 7, 95
  being *friendly versus* being a *friend* 21
  being themselves 102
  dimensions of excellent teachers 85–6

Index

expert teachers 85–90
individual teachers 202–4
personal qualities 101–2, 154
professional development 102–4
professional responsibilities 291–2
quality 94–111
relationships with students 102
roles 94–111
salaries 77, 223–5
'stale' teachers 88
student differentiation of 130–1
student ratings of 128–9
teaching
   a 'battered profession' 71–3
   'core business' 172–3
   educational leaders' influences 144
   evidence base 23–7
   evidence, myth, ideologies, fads, habits, fashions 20–42
   'great' teaching components 94–5
   learning community focus 210
   major developments 319–20
   no evidence base 28–37
   planning, coordinating, and evaluating 150–1
   professional standards, role for 223–5
   quality 66–78
   representations of 85
   student perspectives on 35, 125–31
   teaching and parenting styles 255–7
   what works best? 8–11
teaching for learning
   achievement measurements and variances 47–61
   approaches critique 114–22
   identifying student perspectives 125–31
   quality teachers/teaching 66–78, 94–111
   routine–adaptive expertise, distinction 83–91

schools, role in achievement 3–17
   successful methodology 20–42
teaching strategies 104–8
team leadership 282–5
'thinking hats' (de Bono) 29
trait leadership approaches 135
transformational leadership 145–6
Trends in International Mathematics and Science Study (TIMSS) 54–9, 146
   Australian performance 58–9
   triangulation (data) 156
   trust 169–71
   turnaround school phenomenon 152, 176
   leadership, role of 269–78, 298
   literature review 269–70
   'turnaround' conceptualising 269
   US approach 270–1

understanding, building 40, 105–6
uninvolved leadership 258–9
uninvolved parenting 253

vision 165–9
voice 126
   see also student voice

Wallace Foundation 284–5
   leadership 'action lessons' 302
welfare (of students) 21, 171
wellbeing 152
whole-class discussion 107
widget effect 290
'win–lose' strategies 247–8
'win–win' strategies 247–8

'zero tolerance' 162
zoning (government schools) 4

www.ingramcontent.com/pod-product-compliance
Lightning Source LLC
Chambersburg PA
CBHW051359070526
44584CB00023B/3217